A Consuming Passion

A Consuming Passion

ESSAYS ON HELL AND IMMORTALITY
IN HONOR OF EDWARD FUDGE

Edited by
CHRISTOPHER M. DATE
and RON HIGHFIELD

Foreword by Stephen Travis

PICKWICK Publications • Eugene, Oregon

A CONSUMING PASSION
Essays on Hell and Immortality in Honor of Edward Fudge

Copyright © 2015 Wipf and Stock Publishers. All rights reserved. Except for brief quotations in critical publications or reviews, no part of this book may be reproduced in any manner without prior written permission from the publisher. Write: Permissions, Wipf and Stock Publishers, 199 W. 8th Ave., Suite 3, Eugene, OR 97401.

Pickwick Publications
An Imprint of Wipf and Stock Publishers
199 W. 8th Ave., Suite 3
Eugene, OR 97401

www.wipfandstock.com

ISBN 13: 978-1-4982-2305-8

Cataloguing-in-Publication Data

A consuming passion : essays on hell and immortality in honor of Edward Fudge / edited by Christopher M. Date and Ron Highfield, with a foreword by Stephen Travis

xxiv + 430 p. ; 23 cm. Includes bibliographical references.

ISBN 13: 978-1-4982-2305-8

1. Hell—Biblical teaching. 2. Future punishment—Biblical teaching. 3. Immortality—Biblical teaching. 4. Resurrection—Biblical teaching. 5. Fudge, Edward. I. Date, Christopher M., editor. II. Highfield, Ron, editor. III. Travis, Stephen. IV. Title.

BS680.H43 D182 2015

Manufactured in the U.S.A.   10/13/2015

To Edward Fudge,
whose consuming passion for God's word,
studied faithfulness to God's character,
and deep love for a lost, hurting, and dying world,
have inspired in two generations
a likewise consuming passion, faith, and love.

"As evangelical Christians, it is very easy to claim the Bible as our authority, but fail to carry out the implications of that claim when dealing with difficult issues—especially if that means standing with the minority."

Edward Fudge

Contents

Foreword by Stephen Travis | xi
Preface by Ron Highfield | xiii
Acknowledgments | xv
Abbreviations | xvii
Introduction | xxi

Part 1—The Legacy of Edward Fudge

1 The Legacy of Edward Fudge | 3
   —John G. Stackhouse Jr.
2 My Long Journey to Annihilationism | 17
   —Terrance L. Tiessen
3 "Are You Going to Heaven?" A Journey Away from the Wrong Question | 32
   —Jon Zens
4 Moses, Jesus, and Fudge: How Edward Fudge (and Biblical Theology) Changed What I Preach about Hell | 36
   —Rob McRay
5 "Dear Edward": Letters to a Gentleman Scholar | 53
   —Gregory G. Stump

Part 2—Theology and Philosophy

6 The Extinction of Evil: The Biblical Prerequisite for New Heavens, New Earth | 65
   —Gordon L. Isaac
7 Making the Philosophical Case for Conditionalism | 80
   —James S. Spiegel

8 Paul and the Annihilation of Death | 90
   —Nicholas Rudolph Quient

9 Tempest Theophany, Cosmic Conflagration, and the Vanished Vanquished:
   Toward a Trinitarian Framework for Immortality and Annihilation | 112
   —Peter Grice

10 Divine Sovereignty in the Punishment of the Wicked | 141
   —Adam Murrell

Part 3—Biblical Exegesis

11 The Punishment of the Wicked in Isaiah 66:24 | 159
   —Claude Mariottini

12 Death, Eternal Life, and Judgment in the Gospel
   and Epistles of John | 172
   —Kim Papaioannou

13 Hades in Revelation | 190
   —Roger Harper

Part 4—History and Polemics

14 Eternal Punishment in First-Century Jewish Thought | 215
   —David Instone-Brewer

15 Important Forgotten History: The Roots of Opposition
   to Conditionalism | 245
   —James Kenneth Brandyberry

16 Sic et Non: Traditionalism's Scandal | 257
   —Ronnie Demler

Part 5—The Road Ahead

17 The Future of Hell | 281
   —Glenn Peoples

18 Doctrinal, Biblical, and Psychological Obstacles to Accepting
   Conditionalism: Successfully Rethinking Hell in a Small Christian
   Movement | 296
   —Douglas A. Jacoby

19 The Offer of Life: Conditional Immortality in the Practice
   of Evangelism | 309
   —Ralph G. Bowles

20 How to Talk about the Afterlife (If You Must): Ten Theses to Guide
   Debates among Traditionalists, Conditionalists, and Universalists | 326
      —David C. Cramer
21 Taking Conditionalism to the People | 341
      —Jim Wood
22 Articulating and Promoting Conditionalism in the Twenty-First
   Century | 352
      —Christopher M. Date

Bibliography | 373
Scripture and Ancient Works Index | 389
Subject Index | 409

Foreword

To gain an accurate understanding of human destiny is important for personal faith, biblical integrity, Christian apologetic, and mission. The contributors to this book argue that the perspective known as "conditional immortality" or "conditionalism" expresses the biblical message on this topic. The terminology may be inelegant but the issue is vital.

I began to explore the theme in the 1960s as part of my PhD studies in Cambridge, UK. The initial stimulus came from the brief treatment in J. A. Baird, *The Justice of God in the Teaching of Jesus* (1963). But at that time I could find few books to take me further, except Edward White, *Life in Christ* (1846), LeRoy Edwin Froom, *The Conditionalist Faith of our Fathers* (1965–66), and two privately published works by English authors. Did the fact that they were published privately indicate, I wondered, that mainstream publishers could see no market for such books, or that they feared their reputation would be damaged by publishing works advocating this supposedly novel view of human destiny?

Today, in contrast, there is an increasing wealth of scholarly literature advocating and exploring a conditionalist understanding of human destiny. We have rediscovered the considerable body of nineteenth-century literature from both sides of the Atlantic. We have benefited from significant advances in biblical and theological scholarship. We have been made aware of the pressing need for a Christian apologetic that makes use of the insights of this line of thought.

This new collection of essays is impressive in its variety. There are contributions focusing on interpretation of key biblical passages, on biblical theology, and on questions in theological and philosophical theology. There are personal stories of how contributors have shifted from a traditionalist to a conditionalist perspective, and analyses of why for many this process is such a struggle. There are reflections on how a conditionalist perspective influences one's approach to evangelism, and proposals on strategies that may help the movement to continue gaining ground. In this connection one or two contributors comment on the somewhat enigmatic and unattractive nature of terms such as "conditionalism" and "annihilationism," and offer possible alternatives. There may be more work to be done on this question!

As well as the range of themes, there are other kinds of diversity here also. The authors belong to an assortment of Christian denominations: some are Calvinist, some Arminian. Occasionally they offer critique of each other's arguments. These are healthy signs in a mature and growing movement. As the debates continue—in conferences, on websites, and elsewhere—the challenge will be to resist letting internal debate over details distract from public advocacy of the good news of life in Christ.

Many contributors to this book express warmly their indebtedness to Edward Fudge and his seminal work in presenting the biblical case for conditional immortality. I am glad of the opportunity to echo them and to thank you, Edward, for the clarity, sure-footedness, and comprehensive scope of *The Fire that Consumes*. I only wish you had been there when I started!

Stephen Travis

Preface

Christian theology is disciplined human thought about God and God's relationship to creation, based on God's self-revelation in Jesus Christ, illuminated by the Holy Spirit, and preserved in Scripture. In theology we seek to know God that we might love him, become like him, and live eternally in his presence. God is the beginning and end of all things. All things come from the Father, receive their being through the Son, and live in the Spirit. And all things return to the Father by the Spirit and through the Son. Theology seeks to understand God as the beginning (creation), middle (providence and reconciliation), and end (redemption) of all things, as Creator, as Sustainer and Governor, as Savior, and as Finisher. Hence theologians ought to conduct their work in a spirit of gratitude, reverence, humility, faith, hope, and love. Theology ought not to be carried on as a competitive sport, but as a generous service in Christ's name to his people. Theologians who would be "the greatest in the kingdom" should aim to become "the servants of all."

This book of essays addresses a significant issue within the general topic of eschatology, that is, the nature of divine judgment on the unrepentant and the gift of eternal life given to the saved. However, in the thicket of interpretation and the heat of debate let us not forget that the true subject of eschatology is always God and God's definitive victory over sin and evil and the glorious redemption of creation. Just as God is the beginning, God is the end. God brings all things to their appointed goal, and God himself is that end to which he brings all things. The writers in this book argue that God's victory over sin and evil is total and definitive and that the salvation of the righteous is equally total and definitive. This collection could be considered an extended commentary on Romans 6:23: "For the wages of sin is death, but the gift of God is eternal life in Christ Jesus our Lord." God's total and definitive judgment on finally impenitent and unrighteous people is death, capital punishment. Immortality is not a natural endowment all human beings possess by right but a "gift" bestowed "in Christ Jesus our Lord."

These essays also honor Edward Fudge, whose 1982 book, *The Fire That Consumes*, sparked a revival of interest in the biblical doctrine of hell. I first heard of Edward in the mid-1970s after the publication of his book on Hebrews, *Our Man In Heaven*. I met him in person in 1982 when he moved to Houston, Texas to become editor of a Christian newspaper. Edward, Sara Faye, and their children Melanie and Jeremy became members of the Bering Drive Church of Christ where I served as youth minister. *The Fire That Consumes* had been published that year, and Edward was heavily involved in dialogue with friends of the book and in responding to its critics. I read the book soon thereafter and found it sound in scholarship, comprehensive in scope, and persuasive in argument, especially in its critique of the supposed biblical basis of the traditional doctrine of eternal conscious torment. Edward and I became good friends, and I count myself privileged to have worshiped and served together with him in the same congregation for six years before my move to California. Our many conversations were not limited to the topic of final punishment, but ranged over the entire field of biblical teaching. I soon noticed that Edward's favorite subject was the amazing grace God has bestowed on us in our Lord Jesus Christ. And though Edward Fudge is best known for his work on the nature of hell, I am sure that if he were given a chance to preach one sermon to the whole world the subject would be God's unfathomable love and unspeakable grace bestowed on us sinners in Jesus. And my friend Edward would readily confess himself to be among those sinners saved by grace, rescued by Jesus, and made holy by the Spirit.

So you can see why when I was asked to serve as an editor for a book of essays written in honor of Edward Fudge I agreed immediately and enthusiastically. Thank you, my friend, for your service to God's people. And thank you for setting an example as a theologian who conducts his work in "a spirit of gratitude, reverence, humility, faith, hope, and love" and who, with all God's people, seeks passionately to join that grand movement of all things by the Spirit, through the Son, and to the Father.

Ron Highfield

Acknowledgments

This collection of essays is largely the result of the inaugural Rethinking Hell conference, which took place on July 11–12, 2014 in Houston, Texas, so we would be remiss not to begin by thanking those who came up with the idea to honor Edward Fudge with a gathering to celebrate his theological legacy. The stewards of the Rethinking Hell project—Joshua Anderson, Chris Date, Peter Grice, and Greg Stump—created and put on the conference with help from staff including Joey Dear, Aaron Fudge, Nick Quient, Daniel Sinclair, and William Tanksley Jr.

The event would not have been possible without the generous provision of a venue from our hosts, Mark and Becky Lanier, who have been longtime supporters of Edward Fudge's ministry, and all of the staff at the Lanier Theological Library, including Charles Mickey, Emily Brown, and Curtis Miller. The Stone Chapel, dining hall, grounds, and library buildings were a profoundly beautiful and awe-inspiring locale in which to celebrate our guest of honor and connect with others in the flourishing conditionalist movement. We are particularly grateful for all of those presenters and guests who travelled great distances to be involved in this significant occasion.

We also wish to thank our plenary speakers, John Stackhouse Jr. and Glenn Peoples, along with our other presenters and panelists, many of whom are included in this volume. We are grateful for their willingness not only to carefully construct and share their thoughts at the conference, but also for all of the work that was put into refining their papers for publication in this compilation. We also want to thank those who submitted essays specifically for this book, though they were not able to be present for the conference, as well as Rachel Starr Thomson for her editorial help at Rethinking Hell. The idea for this *festschrift* and the title eventually chosen for the book came from Greg Stump, who also helped with bibliographical research. As with the first book from this project, *Rethinking Hell: Readings in Evangelical*

Conditionalism, this collection would never have moved forward without the tireless efforts of Chris Date, who carefully edited the manuscript along with Ron Highfield. We also thank Pickwick editor Robin Parry for his support and thoughtful input throughout the publication process. The Rethinking Hell stewards also want to acknowledge our supporters Bob Amis and Pamela Poland, whose generosity and encouragement have allowed us to do so much more with this project than we dreamed possible, and who continually inspire us with the hope that the biblical position of conditional immortality might become the predominant view of God's judgment within our lifetimes.

Of course, none of this would have been possible had it not been for the courage, integrity, and conviction of a man who helped so many of us to rethink hell in the first place: Edward William Fudge, who was such a humble, gracious, and delightful guest of honor at our conference and to whom we dedicate this volume. We offer our deepest thanks to Edward and his wife, Sara Faye, along with their extended family, for their willingness to allow us to join together in celebrating the work that God has done through the writing and teaching ministry of Edward on the weekend of his seventieth birthday.

Abbreviations

REFERENCE WORKS

ANF — *The Ante-Nicene Fathers*. Edited by Alexander Roberts and James Donaldson. Buffalo: The Christian Literature Co., 1885–86.

BDAG — *A Greek-English Lexicon of the New Testament and Other Early Christian Literature*. Revised and edited by Frederick W. Danker. 3rd ed. Chicago: University of Chicago Press, 2000.

LSJ — *A Greek-English Lexicon*. Edited by Henry George Liddell et al. Oxford: Clarendon, 1996.

NPNF — *A Select Library of the Nicene and Post-Nicene Fathers of the Christian Church*. Edited by Philip Schaff. Buffalo, NY: The Christian Literature Company, 1887–94.

PERIODICALS

BBR — *Bulletin of Biblical Research*
CTR — *Canadian Theological Review*
EQ — *Evangelical Quarterly*
ExpTim — *Expository Times*
JETS — *Journal of the Evangelical Theological Society*
JQR — *The Jewish Quarterly Review*
JSNT — *Journal for the Study of the New Testament*
JSOT — *Journal for the Study of the Old Testament*
JTI — *Journal of Theological Interpretation*
JTS — *Journal of Theological Studies*
NTS — *New Testament Studies*

VT	*Vetus Testamentum*
WW	*Word & World*
WTJ	*Westminster Theological Journal*

SCRIPTURES AND OTHER ANCIENT SOURCES

ESV	English Standard Version
KJV	King James Version
NASB	New American Standard Bible
NIV	New International Version
NRSV	New Revised Standard Version
RSV	Revised Standard Version

Introduction

It is difficult to find the words to express just how privileged I feel as I write this introduction, having had the opportunity to compile and contribute to this collection of essays in honor of my friend, Edward William Fudge. I first learned of Edward and his work in 2011 when he graciously agreed to let me interview him about the Churches of Christ (COC), among which he was brought up and in which he continues to fellowship today. As I would go on to learn, while Edward is most known for his controversial work on hell, he first drew the ire of many in that tradition for daring to teach that the grace of God unites all genuine believers in Christ, including those outside the COC. As my friend and co-editor Ron Highfield says in the preface to this volume, "God's unfathomable love and unspeakable grace bestowed on us sinners in Jesus" is what most stokes Edward's fire. This consuming passion has proven to be both a blessing and a bit of a curse, for it prompts him to treat his brothers and sisters in Christ in a manner commensurate with his Father's love for them, and simultaneously to go frustratingly against their grain when their traditions distort that love—not altogether unlike Jesus himself. I am inspired more by Edward than by any other pastor, teacher, scholar, or friend, to try and likewise reflect God's love more fully each day than the last, and I will forever be grateful to him for this impact on me.

In my experience it is rare to find someone quite like Edward. I have read the works of scholars with brilliant minds. I have listened to winsome and charming speakers. I have received sage advice from wise old souls. I have been touched by the love of tenderhearted strangers. I have been moved by those with infectious passion. And I have been left feeling ashamed of my own arrogance by the sincere humility of those with far more reason to boast than I have. Seldom, however, have I known someone in whom all these virtues converge as they do in Edward, many of which are captured in the 2012 feature-length film about Edward's life, *Hell and Mr. Fudge*. On the one hand, for example, Edward the scholar begins studying Greek at six years old, and in middle school he crafts a paper defending the New Testament canon when his peers are keen to write about baseball or summer vacation. On the other hand, to those gathered to consider the accusations leveled against him, Edward the jester says, "You know, if I had a couple of slices of bread and some mayonnaise I could make a sandwich with all the bologna here tonight." Edward's heart for others prompts him to invite an African American man to lead a less understanding, Southern, 1970s congregation in prayer, which apparently contributes to his dismissal as pastor. But his love can be matched by his passion, which consumes him during his research project and causes him to put it before his family—a prioritization Edward now regrets, and against which he wisely advises people like me who similarly struggle to balance family and scholarship.

Again, despite his notoriety as an advocate for a minority position on hell, Edward's published works cover a variety of topics. He has published in magazines: on Calvinism and Arminianism in *Christianity Today*; on encouragement from the book of Hebrews in *Leaven*; and on the saving love of God in *New Wineskins*. He has published in the *Journal of the Evangelical Theological Society* on the eschatology of Ignatius and on the Old Testament background to Paul's Areopagus sermon. He has published on guidance from God in his book, *The Sound of His Voice*. In endorsing Edward's book, *The Divine Rescue*, Max Lucado thanks Edward for capturing on paper "the sweetest of stories—God's relentless pursuit of his fallen people."[1] His commentary on Hebrews has been praised by numerous pastors, authors, and university and seminary professors who have called it "scholarly," "discerning," and "theologically-informed" while nevertheless "readable," "accessible," and "within arm's reach for every preacher, elder, Bible class teacher and student."[2]

And yet, despite this diversity of his interests and published works, it is for one issue that Edward is most known. Until about thirty or forty years ago, and for a century before that, evangelicals had thought the nature of hell to be a settled matter. Motivated in America by an understandable reaction to the modernist liberal movement, evangelicals had indiscriminately accused of heresy anyone who questioned the traditional understanding of eternal punishment. Meanwhile in Britain, although not as intolerant of challenges to the traditional view, evangelicals had nevertheless remained

---

1. Fudge, "Divine Rescue: Endorsements."

2. Fudge, "Bible Scholars and Church Leaders Endorse [*Hebrews: Ancient Encouragement for Believers Today*]."

virtually united in affirming the eternal conscious punishment of the lost, with only a handful of notable exceptions. As recently as the last quarter of the twentieth century, Edward and the vast majority of mainstream evangelicals took it for granted that, according to the Bible, those who are not reconciled to God through the blood of Christ by the time they die will go on to suffer the torturous wrath of God for eternity.

But then in 1982, after a year-long research project he was commissioned to undertake, Edward published his findings in *The Fire That Consumes*, reigniting a debate that had been mostly stamped out a hundred years earlier. In his book he offered a powerfully cogent and comprehensive biblical case for the final extinction of the wicked, a view historically called "conditional immortality" by those who believed God will grant immortality only to those who meet the condition of standing united with Christ in faith before the throne of final judgment. And notwithstanding the works of others who shared this perspective both before and after Edward's book, it is *The Fire That Consumes*—now in its third edition—that conditionalists today still identify as the seminal defense of the view that life is found only in Christ.

Despite having been written by an independent lay theologian and published by an obscure private publisher, the first edition of *The Fire That Consumes* was commended in its foreword by the renowned New Testament scholar F. F. Bruce. It was selected as a 1982 Alternate Selection by the Evangelical Book Club and its first printing sold out in just five months. In his foreword to its third edition thirty years later, Professor Richard Bauckham called it "a standard work to which everyone engaged with this issue will constantly return."[3] *Christianity Today* concurred, calling the book "the standard reference on annihilationism,"[4] as did author Gregory Boyd, who lifted it up as the "most thorough and compelling exposition of the biblical basis of annihilationism."[5] Critics, too, turn to Edward as one of the most prolific and influential defenders of conditionalism; he is mentioned by name at least one hundred times in Zondervan's 2004 collaborative defense of the traditional view of hell, *Hell Under Fire*.

In July, 2014, representatives of each of the major views of hell gathered at the Lanier Theological Library in Houston (where three years earlier Edward and hundreds of others had celebrated the release of the third edition of *The Fire That Consumes*) for the inaugural Rethinking Hell Conference, to honor Edward's life and work, and to discuss in an open forum the

---

3. Bauckham, "Foreword to Third Edition."
4. Galli, "Heaven, Hell, and Rob Bell: Putting the Pastor in Context."
5. Boyd, *Satan and the Problem of Evil*, 327 n. 12.

topic for which he is most well-known. Brought together in the pages that follow are eleven of the fourteen papers that were presented that weekend by scholars from around the globe. They were a diverse group of professors, priests, philosophers, pastors, teachers, and students, and they had come from three continents, five countries, and four states of the Union: Canada, New Zealand, Britain, Australia, California, Georgia, Tennessee, and Edward's home state of Texas. But not every conditionalist who wished to join in honoring Edward was able to present, and so many others leapt at the invitation to volunteer their own contributions to this volume as well.

These twenty-two essays cover a wide ground. Although interrelated, they are nevertheless independent and can be read in any order. So we have organized them into parts to assist readers in identifying areas of particular interest.

Long-time friends and fans of Edward may be most interested in part 1, which appropriately focuses on Edward himself. John Stackhouse explains what he sees as Edward's legacy and identifies the work that must be done if conditionalism is to continue to gain ground in the evangelical community. Terrance Tiessen recounts the journey which culminated in his becoming convinced of Edward's view, as well as the role Edward played therein. Jon Zens explains how Edward's work changed his thinking about the oft-repeated question, "Are you going to heaven?" Edward's former pastor Rob McRay shares how Edward changed what he preaches about hell. And Greg Stump reproduces excerpts from a number of noteworthy letters sent to Edward over the years.

Part 2 offers theological and philosophical reasons for embracing conditionalism. Gordon Isaac argues for the final extinction of evil as a prerequisite to the new heavens and new earth. James Spiegel offers a fresh and insightful philosophical case for conditionalism. Nicholas Quient surveys Paul the Apostle's theology of death. Peter Grice presents a theological framework for immortality and annihilation. And Adam Murrell argues from the doctrine of divine sovereignty to the final annihilation of the lost.

More detailed treatments of specific biblical texts are presented in part 3. Claude Mariottini exegetes Isaiah 66:24, which frequently features in debates over the nature of hell. Kim Papaioannou looks at the language of death, eternal life, and judgment in the Gospel and Epistles of John. And issuing a challenge to his fellow conditionalists, Roger Harper concludes from a study of passages in Revelation that while awaiting resurrection and final judgment, in Hades the dead are both conscious and redeemable.

Part 4 contains historical and polemical essays. David Instone-Brewer examines first-century Jewish thought concerning eternal punishment. James Brandyberry documents the important but sometimes forgotten history of the opposition to conditionalism. And Ronnie Demler critiques the maneuvers many contemporary traditionalists make to avoid contradicting the plain language of Scripture.

Finally, part 5 focuses on the future of the hell debate and its impact in evangelism. Glenn Peoples attempts to predict—and shape—the future of the conditionalist movement. Douglas Jacoby leverages his experience in a small Christian movement and shares how he thinks various obstacles to conditionalism's acceptance can be overcome. Ralph Bowles highlights the contribution conditionalism makes to evangelism. David Cramer commends ten principles for respectful and fruitful debate about the afterlife. Documentarian and producer of *Hell and Mr. Fudge*, Jim Wood exhorts those who have embraced conditionalism to take it to the people. And I offer several principles that have guided my work and that I think will help in effectively articulating and promoting conditionalism in the twenty-first century.

The editors of this volume and the Rethinking Hell team are pleased to add these essays to the growing body of conditionalist literature in honor of Edward, whose own work features so prominently therein. Additionally, we wish to add our own words of gratitude, admiration, and love to the voices of our contributors. Many of us were first introduced to the idea of conditional immortality by you, Edward. We owe you a great debt for helping us harmonize the nature of hell with the character of God as laid out in Scripture and for providing a way to share the gospel confidently with skeptics without fear of the all-too-common hell objections. We have found encouragement and inspiration in your example of faithfulness in the face of opposition. We admire you for your humble and winsome, yet cogent and vigorous, articulation and defense of conditionalism, and we seek to follow your example. And those of us who know you personally love you as a dear friend. For these and other reasons, we humbly offer this collection in the hope it blesses you as you've blessed us.

Chris Date

Part 1

THE LEGACY OF EDWARD FUDGE

1

The Legacy of Edward Fudge

— JOHN G. STACKHOUSE JR. —

John G. Stackhouse Jr. was educated in history and religious studies at three of North America's leading institutions: Queen's University in Ontario (BA, First Class Honors), Wheaton College Graduate School in Illinois (MA, with Highest Honors), and The University of Chicago (PhD). Formerly the Sangwoo Youtong Chee Professor of Theology and Culture at Regent College in Vancouver, B.C., he was recently appointed the Samuel J. Mikolaski Professor of Religious Studies and Dean of Faculty Development at Crandall University in New Brunswick. Stackhouse has authored eight books, edited four others, and written over 600 articles, book chapters, and reviews in academic publications, major newspapers, and magazines. And he represents conditionalism in an upcoming "Four Views" book by Zondervan.

John originally presented the following paper as a plenary speaker at the Rethinking Hell conference, 2014.

Normally, when one is asked to give the keynote address on the legacy of the guest of honor, one answers the question, "What is the legacy of Edward Fudge?" And I promise to do so . . . eventually.

Not being normal, however, I want to spend most of my allotted time answering a different question—namely, "Why isn't the legacy of Edward Fudge simply this: that all right-thinking people, or at least all evangelical theologians and preachers, are now conditionalists?" Three decades after the publication of *The Fire That Consumes*, why hasn't conditional immortality carried the field?[1]

---

1. Fudge, *The Fire That Consumes* (1982).

Well, perhaps the solution is simple: it's just a bad book. So its lack of influence needs no further explanation. But it is not, in my view, a bad book. Quite the contrary. I believe instead *The Fire That Consumes* to be one of the most convincing cases ever offered in the history of controversial theology, to the degree that I find it unanswerable.

So why doesn't everybody think so?

In what follows, I will begin by assessing *The Fire that Consumes*. I will demonstrate that it meets a number of high standards for theological argumentation. I will then point out, as academics always do when they honor each other, some of its deficiencies. I will conclude this section by indicating that the lack of commanding influence of this book nonetheless is not due to any putative deficiencies.

I will go on, then, to draw on the work of several disparate theorists—Thomas Kuhn and Michael Polanyi, of a previous generation, and also feminist epistemologist Lorraine Code and sociologist Michèle Lamont, of our own—to indicate something of how paradigms shift, including paradigms in theology. I will apply several of their key contentions then to the career of the doctrine of conditional immortality, and to Edward Fudge's book in particular, to help explain why it has not been more successful.

I will conclude my remarks by suggesting what now might to be done to further the cause of Edward Fudge: to hear the Bible properly and to teach it well.

WHAT EDWARD FUDGE DID RIGHT

Perhaps the most important single thing to say about the style of this book is that it was written by a man who eventually became a successful lawyer. The book commendably presents an actual argument reasoned carefully and plainly from evidence. Such a phenomenon is not to be taken for granted in theology. Indeed, even some of the acknowledged greats in theology have been accused of eschewing argument for mere suggestion or implication or even rhetorical flourish.[2] Theologians who express themselves in this mode generate shimmering tableaux of concepts and phrases that, if they appeal to the intuitions of the reader, give that reader a marvelous experience. If such words do not coincide with the prejudices or aspirations of the reader, however, they will tend to leave one coldly unmoved. Especially is this so in the case of a good lawyer. Eloquence is no substitute for argument in the courtroom.

---

2. Nancey Murphy gives Karl Barth a pretty rough go in this regard throughout *Reasoning and Rhetoric in Religion*.

Well, actually, eloquence quite frequently *is* a substitute for argument in the courtroom! But it is not supposed to be. Nor is it supposed to be in the theological seminar, either—or in the pulpit, for that matter. Edward Fudge takes considerable pains to argue, not merely to announce or assert.

I shall show later that this very strength of the book stands also as a rhetorical weakness. For now, though, let's look at more of its several strengths.

The Fire That Consumes demonstrates a wide range of basic and essential hermeneutical principles. First and foremost, it argues from Scripture and insists that all counter-arguments rely on Scripture as well. Again, this is certainly not to be taken for granted in theological argument in our day, or in any previous day. Not only Protestants, but all Christians in all centuries and places, should similarly insist that theology be conducted fundamentally on the basis of scriptural revelation. So say Augustine and Aquinas, as well as Calvin and Wesley.

Literal interpretation, likewise, is championed rightly in this book, and in an appropriately qualified sense. Literal interpretation properly pays attention to *literature*: genres, and particularly figures of speech, are taken seriously as such. The history of debate over the doctrine of hell is, in fact, rife with proponents of one view or another pressing figurative details for literalistic descriptions while rendering what some would view to be straightforward, even univocal, words and phrases into esoterica that yield only to those with the proper *gnōsis* to understand them. For an example of the former problem, the parable of Lazarus and the rich man is frequently seen to refer to either the intermediate or the final state, while it may well refer to neither, but could instead be simply an illustration, like the story of the Good Samaritan. It might even be, as some have suggested, an instance in which Jesus used a stock set of characters (like St. Peter at the Pearly Gates or the Grim Reaper) to make his particular point on that occasion.

A common example of the latter problem is, as Edward Fudge shows repeatedly, the various words in both Testaments for "destroy," "dead," and the like that pretty plainly mean, at least in most instances, "destroy," "dead," and the like—and yet some interpreters assert instead that they mean "not really destroyed or dead, but kept alive for unending pain."

Proof-texting, the habit of literal interpretation of a primitive sort, is rightly set aside by Edward Fudge for attention to the "whole counsel of God" (Acts 20:27). Indeed, one of the key strengths of the book is its insistence that the Old Testament must constitute the primary, indeed, the governing background against which the New Testament is interpreted, rather than something else: inter-testamental literature, for example, or the reigning philosophy of this or that century of Christian thought. This last point, about taking the Old Testament seriously as the framework for New Testament interpretation, did not arise with N. T. Wright, as some youngsters in the audience might need to recognize, but arose at least as far back as the biblical theology movement of the mid-twentieth century. And it has been crucial to New Testament interpretation at least since then in the modern period.

This hermeneutical point, in fact, cannot be overstated in this discussion. Indeed, I contend that Fudge's case cannot be gainsaid if one takes this principle of interpretation seriously. The cumulative weight of the Old Testament testimony regarding the destiny of the lost is overwhelming: extinction and disappearance. The only way one can plausibly argue, therefore, that the New Testament supports eternal torment, let alone universalism, is to argue deductively, not inductively: from first principles some of which could be derived from Scripture, to be sure, but that also require supplementing from metaphysical presuppositions (such as the immortality of the soul) and moral intuitions (such as the belief that God couldn't possibly allow anyone to suffer in hell forever or even eventually vanish). Instead, however, if one subjects one's metaphysics and morality to the Old and New Testaments interpreted together as the one Word of God—as, I maintain, would be the assumption of the apostles, the Evangelists, and their audiences—then I literally cannot see a cogent case for either eternal torment or universalism.

Having hammered away for a bit, now, about Fudge's commendable championing of the whole canon of Scripture, we can go on to acknowledge that in his work the theological tradition of the church is also given attention. The book repeatedly insists that the idea of conditional immortality is not spoken against in any of the great ecumenical creeds. And early patristic testimony is adduced for what it is worth. Still, Fudge's biblicism correctly dominates over any appeal to any doctrinal symbol or any other theological authority. "What does the Bible say?" is his relentless question. And that is the right question upon which to fixate.

Another one of the book's commendable qualities, therefore, is its attempt to be complete. It takes pains to detail the etymology and definition of terms. Most salient, however, is its attempt to deal with every relevant scripture in both Testaments, as well as all relevant writings in the Apocrypha and pseudepigrapha. Some readers will find this detail to be exhausting as well as exhaustive. But someone has to do this kind of work in order to gainsay any accusation that proponents of conditional immortality are cherry-picking their favorite texts. Indeed, having done this work, Fudge is entitled to accuse the traditionalists (as he calls them) of comprehensively failing to deal with the biblical material. He claims that they dismiss most, if not all, of the Old Testament, and—not coincidentally, but consequently—they misinterpret the relatively small number of New Testament texts they bother to engage. This is quite a damning conclusion to advance, so the advocate for it had better have done a thorough job. But thorough is exactly what Edward Fudge has been.

There are other positive qualities one might note along the way as well. Fudge gives due credit to opponents and to weaknesses on his own side of the argument. He has read deeply enough in the original languages to quibble with various translations and usually to good effect. He has read enough in the secondary sources to note changes in the thought of authorities, such as Isaac Watts and Charles Spurgeon, and ambiguities in figures as important as Martin Luther. He tackles the best, not the worst, of his opponents, even giants such as Augustine and Calvin. He even offers sympathetic explanations of how his opponents could have erred: he points out that there is at least one apocryphal text that does support eternal torment (Jdt 16:17); he sympathizes with his opponents' worries over Jehovah's Witnesses, Seventh-day Adventists, and universalists, in the course of contending with whom the traditionalists have also taken swipes at conditional immortality; and so on.

In sum, therefore, I view *The Fire That Consumes* to be a juggernaut of biblical exegesis that simply crushes any alternative: eternal torment, universalism, or any modification of those views. So the question returns: why hasn't it had more influence?

WHY THE BOOK DIDN'T SUCCEED: THE BOOK ITSELF

Edward Fudge, I'm sure, would be the first to say that his work is not flawless. While I have devoted my attention to the first edition of the book, I'm confident that each subsequent edition, and there have been several, have improved on the deficits of the original. So I will not search for flecks of sandstone in the marble, as I doubt that they are material to the answering the larger question I am raising.

The most significant weakness of the book instead is, to reiterate, also its greatest strength. Its relentless, lawyerly pounding away at Scripture after Scripture makes what I have called a powerfully compelling case. But such argument is not the typical mode of theologians. In particular, Fudge's intense but narrow case for one particular idea (the eventual evanescence of the lost) is not presented within a larger, compelling view of God, providence, and eschatology. Yet such contexts are the frameworks in which most theologians prefer to think.

One might argue instead like this: given a view of God as good—as both holy and benevolent—and I will set out such a view now, on the basis of Scripture, reason, tradition, and so on, it follows that there is a hell and that hell would be thus. And behold! That's what Scripture does in fact say about hell.

The Reformed tradition has been particularly good at this combination of deductive and inductive argument: Calvin, the Westminster divines, Jonathan Edwards, Karl Barth . . . even if sometimes they seem to go pretty light on Scripture—as Calvin does on baptism, for example, or as all of them do on this particular issue! (And I say this as someone who reveres Calvin and who has a portrait of Jonathan Edwards on my office wall.) As many historians and theologians have observed, in the English-speaking world it is the Reformed tradition that has generally set the terms and called the shots and policed the boundaries when it comes to evangelical orthodoxy.[3]

So *The Fire That Consumes* fails precisely as it succeeds: it argues strictly on the basis of biblical exegesis toward a strictly biblical conclusion without connecting it to larger theological themes. It thus does not present its argument in a way that is congenial to the predominant theological mentality. Indeed, while Edward Fudge correctly, in my view, claims that conditional immortality is easily adapted by any orthodox Christian theology—Catholic, Orthodox, or Protestant—the book doesn't actually take much time to show that. And in particular it doesn't offer a winsome theological construct to appeal to the aesthetic as well as the logical sensibilities of the theologians. This quality, I maintain, keeps it from being as persuasive as it might have been—even though, I trust I have made clear, this is not truly a fault of the book or of its author. There is simply a kind of crucial rhetorical deficiency here that has cost the book influence I believe it deserves.

Perhaps significantly in terms of what I am asserting, John W. Wenham did exactly that sort of thing in his earlier book, *The Goodness of God*.[4] Wenham located his discussion of hell in the midst of an exposition of generally accepted evangelical views about God, providence, salvation, and so on. And it therefore might be worth noting that this is the one significant book in the previous generation defending conditional immortality that was indeed published by a mainstream evangelical press. So perhaps I am

---

3. See, among others, Dayton and Johnston, *Varieties of American Evangelicalism*; Olson, *Against Calvinism*; and Worthen, *Apostles of Reason*.

4. Wenham, *The Goodness of God*. I recognize that Clark Pinnock and Robert Brow defended conditionalism also in their book *Unbounded Love: A Good News Theology for the 21st Century*. My sense, however, is that the book made hardly a ripple in the theological conversation. To be sure, as a personal friend of both of these now-departed authors, I would be glad to be proven wrong about this appraisal.

onto something here, and I suggest that further arguments for conditional immortality will have to be embedded in larger discourses of theological concern and interest if they are to catch the attention and win the respect of theologians.

WHY THE BOOK DIDN'T SUCCEED: THE LARGER CONTEXT

What does it take, then, to shift a theological paradigm? We might address this question under three heads: anomalies and felt needs; sponsorship/credentials by way of authorities and networks; and contest with, and attrition of, opponents.

Thomas Kuhn's groundbreaking work on *The Structure of Scientific Revolutions* suggests—if I may ruthlessly dumb down his elegant argument—that people do not change their minds if they don't first want to change their minds.[5] People maintain their current paradigms—the intellectual models that frame and govern their thinking—until anomalies accumulate of such number and weight that the paradigm can no longer accommodate them and it collapses. In that situation of loss, there is a felt need for an alternative and people then look around for one.

In American evangelicalism, however, two factors have oddly combined to prevent serious reconsideration of the doctrine of hell. The first is sentimentality, as depicted in recent books such as Todd Brenneman's *Homespun Gospel*, and Larry Eskridge's *God's Forever Family*.[6] Sentimentality is also most graphically in the phenomenal success of Thomas Kinkade's paintings. I do not mean to score an easy laugh by reference to Kinkade, who is not a favorite among connoisseurs. In my view, the man technically was a competent enough painter: I direct our attention here to the *content* of his work, the *world* he offered to his clients: a never-never land of idyllic cottages, gardens, forests, water features, and peace. This is a safe, calm, orderly, dreamy world into which hell cannot intrude. So it doesn't. And anyone who might want to disrupt the peace of Happy Valley with talk about hell would be guilty of extreme bad manners. So in sentimental evangelical America, we just don't talk about hell—even in church.[7]

---

5. Kuhn, *The Structure of Scientific Revolutions*.
6. Brenneman, *Homespun Gospel*; Eskridge, *God's Forever Family*.
7. Kinkade's world is the world of bestselling Victorian novels depicting the afterlife, such as Elizabeth Stuart Phelps's *The Gates Ajar* and its sequel, *Beyond the Gates*: "We stopped before a small and quiet house built of curiously inlaid woods. . . . It was shielded by trees, some familiar to me, others strange. There were flowers—not too

At the same time, America continues to feel the tensions of the fundamentalist-modernist controversy of a century ago. As American culture has continued to depart in some key ways from orthodox Christian values, there is a widespread fear—and not just among actual fundamentalists—about any further declension. (I would argue that America today is in many respects much more in line with biblical principles of justice and compassion than it was a century ago, but for now we're dealing with a popular perception, whatever the historical reality might be.) In such an atmosphere of apprehension, therefore, any move to the left will be seen as a departure from the "faith once delivered to the saints." This crucial interpretive error—namely, that there is a point in the recent past that offers a benchmark of orthodoxy from which any deviation must be a sign of secularization—shows up among scholars every bit as much as it does among scaremongers on television.[8]

By way of corollary evidence, I point to the fact that the nineteenth century—the century in which evangelicals (and orthodox Christians more generally) ruled their Anglo-American cultures in confidence—is the century in which the idea of conditional immortality enjoyed its widest support. Not coincidentally, it is the nineteenth century that also gives us the rise of kenotic Christology, Christology that, without sacrificing any commitment to the deity of Christ, also attempts to make better sense of the abundant Scriptural evidence for his humanity.[9] With the rise to cultural dominance of liberal Christianity and even outright secularism in the latter nineteenth century and the early twentieth, however, evangelicals retrenched and erected defensive barricades where the battles for orthodoxy were fiercest, among which were, yes, belief in hell in the face of rising universalism and belief in the deity of Jesus in the face of declining Chalcedonian Christology. Intermediate positions such as conditional immortality and kenotic Christology could not be countenanced in the polarization of conflict. Each side would tend to see any mediating positions as compromises unworthy of respect.

---

many; birds; and I noticed a fine dog sunning himself upon the steps" (Phelps, *Beyond the Gates*, 124–25). As historians Colleen McDannell and Bernhard Lang describe the larger scene, "these homes are not located in cities or villages but carefully placed in picturesque surroundings. Heaven has mountains, oceans, and rivers which wind 'quietly in and out in sensuous curves,' with 'forests so thick that it [sic] shuts out the world, and you walk like one in a sanctuary" (McDannell and Lang, *Heaven: A History*, 267–68).

8. For example, see Hunter, *Evangelicalism*. I point to Hunter's work precisely because he is such an eminent scholar whose work has enjoyed wide influence, despite the shortcoming I think is at its heart here.

9. Evans, *Exploring Kenotic Christianity*.

These two factors thus come together: the aching nostalgia for happier times of a disenfranchised counterculture that has its own doctrinal watchdogs to control both the borders and the rank-and-file to prevent any further loss. To put it mildly, such an outlook does not provide a welcoming openness to new theological ideas—even if those ideas can be shown to be in fact very old, even biblical. And this combination of grief and fear—a combination at the heart of George Marsden's magisterial interpretation of American fundamentalism—helps also to explain the bitter *ad hominems* in so much of the literature on this issue ("Your disagreement with us indicates that you refuse to submit to the authority of Scripture and therefore you aren't a Christian, but instead a pathetic apostate desperately conforming your religion to the world"), as fear so easily transforms into anger.[10]

Into this fraught situation comes blithe young Edward Fudge with his openhearted concern just to understand what the Bible says ... and he doesn't know what hit him. No one wanted what he was selling. Quite the contrary: anyone showing up at the theological front doors of American evangelicals offering anything other than what they already knew and trusted would immediately be suspected as a dangerous enemy, not as an interesting and possibly helpful friend. And he was.

A new paradigm, therefore, makes its way in the world only if it enjoys strong credentials and influential sponsorship. Michael Polanyi, Lorraine Code, and Michèle Lamont have all detailed, in their different spheres, how experts change their minds about things.[11] Too rarely, it seems, do even our leading thinkers change their minds merely on the basis of evidence and argument. Instead, scholars themselves typically change their minds because it becomes advantageous to them (to us) to do so: grant money, promotion, influence, and fame all now reside over there instead of here. So we go there. And how do the goodies of intellectual life end up somewhere else? Because networks of influence reposition them.

The best that the conditional immortality option could offer in this regard over the last half-century has been three or four English evangelicals: John Wenham and Philip E. Hughes, acknowledged scholars; John Stott, a giant among international evangelicals, true, but who only reluctantly and "tentatively" offered support for this view—and only on one occasion, to my knowledge, *and* only when provoked in dialogue with David Edwards; and Michael Green, widely respected as a pastor and evangelist, but not as

---

10. Marsden, *Fundamentalism and American Culture*; see also Noll, *The Scandal of the Evangelical Mind*.

11. Polanyi, *Personal Knowledge*; Code, *Ecological Thinking*; and Lamont, *How Professors Think*. I have discussed these matters in Stackhouse, *Need to Know*.

a theologian per se.[12] I am aware that heavy philosophical hitters Richard Swinburne and Anthony Thiselton and front-rank biblical scholars Howard Marshall and Richard Bauckham have argued here and there on behalf of this view as well, but their works are generally located on the top shelf of the bookcase where few even try to reach, and to my knowledge none has put this idea front and center in any of his voluminous publications.

In addition, the conditional immortality people could number the works of LeRoy Edwin Froom (which Fudge himself acknowledges to be both overwhelming and overreaching in its claims); Basil Atkinson (who had no real clout in the theological world and whose book had to be privately published); and Clark Pinnock (whose views on other matters increasingly deviated from the evangelical baseline and so whose support became increasingly a burden as well as a blessing).[13] And then of course there has been Edward Fudge.

Ah, yes, Fudge: a graduate of Abilene Christian University, whose recent ascendancy as a school of some academic standing has come rather too late to help credit Fudge's work; a member of the Churches of Christ, a tradition not widely known as contributing to the broader Christian theological conversation; a man without a theological doctorate; the author of a book published with presses few recognize and without any academic cachet—and the guy's a *lawyer*, of all things. (Calvin himself trained as a lawyer . . . which is a point that might be raised with Fudge's critics in Reformed circles!)

Out of this sort of network, it would seem, not much theological steam could be generated, nor has it been. What then can be done?

WHAT IS TO BE DONE

If we return to Kuhn's work, we find him rather sardonically indicating that the most effective way to win a contest of ideas is to outlive your opponents. Still, one actually needs to convince some people, and especially younger people, of what you say so that there will indeed be someone of your opinion still around when your opponents have passed from the scene. How then to proceed?

First, get a website, and a good one. After all this theological talk, to mention a relatively recent technology not usually associated with intellectual depth can seem jarring. But a moment's thought will tell each of us that

---

12. Edwards and Stott, *Evangelical Essentials*, 312–20.

13. Froom, *The Conditionalist Faith of Our Fathers*; Atkinson, *Life and Immortality*; and Clark Pinnock's contributions to Crockett and Gundry, *Four Views on Hell*.

the first place most people go for information is the Internet, and especially is this true the younger the person in question. So proponents of any view had better have a website, and it must be a good one. Proponents of conditional immortality, therefore, have a considerable stake in the "Rethinking Hell" initiative (rethinkinghell.com), whether they want to have that stake or not. If it is not already, it will soon become the first port of call for anyone investigating this theological alternative. Those who run it therefore have a great responsibility to offer the best possible resources on behalf of the rest of us who confine ourselves mostly to stodgy old technologies of printed articles and books. And the site needs to look good as well, since *all* of the symbols of the site speak to the plausibility of the view it espouses, like it or not.

Second, marshal influential people to speak and write on the question. Among middle-aged North American evangelicals, the magazine *Christianity Today* still has influence. Somebody might talk with editors Mark Galli and Andy Crouch, and CT-associated writers such as Philip Yancey, to see what interest they might have in advancing discussion of this doctrine. Even more radically, just as Nixon went to China, and Reagan improved relations with Gorbachev, is there someone in the Gospel Coalition who in fact is supportive of this view? I would start with Tim Keller and Michael Horton, two influential leaders of that group that have shown themselves capable of theological openness from time to time.

The Evangelical Theological Society has its limitations, to be sure, but it is the place in which one can encounter the most evangelical theologians across the most denominational and confessional lines. Presentations, panels, and publications are the typical ways in which such a view can and should be advanced. (It will not be, contrariwise, terribly helpful to advance the views in the Evangelical Theology Group of the AAR, since many evangelical theologians look askance at this group as flirting shamelessly with heterodoxy. You might as well publish in *The Christian Century*—and I say that as one who has published therein off and on for almost thirty years.)

As for younger people, *Relevant* magazine and similar media can be considered. But my guess is that those younger people who are most interested in serious theological investigation of the doctrine of hell—rather than those who are content with authors who merely raise questions and muse out loud about what might or might not be the case (you know the authors I mean)—will be influenced most indirectly: by influencing their leading teachers.

The most important advance would come, however, only with the cooperation of at least one big-name theological scholar with conservative credibility. In biblical studies, I think of Tom Wright, of course; Christopher

Wright, perhaps; Scot McKnight—although Scot might be too "lefty"/emergent-ish for many; and maybe Richard Bauckham—while in theology itself there is Alister McGrath and . . . well, well-known evangelical theologians are not thick on the ground. Indeed, what is needed most, I suggest, is a new single-volume presentation of the case by a well credentialed theological scholar who can write at the intermediate level and get published by a house that is respected by the target audience: ideally IVP or Baker . . . or even Moody. The recent volume of essays edited by Date, Stump, and Anderson, *Rethinking Hell*, is a fine resource.[14] But I suggest that only the presentation of this doctrine within a comprehensive vision, only a theologically and not merely exegetically presented view, and only a book authored by the right person with the right status will make the necessary impact.

Finally, I suggest that a significant obstacle to the acceptance of the view championed so ably by Edward Fudge is the very term "conditional immortality." If we pay any attention, and we should, to how people change their minds and what ideas tend to stick to those minds, we simply have to realize that names for things really matter. I suggest, then, that we formulate a new term—nay, a new brand.[15]

Annihilationism is obviously a terrible term. It sounds like the unsaved will get off too easily, merely being raised from the dead in order to be immediately extinguished without suffering. Very few people who believe in conditional immortality seem to hold this view, of course, but it is frequently understood to be the view of all of us, and our views are dispensed with as trifling with the concerns of justice. It is also a bad term because it implies belief in an immortal soul that needs killing—and it is belief in an immortal soul that, as Edward Fudge shows, lies behind the error of both the traditional view and many universalisms as well. Annihilationism implies that God must kill something that otherwise would live, which is an odd thing for God to do. And the term seems to open the door to rather stupid irrelevancies such as arguments over "conservation of mass/energy" and the sophistry of "when you burn something it is not annihilated, it simply changes form."[16]

Conditional immortality, however, also has several considerable deficiencies. First, and ironically, it perpetuates the very language of immortality it seeks to combat. Yes, the adjective "conditional" is supposed to govern the noun "immortality," but one can decide for oneself how successfully it

---

14. Date, Stump, and Anderson, *Rethinking Hell*.
15. Heath and Heath, *Made to Stick*.
16. Buis, *The Doctrine of Eternal Punishment*, 125–26; cited in Fudge, *The Fire That Consumes* (1982), 255.

does so. Second, and worse, it focuses on the saved, not the lost—but the argument is about the *lost*, not the saved. So the term literally doesn't aim directly at the subject in question. And third, it doesn't immediately communicate very much at all to those outside this discussion: even theologians, let alone a larger public. So I suggest we need something that does not have these fatal flaws.

I suggest we use the term *terminal punishment*.[17] First, the term assures us that everyone gets what he or she deserves. No one gets away lightly. And who can be against that? Second, the word "terminal" also makes clear that there is no useless prolongation of the sinner's existence in some treadmill of sinning and being consequently punished, forever and ever—the extremity of which makes Sisyphus's fate look mild. There is no grotesque object lesson here regarding the putative glory of God or the dignity of humans in a scene of perpetual torture that in truth burnishes the glory and dignity of neither. (Seriously: according to what biblical definition of greatness does God appear greater because he keeps people alive forever in horror and pain?) And there is no hint of escape, no hint of universalism or restorationism. *Terminal punishment* focuses correctly on the state of the lost who are raised to face the grim reality of atonement: either Jesus pays for your sins or you do. And once the lost person has done so—that is, once he or she has been justly punished and only punished for his or her sins and the moral imbalance or impurity in the universe is restored—that person disappears from the cosmos, having refused to link himself or herself to the only Source of life there is.

This paradigm is easy to explain. It commends itself widely to the intuitions of Christian and non-Christian alike. And, as we all can see, thanks to Edward Fudge, it is abundantly supported by Scripture.

THE LEGACY OF EDWARD FUDGE

It seems to me, in conclusion, that the legacy of Edward Fudge—in the narrow sense of Fudge as "the author of *The Fire That Consumes*," since there has been much more to the man, of course, than this one theological venture, however important—includes the sobering recognition that biblical argument is a *necessary* cause of legitimate theological change but it is not a *sufficient* cause. Despite the self-image of Protestant theologians as those who defer wholeheartedly to the principle of *sola scriptura*, it seems clear

---

17. At the conference, I suggested the term "just punishment." But I became convinced that there needs to be an element in the term that speaks of ending, and several of the conferees liked "terminal punishment," originally coined by Douglas Jacoby.

now, thirty years after Fudge's book was first published, that argument from the Bible, no matter how solid and comprehensive, is clearly not enough to win the day.

What else can be done should be done, therefore, in the service of this important doctrine. But we can pause for a moment now to consider, to the shame particularly of the evangelical theological community, that a clear, winsome, exhaustive, and sensible argument based on Scripture has not been enough to convince us.

That to me—as a theologian, a church historian, and an epistemologist—is the real story of "Hell and Mr. Fudge." And it is up to us to give that story a better ending.

2

My Long Journey to Annihilationism

— TERRANCE L. TIESSEN —

Terrance L. Tiessen is currently Professor Emeritus of Systematic Theology and Ethics at Providence Theological Seminary, Canada. Prior to his twenty-four years on the faculty at PTS, he taught at Tyndale University College (Toronto) and at Asian Theological Seminary (Manila). He served as a missionary in the Philippines for sixteen years. He is the author of Irenaeus on the Salvation of the Unevangelized, Providence and Prayer: How Does God Work in the World?, Who Can Be Saved?: Reassessing Salvation in Christ and World Religions, *and of numerous journal articles and chapters in multi-author books. He blogs at thoughtstheological.com.*

I can think of no one in my lifetime who has contributed more positively to the church's understanding of the Bible's teaching concerning God's final judgment of the wicked than Edward Fudge. His writing has played a critical role in the development of my own eschatology, and so I am delighted to have a part in this book produced in his honor, through the invitation to share how I became an annihilationist.

A NOTE ON TERMINOLOGY

Before I describe my eschatological journey, I will make three comments about my terminology. First, I observe that "hell" is generally used in

English translations of the New Testament to translate *gehenna*. Because it is primarily found in references to discourses by Jesus, it appears in the Gospels but very rarely in the rest of the New Testament. As Anthony Thiselton points out, Paul "never speaks of 'hell,' but regularly of death (Greek, *thanatos*)."[1] In Christian theology generally, however, we have come to use the term "hell" to refer to the final punishment of the wicked, and I continue that usage, even though I realize that it is not precisely the way in which English translations of the New Testament use the word.

Second, I am aware that many who believe that God ultimately destroys the wicked identify their position as "conditionalism." This term highlights the fact that the New Testament always speaks of "immortality" (as it does of "eternal life") as a gift that God gives *only* to those who are saved by Christ. Since immortality and eternal life are exclusively the experience of those with God in the new heaven and earth, we can not legitimately speak of the wicked as living endlessly, that is, as having "immortality." Immortality is conditioned upon faith, hence unbelievers will experience not incorruption, immortality, and endless life, but death of body and soul. As a way of describing the end of the wicked, *annihilation* puts its emphasis on that end itself. And so I call my current understanding "annihilationism," rather than "conditionalism," because many traditionalist theologians also believe in conditional immortality rather than the Platonic view that souls are intrinsically indestructible. They state that souls, like bodies, only exist (or live) if God sustains their existence. God *could* destroy both sinners' souls and bodies (Matt 10:28). But, as traditionalists, they believe that God has chosen to keep sinners alive endlessly, in body and soul. Then they argue that the New Testament does not speak of the unsaved as "immortal," or describe their life in hell as "eternal life," because the experience of continual existence is so radically different for the condemned than it is for the saved.

I concur with Clark Pinnock, who also did not call his position "conditional immortality," because he considered that truth "a necessary, but not a sufficient condition" for his view. "Conditional immortality has to be true for a negative reason—to make the destruction of the wicked conceivable, but it does not positively establish annihilation simply because it would still be possible that God might give the wicked everlasting life and condemn them to spend it in everlasting torment."[2]

Third, I will use the term "traditionalism" to refer to the belief that the nature of hell is eternal conscious torment. Since the time of Augustine, when it became widely believed that souls are indestructible, eternal

---

1. Thiselton, "Claims about 'Hell' and Wrath," 175.
2. Pinnock, "The Destruction of the Finally Impenitent," 67.

conscious torment has been the predominant understanding within the Christian church, so "traditionalism" is a reasonable way to identify this position. I do not use the term derogatorily, or in order to imply that those who believe this doctrine do so only because of their commitment to tradition. I know that this is not the case for Protestant theologians and churches in particular, especially when they are evangelical. I wish there were a more descriptive term, which would represent that belief as helpfully as "annihilationism" represents the alternative view, but I have found none that serves well or that is widely used.

THE STAGES OF MY JOURNEY

As I review the long process of change in my understanding of the Bible's teaching regarding "hell," I now discern five stages in that theological journey. A few other people have told me that their own experience was similar, but no two journeys are ever exactly alike.

Stage 1: Conviction that the traditional view of hell as eternal conscious torment is the orthodox view and is clearly taught in Scripture.

I grew up in the home of missionaries and spent most of my childhood years at the British boarding school that was most commonly chosen by families from Commonwealth nations. In all of my years through high school, I recall being taught consistently that God would punish unrepentant sinners with a conscious and endless suffering so severe that it was analogous to the pain of being burned, but worse because it never stopped.

In my experience at a Bible College and a graduate school of theology, I learned that there were Christians who believed that God would eventually annihilate the wicked. But those who believed this were portrayed as either members of "false cults," like Jehovah's Witnesses, or Protestant Liberals who had abandoned orthodox Christian beliefs on more fundamental points. The Seventh-day Adventists also believed this but they were more difficult to place, and their annihilationism was less problematic than issues like the authority of Ellen White and the doctrine of the "investigative judgment."[3]

---

3. This hierarchy of issues is evident in the 2007 "Joint Statement of the World Evangelical Alliance and the Seventh-day Adventist Church" (http://www.worldevangelicals.org/news/WEAAdventistDialogue20070809d.pdf). In that conversation, annihilationism was not identified as a serious issue between evangelicals and the SDA.

Stage 2: Awareness that some thoroughly orthodox evangelicals were annihilationists, and conviction that this is a viable alternative within evangelicalism, although remaining a traditionalist myself.

I have been a member of the Evangelical Theological Society since 1967, and I've read its *Journal* with significant benefit. I considered it a fair representation of what is going on within evangelicalism, particularly what might now be deemed "conservative evangelicalism," as distinct from fundamentalism on one side and "post-conservative evangelicalism" on the other. Back in 1985, no one was talking about "post-conservative evangelicalism," and *JETS* looked to me like a good mirror of evangelicalism in general, along with *Christianity Today* at the magazine level, though the latter had become rather more popular in style than when I first subscribed under the editorship of Carl Henry.

Consequently, when I read Edward Fudge's article in the September 1984 issue of *JETS*, the realization that at least one evangelical scholar was an annihilationist was rather new to me, so I read that article with keen interest.[4] Not long afterwards, I read the first edition of Fudge's 1982 book, *The Fire that Consumes*, which is now in its third edition. I found Fudge's book to be a very thorough examination of everything the Bible has to say about the nature of God's final punishment of sinners, and I was happy to meet him at an ETS meeting a few years later. In spite of the difficulties he has encountered because of his annihilationist convictions, I found him to be a very gracious man. It became clear to me that a strong biblical case could be made for annihilation, and that the traditional view of eternal conscious torment, though very widespread since Augustine, was not the only option within the evangelical tent. But I was not convinced that the traditional way of reading Scripture in regard to God's final judgment of the wicked was incorrect.

Stage 3: Awareness of the strong antipathy of many evangelical theologians to fellow evangelicals who were annihilationists.

It was not very long after I became aware of Edward Fudge's work that I realized that the stakes could be high for dissenters from the traditional view of hell. To some evangelical leaders this appeared to be a question of orthodoxy. In 1989, the National Association of Evangelicals and Trinity Evangelical Divinity School convened a consultation on Evangelical Essentials, with 650 registered participants, "to unite evangelicals in their commitment

---

4. Fudge, "The Final End of the Wicked."

to the great biblical truths of our faith."⁵ The organizers did not intend to produce a short evangelical creed, nor did they assume that agreement could be achieved if they attempted to produce such a creed. Nevertheless, in the "Preface" to the book they later edited, Kenneth Kantzer and Carl Henry said that they sought to formulate a *"confession of what it means to be an evangelical* [emphasis added]. In a day when this term is used loosely to cover a broad variety of belief and unbelief we trust that a clear statement of those common convictions that constitute our evangelical heritage will prove useful to the church."⁶

At that conference, J. I. Packer did a presentation on "Evangelicals and the Way of Salvation: New Challenges to the Gospel: Universalism, and Justification by Faith."⁷ Along the way, he decided to mention the "challenge" of annihilationism:

> Now we turn to the second proposed revision of historic evangelical soteriology, the view that the question of salvation is less agonizing than we thought because after judgment day the unsaved will not exist. This is universalism in reverse: like universalism, it envisages a final state in which all are saved; unlike universalism, it anticipates, not post-mortem conversion, but annihilation and non-being for those who leave this world in unbelief. The exponents of this view, which for our purposes may be called either annihilationism or conditionalism, are all Protestants or cultists. Having been condemned at the fifth lateran Council in 1513, it is not an option for Roman Catholics. Among the Protestants are some distinguished evangelicals, including recently my fellow Anglicans John Stott and Philip Edgcumbe Hughes, and I think it is currently gaining more evangelical adherents. But the question, whether an opinion is true, is not resolved by asking who holds it.⁸

Packer went on to assert that "conditionalism is never advocated as expressing the obvious meaning of Scripture, for this it does not do. Its advocates back into it, rather, in horrified recoil from the thought of billions in endless torment—a thought to which the memory of Hitler's holocaust, and the modern statistical mind-set, no doubt add vividness."⁹

---

5. Kantzer and Henry, *Evangelical Affirmations*, 13.
6. Ibid., 14–15.
7. Ibid., 107–31.
8. Packer, "Evangelicals and the Way of Salvation," 123–24.
9. Ibid., 124.

At that time, I accepted Packer's assessment that the primary motive accounting for evangelicals being attracted to annihilationism was emotive. I often heard that charge later, but I now know that it is wrong to paint all evangelical annihilationists with that brush. By then, Edward Fudge's calm, reasonable, and exhaustive study of Scripture was in print, without any of the hysterics that Packer said lay behind this trend. Nor could either of Packer's fellow Anglicans, Stott and Hughes, be rightly charged with this. What Packer's remarks impressed upon me, however, was the strength of his conviction that annihilationism is aberrant, unbiblical, and dangerous. In his opinion, evangelicals should be concerned about its arising in their midst. This attitude was re-enforced by an even stronger expression of concern from John Ankerberg, in his official response to Packer's presentation:

> The doctrine of eternal punishment is interrelated with many other doctrines. It conditions our thinking in many areas of preaching and teaching. When friends, such as John Stott, Philip Edgcumbe Hughes, Clark Pinnock, John Wenham, Basil Atkinson and other well-known and reputedly evangelical leaders, reject the traditional view of eternal punishment, *the Church suffers serious or even fatal erosion in its doctrinal foundation* [emphasis added].[10]

Remarks like this from evangelical leaders should not be taken lightly. Any evangelicals who might be otherwise impressed with the strength of the biblical case for annihilationism, as I was, obviously needed to be very cautious about joining the little company who had stuck their heads out. John Stott was clearly aware of this himself, which was why he had not revealed for many years that he did not believe the traditional view of eternal conscious torment. But when David L. Edwards put him on the spot, during their Liberal-Evangelical dialogue, Stott felt compelled to explain that he did not personally affirm that traditional view.[11]

According to a friend who had participated in the 1989 conference, the original draft of "evangelical affirmations" had included a statement regarding hell which described it as eternal conscious torment. Since the book in which John Stott went public about his eschatology had only recently been published, many of the participants were not aware that Stott was an annihilationist until Packer mentioned it at the Essentials conference. But, given the very high regard which evangelicals had globally for John Stott, and given the desire to produce a statement of widely shared evangelical beliefs, many doubted the wisdom of publishing a statement of essential

10. Ankerberg, "Response to James I. Packer," 140–41.
11. Stott, "Judgment and Hell," 51–55.

evangelical beliefs which could not be signed by someone like Stott. Eventually, "Affirmation 9," treating the "second coming and judgment," simply said: "Unbelievers will be separated eternally from God. Concern for evangelism should not be compromised by any illusion that all will be finally saved (universalism)."[12] That was a statement that any evangelical annihilationist could affirm equally with traditionalists.

I know that many people left the conference deeply disturbed by the new respectability given to annihilationism through its having been affirmed by so highly regarded an evangelical leader as John Stott. I even heard of teachers who stopped recommending *any* of Stott's books, on account of what they judged to be his grave error on this important theological matter, and at least one Christian bookstore refused to sell any more of John Stott's books. Once again, the remarkable strength of feeling among evangelical traditionalists against any diversion from that view left a strong cautionary impression upon me.

Stage 4: Conclusion that the annihilationist proposal has sufficient biblical warrant to be a viable evangelical alternative.

In my case, as in that of other evangelicals I know, Stott's "coming out" in this regard added some plausibility to annihilationism. It certainly strengthened in me the conviction that no evangelical church or institution should make "eternal conscious torment" a part of its "statement of faith." In one organization with which I was involved, what had come to light in the "evangelical affirmations" conference led to a proposal that the organization's statement should actually be *tightened up*, since the one already in place would not exclude an annihilationist. I was not alone in opposing that new restriction, so the effort did not succeed. It was inconceivable to me that a broadly evangelical organization like ours would rule out the possibility of membership for John Stott, John Wenham, Philip Edgcumbe Hughes, and other evangelicals who shared their understanding of hell.

In 1989, Eerdmans published Philip Edgcumbe Hughes's book, *True Image: The Origin and Destiny of Man in Christ*.[13] Hughes had been on the faculty at Westminster Theological Seminary when I studied there but, because his specialty was New Testament and my degree was in Systematic Theology, I did not study under him. But he was appointed to give me an exam in reading theological French, and I had high regard for Hughes's scholarship. Since he was on the faculty at Westminster, I knew him to be

12. Kantzer and Henry, *Evangelical Affirmations*, 36.
13. Hughes, *The True Image*.

thoroughly orthodox. So I assigned his book as a text in a seminar on biblical anthropology, and I was not disappointed regarding its contribution to our biblical understanding of human being when viewed in light of Christ's having been the paradigmatic human. As was my usual practice in seminars, I was reading the book for the first time along with the class. So I was as surprised as they were when we got close to the end and met Hughes's biblical argument against inherent immortality of the soul. That was no problem for me, since I had already concluded, as Hughes did, that human souls (like human bodies) exist only because God wills to sustain them, and either or both of them could pass out of existence if God chose to withdraw his support. What took me by surprise was that Hughes went on from his argument for the conditional immortality of the soul to a concise, but fervent, case for annihilation as God's final act of judgment of the wicked. By then, few evangelical theologians defended metaphysical indestructibility of the soul, but I had met very few of them who also rejected the traditional view of hell. Conditionalism (in the narrow sense) was common, and I shared it, but annihilationism was still rather unusual in the evangelical world.

In 1990, Clark Pinnock expressed his outrage regarding the traditional view of hell, and he made a case for annihilationism in an article in the *Criswell Theological Review*.[14] The tide was picking up speed.

In 2006/7, I was asked by the editors of the *Global Dictionary of Theology* to contribute the articles on "Hell" and "Universalism," and I was specifically requested to include the annihilationist understanding in my discussion of hell.[15] That assignment launched me into an extensive reading project. This was my first experience of dictionary article writing, and I quickly discovered that in order to write a good dictionary article one has to be prepared to write a book on the subject. I thoroughly enjoyed my reading, and it considerably expanded my notes for teaching eschatology. I was particularly happy for the impetus to read the latest edition of Edward Fudge's great work on "the fire that consumes." When I was done with the article, I dropped Edward a note to express my appreciation for his contribution to evangelical scholarship in this regard, and I told him that he had *almost* convinced me. Of course, he replied that he was sorry not to have completely succeeded, but it must have been a relief to him to get my kind of response when so many evangelicals were expressing strong abhorrence of annihilationism, even to the point of calling it "heresy."

A few years ago, a group of evangelicals who identified themselves as "conditionalists" began to develop a web site which has become a very

---

14. Pinnock, "The Destruction of the Finally Impenitent."
15. Dyrness, *Global Dictionary of Theology*.

helpful resource for the study of evangelical annihilationism. They call it "Rethinking Hell: Exploring Evangelical Conditionalism."[16] One of its originators, Chris Date, had come upon something I had written in which I had stated that annihilationism should be considered a viable option among evangelicals, and so he asked if I would be willing to write an endorsement of their web site. I was impressed with what I saw of their work up to that point, and I thought that it contributed to the sort of reasonable and charitable evangelical conversation about the nature of hell which I considered to be much needed. So I was happy to provide them with the following statement, which still appears on their site:

> The Christian doctrine of hell is a very important matter for Christians, particularly because it arises so frequently in discussions of God's goodness. Among the four main answers to the question of how long hell persists (universalism, immediate annihilationism, ultimate annihilationism or conditionalism, and eternal conscious punishment), I believe that the last two are supported by the strongest biblical evidence. Although I remain a believer in the fourth and most traditional of the key options, I think that ongoing study of Scripture on this important topic is very healthy for the church, so I am happy to see it encouraged by Rethinking Hell.[17]

Having become aware of the existence of that site, I joined its Facebook group and frequently listened to its podcasts. In the providence of God, this kept the biblical teaching regarding hell on my mind in a way which would not otherwise have happened. By then, I had been telling my eschatology students for some time that I believed in the traditional view of hell, but that I was hanging on to it by my fingernails. I knew already that if one takes the language of Scripture in its natural sense, one very often hears God's warning to the wicked that they will die, perish, be consumed, or destroyed. As I read and listened to the material generated by Rethinking Hell, I realized increasingly how slender the textual support is for traditionalism. Nonetheless, I believe that, in doing theology, biblical texts have to be "weighed," not just counted, and so I was convinced that the key texts which are widely believed to teach that God's punishing process goes on endlessly in hell must be treated very seriously, although they are few in number. It was those texts that had kept me in the traditionalist camp, even though I had felt for quite a long time the weight of the exegetical case for final destruction of body and soul. The very strong emotional response to annihilationism that one

---

16. http://www.rethinkinghell.com.
17. Rethinking Hell, "Endorsements."

encounters from many traditionalist theologians was also intimidating. I find that fear puzzling, given the high respect evangelicals confess for the authority of Scripture over all traditions, and I have seen no evidence that it has dangerous effects in other areas of theology or Christian practice. But this strong antipathy is a reality that cannot be ignored with impunity. I have an indemonstrable hunch that this fear is a major factor accounting for the staying power of traditionalism within evangelical eschatology these days, even though so few evangelical theologians teach that souls are intrinsically indestructible. Unless a longtime traditionalist becomes convinced that the biblical case for final destruction is overwhelmingly clear, agnosticism on this point may seem to be the course of wisdom, or silence may look wise. John Stott's reasons for not revealing his long held belief in annihilationism exemplify this assessment. He had little to gain and considerable to lose by making his position known, so he stayed silent about it for decades.

Stage 5: Belief that annihilationism is what the Bible teaches about the end of the wicked.

When I first reached this stage, I identified myself as "formally agnostic" about the nature of hell, although I had come to believe that annihilationism is the best reading of Scripture's teaching on this subject. I did not think that I feared the wrath of the evangelical majority but I can see how my thinking in stage four may still have been at work, even though the scale had tipped from a tenuously held traditionalism to a lightly held annihilationism. When I told Edward Fudge about this movement in my understanding, he warned me that I should not expect my professed agnosticism to appease traditionalists any more than had been the case when John Stott spoke in those terms. I could see very quickly the likelihood that he was right. Having done so, and considering the strong degree to which I now lean toward an annihilationist reading of Scripture, I see no reason to describe myself any longer as agnostic about the nature of hell.

As was the case when I first became an annihilationist, however, I consider this issue relatively unimportant within the hierarchy of doctrines, and I am convinced that one's stance in regard to this issue affects no other doctrines and no important matters of Christian life and ministry. Christian churches and organizations should affirm that God will raise all people from the dead and will judge them all irrevocably, and that his judgment will result in one of two ends, either eternal life or second death (Dan 12:2; John 5:29; Rev 20:6, 14–15). But I can see no reason why any Christian organization would find it necessary to specify the *nature* of the second death (hell) to which the damned will be consigned.

Annihilationism is not a step down a slippery slope. I see no other dominoes that might fall as a result of one's affirmation of either traditionalism or annihilationism, but I now find the latter to be the most plausible reading of the biblical text, and it is least likely to present a stumbling block in evangelism and apologetics. Clearly, John Stott felt this to be true as well, since he revealed his own annihilationist convictions only when he felt the need to present to David Edwards an evangelicalism that was not subject to Edwards's Liberal critique of the traditional view of hell. I am finding that nothing substantial has changed in regard to my understanding of any other doctrines or any aspects of my Christian life. I continue to feel as strongly as ever the awful horror of hell, as the irrevocable, everlasting, but just judgment of God which will be experienced by all those who choose their sinfulness rather than Christ's righteousness, spurn God's grace, and reject his right to be their king.

I continue to believe in the just proportionality of God's judgment upon sinners. The eight-year-old child who is your neighbor, but who is rejecting God's gracious overtures in whatever way these are given to him, will be no less destroyed in body and soul than the evil tyrants who have inflicted such terrible suffering on many people, but I expect that the process which will bring about that destruction will differ considerably, both in duration and in intensity. Yet I do not find much detail in Scripture concerning the means by which God will bring about the final end of the wicked, and I have no desire to imagine it, even though the righteous souls "under the altar" long for the day of God's vengeance (Rev 6:10). They can do this righteously in a way that we who remain alive and suffering may not always be able to do, so we do best to pray for and seek the salvation of all people, even our enemies, with no desire for their condemnation.

While still a traditionalist, I had gained an appreciation for "reconciliationism," as a way to understand the texts regarding God's ultimate victory (1 Cor 15:28; Phil 2:9-11; Col 1:20) within a traditionalist (rather than a universalist) framework. I looked forward to a time when every knee will bow and every tongue confess that Jesus is Lord (Phil 2:9-11), even those in hell, although it will be an end of their fight against God which involves submission but not repentance. I find this concept equally helpful within an annihilationist perspective, where I postulate the likelihood that the moment at which God finally destroys a wicked person will not come until their conscious punishment has brought them to acknowledgement that Jesus is Lord. The extinction of the wicked is the inevitable result of God's withdrawal, not only of his patient grace, but of his metaphysical sustaining.

When the sin of the wicked has been justly punished temporally, and when they have been brought to a teeth gnashing acknowledgment that Jesus is Lord, God will cease to support their existence as embodied souls.

This is not a doctrine concerning which the classic ecumenical creeds of the church stated a position, and I am grateful that many evangelical bodies, including the World Evangelical Alliance, have chosen not to make it an issue in their statements of faith. This is as it should be, I believe, and I hope to see a time when evangelicals globally will accept that on this point, as on many others which have far more consequence (e.g., monergism and synergism), doctrinal differences regarding the final judgment of the wicked will not hinder Christian fellowship or cooperation in ministry.

It is difficult to reconstruct the process I went through in this last stage of my journey thus far, but two experiences stand out in my memory. The first was reading the article Ralph Bowles wrote regarding the interpretation of Revelation 14:11, and the other was reading the pre-published manuscript of *Rethinking Hell*,[18] when I was asked if I would consider writing an endorsement. Prior to reading that excellent collection of annihilationist readings, I had read many of the items it contained, but reading them all together had a cumulative effect. I wrote my commendation of the book from the perspective of a traditionalist, since that was still my position, but in the months that followed, I gradually found myself moving to general agreement with the conclusion of the authors in that work.

It is now my firm conviction that if people were not previously taught (as many of us were, from childhood) that hell is being consciously tormented forever by God, no one would reach that conclusion from their own careful reading of Scripture itself. There, the end of the wicked is regularly spoken of as death in contrast with life, and the language is almost always descriptive of destruction, perishing or being consumed. As Paul warned the Romans, "the wages of sin is *death* [as readers of Scripture will have heard repeatedly, all the way back to Gen 2:17, through the use of numerous synonyms], but the free gift of God is eternal life in Christ Jesus our Lord" (Rom 6:23 ESV). Likewise James contrasts the two destinies brought about by different actions: "sin when it is fully grown brings forth death" (Jas 1:15), but "the word of truth" brings forth new creatures (Jas 1:18). And Jesus, in what may be the most memorized passage in Scripture, stated that belief in Jesus results in eternal life, but persistent unbelief results in perishing (John 3:16). This drastic contrast between life for the righteous and death for the wicked (even destruction of soul as well as body, Matt 10:28) is so continuous as to be inescapable for an attentive reader of Scripture, who will

---

18. Date, Stump, and Anderson, *Rethinking Hell*.

find remarkably few passages which might give the impression of endless conscious torment for the wicked.

I cannot lay out a chronology of the interpretive moves I made as I came to believe that God finally destroys the wicked, but I am able to identify a few factors which were critical in my journey, including the following:

1. I concluded that it is very unlikely that anyone who only had the Old Testament scriptures would expect that God would finally punish the wicked by causing them to suffer endlessly and consciously. Overwhelmingly, death, ruin, and destruction were the potential fate concerning which God's old covenant prophets warned Israel and the nations. Even in the New Testament, the fire about which Jesus warns sinners is a fire that consumes, not one that perpetually torments (Matt 3:10–12; 7:19; 13:30, 40–42, 49, 50). The opposite of the life which God gives the righteous is death or destruction, not endless torment (cf. Matt 7:13, 14).

2. I became more aware of the diversity of understanding concerning the final end of the wicked during the inter-testamental period, and I could see that the idea of endless conscious torment was the consequence of Greek philosophical influence rather than Old Testament exegesis. I also realized that this diversity continued into the thought of the early theologians of the Christian church, until consensus grew that human souls can not be destroyed, after which eternal conscious punishment was an inevitable theological deduction.

3. The fact that I had believed in the conditional immortality of the soul from the earliest period of my formal theological formation had always made annihilationism a possibility for me, so I was a traditionalist because I believed the Bible taught the endless conscious punishing of the wicked, not because of my theological anthropology. Consequently, my traditionalism depended upon the biblical texts which seemed to indicate that God keeps the condemned alive forever, in parallel with the endlessness of the joy of the saved, although the quality of that life was so vastly different that neither "immortality" nor "eternal life" were ever ascribed to the wicked. Those texts were not numerous (Matt 18:34, 35; Mark 9:43–48; esp. Rev 14:10–11; 20:10), but they were critical anchors for my traditionalism.

4. Consequently, key factors in undermining my traditionalist reading of the New Testament were new grammatical and lexicological understandings. Among these, the most important were the following:

a. I gained a better understanding of the significance of the range of meaning of *aiōnios*, which is commonly translated "eternal." It can have the sense of "age long" or refer to something derived from God, the Eternal One, so that it describes qualitatively rather than quantitatively (cf. Rom 16:25-26, and phrases like "eternal life" and "eternal fire" [Matt 18:8 and 25:41; cf. Jude 7 and 2 Pet 2:6]). When I revisited Edward Fudge's work, I realized more keenly the importance of the fact that "when the [NT] word *aiōnios* modifies words which name acts or processes as distinct from persons or things, the adjective usually describes the issue or result of the action rather than the action itself."[19]

> This is indisputably true in four of the six New Testament occurrences. There is eternal salvation [Heb 5:9] but not an eternal act of saving. There is eternal redemption [Heb 9:12] but not an eternal process of redeeming. The eternal sin [Mk 3:29] was committed at a point in history, but its results continue into the coming age which lasts forever. Scripture pictures eternal judgment [Heb 6:2] as taking place "on a day," but its outcome will have no end. In the light of this usage, we suggest that Scripture expects the same understanding when it speaks of "eternal destruction" [2 Thess 1:9] and "eternal punishment" [Mt 25:46]. Both are acts. There will be an actual destroying and the punishing will issue in a result. That resultant punishment of destruction will never end.[20]

This awareness opened the door to the possibility that the eternality of punishment might lie, not in its temporal endlessness, but in its effective irreversibility, particularly when we consider the metaphors of fire and consumption by worms which are regularly used in Scripture to denote total destruction (cf. Ezek 20:47-48; Amos 5:5-6; Mal 4:1-6; Matt 3:12). Eternal punish*ment* need not connote eternal conscious punish*ing*; indeed it *cannot* do so, if God grants eternal (in the sense of endless) life exclusively to those whom he saves in Christ, which can only be denied through contorted readings of the clear statements of the New Testament.

b. I gained a stronger appreciation of the interpretive importance of the Old Testament incidents and language which were in the minds of the authors of New Testament texts, particularly in

---

19. Fudge, *The Fire that Consumes* (1982), 49.
20. Ibid., 49-50.

Revelation, where some of the most important texts which purportedly support eternal conscious torment are found. These included highly important references to unquenchable fire, smoke that rises forever, and worms that never die. I saw more clearly how New Testament descriptions of the punishment of the wicked, which had seemed to connote an endless process, were drawn from Old Testament descriptions of God's judgment of opponents like Sodom and Gomorrah (2 Pet 2:6) and Edom (Isa 34:10; cf. Rev 14:11).[21] These judgments were clearly temporary but unstoppable until God was finished with them, and their destructive effects were never ending. The language of Isaiah 66:24, as cited by Jesus in Mark 9:44–48, has been particularly important in the church's traditional perception of hell. But, as Edward Fudge noted, it is likely reminiscent of the historical incident in Isaiah 36–37, which alerts us to the significant fact that, in both Isaiah 37:36 and 66:24, the enemies go out and see dead bodies or corpses, as they view their enemies' destruction, not their misery.[22]

Other essays and books have dealt with these interpretive issues in great detail, and I cannot do them justice here without writing another book. But these were key factors in my eschatological development.

I hope that this brief theological autobiography in relationship to one small, but very significant part, of Christian doctrine will be of some help to others. I write it because I have benefited from hearing others tell about aspects of their theological journey. To really grasp the immensity of the loss that God's enemies will ultimately experience, we need to know what God has in store for those who love him and are loved by him. All Scripture is profitable, and we should not shrink from declaring the truth that those who fight God all their lives will be very severely punished. God can use those warnings as means of graciously drawing people back from the brink of hell. But we must not neglect to paint just as clearly, for those who are rejecting God's grace, a biblical picture of the wonderful and endless life that God has planned for his children by faith, in the new heaven and earth which will be more glorious than anything we can possibly imagine. No decision human beings make in their entire lives is more important than the one that will finally determine whether they experience endless joy with God through Christ in the new earth, or lose all of that and perish in the second death.

---

21. See particularly Bowles, "Revelation 14:11," 141–42, 146–48.
22. Fudge, *The Fire that Consumes* (1982), 110–11.

3

"Are You Going to Heaven?"
A Journey Away from the Wrong Question

— Jon Zens —

Since 1977, Jon and Dotty Zens have traveled to encourage relational fellowships both domestically and internationally. They bring Christ as the Foundation, and help with the expression of Christ's life in the community. From 1970–1975 and 1985–2000, Jon worked in three manufacturing facilities in aerospace production planning, inside sales, inventory control, engineering support, human resources, purchasing and shipping/receiving. Jon has been the editor of Searching Together *since 1978, and is the author of numerous books. He has a BA from Covenant College, an MDiv. from Westminster Seminary, and a D.Min. from the California Graduate School of Theology.*

The first church I was a part of in Southern California had a visitation program. For many months in 1965 I went with another member house-to-house. At every opportunity we asked those who answered the door, "If you died tonight, would you go to heaven?" After many years into my pilgrimage, I realized that is the wrong question to ask. In a sense, my path away from this question began when I met Edward Fudge.

In the strangest of circumstances, I met Edward in 1979 at a Nashville Holiday Inn where Robert D. Brinsmead was doing sessions over a weekend. Edward may have thought that my theology fostered melancholy because when we shook hands his first words to me were, "Jon, are you a happy man?"

Prior to that brief encounter in Nashville, I had prepared an article that took issue with a piece published by Edward in *Christianity Today*, "Putting Hell in Its Place."[1] My article was titled, "Do the Flames Ever Stop in Hell?" and appeared in the *Free Grace Broadcaster*.[2] In 1978 I believed in eternal torment, and the brunt of my conviction was based on the fact that the Greek word αἰώνιος, translated "eternal," was used to describe both bliss and punishment.[3] Little did I know that this belief would be challenged as my journey progressed.

Beginning in 1977, I began to move away from a Law-based theology into a Christ-centered outlook rooted in the New Covenant. In 1982 I was reflecting on the Holy Spirit's work in revealing Christ to us, and my research came upon the invasion of Greek philosophy into the early church fathers' discussion of the Trinity. My published article cited K. R. Hagenbach who noted in 1864 that the thinking of the early fathers "frequently yielded to speculation, and was mixed up with foreign [philosophies]."[4]

Somewhere in all this, I began to see that the traditional view of the "Immortality of the soul" was not anchored in the Bible, but in philosophy. I read Oscar Cullmann's small, but classic book on the immortality of the soul.[5] So much theology was built on the assumption that each person had an "immortal soul," yet the New Testament seemed to point in other directions.

"Immortality" is used five times in the New Testament—of God, Christ, and believers. To suggest that unbelievers are "immortal" in any way flies in the face of this revelation. In their "witness," the early church spoke about "the resurrection of the dead," not about "going to heaven." John tells us that "no one has ascended to heaven" except Christ (John 3:13), and Peter mentions specifically that "David did not ascend to heaven," but Christ did (Acts 2:34).

If people's spirits leave their bodies when they die and go straight to heaven or hell, then what is to be made of a passage like Matthew 25:31–46? These verses describe the future appearance of resurrected humans before Christ on the last day. At this time their final destiny, one of bliss or of

---

1. Fudge, "Putting Hell in Its Place."
2. Zens, "Do the Flames Ever Stop in Hell?"
3. See, for example, Matt 25:46.
4. Hagenbach, *History of Doctrines*, 117.
5. Cullmann, *Immortality of the Soul or Resurrection of the Dead?*

judgment, is proclaimed by the Lord. If their spirits had already been in the bad or good place for periods of time, then what sense would the Lord's words make? They could rightly point out, "You're just telling us what we already known for some time," which would in effect render Jesus' assignment of destinies superfluous and meaningless. It is not at death, but in the final resurrection of the just and unjust that their ends are announced by Jesus Christ.

If one's "spirit" goes to "heaven" when death occurs, it can't be as is stated at many Christian funerals, "so-and-so is not in a wheelchair now, but dancing with the Lord." One can't do such things without a body.

Someone has said, "We are not human beings having a temporary *spiritual* experience, but rather we are spiritual beings having a temporary *human* experience." This kind of thinking permeates traditional theology, and certainly contemporary Christian music and literature. However, this perspective fails to measure up to the *holistic* view of humans offered by the Bible. It sees us not as persons divided up into parts, but always connects us with *bodily* existence. Thus, the common idea that at death the human spirit leaves the body and "goes to heaven" is very confusing. Paul viewed dead saints as "asleep," awaiting the future resurrection. The Scriptures do not contemplate believers being apart from their bodies. The "spirit leaving the body at death" is a pagan idea, not a biblical one. Paul's repeated word is "asleep." We "sleep" until resurrection day.

Reading and later re-reading Richard Gaffin's *The Centrality of the Resurrection* confirmed to me that the overwhelming emphasis in the New Testament is on resurrection—first Christ's, then ours at the end of this age.[6] Just as Christ suffered and then entered glory via resurrection, so we suffer in the present age and then are glorified in resurrection on the last day. Paul is specific that our bodily "glorification" will take place in the context of Christ's return in glory, not at the moment a believer dies. "Glorification" is about all of God's people being handed over to the Father by Christ, not the individual deaths of believers one-by-one. The author of Hebrews tells us that those of faith in the old era were not looking for "life after death," but rather a "better resurrection" (Heb 11:35).

Another domino that fell was the assumption that by "eternal punishment" Jesus meant that the judgment of the wicked would consist in eternal torment. I began to notice that the preponderance of images used in the New Testament involved "perishing" and "destruction." Gathering the wheat and burning up the chaff did not seem compatible with people burning forever. A key picture Jesus used for judgment was that of Gehenna, a

---

6. Gaffin, *The Centrality of Resurrection*.

garbage dump outside of Jerusalem in which the smoke never stopped, and what was thrown into it was totally consumed.

As I spent time reflecting on the fate of those outside of Christ, the clear pattern of utter "destruction" emerged. It was at this time, probably around 1988, that I finally pulled Edward Fudge's *The Fire that Consumes* off the shelf and read it.[7] This masterful book confirmed and expanded the conclusions I had been coming to. While I had rejected Edward's views in 1978, *The Fire that Consumes* brought home the truth to me in a powerful way years later.

In 2009, a quarterly journal I have edited since 1978 called *Searching Together* published an issue under the theme, "Then What?" It featured two articles: "Heaven to Earth: The Believer's Hope in the Resurrection" by David D. Flowers, and "Death and Resurrection in Scripture" by W. F. Bell. Needless to say, what was presented caused quite a discussion! Then when Rob Bell's *Love Wins* was released, a number of people encouraged me to write a response to it. This resulted in my little book, *Christ Minimized?* and Edward Fudge was kind enough to write an excellent foreword.[8]

I am so thankful for the loving labors and kind spirit Edward has manifested for many years. He has contributed to my growth in Christ in a singular way since I met him in 1979. Even though we have only met face-to-face once, I feel like I have always had a true, supportive friend in him.

---

7. Fudge, *The Fire That Consumes* (1982).
8. Zens, *Christ Minimized?*

4

Moses, Jesus, and Fudge
How Edward Fudge (and Biblical Theology) Changed What I Preach about Hell

— Rob McRay —

Rob McRay is a graduate of Abilene Christian University (Biblical Studies) and Wheaton College Graduate School (Theological Studies) and has done graduate study in New Testament backgrounds at the University of Chicago. He served as a senior minister for thirty years, and is currently the Executive Director of Youth Encouragement Services, a nonprofit serving inner city youth in Nashville. Rob is also an adjunct instructor in Bible at Lipscomb University.

Rob originally presented the following paper at the Rethinking Hell conference, 2014.

INTRODUCTION: THE POPULAR PROBLEM WITH HELL

About ten years ago, Jan walked into my office loaded with questions. She had been coming to our church with the man she was dating. She was in her late forties and turned off with Christianity. Something in my preaching intrigued her enough that she decided to come with her questions and see what I'd say. But she was pretty confident that the conversation would end as a number of previous conversations with other preachers had ended.

Jan had largely rejected faith in God and the Bible because she could not accept certain doctrinal positions that she thought all Christians were expected to accept. Chief among them were the views that the earth was created in six twenty-four-hour days and the view that people would burn in hell for all eternity. She felt that such views, which she had heard from so many other preachers, required her to shut off her brain and blindly accept ideas which seemed absurd to her. We talked for at least an hour and a half, and when she got up to leave she said, "You know, you did not say anything I expected you to say."

Jan's reaction to eternal torment is almost universal in my experience. Among unbelievers, Christians are commonly viewed as judgmental.[1] In my experience, the traditional doctrine of hell is a significant reason for that opinion. People often remark, "So you think I'm going to burn in hell because _____," or, "How do you believe in a God who will burn people forever?" Among Christians, a similar reaction to eternal torment is sometimes only tempered by church members' fears of criticizing a view for which they have no alternatives—after all, rejecting the doctrine of hell might send you there! But the overwhelming majority of church members I have taught have been eager for an alternative. Personally, they find the doctrine of eternal torment abhorrent, but feel they have been forced to accept it as an abhorrent truth.

Some Christians react when I tell Jan's story by saying, "So you are changing your teaching on hell to make it easier to swallow by worldly people." Albert Mohler, in *Hell under Fire*, asks what has happened that has led so many evangelicals to reject the traditional view. He says, "the answer must be found in understanding the impact of cultural trends and the prevailing worldview on Christian theology."[2] In the same volume, my former classmate at Wheaton, Robert Yarbrough, contends, ". . . we should be wary of the temptation of our era to dilute the Bible's message about hell because it is currently acceptable, not only in society but increasingly even in the church, to pick and chose [sic] what one wishes to believe."[3]

This is too easy a dismissal of the critics of the traditional view. Too often voices of reform are disdained as just following the present age. If someone advocates for changes in the role of women in the church, it must be because they are following cultural trends and influences, not because they considered the biblical evidence from Judges 4 to Galatians 3 and

---

1. See the disturbing research in Kinnaman and Lyons, *unChristian*. The authors do not address the popular reaction to the doctrine of hell.
2. Mohler, "Modern Theology," 36.
3. Yarbrough, "Jesus on Hell," 71.

honestly came to a different conclusion. If someone promotes an ecumenical spirit of unity over continued dogmatic division, it must be because they caved in to the popular notion that love is all that matters, not because they have wrestled with John 17 and 1 Corinthians 13 and objectively assessed the demands of these texts.

It may well be true that some critics of the traditional view of hell are merely under the influence of the spirit of this age. But that was certainly not the case for Edward Fudge, as his story, told in the new film "Hell and Mr. Fudge," dramatically represents.[4] Nor was it true in my case. Biblical theology drove me away from the traditional view in search of some other answer, and Edward helped put the pieces together.

The problem we have with the traditional view is not the result of a rejection of biblical authority or a biblical worldview, nor a refusal to accept the plain meaning of the text—I think both sides of the debate over hell accept biblical authority and are honestly trying to interpret individual texts. The key issue, I suggest, is whether our interpretations of individual texts are consistent with the broader scope of biblical theology.

THE CONTRIBUTIONS OF EDWARD FUDGE

This point, I think, is the most significant impact of Edward's teaching. Edward lamented for a time that his legacy would be bound up forever in hell. In recent years I think he has come to peace with that possibility, and taken some comfort with knowing he has made a significant impact on a very serious topic. But I suggest that his work should be less remembered for explaining the meaning of eternal punishment, and more for preaching the love and grace of God.

Edward's work has made several important contributions to the discussion of this topic. Among these are the sheer scope and detail of his research and arguments (the words "encyclopedic" and even "exhausting" come to mind). I know of nothing on this subject quite like *The Fire That Consumes*. Another contribution has been his helpful exegesis of key texts: considering anew what various passages actually say and how they are best understood in context, and pointing out how the traditional view requires strained readings of some texts. Also helpful has been his contention that the traditional view of hell originates more in Greek philosophy than in the Scriptures themselves.

Most important, however, has been Edward's stressing of the incompatibility of the traditional view with the character of God. He has rightly

---

4. See Fudge's response to such charges in Fudge, *The Fire That Consumes*, 2–3.

argued that eternal torment is irreconcilable with God's self-revelation as loving Father.

In 1991 I sat in a classroom at the Bible lectureship at Pepperdine University and listened to Edward give a lecture on his views. My father had introduced me to some of his ideas earlier, but this was my first opportunity to hear Edward make his case. Several of the contributions I just mentioned were evident in his presentation, but one story would forever change how I approached this subject.

Edward asked us to imagine that we left our children with a babysitter. In order to get our children to behave, the sitter threatened that, if they were not good, when we returned we would take matches and burn the bottoms of their feet, and take toothpicks and drive them under their fingernails, and take knives and peel off their skin, and continue to do this over and over and over again. The images made us visibly cringe. I didn't even want to hear it, much less imagine it.

Then he said, "Now I want you to imagine returning home to learn that is what this sitter, to whom you had entrusted your children, was telling the children whom you love. How furious would you be with that sitter? How hurt would you be to think that is what your children had been led to believe about you?" This, Edward said, is what we preachers have been telling the children of God about their Heavenly Father.

This illustration stunned me. I knew immediately that I could never again teach the traditional view of hell—not unless I could reconcile that doctrine with the image of myself as a sitter to God's beloved children. That is not an emotional reaction to a disturbing sermon illustration. It is rather the conviction that came with clearly seeing the impact of teaching a doctrine at odds with biblical theology—with the self-revelation of God—as I hope to show in this paper.

BIBLICAL THEOLOGY AND THE STORY OF GOD

By "biblical theology" I do not mean a "theology based on the Bible," as any Christian theology should indeed find its basis in the teachings of Scripture. Rather, I mean "biblical theology" as distinct from "systematic theology" or "dogmatics." As Roy Zuck explains, "biblical theology seeks to find its theological categories and emphases within the Bible itself and not from rational or classical patterns derived from without and imposed upon Scripture."[5] Systematic theology considers biblical data and arranges and categorizes and explains that data, using philosophical approaches that may or may

---

5. Zuck, *Biblical Theology*, 1.

not be consistent with the theology of the biblical documents themselves, and which may impose meanings on the textual data inconsistent with the original theological contexts. While there is a place for systematic theology, and the consideration of church tradition, natural theology, and other influences employed in that discipline, biblical theology confines itself to the themes and concepts found in the Scriptures themselves. Edmond Jacob further suggests that dogmatics must constantly reassess its conclusions based on the results of the work of biblical theology.[6]

If we allow the Bible itself to set the categories for how we describe God, we must begin by recognizing that the Bible does not attempt to define God in philosophical terms or to present philosophical arguments for God's existence.[7] The Scriptures do not focus on explaining the nature of God using categories such as omnipresence, omnipotence, omniscience, essence, or even Trinity. (That is not to say that such concepts are not true, or that they are not themselves based on biblical statements and ideas. It is simply an acknowledgement that there are no treatises in Scripture on the nature of God as we might find in a creed or a systematic theology.) We should not, therefore, let philosophical assumptions determine God's nature and what he must do, but rather let the Bible define God using its own categories.

In the Scriptures God reveals himself in two ways: by descriptions of God's character (we will return to this below), but even more by the story of what God has done—by his acts which themselves reveal his character. The Scriptures do not "bring us ideas about God, but acts of God."[8] As Hasel points out, "God introduces and identifies himself by great events in deeds and words, and it is around them that Israel responds in praise and worship, and that Biblical literature originates."[9] Biblical theology is, therefore, "primarily a story about God," a "description and interpretation of the divine activity," not a "system of abstract truths."[10] Consequently, as Westermann

---

6. "Dogmatics does not confine itself solely to the Bible, it takes much account of the contributions of philosophy and natural theology, as well as that of Church tradition; but if it wishes to remain 'Christian' it will always have to make fresh assessments of its declarations by comparing them with the essential biblical data, the elucidation of which is precisely the task of biblical theology, itself based on well-founded exegesis." (Jacob, *Theology*, 31)

7. "The Bible is not concerned to prove God or to discuss theism in a philosophical manner. It assumes a personal, powerful, self-existent being who is creator of the world and of man, and who is concerned about man." (Ladd, *Theology*, 26)

8. Jacob, *Theology*, 32.

9. Hasel, *Old Testament*, 100.

10. Ladd, *Theology*, 26.

contends, if the Scriptures present God through a story, the structure of a biblical theology "must be based on events rather than concepts."[11]

THE CORE OF BIBLICAL THEOLOGY

It is perhaps all but universally recognized that the theology of the New Testament centers on the death and resurrection of Jesus. The problem of the center of OT theology, however, has been widely debated. Kaiser points to the promise of God; Eichrodt, the covenant theme; Von Rad, the narration of the mighty acts of God; and so on. Hasel argues that none of these can account for the theological perspectives of all the Old Testament scriptures, especially the Wisdom literature, and suggests that the center is simply God![12]

I obviously cannot settle that debate, but I will contend (somewhat in keeping with Von Rad) that Old Testament theology centers in the story of God's mighty acts, acts that reveal God's nature especially as a God of steadfast lovingkindness. A few of these mighty acts principally serve to shape the story of God and how he is revealed to Israel. These few rise above the litany of all the great things Yahweh has done to become common expressions of faith, sources of revelation and exposition about God and his relationship to his people, and foundations not only for the theology of the Old Testament but also for the New.

First among these is, of course, the creation which first reveals God and his purposes for humanity.[13] Next, the promise to Abraham not only points to the exodus and shapes much of the language of the New Testament, but in some ways provides a limited three-part outline of the rest of the story of the Bible: the formation of the nation of Israel, the settlement of the Promised Land, and the blessing of all nations through Israel and the

---

11. "If we wish to describe what the Old Testament as a whole says about God, we have to start by looking at the way in which the Old Testament presents itself; this can be recognized by everyone: 'The Old Testament tells a story' (Gerhard von Rad). With that statement we have reached our first decision about the form of an Old Testament theology: if the Old Testament narrates what it has to say about God in the form of a story, then the structure of an Old Testament theology must be based on events rather than concepts." (Westermann, *Old Testament*, 11–12)

12. Hasel, *Old Testament*, 99–103.

13. The flood is not a central, defining event in biblical theology on a level with the others in my list. Outside of the Genesis narrative and genealogies, Noah is only mentioned seven or eight times in Scripture. Rather, the Noah story is part of, or perhaps a sequel to, the creation narrative itself. God's good creation plunges into sin, and God destroys and recreates the earth and humanity.

Messiah.[14] Third, the exodus narrative from Egypt to the Promised Land is not only the greatest of the mighty acts; it is, in fact, a *collection* of mighty acts revealing God. The exodus not only serves as the foundation event for the faith of Israel, but also serves as the setting for the gospel event when Jesus chooses Passover as the occasion for his death and resurrection. Fourth, God's selection of a shepherd boy to be king and calling him to shepherd the people provides the standard against which future Israelite kings would be measured, transforms Israel's language of worship and leadership, and is the source of much of the Messiah and kingdom language in the Gospels. Finally, the exile dominates much of the Old Testament, affirms what the exodus narrative revealed about God, provides the context for much of the message of the prophets, and shapes most of the eschatological language of the New Testament (including the teachings about final punishment). Each of these events serves to reveal God and to shape the way the story of God is told.

Of these, the exodus event is unquestionably the foundational event.[15] The story of Moses from the burning bush to the Promised Land is *the* great narrative of God's self-revelation in the Hebrew Scriptures. God's declaration that "I am the LORD your God who brought you out of Egypt" not only opens the Ten Commandments, but is repeated over seventy times throughout the Old Testament.[16] In a manner somewhat parallel to the New Testament, the Torah is the foundation narrative revealing Yahweh as the God who brought Israel out of Egypt, much like the Gospels reveal that God is the one who raised Jesus from the dead.[17] These two affirmations—God

---

14. The promise to Abraham had three parts: his descendants would become a great nation, they would be given the land of Canaan, and through them God would bless all nations.

15. Contra Westermann (who questions the unquestionable): "It is the task of a theology of the Old Testament to describe and view together what the Old Testament as a whole, in all its sections, says about God. The task is not correctly understood if one takes one part of the Old Testament to be the most important and gives it prominence over the others; or if one regards the whole as determined by one concept such as covenant or election or salvation; or if one asks, to begin, what the theological center of the Old Testament is. The New Testament obviously has its center in the suffering, death, and resurrection of Christ, to which the Gospels are directed and which the Epistles take as their starting point. The Old Testament, however, has no similarity at all to this structure." (Westermann, *Old Testament*, 11)

16. Its classic expression is found in the creedal affirmation at the offering of the first fruits: "And the Lord brought us out of Egypt with a mighty hand and an outstretched arm, with great deeds of terror, with signs and wonders. And he brought us into this place and gave us this land, a land flowing with milk and honey." (Deut 26:8–9)

17. By placing the exodus narrative at the foundation of Old Testament Scripture and theology, I am not speaking of the date of the compositions of the Pentateuch as we

brought Israel out of Egypt and raised Jesus from the dead—serve as the core of the Bible's revelation of God. Thus the center of each Testament is a mighty act in which the love of God is demonstrated through his faithful act of saving his people and keeping his promises.

This framework will serve to help us describe two great themes in Old Testament theology, each of which is particularly relevant to the discussion of hell: God's steadfast love and his justice.

BIBLICAL THEOLOGY AND THE *CHESED* OF GOD

God's character is revealed and described in the Scriptures with terms such as "holiness," "faithfulness," "justice," and "love."[18] Chief among these, of course, is his love. The story of God's deliverance of Israel from Egypt includes the most significant theological statement of the Old Testament—God's description of himself:

> The LORD passed before him, and proclaimed, "The LORD, the LORD, a God merciful and gracious, slow to anger, and abounding in steadfast love and faithfulness, keeping steadfast love for thousands, forgiving iniquity and transgression and sin, but who will by no means clear the guilty, visiting the iniquity of the fathers upon the children and the children's children, to the third and the fourth generation." (Exod 34:6–7, RSV)

This statement is quoted repeatedly throughout the Old Testament (though not nearly as often as the statement that God brought Israel out of Egypt). Moses quotes it in the wilderness (Num 14:17–18), and Jonah at Nineveh (Jonah 4:2)—though for conflicting reasons. Nehemiah cites it in his great prayer (Neh 9:17), the Psalmist declares it in worship (Pss 86:15; 103:8; 145:8), and Joel cites it in his preaching (Joel 2:13).

These descriptions of God's character use a word that is notoriously difficult to translate into English. The Hebrew *chesed* was translated as "lovingkindness" by the American Standard Version, "steadfast love" by the

---

have them, any more than the assertion of the primacy of the death and resurrection of Jesus requires that the Gospels were written prior to the epistles. The point is not which books were written first, but that the story and Torah of Moses preceded the preaching of the prophets, and that the exodus event and giving of the Torah are foundational to the prophetic message and ministry, to the worship of the Psalms, and to the histories of Joshua–Kings and Chronicles–Nehemiah.

18. We could use the term "God's nature," but this would confuse the biblical focus with philosophical efforts to describe what God is, whereas the Scriptures are concerned with who he is and how he acts toward humanity.

Revised Standard Version, and simply "love" by the New International Version.[19] The word *chesed* suggests the kindness freely shown by God out of his own mercy, especially in the context of his covenant relationship of love. It is very close to Paul's use of "grace."[20]

While the Exodus 34 text includes a word of judgment, that judgment is poured out only to the third and fourth generation, not infinitely. More importantly, "to the third and fourth generation" is contrasted with showing steadfast love to "thousands." As Olbricht stresses in his brief but excellent Old Testament theology written for use by Bible students, "Despite popular opinion, the primary characteristic of God in the Old Testament is love. His love is intense and unremitting. His love is forever. This point cannot be stressed too much. The wrath of God is a secondary characteristic."[21] This theme continues, of course, as the heart of New Testament theology, especially in the Johannine focus on love (esp. John 3:16, 1 John 4:7–16) and the Pauline emphasis on grace (esp. Eph 2:1–10).

It is no coincidence that the two most significant statements about God in the Old Testament both come from the Exodus narrative. God's character is revealed primarily through his great acts. And so, God's steadfast love is most especially revealed through is merciful act of deliverance, just as in the New Testament God's love is most clearly seen in the death and resurrection of Jesus. "The love of God is obvious, not because of some misty sheen that hangs over the universe or an ecstatic emotion that overpowers the human heart, but because of his concrete, dramatic acts of salvation on behalf of his people."[22]

In my opinion, the greatest challenge to the traditional view of hell is that it elevates other qualities of God above the primary scriptural description of God as one who abounds in mercy and love. Even if it may be argued that God's justice and holiness require severe punishment of wickedness, the idea that God would deliberately create billions of human beings whom he knows will sin, and then keep them alive for all eternity to suffer the unspeakable torments of hell, is incredibly difficult—I would say impossible—to reconcile with the central, overarching description of God throughout Scripture. The story of the Bible is the story of a God on a mission to save

---

19. The problem with the overly simplistic rendering of the NIV is that it confuses *chesed* with the common word for "love" (*ahab*), calling up notions of feeling and emotion, whereas *chesed* connotes acts of mercy and kindness.

20. In fact, the Complete Jewish Bible uses "grace" to translate *chesed* in Exodus 34:6.

21. Olbricht, *He Loves Forever*, 11.

22. Ibid., 16. Olbricht points to Psalm 136 as an example of God's mighty acts declared as evidence of his steadfast love.

humanity out of his merciful lovingkindness. It is a story that begins and ends in the garden. Eternal torment seems terribly out of place in that story.

THE THEME OF JUSTICE AND DIVINE PUNISHMENT IN THE OLD TESTAMENT

Now we turn to the theme of God's justice, especially as it relates to the question of hell. Some say God's justice demands the eternal torment of the wicked, but that argument is inconsistent with what the Scriptures say about God's justice.

According to the principles of justice laid out in the Torah, punishment must fit the crime—life for life, eye for eye, tooth for tooth (Exod 21:22-25; Lev 24:17-21; Deut 19:16-21). This principle, commonly referred to as the *lex talionis*, not only required that justice be meted out in a manner as severe as the offense, it also prevented punishment from exceeding the severity of the offense. So murder required capital punishment, but one could not be executed for theft. Furthermore, humane considerations restricted the extent of corporal punishment, guarding against the debasement of the one punished (Deut 25:1-3).

If, under the Torah, a thief could not be executed, and if corporal punishment had to be limited, how is infinite suffering a just punishment for *any* sin? If the *lex talionis* ("life for life") were applied quite literally to perhaps the worst murderer in human history, Adolph Hitler, you could perhaps sentence him to die some 10,000,000 times—I'm not sure how you would do that, but once you did, presumably it would be finished; or, you could sentence him to 10,000,000 consecutive life sentences totaling over 700,000,000 years—but no more. However, according to the traditional view, 700,000,000 years is just a drop in the bucket of the eternity that awaits him. An eternity of suffering is simply incompatible with God's justice as defined in the Torah.

We should further note that this is an application of Old Testament justice which does not yet take into account the grace of Jesus! If the Sermon on the Mount replaces the *lex talionis* as a principle of justice (and I'm not convinced it does), it does so with the extension of mercy, not the extension of punishment to infinite extremes.[23] Jesus clearly moves in the opposite direction of eternal torment.

Next to the exodus, perhaps the most significant mighty act of God in Old Testament theology is the exile—more Old Testament books are

---

23. In my opinion, Jesus was speaking to personal revenge more than to the duly authorized execution of justice. Still the point remains a relevant consideration.

connected to the exile than any other biblical event.[24] The exile reveals who God is, demonstrates his justice, and promises his mercy and restoration. These texts present a view of God's justice that support conditionalism, but not eternal torment (nor universalism).

The exile demonstrates God's justice in the destruction of the wicked. The principle of the *lex talionis* continues in the prophets as the standard of God's own just actions in punishing the nations. Jacob observes:

> Whether judgment on the nations or on Israel is concerned, the law which guides the exercise of judgment is always the "lex talionis": "Thou hast pillaged—thou shalt be pillaged" (Isa 33:1); "Those who devour you shall be devoured" (Jer 30:16); "Do unto her as she [Babylon] hath done" (Jer 50:29). The people forsook Yahweh and so Yahweh will forsake them (Hos 1:9; 2:4; 4:6). The wicked will reap what they have sown (Isa 3:10–11). This is why the prophets were able to see, in the exile, the just punishment of God against a people who had forsaken him (Jer 5:19; 18:10–13).[25]

God himself is seen in the exile as acting according to his own principles of justice set out in the Torah. Again, the idea that God's justice requires unending suffering is simply out of character with the biblical evidence.

The exilic texts inform most of the apocalyptic and prophetic material in the New Testament, including Jesus' descriptions of Gehenna. The language of unquenched fire and perpetual worms draws on the image of the piles of rotting and burning corpses after the siege and destruction of a city (Mark 9:47–48; cf. Isa 66:24). Jesus employs language common in the Old Testament for the destruction of wicked nations when he states very plainly, "Do not fear those who kill the body but cannot kill the soul. Rather fear him who can destroy both soul and body in hell" (Matt 10:28). The common argument that the word "destroy" in Greek doesn't always have to mean "destroy" would not likely make sense to those listening to Jesus in Hebrew or Aramaic. It's hard to imagine that Jesus' Jewish audience would have understood him to say anything other than that God will kill the soul in hell.[26]

---

24. The works of Samuel–Kings and Chronicles explain why the exile happened; Ezra, Nehemiah, and Esther are set during the exile and return; and all, or nearly all, of the prophets either predict the exile or are written during the exile or its aftermath. We could add that some of the Psalms are connected to the exile, placing the final compilation during the exile or return.

25. Jacob, *Theology*, 322.

26. There is widespread discussion of whether "destroy" in Greek (*apollumi*) implies annihilation or may refer to eternal suffering, but I have not found anyone discussing whether such a connotation was possible in Aramaic or likely to be understood by

Jesus' parable of the Rich Man and Lazarus draws on themes common in the prophets of the exile. It is a harsh and straightforward text, but not about the nature of eternal punishment. As Edward has noted, whatever we are to make of the torment of the rich man, it occurs while his brothers are still living. The point of the Lazarus story is painfully clear—so painfully clear that we seem to want to avoid its clear message by shifting the focus of the discussion. The parable is not a text on whether hard hearts will believe the gospel, even if Jesus returns from the grave; nor is it a text elucidating the intermediate state of the dead. We have misread the parable as a discussion on faith or misused it as a proof-text for debates on eternal torment, perhaps to avoid facing its fearful condemnation of the same charges made by the prophets. For example, Amos condemned Israel to be exiled for selling the needy for a pair of sandals (Amos 2:6); and even more to the point, Ezekiel condemned Judah to destruction for being worse than Sodom, who "had pride, excess of food, and prosperous ease, but did not aid the poor and needy" (Ezek 16:49)—the precise point of the Lazarus parable.

Further, the exile also demonstrates God's unending love for his people, offering his promises of hope and restoration even in the midst of terrible judgment. Some of the most beautiful words in Scripture are: "The steadfast love of the Lord never ceases, his mercies never come to an end; they are new every morning; great is your faithfulness." These words come from—of all places!—Lamentations, following a bitter lament on the horror of the siege and destruction of Jerusalem.[27] Even in the midst of God's terrible judgment, his steadfast love and mercy are declared.

One important image of God's merciful love is found in the prophets' descriptions of God as the husband of an adulterer. If a husband has an unfaithful wife he may divorce her, he might be tempted to kill her, but he doesn't tie her up in a dungeon and torture her for years and years. However, the teaching of the prophets is that God takes her back—in violation of his own law![28] If anything, this image of God's love supports universalism, but in no way suggests that God would employ eternal torment as just punishment.[29]

Jesus' followers.

27. Olbricht, *He Loves Forever*, 15.

28. See Jer 3 and Hos 1–3.

29. Olbricht contends that the very wrath of God poured out in his acts of judgment is a demonstration of his love: "The wrath of God neither supersedes love nor is independent from it. In fact, it is precisely because of God's intense love that his wrath pours forth on people who obstruct his efforts to achieve intimate communion with man" (Olbricht, *He Loves Forever*, 11). Comparing God to the anger a husband feels toward an unfaithful wife, he writes: "Likewise, God shows by his wrath that his love for

Two of the most severe acts of God's judgment in Scripture are the flood and the punishment of the Canaanites, which each destroyed countless men, women, and children. (I think the genocide of the Canaanites is at the top of the list of questions I wish I could ask God.) These events are very disturbing, but they pale in comparison to the traditional view of hell. The destruction of the Canaanites was a one-time event linked to specific circumstances within the mission of God to save mankind, not a paradigm for how God dealt or will deal with other peoples. Both the flood and the judgment on Canaan were finite, not infinite. The flood drowned and destroyed; it was not eternal water boarding. If these events suggest anything about how God may exact final judgment on the world—and Peter does, indeed, compare the flood to the end of the world destroyed by fire (2 Pet 3:5–7)—they point to annihilation.

A biblical theology of God's justice, based on the evidence of the Torah, the prophets, and God's terrible judgment in the exile, requires that God's justice not exceed the sin he judges, and that at worst he destroy the impenitent. Eternal torment seems entirely inconsistent with what the Scripture teaches about God's principles of justice and his own acts of judgment. To construct a view of justice which not only contradicts this evidence, but contradicts the overarching description of the nature of God, must be seen as a misreading of the story of God.

THE PROBLEM OF LANGUAGE ABOUT HELL:

Packer accuses opponents of the traditional view of describing that view as terrible and dreadful, suggesting that we think traditionalists have not considered the impact of their words:

> What troubles me most here, I confess, is the assumption of superior sensitivity by the conditionalists. Their assumption appears in the adjectives (awful, dreadful, terrible, fearful, intolerable, etc.) that they apply to the concept of eternal punishment, as if to suggest that holders of the historic view have never thought about the meaning of what they are saying.[30]

But I believe Packer misses the point. Traditionalists have certainly thought about it, and often acknowledge the dreadful nature of what they

---

wayward humanity is undying and deep. His sanctions against humans are the result of his incessant desire to bring man back into his fellowship (Amos 4:6–12)." (Ibid., 14–15)

30. Quoted in Mohler, "Modern Theology," 32.

believe to be the truth. They intentionally use language that is dreadful and terrible—because that is what they believe about hell.

Mohler describes the language of Wenham's critique of the traditional view as "impassioned, almost hysterical";[31] Yarbrough sets aside Fudge's language as "overwrought rhetoric."[32] But the language of Wenham and Fudge is no more impassioned and overwrought than traditionalists' fervor in describing eternal torment.

One of the most famous sermons on hell from my own church fellowship was given some fifty years ago by Jimmy Allen, long-time teacher of Bible at Harding College. He contended that because God is light and hell is darkness, God is not in hell.

> But there is one place where God is not. God is not in Gehenna. God is not in the place of everlasting destruction. God is not in Hell. Where God is not is bound to be what the Bible calls Hell. That must be Hell, if God isn't there. There won't be any God to listen to your oft-repeated prayers in torment. There won't be any God to listen as you scream and beg for mercy. None will be granted because God will not be there.[33]

Allen goes on to quote an earlier well-known preacher from our fellowship:

> Brother Marshall Keeble ... once said that a man could build the hottest fire possible, remove the damned from Hell, place them in the man-made fire and in ten seconds they'd freeze to death. That has a note of levity in it, but I believe he was right. My friends, if Hell is just one tenth as bad as the description found in the Bible, that should be enough to produce fear in the heart of anyone. But, the truth of the matter is, it's a thousand times worse than any description found in God's word.[34]

Mohler himself quotes an unnamed medieval preacher warning his congregation of the danger of hell:

> Fire, fire! That is the recompense for your perversity, you hardened sinners. Fire, fire, the fires of hell! Fire in your eyes, fire in your mouth, fire in your guts, fire in your throat fire in your nostrils, fire inside and fire outside, fire beneath and fire above,

---

31. Ibid., 30.
32. Yarbrough, "Jesus on Hell," 78.
33. Allen, *What is Hell Like?* 233.
34. Ibid., 237.

fire in every part. Ah, miserable folk! You will be like rags burning in the middle of this fire.[35]

He quotes Jonathan Edward's warning that there is no escape from hell:

> Consider how dreadful it will be to suffer such an extremity forever. It is dreadful beyond expression to suffer it half an hour. O the misery, the tribulation and anguish that is endured![36]

He also cites the words of Charles Spurgeon making a similar point:

> Suffice it for me to close up by saying, that the hell of hells will be to thee poor sinner, the thought, that it is to be forever. Thou wilt look up there on the throne of God, and it shall be written "For ever!" When the damned jingle the burning irons of their torments, they shall say, "for ever!" When they howl, echo cries "for ever!"[37]

If conditionalists describe the traditionalists' view of hell as "dreadful," it is because that is precisely what the traditionalists themselves say. The question is not whether the traditional view is dreadful; the question is whether such a dreadful view is in fact consistent with biblical theology.

Mohler contends that conditionalists such as Pinnock assume a moral superiority and imply that traditionalists lack sensitivity and human compassion.[38] However, I suggest that while traditionalists do not necessarily lack human compassion, the position itself lacks divine compassion (i.e., it does not represent the merciful compassion of God declared so often in Scripture), and professing the position often leads the professors to say things that do lack compassion.

THE IMPACT OF SUCH LANGUAGE

Our church members are longing for another way to understand hell. You can blame it on the culture, but I suggest it is something deeper, something rooted in the work of the Spirit of God. As churches have rightly chosen to emphasize grace, and as they have sought unity rejecting the centuries of making war against each other over alleged heresy, Christian people have sensed an inconsistency between their view of God's gracious love and their view of eternal torment. That move, I think, may be attributed to the Holy

---

35. Mohler, "Modern Theology," 18.
36. Ibid.
37. Ibid., 28.
38. Ibid., 34, n. 76. Some of Pinnock's comments could be taken that way.

Spirit.[39] Whenever I have presented to Christians what I have argued here, there is a great sense of relief on the part of many. They say they wish they had seen this long ago.

But more serious even than the longings of believers, who want to believe the Bible and also believe in a merciful God, is the impact of the traditional view in driving people away from God. Yes, some have been terrified into conversion by the impassioned rhetoric of preachers like Jonathan Edwards. However, I suggest that in this day many more have been and continue to be driven away from faith because they cannot conceive of nor accept a God who would do what preachers have described. It turns away seekers like Jan, and presumably seals their fates in the very hell that has caused them to reject faith in God.

CONCLUSION: MOTIVATING BY GOD'S LOVE FOR US, NOT OUR FEAR OF GOD

Some say that without the fear of eternal torment in hell, people will not be motivated to be saved. But in my experience the opposite is true. Would not people naturally fear total annihilation? Would people really choose to cease to exist? That is contrary to human nature. We are driven at the most basic level by the instinct to survive. Our task is to present people with the choice between eternal life with a loving Heavenly Father or the ultimate and final death penalty. As Moses said to Israel in his final sermon: "I set before you life and good, death and evil . . . choose life" (Deut 30: 15–30). If we have to resort to terrible visions of eternal torture to motivate people to choose life, perhaps something is wrong with the way we present life.

Most people are motivated in life more by love than fear. Yes, fear has its place, but that is not the most powerful motivation for change. The fear of the Lord may be "the beginning of knowledge" (Prov 1:7), but as John the Beloved declares, "Perfect love casts out fear . . . he who fears is not perfected in love" (1 John 4:18). As we have seen, the very story of God itself motivates more by love than fear. Should not our appeal be rooted in the heart of God? I once read a story of a monk who would carry around a set of keys and a bucket of water. When asked why, he would say he wished to lock the doors of heaven and put out the fires of hell, so that people would serve God neither from desire for reward nor fear of punishment, but solely out of love.

39. I am not implying that the traditionalists do not have the Holy Spirit, only that I think the discomfort so many Christians feel with the traditional view may be the prompting of the Spirit. (I wish we could move past the need to make such disclaimers.)

After a few months of conversations with Jan, I had the great joy of baptizing her into Christ, and not long after I performed her wedding ceremony. Two years later, following a battle with cancer, I preached her funeral. Jan is with the Lord not because she was scared she would be tortured forever—but because she learned of the steadfast love of the Lord.

And that was not so much because of me as because of Jesus, Moses, and Fudge.

5

"Dear Edward"

Letters to a Gentleman Scholar

— GREGORY G. STUMP —

Gregory G. Stump graduated with an MA in Theology from Fuller Theological Seminary and currently serves as a pastor in a Baptist church in Southern California, where he lives with his wife, Michele, and three dearly loved children. He is the co-editor of Rethinking Hell: Readings in Evangelical Conditionalism *and serves as a steward of the Rethinking Hell project. After meeting Edward Fudge in 2011 at a debate on the nature of hell that Stump had helped to organize at Biola University, he was privileged in July of 2014 to lead out on organizing the inaugural Rethinking Hell conference as a celebration of the life and ministry of his theological hero.*

On Friday, July 11, 2014, Edward Fudge was a few days from turning seventy years old and found himself the guest of honor at a conference celebrating his legacy, surrounded by one hundred and fifty of his family, friends, and admirers from all over the world who had gathered to honor his life and Christian scholarship. His magnum opus, *The Fire that Consumes*, had been reprinted only a few years before in a handsomely designed, revised and expanded third edition, which had quickly found a new generation of readers, and answered decades' worth of critical responses of to his view of God's final judgment. A year before this gathering, a feature film based on his life and ministry called *Hell & Mr. Fudge* had also been released, playing in theaters around the U.S. at screenings organized on a grass roots level after Christian film distributors had apparently found the content to be too controversial. These last few years for Fudge had been a series of vindications of his calling as a young man to the study of Scripture and theological reflection, and had demonstrated a wide-reaching recognition of his persevering and consuming passion for truth that had, in the course of time, influenced so many Christian thinkers, ministers, and followers of the Lord he served. And so this gathering in the heat of a Houston summer was another capstone of Fudge's ministry, intended to honor his theological work and continue his legacy for years to come.

At this conference, however, there was also a small exhibit that may have gone unnoticed by many of the attendees.[1] It was a collection of letters addressed to Edward Fudge from various scholars, friends, and readers from more than forty years of his life. In contrast to the highly respected and widely admired scholar who was being honored in 2014, these letters, spanning from 1972 to 2000 revealed a young writer struggling to engage both scholarly and popular Christian audiences with his untraditional understanding of hell. This collection of letters to Edward Fudge painted a portrait of the recipient as being a man of insight, conviction, and honor, both from admirer and opponent alike. However, they not only captured an era in one man's life, but also illustrated an age of written communication that had largely been lost in the twenty-first century: aerogram letters on blue paper sent from overseas; correspondence from professors on seminary letterhead printed by a manual typewriter; and handwritten epistles using cursive penmanship.

The first letters in the collection were from 1972, sent from the eminent British biblical scholar F. F. Bruce, to whom Fudge had written to request a foreword for his exposition of the book of Hebrews entitled *Our Man in Heaven*, which Bruce supplied, indicating that it was his "pleasure to commend" the book.[2] The letters between these two men continue in the collection until just a few years before Professor Bruce's death in 1990. On January 18, 1975, Bruce acknowledged his receipt of a letter from Fudge, "together with your paper 'Is the eternal punishment of the lost literally unending?'"

> As for your paper, I am sure that you are right in emphasizing that eternity is different in character from time, and that therefore ideas like "unending," which relate to our experience of time, are inapplicable in the context of eternity. The trouble is that we ourselves are children of time at the present, and therefore find the vocabulary of time natural and intelligible, whereas it takes a considerable effort to try to think in terms of eternity.

---

1. Many thanks to Carisse Berryhill of Abilene Christian University for curating this exhibit for the 2014 Rethinking Hell Conference.
2. F. F. Bruce to Edward Fudge, November 20, 1972, Correspondence.

But you rightly say that "the categories don't fit," any more than they do with regard to marrying and giving in marriage in the resurrection age.[3]

Bruce later wrote the foreword to the first edition of Fudge's book, *The Fire that Consumes*, which argued that the punishment of the lost was not unending, but rather resulted in their destruction. Though Bruce did not identify himself as being fully convinced of conditionalism in his foreword, it is clear that he vouched for Fudge's scholarly work, as seen in a letter from 1975, when, at a time when Fudge was applying for a doctoral program, Bruce indicated that he had sent a "few words" to the university "in hope that they may lend some support to your application."[4] Bruce continued to bless Fudge's work, even when his field of study turned to the law, as he noted at the conclusion of a letter in 1987, only a few years before his death: "With all good wishes to yourself and your family—bearing in mind your spiritual ministry and your law studies. As Billy Graham used to say, 'The Lord bless you—real good!'"[5]

Another important figure in Fudge's correspondence was the British biblical scholar and minister John Wenham, who later wrote the foreword to the second edition of *The Fire that Consumes*. Shortly after Fudge's first edition had been published, Wenham, who had promoted the idea of conditionalism in his 1974 work, *The Goodness of God*, wrote to him with congratulations, thanks, and questions:

> I have seen two very favorable reviews of your book and I write to congratulate you on its publication—what a relief it is when that hurdle is negotiated. . . . I have used my MS copy to help a man deeply depressed, mainly over wrong ideas about hell & therefore of God. We meet twice a week to read the Word. I'm earnestly praying for his conversion. . . . Have you had much vitriol from right-wing critics, or is Conditional Immortality beginning to be accepted in Evangelical circles?[6]

The answer to both of Wenham's questions was a mixture of yes and no. Fudge's book received a variety of responses, from condemnation to interest to great joy. One church leader, Gene Getz of the Dallas Center for Church Renewal, wrote:

---

3. F. F. Bruce to Edward Fudge, January 18, 1975, Correspondence.
4. F. F. Bruce to Edward Fudge, July 31, 1975, Correspondence.
5. F. F. Bruce to Edward Fudge, September 9, 1987, Correspondence.
6. John Wenham to Edward Fudge, October 8, 1982, Correspondence.

> I'm definitely interested in seeing a copy of your new book. . . . It sounds very interesting. Frankly, I hope that you are accurate. Eternal punishment has always been a very difficult concept for me to accept. However, I do accept it, though I must admit that every emotional fiber within my being wants to resist the reality of an eternal Hell. However, I'm firmly committed to Scripture and what it teaches, and therefore I take by faith ay area of theology that is difficult to comprehend or understand. I'll be very much interested to see what you have concluded and what the biblical basis is.[7]

Another reader, William Pace, who worked for a missions organization called TEAM (The Evangelical Alliance Mission), told Fudge,

> I have read with great interest your book, *The Fire that Consumes*, and appreciate your clarity and fairness—and humor! The question of the destiny of the unbeliever has long troubled me, and your book has opened up an entirely new line of thought. I found very little that I disagreed with, but propose to read through the book again before coming to a conclusion.[8]

However, Fudge had greater difficulty finding a favorable hearing from readers who had institutional commitments to uphold. For instance, William Barker, the President of Covenant Theological Seminary wrote, "Your book *The Fire That Consumes* looks like a very interesting study although it appears to contain teaching that is contrary to our understanding of the Scriptures. . . . We will probably confine notices in *Threshold* [the seminary newsletter] to publications by our graduates that are in clear accord with our doctrinal standards."[9] Another example is found in a letter from Lyn Cryderman, the managing editor of *Christianity Today*, in regard to an advertisement that one of Fudge's supporters had sought to run:

> You should know that all of us connected with the editorial process are trying to be open to God's leading regarding your view of hell. At our last senior editors meeting, it was decided that CT could advertise your book, but that the particular advertisement submitted by Desmond Ford was promoting more than a book. In other words, if you want to run an ad that says, "Here's a new book examining a controversial interpretation of hell and punishment," I think we would run it. But for us to run an ad that knowingly called into question one of CT's statements of faith

---

7. Gene Getz to Edward Fudge, June 11, 1982, Correspondence.
8. William Pace to Edward Fudge, July 28, 1983, Correspondence.
9. William S. Barker to Edward Fudge, August 23, 1983, Correspondence.

would be understandably out of bounds. We still have a board of directors to answer to.[10]

Fudge's supporter, Desmond Ford, was an Australian theologian who had received a PhD in New Testament from the University of Manchester under F. F. Bruce[11] and who shared Fudge's views of conditional immortality. A year after the release of Fudge's book, Ford had written to him:

> Yesterday it was a feast to spend some time in *The Fire that Consumes*. I am deeply impressed with it and rejoice at your courage, humility, and scholarship. I believe the book will bring glory to God. Now that the book is on a ministerial book-list many more may be blessed—whole congregations as well as their leaders. What impresses me so much is that as I listen to Billy Graham, Pat Robertson, etc. they all take for granted the Platonic view of man and seem not to suspect that the biblical view could be otherwise. I had wondered how they could be reached. Your book is part of the solution. Sometime if you find time to write please tell me how your book with its untraditional stance yet got such deserved but unexpected favor in placement on a book list? I am so glad it has and am sufficiently selfish to desire to know how it is done apart from the obvious answer: write a book of superlative quality.[12]

Another letter, from Leonard George Goss, the editor of the Evangelical Book Club, answers Ford's question of how *The Fire that Consumes* came to be placed on the "ministerial book-list":

> Here is my quote ... for the jacket copy of the new printing of your *The Fire That Consumes*.... I think the quote will effectively recommend the nontraditional approach to our membership. It might interest you to know that after my graduation from Trinity Evangelical Divinity School, and upon my licensing in 1975 by the Evangelical Free Church of America, my doctrinal statement in the paragraph on eschatology outlined my acceptance of conditionalism. Some pursed lips and furrowed brows, but no real objections from my examining panel! P.S. If I did not mention this on the phone, I'm glad to use your book. It is important enough to expose as widely and broadly as possible.[13]

---

10. Lyn Cryderman to Edward Fudge, November 5, 1990, Correspondence.
11. Good News Unlimited, "Reflections on Adventism."
12. Desmond Ford to Edward Fudge, October 5, 1983, Correspondence.
13. Leonard George Goss to Edward Fudge, November 10, 1982, Correspondence.

With the foreword from F. F. Bruce and the recommendation of the Evangelical Book Club, Fudge's work came to the attention of many Christians thinkers, including another PhD student of Professor Bruce who had himself become a highly regarded evangelical theologian—Clark Pinnock—who had written an article entitled "The Destruction of the Finally Impenitent" in the *Criswell Theological Review* that supported the conditionalist view. Pinnock wrote to Fudge in 1989, "I'm glad you liked my article. It owes a lot to you.... I am delighted that *Fire that Consumes* is selling briskly. It's a much needed book."[14] Colin Brown, a professor of systematic theology at Fuller Theological Seminary, had begun using Fudge's book in his classes. He wrote to Fudge, "I am truly glad to be able to include your book in my list of recommended reading.... I attempted to say something on the subject in the article on Punishment, *kolasis*, in *NIDNTT* 3:988–1000. I wish that I had had your book to help me."[15]

Sometimes, however, it was the case that Christian thinkers had a copy of Fudge's book, yet had not read it before writing on the topic of conditionalism. The most significant example of this situation is seen in a letter from the British evangelical statesman John Stott to Edward Fudge in 1990.

> Your name is, of course, very familiar to me, and I obtained a copy of your book soon after it was published. At the same time, albeit with some embarrassment and shame, I have to confess that I have not yet read it! But I intend to do so at the soonest possible opportunity. I have exchanged letters with Professor Bruce and John Wenham recently on this topic, and I know that F. F. Bruce contributed the Foreword to your book. I am delighted to read that it is now undergoing a fourth printing.[16]

In 1988, Stott had addressed the issue of the fate of the unsaved in a written conversation with David Edwards, published as *Evangelical Essentials: A Liberal-Evangelical Dialogue*, with Stott tentatively endorsing the annihilationist view. However, it is clear from reading Stott's chapter on the topic that he did not quite understand the terminology involved in the discussion on conditional immortality—a shortcoming which may have been avoided had he found time to read Fudge's book![17]

---

14. Clark Pinnock to Edward Fudge, December 19, 1989, Correspondence.
15. Colin Brown to Edward Fudge, May 4, 1988, Correspondence.
16. John Stott to Edward Fudge, January 5, 1990, Correspondence.
17. John Wenham points out that he found "Stott's way of distinguishing annihilationism and conditional immortality ... somewhat confusing" in his chapter "The Case for Conditional Immortality" in *Universalism and the Doctrine of Hell*, 166.

Some of Fudge's theological opponents who had read *The Fire that Consumes* found much to admire, even as they disagreed with him and publicly repudiated his work. John Blanchard, the author of *Whatever Happened to Hell?* wrote to Fudge in reply to a letter, "I deeply appreciate the spirit of your letter—as I do that shown in your book. May the Lord graciously continue to bless you in all your work and witness for Christ."[18] Another traditionalist author, John Gerstner, who severely criticized Fudge's conditionalism in the book *Repent or Perish*, also replied more charitably in a private letter than he had in his public work:

> Thank you for your most gracious and interesting letter and restatement of some of your views stated in *The Fire That Consumes*. I honor you for honoring the Word of God. Though I profoundly disagree with your interpretation I have no doubt that it is an honest one and that you sincerely hold to what you believe the Bible to teach because the Bible teaches it (you believe).[19]

A professor of systematic theology from Dallas Theological Seminary, Robert Pyne, also wrote:

> Again, I apologize for not yet working through your book. I hope to do so in the very near future and look forward to continuing dialogue with you at that point. I appreciate the spirit of your letter and the heart for evangelism and biblical integrity that is so apparent in your efforts. It's a pleasure to "warmly disagree" when so many discussions make a mockery of the love which should be so evident in the body of Christ.[20]

Another theological opponent named Kendall Harmon, who delivered a paper entitled "The Case against Conditionalism: A Response to Edward William Fudge" at the Fourth Edinburgh Conference on Christian Dogmatics, responded to a letter from Fudge:

> As you correctly gathered from the title of my paper, I did not agree with your book. However, I have mixed feelings about this since (a) I agree with you that the conditionalist argument has been inadequately considered, which I note in a footnote, and (b) this places me in danger of being associated with other recent critiques of conditionalism, which I have found to be particularly unbecoming in tone and style (Morey and Gerstner

---

18. John Blanchard to Edward Fudge, May 24, 1993, Correspondence.
19. John Gerstner to Edward Fudge, July 11, 1990, Correspondence.
20. Robert A. Pyne to Edward Fudge, January 16, 1991, Correspondence.

especially). I am interested in genuine dialogue about these matters, and I hope that you can tell in my paper that I read your book and that I tried to be fair.[21]

Edward's friend John Wenham, who was also at the Edinburgh Conference to deliver a paper supporting conditionalism, had a different take on Harmon's paper, as he wrote to Fudge in November 1991, "Edinburgh was a good time & we conditionalists got a good hearing, and some of the traditionalists (e.g., Henri Blocher) yielded a lot of ground.... Kendall Harmon's paper surprised me. I thought that he had raised some points which merited clarification, but to me it seemed no *answer* to you. But he seemed to think that he had effectively shown you seriously wrong."[22]

Fudge's critics, for all of their work in attempting to refute him, did not silence his perspective or put an end to the momentum that he had sought to build over many years in his speeches, debates, sermons, articles, books, and correspondence. Instead his work continued on into multiple printings and editions, gaining favor and acceptance from a wide variety of scholars. In January of 1993, Fudge received a reply to a letter he had sent to a professor of religion at the University of Manitoba:

> Thank you very much for your note of 14 January 1993, received today. I have not yet read your good book. I say "good" because of those who have recommended it to me—directly or in their writings. I look forward to reading it over the next year or so as I will be exploring the relationship of Christianity and other religions and your work bears on an important tangent upon this subject. I might say, by the way, that I lent your book to a friend who had read Gerstner's book, and he found yours a delightful and refreshing alternative![23]

This correspondent later became an influential evangelical spokesman, prolific Christian writer, and professor of theology and culture at Regent College in Vancouver, Canada. At some point, he also embraced conditionalism and, in 2014, was the featured plenary speaker at the Houston conference in honor of Edward Fudge, as well as the author of the opening chapter in this volume: John Stackhouse. His eloquent speech commending Fudge and his work on final judgment told a story of God's work through one man's dedication to pursue the truth no matter what the cost might be, as well as serving as a challenge to raise up a new generation who could

---

21. Kendall Harmon to Edward Fudge, August 17, 1991, Correspondence.
22. John Wenham to Edward Fudge, November 23, 1991, Correspondence.
23. John Stackhouse to Edward Fudge, January 18, 1993, Correspondence.

continue to advance conditionalism (even if under another name) in the academy, church, and world.

However, that small exhibit of letters to Edward Fudge also told a story to this next generation of the gracious, yet tenacious perseverance of a young, independent scholar who pointed anyone who would listen back to the Word of God in order to understand God's true character and his just judgment of all people. John Wenham had written to Edward in 1991 with a humble sense of hope for the future: "Maybe we are entering upon a new phase of serious discussion. If Conditional Immortality is right, we might do much to relieve the church of a hideous burden."[24] Though Wenham did not live to see that day, through the continuance of Edward's influence, the church may very well experience this unburdening in the days to come.

---

24. John Wenham to Edward Fudge, March 22, 1991, Correspondence.

Part 2

THEOLOGY AND PHILOSOPHY

6

The Extinction of Evil
The Biblical Prerequisite for New Heavens, New Earth

— Gordon L. Isaac —

Gordon L. Isaac was educated in systematic theology and religious studies at Western Theological Seminary (MDiv), Luther Theological Seminary (M.Th.) and Marquette University (PhD). He presently serves as the Berkshire Associate Professor of Church History and Advent Christian Studies at Gordon-Conwell Theological Seminary where he regularly offers seminars on Martin Luther and Dietrich Bonhoeffer. He is author of Left Behind or Left Befuddled: The Subtle Dangers of Popularizing the End Times. *He has lectured internationally and his articles have appeared in a number of journals including* Concordia Theological Quarterly *and* Luther Digest. *He is presently working in a monograph on Martin Luther.*

I have had the good fortune to become acquainted with Edward Fudge. We have met at various conferences on both West and East coasts and on every occasion I have found Edward to be of congenial and magnanimous spirit. Although a man of some learning, his erudition rests lightly due to his ease in engaging others, even others with whom he may disagree. He is pastoral in his approach, yet he is not one to eschew theological inquiry. But beyond these few meetings it is perhaps through his writings that I have gotten to know him best. I have learned from his thorough research and for this reason I am particularly pleased to offer a small token of my appreciation for his accumulated contributions to the church.

The topic of this article, in the first instance, follows a line of inquiry that flows directly from the work of Edward Fudge. If the weight of the argument of *The Fire That Consumes* is accurate, and the final end of the wicked is death and not eternal conscious suffering for all eternity, then there surely must be consequences of this mode of thinking. I want to suggest that one advantage in standing with Fudge and his understanding of the final judgment along these lines touches on the matter of sin and the extent of reconciliation. Will the renewal and cleansing of the world be partial or complete? Seeing the destruction of the wicked as a key element and first step in overturning of all wickedness and evil brings us to a new vision of the extent of the reconciliation that God has undertaken in the work of Jesus Christ on behalf of humanity. The intent of this article is to explore something of what this might mean as we reflect on the time that comes for "God to restore everything, as he promised long ago through his holy prophets" (Acts 3:21).

In the second instance, I am pleased to take up the terminology suggested by John Stackhouse, who in his article included in this volume, recounts the unsatisfactory nature of the various options presently in use. He points out that the use of the term *annihilationism* causes hearers to believe that justice is being trifled with, that there is no real punishment and thus no real hell. Along these lines I remember a conversation that I had with a Christian who discovered that I believed in annihilationism. He informed me that I did not believe in hell. As I remember the conversation, I replied by saying, "On the contrary, I believe in hell. In fact, I believe in a hell that is much hotter than the hell that you believe in! Those who go into the hell I believe in are actually burned up!" *Conditional immortality* as a label could well arouse the suspicions of the ardently Reformed who prefer to describe the grace of God without recourse to the matter of human decision or anything close to what is conditional. Some whose sensibilities lie along these lines have used the phrase *conferred immortality* to indicate that the gift of eternal life is not something inherent in the individual but is rather the gift of God through the work of Jesus Christ. But even so, Stackhouse is right to point out that the more telling problem with this concept is that it refers to the saved when in point of fact the discussion has to do with the lost. In response he proffers the phrase *terminal punishment*, coined by Douglas Jacoby, for it conveys the seriousness of the act of judging and it indicates that the process will have an end and will be final.

How shall we begin? What is the problematic that we need to address? Simply put, the traditional view of punishment that consists in eternal conscious suffering of the wicked does not leave room for the biblical concept of the extinction of evil. While a traditional view may attempt to claim that evil has been dealt with in the way that God has seen fit, it does not finally sweep the field clear; evil continues to exist. Ultimately one would have to speak of the ongoing nature of rebellion against God. If the wicked are indeed collected together and placed in hell, it is reasonable to assume that their cries of blasphemy make their way to the ears of the holy God for all eternity. This is hardly a vision of the final victory of God that the Scriptures assert.

In fact, we are informed by proponents of the traditional view that it is quite likely that the unregenerate who will purportedly be incarcerated in hell will continue to heap up sin and its consequent guilt, and it is perhaps for this reason that the punishment is ongoing.[1] Given this situation, it would seem that even after judgment, the Triune God will not rule his universe without opposition. The prayers of countless Christians over the ages, "Thy Kingdom come, Thy will be done in earth, as it is in heaven" will come to naught. This brings us to the intolerable situation where it is hard to imagine that God has "become all in all" (1 Cor 15:50). Rather, there is much left undone; there are many for whom there is no final resolution; and creation itself is not relieved of its frustration and bondage to decay (Rom 8:21). In short, traditionalist arguments for the eternal duration of judgment trump the larger vision of Scripture that holds out to us a time when evil in all its forms will be extinguished and earth shall become the unsullied home of righteousness (1 Pet 3:10).

Henry Constable, an author from the nineteenth century, says that the commonly accepted doctrine of an eternal hell does not put an end to evil.

> It merely removes it from one part of God's world to another, and, as a direct consequence of this removal, intensifies it in its new habitation. "There is to be an end of evil," says Tertullian, "*when the chief thereof, the devil, shall go away into the fire which God hath prepared for him and his angels.*" Strange end of evil! As if evil was terminated by its change of locality, or as if evil was no evil when it was in hell! This is no restoration of all things.[2]

This colorful expression put forward by Constable uses the dictum of Tertullian that states, "there will be an end to evil," but could just as easily be taken from any number of scriptural texts that witness to the putting away of evil and evildoers in order to make way for the renewal of heaven and earth at the end of human history.

---

1. This, according to D. A. Carson as cited in Morgan, "Annihilationism," 212.
2. Constable. *Future Punishment*, 178.

In what follows I wish to argue for a biblical vision of judgment that flows out of the goal of Christian hope—new heavens/new earth. I will seek to show that establishing the new heavens and new earth includes an end to sin and to all evil, which in turn requires the death of evildoers—what some of us refer to as terminal punishment. In order to set forward this case I will proceed in three steps. First, some biblical foundations regarding the final consummation and the establishment of the new heaven, new earth will be set forward. With this biblical vision firmly set in place, other important questions find their appropriate resolution. Second, in view of the biblical data, some clearing of the ground is necessary. Assumptions that have grown up without the big picture of God's redemption will be shown for what they are—impositions on the text. And third, a closer look at a cosmic eschatology focused on the restoration of all things is in order with comment on a few of its advantages.

BIBLICAL FOUNDATIONS: NEW HEAVENS, NEW EARTH

Of all the individuals who speak of new heaven, new earth in our times, none is more prominent or compelling than N. T. Wright. He maintains that the great weight of biblical theology focuses the renewal of heaven and earth.[3] He builds his case on a number of Scriptures but focuses especially on Romans 8.

As is his custom, Wright sets out his thesis over against what he sees as common misunderstandings. In this case he complains that if you read Romans simply as a book about how humans "get saved," in the sense of "going to heaven when I die," Romans 8:18–28 will function as a kind of odd apocalyptic addendum. That is what happens, he goes on to say, in much contemporary "radical" scholarship and in many evangelical readings. But Paul's argument regarding a new heaven and new earth is intentional and actually serves as the climax of his thought in Romans 1–8 as a whole.[4]

Turning to Romans 8:18–28 we find the apostle speaking of the hope of creation (vv. 18–22), the hope of human deliverance including the redemption of our bodies (vv. 23–25), and the intercession of the Spirit according to will of God (vv. 26–28). This passage takes each in turn, highlighting the oppression of sin and futility that will ultimately be overcome in the freedom that is established through the return of Jesus Christ. Paul's main focus is on future glory, not present suffering, although that is also in view.

3. Wright, *New Heavens, New Earth*, 12–27.
4. Ibid., 12.

The apostle paints a picture full of "eager longing." The hope of creation is that it will be "set free from its bondage to decay." We could say that the created order is straining forward on tip-toe anticipating its release. While there may be some who think that redemption applies only to human beings, we cannot accuse St. Paul of such a position.[5] In Paul's view, the redemption of God is of cosmic proportions extending to the farthest corner of his creation.

The apostle also paints a picture of redeemed humanity. Here too, he speaks of eager anticipation. What is of particular significance is his assertion that we look forward to "the redemption of our bodies." This hope would have sounded very strange in the ears of most of his first century audience. The Greeks were offended by the created world; they thought it evil. For them, salvation consisted in escape from the body and escape from the world. Death was anticipated for it would release the immortal soul into the untrammeled realm of spirit. But for Paul, salvation is not release into some kind of bodiless abstract existence. With the hope of the redemption of our bodies he takes his stand with the Jewish and Christian concept of salvation that treats the individual as a psychosomatic unity.

Finally, St. Paul speaks of the role of Spirit in all of this. As a close reading of the passage reveals, all three are in the midst of groaning: creation, humanity, and the Spirit. But it is the Spirit, whose "groanings are too deep for words" (Rom 8:26), who intercedes and brings all things to rights. In the logic of the passage, even as Moses led the people of Israel into the Promised Land, so the Spirit who intercedes will bring us into the "Promised Land" of an earth made new.

Once the grand vision for the redemption of creation and a redeemed humanity taking up residence in the midst of it is set in place, certain implications follow. A proper Christian understanding of heaven is retrieved from its worst caricatures—that see it as a place located somewhere off in outer space. Or, equally bad, a view in which heaven is seen as reserved for a few disembodied souls. "A proper Christian understanding of heaven," in the words of N. T. Wright, "is not as 'a place remote from the present world' but rather as a dimension, normally kept secret, of present reality."[6]

An excellent scriptural example of how this works is found in 2 Kings 6:5–19 in which Elisha and his servant are surrounded by the Syrian army. Not surprisingly the servant cries out to his master saying, "Alas, my master! What shall we do?" Elisha for his part responds by saying, "Do not be afraid,

---

5. For details on various exegetical positions on this point see, Russell, "New Heavens and New Earth," 159–73.

6. Wright, *New Heavens, New Earth*, 15.

for those who are with us are more than those who are with them." Elisha then prays that the eyes of his servant would be opened. As the servant looks up he is allowed to see the chariots of God surrounding the city. The prayer of Elisha unveils what all along had been there. In like manner, this is how the language of "heaven" functions in the book of Revelation when the seer speaks of heaven being opened (Rev 4:1). News from the heavenly realm is not meant for an End Times calendar but is intended to show what is going on now in the heavenly realms in a way that will strengthen the saints for their work in their present part of ministry responsibility.[7]

God rules both in heaven and on earth. In heaven God rules without opposition. On earth God rules, but there is opposition. When Christians pray in the Lord's Prayer, "Your kingdom come, your will be done in earth as it is in heaven" (Matt 6:10), the prayer is for the uncontested rule of God. The coming kingdom of God is the extension of God's rule to the ends of the created order. Or, as the Christmas carol has it, "far as the curse is found." Scripture is the account of what God has to say about evil and about what God has undertaken through his Son to overturn evil for all eternity.[8] The redemption of creation and humanity in the midst of it will be complete without reservation, without exception. In short, redemption of heaven and earth takes place in such a way that God rules in both without opposition.

Envisioning redemption as the establishment of new heavens and a new earth, not only shapes the way Christians think about heaven but it also has something to say about how we use the "soul" language of Scripture. If we are grasped by the embodied character of salvation, then it is no longer possible to talk about the "soul" being the "real you." Speaking of the body as the prison-house of the soul comes dangerously close to blasphemy against creation and an undermining of the goal of salvation, which is the integration of a world gone wrong.[9] Everywhere in Scripture humans are understood to be a psychosomatic unity. G. E. Ladd says it well: "such terms as body, soul, and spirit are not different parts of man as in Greek dualism, but are simply various ways of viewing man as a total entity."[10]

This has been an all too short treatment of this topic but a few salient points emerge. First, once the vision of the new heaven, new earth is set forward as the goal of Christian hope, other considerations take their proper

---

7. For a treatment of this subject see Bauckham, *Theology of the Book of Revelation*.

8. Wright, *Evil and the Justice of God*.

9. Unfortunately, even Jean Calvin fell prey to this error. He writes, "And when Christ commended his spirit to the Father [Luke 23:46] and Stephen his to Christ [Acts 7:59] they meant only that when the soul is freed from the prison house of the body, God is its perpetual guardian" (Institutes I.15.2).

10. Ladd, *The New Testament Pattern of Truth*, 103.

place. Popular ideas of "going straight to heaven when I die" are called into question, as are several other forms of dualism. Second, this holistic rendering of salvation in which we are reminded of the goodness of God's world places the emphasis on God's intention to renew creation fully and to expunge all sin and evil from it. Third, the Jewish and Christian concept of salvation stands opposed to any dualism that would deny the redemption of creation, or any dualism that would treat human existence as something other than psychosomatic unity.

CLEARING THE GROUND: ELEMENTS THAT DO NOT FIT

"Putting the cart before the horse" is an idiom indicating an improper ordering of things, of having things mixed up. A rough equivalent would be to say, "You're eating your dessert first!" Or, it would be a case of putting the cart before the horse if one were to choose what to wear before being invited to an event. It simply wouldn't do to choose to wear a fine coat and tie only to discover that one had been invited to the beach!

The same is the case with our Christian thinking. If we get things out of order it can make a big difference. If we begin our thinking with new heavens, new earth we are much more likely to get things right rather than starting with another set of presuppositions and only then trying to fit Scripture's witness into the system. Unfortunately, this reversal of order seems to be the case with the position that maintains eternal conscious suffering of the wicked.

The language of Scripture points to God's judgment as that event by which the world will be cleansed from evil and evildoers. But, the eternal conscious suffering of the wicked and the hermeneutics of the immortal soul, upon which it is based, excludes this biblical position. Leading with this view obfuscates the vindication of the action of God in the final consummation. It is a case of putting the cart before the horse.

The idea of the immortality of the soul subtly but unalterably changes the nature of the final consummation. The logic of the matter is quite simple. If all souls are indestructible, then they must be housed somewhere. In the case of the righteous, the soul will have "heaven" as its resting place. In the case of the wicked, the soul will have "hell" as its eternal abode. Incredibly, salvation becomes a matter of destination, a matter of going "up" to heaven or "down" to hell. As a corollary, the intent of it all is to assign rewards and punishments, for in this structure, since souls are indestructible, it comes down to a matter of happiness or misery. But this is not the language that Scripture uses to describe salvation.

Further, if the soul already possesses eternal life in itself, once again we find that the nature of the work of Christ is subtly altered. Christ comes not to give life but to arbitrate between good people and bad people who already are the possessors of eternal life. He becomes the dispenser of rewards and punishments and Christianity is reduced to a certain kind of religious sentiment that should be imparted or a morality that will be tested at the end of time.

In the Old Testament the witness of Scripture is to the two ways: the way of the righteous that leads to life, and the way of the wicked that leads to death. In Deuteronomy 30, the two paths of life or death are laid out before the people. Keeping the statutes and commandments of the Lord God leads to prospering and multiplying while worshiping other gods and turning away leads to something opposite. "I declare to you today, that you shall surely perish" (Deut 30:18). Psalm 1 is another good example. The psalm begins by saying, "Blessed is the man who walks not in the counsel of the wicked, nor stands in the seat of scoffers; but his delight is in the law of the Lord, and on his law he meditates day and night." The psalm goes on to describe the blessed man in terms of prospering, of fruitfulness, and perseverance. In short, this is the path of life! The wicked, however, are likened to chaff and at the end of the psalm these words make the difference between the two ways quite clear, "for the Lord knows the way of the righteous; but the way of the wicked will perish." The Old Testament pattern is the two ways, that of the righteous and the wicked resulting in either life or death.

The New Testament is similar—full and overflowing with these two alternatives. Jesus speaks of the narrow gate that leads to life and the wide and easy way that leads to destruction (Matt 7:13). The force of his parables and his discourses is eternal life, the life which he alone could give, and which he would freely give to all who would place their trust in him. The life of the Son is life indeed and is the only escape from death and destruction. So it is that he says, "I am the way, the truth, and the life" (John 14:6). "For unless you believe that I am he, you will die in your sins" (John 8:24). "For God so loved the world, that he gave his only Son, that whoever believes in him should not perish but have everlasting life" (John 3:16). "And do not fear those who kill the body but cannot kill the soul. Rather, fear him who is able to destroy soul and body in hell" (Matt 10:28).

The theology of St. Paul on this point continues in the same vein. "The wages of sin is death, but the free gift is eternal life through Jesus Christ our Lord" (Rom 6:23). And again, "For the one who sows to his own flesh will from the flesh reap corruption, but the one who sows to the Spirit will from the Spirit reap eternal life" (Gal 6:8). More examples could be heaped up but the point is clear: it is always life and death. Here it should be noted that he speaks of eternal (*aiōnios*) life but the apostle never speaks of eternal death, but—death. He never joins the term *aiōnios*, eternal, with it, as he does with life, neither does our Lord, nor do any of the sacred writers, for this death is of itself a finality. It is not a never-ending reality, a progressive form of being as life is, but an end, a cessation of life. Therefore the contrast of Scripture is always between eternal life and death.[11]

The harmony and unanimous witness of Old and New Testaments to the two ways is impressive. This is an important background that gives context to the singular texts of the book of Revelation that speak of the second death and the book of eternal life. As early as the second chapter mention is made of the second death. "He who conquers shall not be hurt by the second death." The first death that all humans are subject to can be overcome in resurrection. But from the second death there is no return. "But as for the cowardly, the faithless, the detestable, as for murderers, the sexually immoral, sorcerers, idolaters, and all liars, their portion shall be in the lake that burns with fire and sulphur, which is the second death" (Rev 21:8). This is a vision of terminal punishment as the Bible portrays it. A few observations are in order in light of the biblical data that shows the two ways to be the overwhelming language of Scripture with respect to salvation.

First, the Bible is not a story about misery and happiness, but a drama of death and life. Any presupposition that alters this fact is an imposition that does violence to the text of Scripture. Evangelical theology that is reminded of this fact cannot help but be more robust because of it. How would our preaching be changed if it more truly reflected the great drama of the narrative of Old and New Testaments in fresh ways because of our commitment to this truth? The goal and the hope toward which we are moving is the new heavens and the new earth. The eschatological element of the faith is caught up in this fact, and as such calls into question any presuppositions that would freeze the dynamic or cloud this truth.

Second, any view that does not allow the words of Scripture to mean what they say is suspect and in need of revision. When the term *death* is read to mean a punishment that never ends, the lexical meaning of the term is stretched beyond credulity. It is a strange dying that does not eventuate in death itself, the cessation of life. When the word *destroy*, even when in parallel with the term *kill*, is defined as an event of ongoing duration, clearly a presupposition is exerting an unnecessary influence.

---

11. Pettingell, Τὰ Μέλλοντα, 124–28.

Third, continued dependence on a doctrine of inherent immortality of the soul is in direct conflict with the biblical data.[12] There is an immortality that is spoken of in Scripture but it is an immortality that is brought to light in the gospel. Rather than starting with inherent immortality, the Bible begins with the fragility and temporality of human existence. Life is a gift of God given to all people, eternal life is granted to those who are united to Christ through faith. Those who are not found in Christ are not suited for immortality but will be subject to the second death.

NEW HEAVENS AND NEW EARTH: A WORLD WITHOUT EVIL

Catching a vision for the new heavens and the new earth begins in the Old Testament. There is clearly not enough space in a short article to be comprehensive on such a topic but a good place to begin is the powerful depiction of the prophet Isaiah. Chapters 65 and 66 craft an image of hope and abundance all secured by justice and recompense to those who would place themselves above God's purposes. As a surety the presence of the Lord himself will bring it to pass. The passage begins with resonant power.

> For behold, I create new heavens and a new earth, and the former things shall not be remembered or come into mind. But be glad and rejoice forever in that which I create; for behold, I create Jerusalem to be a joy, and her people to be a gladness. (Isa 65:17–18).

The remainder of the chapter is a listing of various earthly delights all pointing to the goodness of embodied existence made possible by the creative action of God. "They shall build houses and inhabit them; they shall plant vineyards and eat their fruit" (v. 21). The vision is of fullness of life, and toward the very end of the chapter the newness of creation is put forward in the striking image of the wolf and the lamb grazing together! The prophetic vision is of the world to come, not something that fits into the paradigm of the old order. The old enemies of sin, death, and systemic evil will be swept away to make space for the realization of the kingdom in its fullness.

Malachi also presents us with a picture of a brand new playing field. The great day of the Lord is set out with somber reality.

---

12. For further discussion on the question of the immortality of the soul see, Brown, Murphy, & Malony, *Whatever Happened to the Soul?*; Murphy, *Bodies and Souls*; and Green, *Body, Soul, and Human Life*.

> For behold, the day is coming, burning like an oven, when all the arrogant and all evildoers will be stubble. The day that is coming shall set them ablaze, says the Lord of hosts, so that it will leave them neither root nor branch. But for you who fear my name, the sun of righteousness shall rise with healing in its wings. You shall go out leaping like calves from the stall. And you shall tread down the wicked, for they will be ashes under the soles of your feet, on the day when I act, says the Lord of hosts. (Mal 4:1–3).

The Lord will enter into judgment with his world. The arrogant and all evildoers will be stubble—reduced to ashes under the feet of the living. The goal of the judgment of God is to cleanse the world of anything that stands in opposition to his loving perfection. The burning action of God is to assure that the stain of sin and systemic evil can never more establish estrangement between God and creation. The meeting between divine holiness and the arrogance of this present age could end in no other way. Judgment is necessary and terminal; it is necessary in order to bring all things back into right relationship with the triune creator; it is terminal to put a final end to evil. Only in this way is it possible for the earth to become the home of righteousness (1 Pet 3:10).

The work of judgment leads to the healing that comes through the sun of righteousness. So, at the final resolve Malachi begins to speak the language of joy. "You shall go out leaping like calves from the stall" (v. 2). This is truly the picture of a young and expectant new creation ready for the experience of unhindered life. Joy is possible precisely because that which is wicked no longer has a hold on reality.

Turning to the New Testament we find that the vision of the new heavens and new earth are centered in the Messianic ministry of Jesus.[13] At the very outset of his work, an instructive moment is recorded for us. In the very first miraculous encounter Jesus heals a man with an unclean spirit (Mark 1:21–28). The authority of Jesus elicits confession, obedience, and ultimate compliance. The demon recognizes Jesus for who he is—the Holy One of God. The demon's statement, "I know who you are" is consistent with the information Mark provides in 1:34, that the demons "knew him." Mark indicates that they are reliable spokesmen for understanding who Jesus is because of their supernatural insight.

What is fascinating in the account is what the demon says just prior to being cast out. "What have you to do with us, Jesus of Nazareth? Have

---

13. Goppelt, *Theology of the New Testament Volume 1*, 139ff.

you come to destroy us? I know who you are—the Holy One of God."[14] The introductory formula is used a number of times in the Septuagint and in the New Testament.[15] The force of the utterance comes to this, "What have we in common? Or "What business do we have with each other?" It may even carry the idea, "Go away leave me alone!" It indicates difference between the parties and in the Old Testament was used as a challenge to those who came in battle (e.g., 2 Chr 35:21). It is as though the presence of Jesus is an encroachment on enemy territory. In this account there is instant recognition that they are on opposite sides. The next question is telling in that the demon remonstrates for his threatened community, saying, "Have you come to destroy us?" Demonic anxiety corresponds to the Messianic ministry undertaken in Holy Spirit—the sweeping clean of heaven and earth. The final end of the demonic powers is certain, and their doom is sure. They do not need to be told of their end, it is already evident. And in Jesus, the prosecutor of the Messianic ministry, the demonic world is plundered. The destruction of Satan's rule is a natural consequence of the in breaking of the kingdom. As 1 John 3:8 puts it, "The reason the Son of God appeared was to destroy the works of the devil."

Not only do we have the overcoming of the demonic forces in the Messianic ministry but we also see the overcoming of sin and evildoers.[16] The parable of the weeds and its explanation in Matthew 13 sets forward the salient points. The parable is of the sower who sowed good seed in his field, but at night weeds were sown among the wheat. They were both allowed to grow until harvest time. The word of Jesus is given to answer the questions of the disciples.

> He who sows the good seed is the Son of man; the field is the world, and the good seed means the sons of the kingdom; the weeds are the sons of the evil one, and the enemy who sowed them is the devil; the harvest is the close of the age, and the reapers are angels. Just as the weeds are gathered and burned with fire, so will it be at the close of the age. The Son of man will send his angels, and they will gather out of his kingdom all causes of

---

14. For parallels see, Luke 4:33–34, and also Matt 8:29ff, and Mark 5:7ff.

15. Maynard, "ΤΙ ΕΜΟΙ ΚΑΙ ΣΟΙ."

16. The Messianic vision outside the canon also has in view the cleansing work of the Son of Man. First Enoch 69:27 reads, "And he sat on the throne of his glory, And the sum of judgment was given unto the Son of Man, And he caused the sinners to pass away and be destroyed from off the face of the earth, And those who have led the world astray." The text goes on to say that "henceforth there shall be nothing corruptible," and "all evil shall pass away before his face." Charles, *The Old Testament Apocrypha and Pseudepigrapha*, 2:235.

sin and all evildoers, and throw them into the furnace of fire; there men will weep and gnash their teeth. Then the righteous will shine like the sun in the kingdom of their Father. He who has ears, let him hear (Matt 13:37–44).

The close of the age is what is in view. Jesus explains the elements of the story to paint a picture of final resolve. The angels are reapers who gather from the four corners "all causes of sin and all evildoers." The focus here is not exclusively with the demonic powers as in Mark chapter 1, but on evildoers. Here human agency and the "sons of the evil one" mark a contrast with "the sons of the kingdom." And just as weeds are gathered and burned with fire, so it is at the close of the age. This is an image of the cleansing of the threshing floor and a destruction of that which would thwart the purpose of the master. Incineration is meant to rid the world of that for which there is no use. Even though mention is made of those who will "weep and gnash their teeth" the cleansing of the threshing floor is the object. It should be pointed out that the phrase "gnashing of teeth" does not reflect pain so much as it refers to those who so hate the will of God that they gnash their teeth in rage against it.[17] In this New Testament usage the phrase may best be interpreted as "despairing rage." That there is pain and anguish in the moment of final judgment is no surprise, nor is there any reason to think that the ultimate intended purpose of the consuming fire is not reached.

What we have seen in these two brief encounters in the life of Jesus is that the Messianic ministry aims to disarm the demonic forces and any human agency that would stand against the one will of God. The opposition to the good is ultimately overcome in the reconciling work of Jesus Christ who is the Alpha and the Omega. The first and last word of God in Christ is to say that the reconciliation of the world to himself will be complete without remainder. The healing of the nations and indeed of the world will not be complete without it.

If we accept this compelling and expansive vision of the redemptive work of Christ, certain advantages follow. First, it highlights the solemn fact of the final judgment. As Scripture says, "It is a fearful thing to fall into the hands of the living God" (Heb 10:31). The Last Day will come, and it is inexorable in its solemn and holy work. The separation of the sheep and the goats is one of the many figures that Scripture uses to depict the culmination of the Second Coming of Christ. The cleansing of the threshing floor with its separation of the wheat and the chaff is another. But in the midst of the process of separation there is also the work of bringing all things together. It is good to be reminded that judgment is the removal of the separation of the

---

17. Fudge, *The Fire That Consumes* (2011), 131–34.

church from Christ and a relegation of sin and death to the past. The judgment against sin has already been accomplished in the one work of Christ. The final judgment will serve the purpose of applying the forgiveness of sins to those outstanding events between nations, institutions, and persons that have remained unresolved in time. The judgment is thus the act that restores the community to its proper functioning. As such, the judgment of God is to be longed for, for God alone is worthy to open the seal of history and to unravel the skein that sin and systemic evil have tangled. The judgment of God brings justice. It is healing and brings good—it is not merely the dispensing of punishments and it is certainly not a matter of sorting out worthy and unworthy human specimens.[18]

Second, it challenges the false notions of "destination" imposed by the Greek doctrine of the immortality of the soul. It returns us to the biblical terminology of the two ways—death and life. Immortality, when claimed for humans even in a derivative form, has the tendency to skew a biblical view of judgment and deflect the mercy that God delights in showing his people into a retribution magnified by eternity. God alone has immortality (1 Tim 6:16), and only those who are fit for the coming kingdom will inherent the life that comes in Christ alone. The soul is not innately immortal. Life is the gift that comes in Christ and only those who have the son have life. The work of Christ is not a matter of determining who will experience misery and who will experience happiness. Jesus is the life giver. He is the one who delivers from sin and death itself, and the only source and giver of eternal life to all who receive it at his hands. As Scripture puts it, "The wages of sin is death, but the free gift of God is eternal life in Christ Jesus our Lord."

Third, it enables us to take seriously the cleansing of the cosmos from sin and evil. It solves the problem of evil, insofar as it can be solved in this lifetime, by showing that it is not an integral and perpetual part of the Divine economy, but is only incidental and transitory. It will pass away forever. Since this is the case, the plausible objection that many have been accustomed to level against the Bible and its Author is removed. When we stand with Edward William Fudge and the conclusions derived from Scripture, we no longer have to sully the nature of God with the outrageous assertion of the eternal conscious suffering of the wicked.

It is an interesting fact of the biblical record that Genesis begins in a paradise garden produced at the hand of a God who delights in overflowing abundance. At every stage of the creative event, the Spirit is ready to add his breath of life to the proceedings. Whether it is a matter of the expanse

---

18. For a helpful discussion of judgment see, Jenson, *Systematic Theology Volume 2*, 322–37.

of waters crashing into continental sized landmasses, or a matter of minute vegetation sprouting up, all is orchestrated with fine-tuning and the word of the Lord that allows everything its time and its place. It is a fine habitation, or perhaps better we should say "temple" fit for the presence of the Triune God and all the beauty of his entire creation, including mankind.

The wonder and beauty of the original creation is matched and exceeded at the end of the canon as the book of Revelation concludes with a vision of the new heaven and new earth. "Behold, I am making all things new" (Rev 21:5). This is the prerogative of the one who is the Alpha and Omega, the beginning and the end. No temple is found or needed in the New Jerusalem and in this vision there is no need for sun for the glory of the Lord is sufficient. In this unparalleled garden the river of life is flowing. "No longer will there be anything accursed, but the throne of God and of the Lamb will be in it, and his servants will worship him" (Rev 22:3).

The correspondence between these two gardens is not merely striking; it is instructive. The original garden and all that is in it is created good, indeed, very good. The last garden and all that is in it is good, indeed, very good in that every mark of the sin that despoiled the original creation is remedied. All taint of evil is vanquished and eliminated. The presence of the Lord is no longer hidden but has come forth to give healing and salvation in every dimension of life.

> The plan of redemption will eventuate in the recovery of our material universe from satanic domination, and its restoration to its primal conditions; and our marred and blasted creation shall once more blush in Edenic beauty, with *redeemed* man in full fruition of his ancient immunities and glories; and EARTH cleansed from the *virus* of the curse, regarnished and put in its native attire, will be the future and unchanging home of ransomed saints.[19]

Judgment is not the last word, it is the word before the last word. Once holy judgment is rendered, evil shall be extinguished in all its various forms, moral, social, and personal, and the depredations it has caused will be righted for all time. The righteousness of God will no longer be by faith but will be evident to sight. In that moment the last word of God will sound forth, "Behold I make all things new" (Rev 21:5). And we, as the ransomed saints shall reign in an earth made new.

---

19. Stockman, *Our Hope*, 126.

7

Making the Philosophical Case for Conditionalism

— James S. Spiegel —

James S. Spiegel (PhD, Michigan State University) is a Professor of Philosophy and Religion at Taylor University in Upland, Indiana. His publications, which primarily explore issues in ethics and philosophy of religion, have appeared in such journals as Sophia, Faith and Philosophy, Theory and Research in Education, *and* Philosophia Christi. *Jim has also published numerous books, including* The Benefits of Providence *(Crossway, 2005),* Faith, Film, and Philosophy *(InterVarsity, 2007),* The Love of Wisdom *(B&H, 2009), and the award-winning* How to be Good in a World Gone Bad *(Kregel, 2004). Jim and his wife, Amy, blog together at www.wisdomandfollyblog.com. They have four children and live in Fairmount, Indiana.*

These are exciting times for the doctrine of conditional immortalism. Recent Rethinking Hell initiatives have generated, or perhaps are being generated by, what is apparently the most significant organized pro-conditionalist movement in history. I am personally enthused by the prospect that what has historically been a recondite perspective on hell will eventually become a major alternative position within the church. If we do our work properly, conditionalism will continue to garner respect among scholars and lay people alike for how it coherently accounts for the biblical record while avoiding the most difficult problems plaguing the traditional view. However, while theologians and biblical scholars are plentifully engaged, not enough philosophers are involved in this effort. This is a handicap and needs to be rectified. In what follows, I will briefly explain why it is important that philosophers contribute to the project of making the case for conditionalism, then I will review some important philosophical arguments for conditionalism, all of which are potentially fruitful areas where further philosophical work may be done.

WHY WE NEED PHILOSOPHICAL CONTRIBUTIONS

For all of the biblical exegetical and hermeneutical issues involved in the hell debate, many of the most decisive inferences made by defenders of the various views are philosophical in nature. What is the purpose of punishment? What counts as a just punishment? What is evil? What is the nature of human responsibility and what are its limits? What is freedom? What is infinity? What is cruelty? Fairness? Malice? All such questions are philosophical, and their proposed or assumed answers figure prominently in discussions about hell and defenses of the various views. This is why philosophers must play a critical role in this theological discussion.

In the Anselmian tradition, I maintain that philosophy is properly a handmaid to theology, serving the "queen" of the disciplines rather than usurping her authority. This means, to mix my metaphors, being a watchdog of sorts, identifying and correcting fallacious reasoning and muddled thinking as it threatens to corrupt our reflection on theological matters. It means rigorously defining terms, clarifying concepts, and tackling hard issues pertaining to logical relationships between truth claims. In general, philosophers' involvement in theology is good for both theology and philosophy. Both disciplines are strengthened because theology always needs philosophical rigor and, even more obviously, philosophers and philosophy need theological schooling—guidance, correction, enlightenment, and edification by the queen!

If these remedial observations about philosophy and theology apply generally, then they are especially true regarding the doctrine of hell, which is more pregnant with philosophical issues than most theological doctrines. (And, yes, in this case pregnancy *is* a matter of degrees.) More specifically, it seems to me that the state of the current debate is especially ripe for greater involvement by philosophers. There are many significant pro-conditionalist arguments, and they deserve extensive, rigorous philosophical treatment. In the remainder of this essay I will adumbrate five such promising arguments. My purposes are to (1) demonstrate how strong the philosophical case is for conditionalism, at least vis-à-vis the traditional view of hell and, in doing so, (2) offer an invitation to theologically interested philosophers to contribute to the discussion by clarifying, improving, and extending these arguments or perhaps challenging or rebutting some of the arguments or concepts they involve.

FIVE PHILOSOPHICAL PROBLEMS WITH THE TRADITIONAL VIEW

The following précis of pro-conditionalist philosophical arguments is not intended to be exhaustive. I have chosen only the more obvious issues, which happen also to be ones where further work may contribute significantly to the case in favor of conditionalism. Some of these issues are metaphysical in nature, while others are essentially moral.

The Problematic Status Principle

One major area of philosophical debate about hell concerns the justice of the traditional view of hell. Specifically, how could the sins of human beings possibly warrant everlasting conscious torment? As finite creatures living relatively brief earthly lives, endless suffering would appear to be wildly excessive. Given the retributive principle of *lex talionis*, only punishment of fixed duration and intensity, perhaps varying among the damned depending on the extent of their offenses, would be more appropriate for the moral crimes of the damned.

To this complaint, traditionalists have a long-standing response, which appeals to the notion that in assessing the justice of a punishment one must take into account, among other things, the moral and metaphysical status of the person offended. Accordingly, this idea has become known as the "status principle." Thomas Aquinas explains as follows:

> The magnitude of the punishment matches the magnitude of the sin; according to the measure of the sin, shall the measure of the stripes also be. Now a sin that is against God is infinite; the higher the person against whom it is committed, the graver the sin—it is more criminal to strike a head of state than a private citizen—and God is of infinite greatness. Therefore an infinite punishment is deserved for a sin committed against Him.[1]

The status principle has been just as confidently deployed in the Protestant camp. Jonathan Edwards writes:

---

1. Aquinas, *Summa Theologica*, 25.

> Our obligation to love, honor, and obey any being, is in proportion to his loveliness, honorableness, and authority.... But God is a being infinitely lovely.... He is a being of infinite greatness, majesty and glory; and therefore is infinitely honorable.... His authority over us is infinite; and the ground of his right to our obedience, is infinitely strong.... So that sin against God being a violation of infinite obligations, must be a crime infinitely heinous; and so deserving of infinite punishment.[2]

While the status principle has some appeal at first blush, it lacks nuance and consequently has counter-intuitive implications. For given this principle it follows that even the slightest sin, such as one brief inordinate desire, would warrant endless torment. This seems radically excessive, even granting the infinite goodness and majesty of God. Surely the nature of the sin itself should contribute to an overall reasonable assessment of the severity of any offense as well as its appropriate punishment. However much we should consider the nature of the person(s) offended, surely the nature of the sin matters as well.

Thus, some traditionalists point out, in defense of the status principle, that there is a vast distinction to be made between harming an animal, such as a dog, as opposed to offending a human being. This is certainly true. But what is also crucial to consider when weighing the severity of the two offenses is exactly what the offenses were. If I tortured the dog for days, while my offense against the human being was that I made a rude gesture, then the former is surely a worse offense than the latter. Despite the fact that a human being is far greater in terms of dignity and moral worth, my offense against the dog deserves more severe censure than does my offense against the human. This example shows that the status of the offended party is not the sole relevant matter to consider when assessing the relative severity of moral offenses.

These are just a couple of reasons why we should be suspicious of the status principle and, in turn, the status *argument* for the traditional view of hell. Too often, traditionalists have appealed to these problematic ideas in full confidence that by doing so they have disarmed their critics. This is far from true, however, as just this brief reflection demonstrates.

Which Punishment is Actually Infinite?

Now let's suppose that despite these problems the status argument actually succeeds in its intended aim to show that the damned deserve an

---

2. Edwards, "The Justice of God in the Damnation of Sinners," 342–43.

infinite punishment. Even so, there is another major problem lurking for the traditionalist. The problem is that eternal conscious torment (ECT) doesn't satisfy the demand of infinite punishment, since the damned can never suffer infinitely. When it comes to any suffering, this can vary in two ways—intensity and duration. Since humans are finite creatures, an infinite intensity of suffering is impossible (which might explain why traditionalist theologians have never seriously conjectured in this direction). But when it comes to an actually infinite *duration* of punishment for the damned, this too is impossible. For at any given moment in their hell career, the damned will have only suffered for a finite duration. Their future in hell is infinite, of course, but this is so only in the sense of potentiality, as, for instance, my baseball card collection is potentially infinite but always actually finite. So it turns out that the traditional view of hell actually does *not* affirm infinite punishment as advertised. ECT may be everlasting, but *the actual suffering of the damned is always finite.* Therefore, in making the status argument for infinite punishment for the damned, the traditionalist thereby sets up a requirement that cannot be met by ECT.

But the situation gets worse for the traditionalist, for not only is ECT inadequate to meet the demands of the status principle, there are plausible reasons to believe that annihilation *is more* appropriate to satisfy this requirement, in that it is a more extreme punishment than ECT. First, annihilation of the self in hell is complete and final for all eternity, unlike ECT which is an on-going, perpetually unfinished process. Second, annihilation of the wicked involves complete removal of goodness in a person, whereas with ECT the damned always retain some goodness, so far as they still exist and retain the *imago Dei*. Lastly, annihilation involves the obliteration of an entire being or substance, whereas in ECT all that is truly eliminated are certain qualities of that being, viz., positive or pleasant states of consciousness. For all of these reasons, annihilation appears to be a more severe punishment than ECT and, thus, a more appropriate punishment, if we assume that the damned deserve infinite punishment.

Here some traditionalists will object that annihilation of the damned doesn't really count as genuine punishment, since the person who is extinguished is no longer around to experience the punishment. Thus, Andy Saville asserts that "for a punishment to be retributive it must be experienced, but extinction can only be experienced in prospect, and this cannot be a complete apprehension of it in its infinite extent . . . since a finite mind could not fully grasp the prospect of an infinite future, and thus not experience an infinite loss."[3] Shawn Bawulski offers the same objection, insisting that

> The only penal aspect related to *annihilation* is the dreadful anticipation of the upcoming annihilation. Yet if the antecedent period of punishment is finite and the anticipatory period of dread is finite, even if the annihilation is permanent and in that sense infinite in consequence, the punishment itself is finite. Thus, I conclude that annihilation should not be considered an infinite punishment.[4]

What are we to say in response to this? Well, it appears that Saville and Bawulski beg the question with this argument, since they never actually argue for their crucial premise that all punitive measures must somehow be experienced by the punished person. Why assume this? In ordinary human experience that is certainly not the case, as persons who suffer the death penalty do not, from an earthly standpoint, experience their punishment after their execution. Yet it makes sense to say that their punishment remains effective even after they have perished. Similarly, it seems reasonable to suggest that an analogous "execution" of the person in hell remains punitive for all eternity, despite the fact that the perpetual effects of this punishment are not experienced by the person who has been annihilated.

These brief reflections show, then, that (1) the traditional view of hell as ECT cannot meet the demands of the status principle, assuming this principle does indeed entail that the damned are due infinite punishment and (2) there are good reasons to think that the conditionalist concept of annihilation of the damned is actually a more fitting punishment, given the standard traditional interpretation of the status principle.

The Problem of Infinite Evil

A third philosophical problem for the traditional view concerns some disturbing implications of ECT regarding the problem of evil. Now evil is generally conceived, following the standard Augustinian account, as a privation of good. And there are two forms that such privation takes, namely natural evil, or suffering, and moral evil, or sin. Now the troubling implication for

---

3. Saville, "Arguing with Annihilationism," 73–74.
4. Bawulski, "Annihilationism, Traditionalism, and the Problem of Hell," 66–67. Emphasis in original.

the traditional view of hell is that ECT has the outcome that both forms of evil are eternal.

Traditionalists maintain that the sins of the damned warrant ECT, but they are divided as to exactly how this is so. Some, following Anselm, Aquinas, and Edwards, affirm the Infinite Seriousness Thesis (IST), which says that human sins on earth are infinitely heinous and thus deserve infinite punishment. This rationale typically appeals to the status principle. But if IST is true, then given the fact, as pointed out in the previous section, that the punishment delivered in ECT is itself never actually infinite but at every moment finite, then for every person in hell, there will always remain *unpunished* sin. That is to say, for each damned soul there is *eternal moral evil*. Not only this, but for each person in hell, this outstanding moral evil is *infinite*, given IST. If earthly sin is infinitely heinous, thus requiring infinite punishment, then however long the damned have suffered in hell, the duration of their torment has been finite. And to subtract any finite number from infinity still leaves an infinite number. So the sin for which they are being tormented remains infinite. Therefore, the unpunished moral evil of the damned remains infinite for eternity. Thus, given IST, the traditional view of hell entails that *for each person in hell there exists eternally an infinite amount of moral evil*.

This appears devastating for the IST option. Apparently, the only recourse for the traditionalist is to opt for the Continuing Sin Thesis (CST), which rejects the notion that earthly sin is infinitely heinous and instead proposes that the damned sin perpetually in the afterlife. C. S. Lewis seems to hold such a view, as he writes that "the doors of hell are locked on the *inside*. . . . [The damned] enjoy forever the horrible freedom they have demanded, and are therefore self-enslaved."[5] More recently, Charles Seymour has advocated CST, proposing that, "the damned have the freedom to sin even after death. If they choose to sin continually, it is fair that they suffer continually."[6] And Michael Murray reasons as follows: "those who are judged and sentenced to hell might not have a sentence which initially merits an infinite punishment. But their unchecked sinful desires continue to lead them to sin even in hell and so continue to mount penalties which are never satisfied."[7]

Now CST is an improvement on IST, since it recognizes the finitude of human sin and thereby reduces the amount of deserved punishment to a finite quantity. Nevertheless, CST is deeply problematic. For one thing,

---

5. Lewis, *The Problem of Pain*, 115–16.
6. Seymour, "Hell, Justice, and Freedom," 78.
7. Murray, "Heaven and Hell," 293.

it appears to be an *ad hoc* theory, proposed merely as a way of resisting an objection rather than as a claim independently supported by evidence. In fairness, some advocates of the view have argued for the thesis. D. A. Carson asks, for instance, "are we to imagine that the lost in hell love God with heart and soul and mind and strength, and their neighbors as themselves? If not, they are breaking the first and second commandments."[8] This is a terribly weak (implied) argument, however. For given the extreme torments of hell, loving God wholeheartedly seems psychologically impossible. Imagine placing your open palm on a red-hot oven burner, holding it there for, say, ten seconds. How single-mindedly would you be able to love God during that time? Arguably, you would be a bit too distracted by the tactile experience to effectively love God and neighbor.

This suggests a further problem with CST, which takes the form of a dilemma. If, as Carson would have it, we can know with confidence that the damned will sin in perpetuity, this implies that they really are no longer free in hell, given a libertarian view of freedom. And without such freedom, again assuming the libertarian perspective, there can be no sin. But if the damned do retain libertarian freedom, then we can't rule out post-mortem repentance, a cessation of sin in hell, and ultimately salvation. Both of these options are unsavory ones for libertarian traditionalists, as neither can secure grounds for perpetual punishment in hell.

But even if these problems could be overcome somehow, there is another insurmountable reason to reject the Continuing Sin Thesis. Like IST, CST entails the eternal existence of evil. If the damned persist in their sinning even while being tormented for past sins, then there is always more sin awaiting retribution. This means *there is never a moment in which there is no unpunished sin*. So, given CST, *moral evil exists eternally*. Notice that CST improves upon IST in the sense that it does not imply that this eternally existing moral evil is infinite. But this is small consolation for the traditionalist, since even finite moral evil existing eternally is devastating for their view. For this suggests something more like Zoroastrian cosmic dualism than biblical Christian theism.

The Problem of Injustice

By now, perhaps, the traditionalist horse is, philosophically speaking, dead. Still, I propose to beat that horse just a bit more, beginning with some attention to the fact that this view is (ahem) saddled with a serious problem of injustice. Again, the traditionalist either affirms or denies IST and CST. If

---

8. Carson, *The Gagging of God*, 534.

she denies both IST and CST, then ECT is unjust because it is a punishment too severe for the moral crimes of the damned. For if all human earthly sin is finite and the damned do not continue to sin in hell, then there is no warrant for their being subjected to ECT. The finitude of their sin implies that at some point the damned would have suffered enough for a punishment equal to the severity of their earthly sin. If the traditionalist affirms IST, then ECT is unjust because it is insufficient as a punishment, since, as shown above, the damned never suffer enough to equal the infinite severity of their sins, since at any moment in eternity, they've only suffered finitely. And if the traditionalist resorts to CST, then God must ensure that the damned never stop sinning in hell in order to guarantee no one deserves to escape for all eternity. But this is unjust, as it is to force the damned to keep sinning. The final alternative of affirming both IST and CST is not even worth consideration for the traditionalist, as it inherits the difficulties of both IST and CST and is thus only doubly problematic.

So the traditionalist faces a particularly nasty quadrilemma of injustice. Whether she affirms IST and CST, denies both, or affirms one or the other, her position entails that ECT is extremely unjust.

The Problems of Cruelty, Malice, and Callousness

The last philosophical problem with traditionalism I want to discuss regards an objection often made against ECT but never, to my knowledge, developed in detail. It is the claim that such punishment would be cruel. To act cruelly is to willfully inflict undeserved, unconstructive pain on another sentient being. Given this basic understanding of cruelty, further problems with some forms of traditionalism appear. First, if the traditionalist denies both IST and CST, then the excessive punishment this involves (per above) is cruel. Furthermore, if God is *pleased* by this punishment, as traditionalists sometimes explicitly affirm, then he is malicious. For, as Kant puts it, "A malicious man is pleased when others suffer, he can laugh when others weep."[9] And if God does not have any feelings about it, then he is callous. Now neither cruelty, malice, nor callousness can be reconciled with the love and goodness of God. So the traditional view is unacceptable given IST.

However, some traditionalists who opt for CST have similarly serious problems. For, as we've seen, on this view God must somehow ensure that all of the damned continue to sin for all eternity, which given a libertarian view of freedom, is inconsistent with human freedom and moral responsibility. To coerce a person to sin is unjust. So any suffering that God brings

---

9. Kant, *Lectures on Ethics*, 223.

upon such a person would be cruel. And depending on whether or not God is pleased or indifferent to this, he would be malicious or callous. So, given a libertarian conception of freedom, the traditional view allied with CST, too, is irreconcilable with the love and goodness of God.

These are serious, even devastating problems for traditionalists of various stripes, as any traditionalist libertarian who rejects IST and CST essentially guts the Christian moral conception of God. Apparently, the only traditionalists who escape these particular problems are those who affirm IST and the compatibilist who affirms CST, though there might be some other problems lurking here as well that have not occurred to me. (Here is yet more philosophical work waiting to be done!) However, if these traditionalists do evade problems here, they nonetheless remain burdened with all of the problems discussed in the previous sections.

CONCLUSION

Much more could be said about each of the arguments I've discussed. But I hope this brief review at least demonstrates that there are several promising lines of philosophical argumentation to be developed in support of conditionalism. If universalism is untenable for biblical reasons, then we might say that the traditional view of hell is unsalvageable on moral grounds, as its concept of ECT in hell is extremely unjust, it implies the eternal existence of evil, and it is at odds with the love and goodness of God. What makes conditionalism the most attractive alternative among the views on hell is that, all things considered, it makes the most sense of both theological and philosophical concerns. The theological virtues of conditionalism have been far more widely understood than its philosophical merits. Hopefully, this will change soon as more philosophers begin to tackle some of the issues discussed here.

8

Paul and the Annihilation of Death

— Nicholas Rudolph Quient —

Nicholas Rudolph Quient is a graduate of Saddleback College, Biola University, and is currently a Masters student at Fuller Theological Seminary where he studies biblical languages, New Testament exegesis, and systematic theology. He is an avid student of the writings of Paul and hopes to pursue a PhD in New Testament Studies upon graduation.

Nick originally presented an early version of the following paper at the Rethinking Hell conference 2014.

Death. It's a topic that spills across your news feed or your daily newspaper. One cannot escape the deluge of information about suffering and terror in our world. My goal in this paper is this: to bring the Old Testament, Apocrypha, and ultimately Paul into the conversation about death and the doctrine of annihilationism or conditional immortality. This is a massive topic but hopefully by examining the primary biblical literature before 1 Corinthians 15, we can properly understand Paul's theology of final punishment, which is based on his view of God's chief enemy: death.[1]

---

[1]. The more I read and research, the more I realize how large the ocean of data is. I wish I could delve more into issues such as Pauline anthropology, the differing Hebraic ideas of death and resurrection, and the exegetical and theological insights of Philo and Josephus. Alas, time and space do not provide room for such exploration.

HUMANITY AND DEATH IN THE OLD TESTAMENT

Death did not have the dominion over humanity at its beginning. Before this collapse, we were "fully alive," according to Joel Green's interpretation of Genesis 2:7.[2] Within the primeval estate of Eden, the loss of the tree of life is the beginning of the end for humanity. The end result of disobedience is death, as Genesis 3:19 states: "By the sweat of your face you shall eat bread until you return to the ground, for out of it you were taken; you are dust, and to dust you shall return." The imagery of returning to the earth indicates something quite clear: male and female are now marked by mortality. We see this in Genesis 6:3, as human wickedness is more fully formed, where YHWH asserts "my spirit shall not abide in mortals forever, for they are flesh; their days shall be one hundred twenty years." This assertion confirms that flesh is mortal, and that for life to continue the spirit of YHWH must abide within us.

The death of the whole person is confirmed in the following flood narrative from Genesis 6–9. Yet even this catastrophe is not enough to assuage death, as sin and the loss of life continue in a fatal tango throughout the rest of the Old Testament. Metaphorically, Eve is then a witness to the first murder, as son is slaughtered by son in Genesis 4. Sodom and Gomorrah are used often in key examples throughout the Testaments in the context of divine judgment and absolute annihilation.[3] We see the anguish of Hagar in Genesis 21 as she leaves Ishmael to die, and one is hard-pressed to not imagine the sufferings of mothers everywhere who witness the death of their children; especially in parts of the developing world. A similar story is told in chapter 35 where Rachel dies in childbirth to Benjamin, the "son of my sorrow" (Gen 35:16–21). The book of Genesis never hides us from the face of death, and the mortality of human beings is shown to be anything but a celebration. According to John Goldingay,

> Human beings are born, they grow, they mature, they grow old, and they die. The process is built into their nature, like the pain of childbirth. Yet we have seen that coming into a friendship

---

2. Green, *Body, Soul, and Human Life*, 61–65, 64.

3. Sodom and Gomorrah is referenced over forty times throughout the Testaments and it is universally acknowledged negatively. It is most often used as a type of divine judgment. Cf. Deut 29:23; 32:32; Isa 9–10; 13:19; Jer 49:18; 50:40; Lam 4:6; Ezek 16:46–49; (vv. 50, 53, 56 is one of the few examples where the example of Sodom is reversed, though it is predicated on the idea that Sodom was a negative example to begin with); Amos 4:11; Zeph 2:9; Matt 10:15; 11:23–24; Luke 10:12; 17:29; Rom 9:29; 2 Pet 2:6; Jude 7; Rev 11:8; 3 Macc 2:5; 2 Esd 2:8. Lest the context be limited to this life, any judgment that commences with the death of the physical body and climaxes in an eternity of conscious torment surely bears the greater burden of proof.

with God had the equally natural potential somehow to defy the logic of humanity's creation. The tree of life stood for that possibility. Access to that is now ruled out. YHWH God determines to expel Adam from the garden so that he cannot eat of its fruit and thereby live forever.[4]

Human death occurs as a result of the fall, and is therefore an unnatural reality. Death simply is the natural down payment of sin. Death occurs when YHWH doesn't allow humanity to pursue continued immortality.

The Old Testament law codes stress death as the ultimate and irrevocable punishment for sin.[5] Beyond this we read reflections about the nature and presence of death by David (2 Sam 22:5) as "encompassing," and Job speaks of it as irresistible (Job 14:1). The Wisdom literature is pregnant with such imagery. Mortals die, are laid low, expire, wither, and waste away (Job 14:10–14). As mortals, our days are like grass (Ps 103:15), and we "return to dust" (Job 34:21; Ps 22:15), even under the eyes of YHWH. "Like sheep they are appointed for Sheol; death shall be their shepherd; straight to the grave they descend; and their form shall waste away" (Ps 49:14).[6] Samuele Bacchiocchi says of the Old Testament's view of the soul and death that "death is seen in the Old Testament as the emptying out of the soul of all its vitality and strength."[7] To die, then, is to be gone. You cease to be alive in any sense of the word. However, the hope is that "in the path of righteousness there is life, in walking its path there is no death" (Prov 12:28).[8]

Issues of life and death often arise in the Old Testament when the theme is worship. The anxiety of Israel can often be wrapped up in the phrase "in *Sheol* who can give you praise?" (Ps 6:5). "Sing praises to YHWH, who dwells in Zion" (Ps 9:11a) because "you are the one who lifts me up from the gates of death, so that I may recount all your praises, and, in the gates of daughter Zion, rejoice in your deliverance" (Ps 9:13–14). Psalm 115:17 continues with "the dead do not praise YHWH, nor do any that go down into silence." The rhetorical question asked of YHWH in Psalm 88:10–11 is, "do you work wonders for the dead? Do the shades rise up to praise you? Is your steadfast love declared in the grave . . . ?" The dust cannot praise YHWH (Ps 30:9) and those in Sheol cannot thank nor praise YHWH (Isa 38:18).

---

4. Goldingay, *Old Testament Theology*, 143.

5. A mere sampling includes cursing parents (Exod 21:17) and striking them (Exod 21:15); kidnapping (Exod 21:16); bestiality (Exod 22:19); prostitution (Lev 21:9) and murder (Num 35:18–21).

6. Ps 49:20 speaks of mortals being "like the animals that perish." 2 Pet 2:12 clearly has this text in mind, and uses it in a similar manner.

7. Bacchiocchi, *Immortality or Resurrection*, 55.

8. The NIV translates "no death" here as "immortality."

More tragically, who can tell others of YHWH's deliverance if one sleeps? Who can see his righteousness if no one sings his praises? Only YHWH's steadfast love can deliver humanity from death and famine.[9] As it is, dead people don't praise YHWH. What is needed—what is required—is resurrection. Resurrection is desired, not only for the sake of renewed life but that relationship with YHWH may continue. Worship and communion with the God of the living is often the end goal, the destiny of dusty humanity.[10]

YHWH takes no pleasure in death (Ezek 18:23, 32; 33:11), for what community can praise him in the slumber of death? What community can proclaim his steadfast love if they aren't among the living? What community can showcase YHWH's power to overcome death when "the living know that they will die, but the dead know nothing?" (Eccl 9:5). Death is impartially applied to animals and humans in Ecclesiastes 3:19.

HUMANITY AND DEATH IN THE APOCRYPHA

The imagery of worship is also picked up in the Apocrypha, where Sirach 17:27–28 states, "who will sing praises to the Most High in Hades in place of the living who give thanks? From the dead, as from one who does not exist, thanksgiving has ceased; those who are alive and well sing the Lord's praises."[11] Because of this, Sirach 17:30 asserts, "for not everything is within human capacity, since human beings are not immortal." Similarly in Sirach 22:12, "mourning for the dead lasts seven days, but for the foolish or the ungodly it lasts all the days of their lives." Because of this we "do not rejoice over anyone's death; remember that we all must die" (Sir 8:7). In fact, the most powerful anthropological statement recorded in the literature is from the Wisdom of Solomon 7:1–6, which deserves to be quoted in full:

> I also am mortal, like everyone else, a descendant of the first-formed child of earth; and in the womb of a mother I was molded into flesh, within the period of ten months, compacted with blood, from the seed of a man and the pleasure of marriage. And when I was born, I began to breathe the common air, and fell upon the kindred earth; my first sound was a cry, as is true

---

9. Ps 33:12–22, 19.

10. The most explicit statement regarding resurrection in the Old Testament is Daniel 12:1–3.

11. The beginning of Sirach 17 is a brief commentary on the creation accounts in Genesis 1–2. For example, "The Lord created human beings out of earth, and makes them return to it again. He gave them a fixed number of days, but granted them authority over everything on the earth [or it]."

of all. I was nursed with care in swaddling cloths. For no king has had a different beginning of existence; there is for all one entrance into life, and one way out.

Humanity descends from the past, is born of blood and seed and pleasure, and "breathes the common air" (v. 3). The mortality described is purely physical and universal in scope: "there is for all one entrance into life, and one way out" (v. 6). Death is unquenchable, impartial, unflinching, embracing servants and kings, women and men, old and young.[12] It kills all who flee, and consumes each that fights against the inevitable.

PAUL AND THE IMMORTAL GOD

Paul affirms the sole immortality of God (Rom 1:23; 1 Tim 1:17; 6:16), and believed that anything that was not God was not immortal. The distinction between "images resembling mortal human beings or animals" and God (Rom 1:23) illustrates this point. This God brings immortality (*aphtharsia*)[13] through the gospel and "abolishes death" (2 Tim 1:10).[14] It is in this God that Paul personally believes and in whom we seek immortality (Rom 2:7). If God alone is immortal, it means that nothing else is (1 Tim 6:16).[15] Immortality is an attribute of God, an ontological fact. In this God "we live and move and have our being" (Acts 17:28), and to "those who by patiently doing good seek for glory and honor and immortality, he will give eternal life" (Rom 2:7). Paul's theology of immortality begins with God, the source of all life. Thus, conditional immortality is fundamentally theocentric.

---

12. Job 14:1 states, "A mortal, born of woman, few of days and full of trouble." The chapter continues in verse 10 where "mortals die, and are laid low; humans expire, and where are they?"

13. *BDAG*, s.v. "ἀφθαρσία," defines it as not being subject to decay; immortality. In the most likely sense, it means believers won't experience the decay of death and it supposes that God cannot experience such things.

14. The Common English Bible renders this as "[Jesus Christ] destroyed death and brought life and immortality . . . ."

15. A contemporary Hellenistic Jew, Philo of Alexandria asserts that man is "Mortal as to his body, but immortal as to his intellect" (*On The Creation*, XLVI, 135). He speaks of "death" more in terms of physical death, while the soul continues on. One gets a distinct sense that death for Philo is like tax season for us; more inconvenient than anything else.

PAUL AND THE MORTAL PERSON

Modern science has issued a serious challenge to the mainstream Christian conception of a partitive nature of the human person;[16] namely that "humans are composed of two parts, a body and a soul, or a body and a mind."[17] Biblical studies, however, offers a more holistic account of the human person.[18] Samuele Bacchiocchi points out that, "it is noteworthy that Paul never uses *psyche*—soul to denote the life that survives death."[19] Paul uses the phrase "eternal life" predominantly in Romans (2:7; 5:21; 6:22, 23) and Galatians (6:8), though it appears in Acts (13:46, 48) and the other epistles such as 1 Timothy (1:16; 6:12) and Titus (1:2; 3:7) for a total of eleven times. In each instance it presupposes at least two connected foundations: it is soteriological, and it is the gift of God to those "in Christ."[20] The phrase "eternal life" is never positively, neutrally, or negatively used of those not "in Christ." The very use of the expression "eternal life" suggests that the notion of immortality is connected to soteriology. F. F. Bruce notes, "Paul evidently could not contemplate immortality apart from resurrection; for him a body of some kind was essential to personality."[21]

The general trajectory of Judaism held that "*nephesh*" [or "soul"] was that which gives life to the human person and not a separate entity within the person.[22] For Paul, human life is intimately connected with the ethical dimensions of his admonitions regarding sexuality, gender and purity. Within 1 Corinthians alone we see several strong affirmations of bodily purity, such as the rejection of incest (5:1–5), warnings about sexual immortality (6:1–11), rules for marriage and intimacy (7:3–4), and instructions

---

16. Cf. Murphy, *Bodies and Souls, or Spirited Bodies?* 39–70; Joel B. Green, *Body, Soul and Human Life*, 1–29. See also Brown, Murphy, & Malony (eds.), *Whatever Happened to the Soul?*

17. Murphy, *Bodies and Souls, or Spirited Bodies?* 2.

18. Schwarz, *Eschatology*, 271–80.

19. Bacchiocchi, *Immortality or Resurrection?* 89–95.

20. Universalism is beyond the scope of this paper, but it deserves a brief mention here. I consider Romans 5:12–21, 11:32–36, and Philippians 2:5–11 to be reasonable proof texts in support for universalism, though I do think they can be accounted for within an annihilationist framework. For a succinct explanation of these texts, see Gundry-Volf, "Universalism," 956–61.

21. Bruce, *Paul, Apostle of the Heart Set Free*, 311.

22. Kreitzer, "Resurrection," 805–12; 810. He also states, "In mainstream Jewish thought human beings do not have souls, they are souls. This anthropological underpinning has tremendous implications for a doctrine of the resurrection in that it refuses to surrender the somatic component of a human being." As this paper progresses it will be shown how much I agree with Kreitzer.

concerning the mutuality of men and women in the assembly (11:2–16). All of these texts indicate not only the necessity of bodily cruciformity but also a desire to be united into one body, the Bride of Christ.[23] Sin affects not only the individual but the community as Paul makes clear in the section on the Lord's supper (11:17–34).

One of the classic proof texts for anthropological dualism is 2 Corinthians 5:1–10, and Michael Gorman points out two foundational Pauline affirmations within: "(1) that the believer's temporary, mortal body will be replaced with a permanent one; and (2) that present suffering will be replaced by future glory."[24] These affirmations are meant to encourage believers in Corinth so they "do not lose heart" (4:16). The longing for "that what is mortal may be swallowed up by life" (v. 5) is a clear indication not only of the mere hope of resurrection, but a confident assertion like the one in 1 Corinthians 15:54–55. Our confidence rests not in our own nakedness, but in the tent made for us by God: a tent, temporary and fragile, mortal and subject to destruction (5:1–4).[25] What we do "in the body" (v. 10) factors into our final judgment, thus further emphasizing the preciousness of God's temple, given to us. We long for the "redemption of our bodies" (Rom 8:23). Because Paul affirms the centrality of the human person in redemption, Paul believed that eschatology was primarily ethical and relational.[26] No longer will our bodies "sink down into the dust" where "our bodies cling to the ground" (Ps 44:25). The mortality of humanity requires the ability of God to redeem the bodies of his people from death, for without God's intervention, we die in our sins.

For Paul, the body appears is intrinsically tied to the person, considered as a unified whole. This view expresses Hebraic eschatology, not Greek anthropology.[27] To be "naked" in Jewish thought is not only undesirable, it

---

23. My thanks to Michael J. Gorman for the term and his wonderful book *Cruciformity*.

24. Gorman, *Apostle of the Crucified Lord*, 301–5, 303.

25. Ibid., 303.

26. This includes the passage in Philippians 1:23, where Paul speaks of wanting to "depart and be with Christ." Paul's relationship with the risen Messiah is relational, and says nothing of his anthropological commitments. His Christology here is fundamentally about relationship, not ontology. Bacchiocchi points out that "Paul was not giving a doctrinal exposition of what happens at death." He also mentions that when believers sleep, they "experience what may be called 'eternal time.'" (*Immortality or Resurrection?*, 178–86, 179.) In my own words, when one sleeps, time becomes irrelevant. In the twinkling of an eye, we shall be in Christ's presence. Time is, then, entirely in the eye of the beholder.

27. Ellis, *Christ and the Future in New Testament History*, 158.

is shameful as we see in Hosea 2:3 and Isaiah 20:2–4.[28] What is significant about the entire sequence in 2 Corinthians 5:1–10 is that the judgment of God is imminent in verse 10. The statement about "life in this tent" (v. 4) indicates our present condition, illustrating the oncoming giving of eternal life, guaranteed by the Spirit in verse 5 where "what is mortal may be swallowed up by life." Immortality that encompasses and empowers physical bodies is utterly a gift of God, and when the naked body is clothed, it is with Christ (v. 3).[29] This is juxtaposed powerfully in Job 26:2: "Sheol is naked before God, and Abaddon has no covering," which illustrates helplessness before YHWH, and demands God's sovereign creative action in our resurrection.

As Jürgen Moltmann points out,

> Soul and body are not analysed as a person's component parts. When, according to the Yahwist's creation narrative, God breathed his breath into the lump of earth, we are told that "man became a living soul" (Gen. 2.7 AV). He does not *have* a soul. He *is* a living soul . . . the person is always affected as a whole, though he assumes a difference specific form in different relationships. Nor does he find in his God any opportunity for withdrawing to an immortal, spiritual substance, so as to surmount the happiness and pains, life and death of his body.[30]

Given Paul's pervasive dependence on the Old Testament, his views about anthropological monism seem coordinate with the mainstream thrust of the Old Testament, "which views man as a unity and pictures the whole person as going into the grave."[31]

According to Michael Gorman,

> If Christ's "resurrection" and ours were simply about the survival of the soul or something similar, then what one does to and with the body would matter much less, if at all. However, because Christ's resurrection was a resurrection and transformation of his embodied self, and because our resurrection will likewise be a resurrection and transformation of our embodied

---

28. Ellis points out several other texts: Ezek 23:26, 29; Isa. 47:3; Dan 4:30b (LXX). See his *Christ and the Future in New Testament History*, 158 n. 63 and 159.

29. This demands that the Corinthian Christians return to 1 Corinthians 15, where Paul has already laid out much of this material.

30. Moltmann, *God in Creation*, 256–57.

31. Ellis, *Christ and the Future in New Testament History*, 188.

selves, what we do with and to our bodies has tremendous, even eternal, significance.³²

The nature of Paul's anthropology coheres strongly with his passionate defense of *bodily* resurrection in 1 Corinthians 15. As the first human beings were drawn from the dust, so are the righteous who believed in the power of God. Human life, as it is, is not *ex nihilo*. The imagery of being (re-)made from preexistent matter is not an image foreign to Scripture (Gen 2:7). Specifically for Paul, the restoration of the flesh is of paramount concern here. E. Earle Ellis notes, "Paul's hope . . . is . . . in the abiding Christ; not in the immortal soul of Platonic idealism, but in 'the God who can bring the dead to life and can call to himself those that do not exist as though they did' (Rom. 4:17)."³³

DEATH, SIN, AND DESTRUCTION IN PAUL

To be "destroyed" in Pauline thought involves several factors, and is subject to a mosaic of varying imagery. In Galatians 1:8–9, Paul begins by cursing of those who have challenged his gospel of God. At the climax of verses 8 and 9 Paul uses the word "*anathema*."³⁴ It is generally translated "cursed" or "eternally condemned."³⁵ If we look to the LXX, we find several uses of it.³⁶ For example, in Numbers 21:3, the context is death. The curse was destruction, as the Canaanites and their city were destroyed.³⁷ A similar account in found in Judges 1:17, where the Canaanites in Zephath are "devoted to destruction" (NRSV), using "*anathema*." The same idea occurs in Joshua 6:17 and 7:12; both indicate complete physical destruction of the enemies of Israel.³⁸ In this same epistle (Gal 6:7–8), the operative phrase is "Do not

---

32. Gorman, *Reading Paul*, 107.
33. Ellis, *Christ and the Future in New Testament History*, 164.
34. See also Fudge, *The Fire That Consumes* (2011), 199–203.
35. *BDAG*, s.v. "ἀνάθεμα," offers three definitions: 1) that which is dedicated as a votive offering; 2) that which has been cursed, cursed, accursed; 3) the content that is expressed is a curse, a curse. Most of the examples are found in definition 2, and it is within this definition that we find Gal. 1:8 being placed.
36. Paul was most likely trained with the LXX, and it is most probable that he didn't choose this word in isolation of its Old Testament contexts.
37. The CEB footnote in verse 3 says that "*Hormah*" means destruction. The same is found in Judges 1:17.
38. In Joshua 7:12, we see that the Israelites turned their backs to their enemies, in the same way they are told to turn away from false gods; things (cities, enemies, false gods and idols) to be burned and devoted to destruction. The curse of God through the LXX is that of destruction and death.

be deceived; God is not mocked, for you reap whatever you sow. If you sow to your own flesh, you will reap corruption from the flesh; but if you sow to the Spirit, you will reap eternal life from the Spirit" (NRSV). Paul's use of *"phthora"* (corruption) here is key. Bauer's lexicon offers several definitions but identifies its meaning in Galatians 6:8 as: the "total destruction of an entity, *destruction*.[39] Namely, those who sow according to their flesh will reap corruption and not inherit "eternal life" in the Spirit.

Those who oppose the reign of God are subject to "wrath" (1 Thess 1:9–10)[40] and "eternal destruction from the presence of the Lord" (2 Thess 1:9).[41] The use of *"olethros"* in 1 Thessalonians 5:3 indicates that Paul has in mind "a state of destruction, ruin, death."[42] The use of this word as "eternal death" in *Testament of Reuben* 6:3 illustrates that the concept of "death" means destruction, the loss of life.[43] In both Testaments, death is seen as the ultimate punishment for sin.[44] Paul is simply picking up the language of destruction already found in his Scriptures, and the Old Testament rarely speaks in the language of eternal conscious torment.

---

39. BDAG, s.v. "φθορά," offers these other definitions: 1) Breakdown of organic matter, dissolution, deterioration. 2) Destruction of a fetus, abortion. 3) Ruination of a person through an immoral act. 4) Inward depravity, depravity. Included with Gal 6:8 under "total destruction of an entity" is 2 Peter 2:12, where the destruction of "brute beasts" or false teachers happens.

40. In speaking of *"orgē,"* J. Fichtner, as cited in Fudge, *The Fire That Consumes* (2011), 190 n. 16, writes, "the wrath of YHWH aims at destruction, at full extirpation."

41. What makes this difficult is that the New Testament uses of *"olethros"* (destruction) are found only in Paul's writings, and the context is either ambiguous or clearly in favor of annihilationism. The noun *"olethros"* appears with the adjective *"aionios,"* thus modified. The meaning of *"aionios"* has either a qualitative state or quantitative. Both meanings are possible, but conditioned via context. Almost instantly, given the lexical support for *"olethros"* indicating destruction, it appears that *"aionios"* would fit far stronger in the category of qualitative. For example, *"aionios"* modifies several nouns throughout the New Testament: "punishment" (Matt 25:46); "death" (Rom 1:32; 6:21ff; 7:5; 8:6; 1 Cor 15:21f, 56; 2 Cor 2:16; 7:10; Jas 1:15; 5:20; 1 John 5:16; Rev 2:11; 20:6, 14; 21:8); "fire" (Jude 7; Matt 18:8; 25:41). In each context, the author is speaking of the quality of (or the lack of) life experienced, with Jude 7 being an excellent example of *"pur aionios,"* resulting in utter extinction upon the inhabitants of Sodom and Gomorrah. The fire didn't remain, though the awful effects echoed throughout history.

42. BDAG, s.v. "ὄλεθρος." Also of note is the use of *"oluthrios"* on this same page, including their definition: "pertaining to being totally destroyed, deadly, destructive." "Obliteration" or "annihilation" is a fitting transliteration.

43. Borchert, "Wrath, Destruction," notes that *"Olethros aionios* in 2 Thessalonians 1:9 seems to mean 'eternal destruction' or the opposite of eternal life." He concludes with, "the usual meaning in Paul is 'final and hopeless judgment.'"

44. Gen 2:17; 3:17; Ezek 18:4. The verdict upon humanity is death, a "return to the ground . . ." in Gen 3:19.

We see this same annihilation in 2 Thessalonians 2:3–4. Since we can't know the identity of the "lawless one" in 2:3–4 we won't spend time on decoding *its* identity.[45] What is compelling is that this "lawless one" is "destined for destruction (*olethros*)" (v. 3), because he opposes God and declares himself to be God (v. 5). There seems to be a theme here: humanity desires to be like God in Genesis 2, and so does this Lawless One. The results of such hubris are most commonly a loss of the prospect of immortality and, always, life itself. In the same sense (though far stronger in terms of action), Jesus will "destroy" or "consume"[46] him with the breath of his mouth, annihilating (*katargesei*) him by the manifestation of his coming (v. 8). The Parousia of Jesus results in the "annihilation" of the Lawless One[47] and the Lawless One perishes.[48] The definition Bauer gives *katargesei* is "to cause something to come to an end or to be no longer in existence."[49]

Instead of asserting metaphysical abstractions, Paul deals in very human contexts and speaks of sin and death and life in strongly human terms.[50] Anthony Thiselton is quick to point out that Paul "does not even speak of 'hell,' but occasionally of 'destruction.'"[51] The imagery employed by Paul to this point is a reflection of Old Testament judgment, with death as the end result of unrighteousness.[52] Two key examples may suffice.

First, Isaiah 30:27 speaks of YHWH's judgment of Assyria as such:

---

45. Chrysostom (*Homilies on 2 Thessalonians* 3) and Augustine (*The City of God* 20.19.2) believed it was the antichrist. Cyril of Jerusalem calls them "masked heretics," *Catechetical Lectures* 15.9. Thankfully, we aren't as interested in this question as they were.

46. Other sources read "consume" in the NRSV footnotes; an apt image of Jesus.

47. Ambrose speaks of the "Lawless One" as one that is "slain" by Jesus, *Of The Holy Spirit*, 3.44.

48. Marshall, "The New Testament Does Not Teach Universal Salvation," 70, notes, "whenever Paul uses 'destroy' (*appolumi*) of human beings he refers to a judgment upon them that destroys them with no suggestion that their sinful nature is destroyed but they themselves are spared." See n. 37. He notes several scriptural passages: Rom 2:12; 14:15; 1 Cor 1:18; 8:11; 15:18; 2 Cor 2:15; 4:3, 9; 2 Thess 2:10. Cf. Phil 1:28; 3:19; 1 Tim 6:9.

49. BDAG, s.v. "καταργέω."

50. His personification of death and sin through the epistle to the Romans illustrates this.

51. Thiselton, *The Living Paul*, 146.

52. See Bacchiocchi, *Immortality or Resurrection?* 41–78, 134–42, 157–69, 197–9, 227–9. Fudge, *The Fire That Consumes* (2011), 44–84; Fudge, "The Final End of the Wicked," 31–32; Ellis, *Christ and the Future in New Testament History*, 186–90; Pinnock, "The End of the Finally Impenitent."

> See, the name of the Lord comes from far away, burning with his anger, and in thick rising smoke; his lips are full of indignation, and his tongue is like a devouring fire; his breath is like an overflowing stream that reaches up to the neck—to sift the nations with the sieve of destruction, and to place on the jaws of the peoples a bridle that leads them astray.

The language of "comes from far away," "rising smoke," "devouring fire," and "breath" indicates that Paul may have this text in mind. This imagery is found throughout Scripture and usually indicates destruction (Sodom and Gomorrah in Genesis 19); and when it comes from God, most of the time it destroys and consumes, leaving smoke that rises.

We find the next example in Isaiah 66:15 where Christ comes in "fire" and to "pay back his anger in fury." Verse 16 continues with "For by fire will the Lord execute judgment, and by his sword, on all flesh; and those slain by the Lord shall be many."[53] As is clear from this text the Old Testament doesn't envisage eternal conscious torment. It envisages the destruction of cities, of groups, and of the entire person.

Similarly in 2 Corinthians 2:15–17, the immediate contrast is between "those who are being saved" and "those who are perishing."[54] In Romans 5:12–21, the operative phrase is "justification and life." Just as death reigned through Adam, justification and life come to all "in Christ" (v. 18).[55] We have already seen in Romans 2:7 that there are those who do not seek "for glory and honor and immortality" and therefore cannot be justified and thus receive "life." Grant Osborne notes,

> the eschatological rewards is seen in the fact that *believers* [emphasis added] seek glory, honor and immortality by their good works. These three rewards refer to the gifts that God will bestow on the faithful at the final judgment when he will give eternal life to those who have so lived. These three define the meaning of eternal life for the faithful.[56]

---

53. See also Fudge, *The Fire that Consumes* (2011), 193.

54. BDAG, s.v. "ἀπόλλυμι" (destroy, death), is in the middle voice ("*appolumenois*"), showcasing the perishing of those who are not saved. Since this is being applied to human beings, to "ruin" them doesn't seem contextually applicable. When it appears to apply to people, it often means to kill (2 Pet 3:9; 1 Cor 10:9).

55. It is clear that not all seek for glory and honor and immortality. To do so would place them within the accessibility of Christ's decisive act of reconciliation. Paul's concern with the immediate nature of the present life appears to exclude a universal salvation, though it cannot be said to be an improbable interpretation of Romans 5.

56. Osborne, *Romans*, 65. See also Witherington and Hyatt, *Paul's Letter to the Romans*, 82 (as regards v. 7): "Paul is arguing that those who persist in doing good have the prospect of receiving from God glory, honor, peace, immortality, and everlasting life . . .

According to Paul in Romans 5, the first human beings triggered a chain of horrific events that resulted in death, a fate that awaits all of us. Since they sinned and brought death, we now suffer the consequences.[57]

Thus, under sin and death, we no experience the fullness of our humanity. Because of sin and death, human beings lack life suited for the age to come, and we lack full relationship with God and with each other. Because of this the fully human and fully divine Christ undoes the dominion of death by becoming obedient to death, even such a death as on a cross (Phil 2:8), liberating us from the slave-masters of death, allowing us to rise again, with sins forgiven and lives reconciled with God and within community. To refuse to seek the kingdom of God and be united to Christ is to fail to "inherit God's kingdom," to suffer "wrath" (Eph 5:5–6), and to be "destroyed" (Phil 1:28; 3:19). While resurrection is not a concept alien to the Old Testament (cf. Dan 12:2), the theme is certainly not dominant.[58] However, with Paul, the thought of resurrection becomes more than just speculation; it is foundational to his gospel. This belief in resurrection has the authority and power to affect even those who sleep, thus defeating death.

PAUL, RESURRECTION, AND THE ANNIHILATION OF DEATH[59]

Calvin Roetzel poses a rhetorical Corinthian response to Paul, which in turn yields 1 Corinthians 15. His reconstruction is this:

> Through baptism we have already passed from death to the resurrected life. If we have already died, and have been raised with Christ, then, as you said, today is the day of salvation. Also, the whole idea of the resurrection of the body is disgusting. Which body? The old body or the young one? The sick body or the

---

Paul is talking about the eschatological reward or blessing for the godly . . . ."

57. 2 Esdras 3:10–26; 7:117–9.

58. Goldingay, *Theological Diversity and the Authority of the Old Testament*, 55–58; Nickelsburg, *Resurrection, Immortality, and Eternal Life*, 23–38. Nickelsburg concludes, "For Daniel, resurrection has a judicial function. . . . Daniel does not conceive of a general resurrection of all humanity, but of those particular people whose unjust treatment in this life presents a problem for the writer." See also 37 n. 63. Bassler, *Navigating Paul*, 87–88, offers a brief survey of Hellenistic Judaism and concludes that the topic is diverse and ambiguous.

59. Major commentaries consulted for this section include Fee, *1 Corinthians* (1987); Thiselton, *1 Corinthians: A Shorter Exegetical & Pastoral Commentary*; Witherington, *Conflict and Community in Corinth: A Socio-Rhetorical Commentary on 1-2 Corinthians*; Johnson, *1 Corinthians*.

healthy one? How can you say we must prepare for the resurrection of the dead and the judgment of the resurrected? How can those who have already died with Christ and been raised up die again? Also, what do you mean by the 'resurrection of the body?' The whole idea of the resuscitation of a rotten corpse is repugnant. Salvation brings release from our bodies; and did you not say that flesh and blood cannot inherit the kingdom of God? What good is salvation if we are still imprisoned in our bodies?[60]

Roetzal's reconstruction offers us a chance to look through one of the most pregnant chapters in all of Paul as it gets to the root of the problem: the disbelief in the necessity of bodily resurrection. 1 Corinthians 15 asserts three fundamental principles: first, the fact of resurrection of Christ in verses 1–11; second, the resurrection of the dead, with emphasis on salvation in Christ in verses 11–34; and third, verses 35–57, where Paul describes the nature of resurrection and the ultimate victory of the Triune God over the sting of death.

15:1–11

Paul introduces a tradition that comes from the witnesses of the resurrected Christ (vv. 1–4) with the purpose of correcting Christians.[61] Of particular emphasis is the death for sins,[62] the burial of the dead,[63] and the raising[64] on

---

60. Roetzel, *The Letters of Paul*, 95. See also Bassler, *Navigating Paul*, 87. "Because the Corinthian position as rooted in a view of the body as inherently mortal and corruptible and therefore incapable of resurrection, Paul devotes a large portion of his argument to the question of how dead bodies are raised (vv. 35–57)."

61. Johnson, *1 Corinthians*, 282. Of note are three opinions on why Paul feels the need to remind the Corinthians (notice that he doesn't prove the historicity of the resurrection; he assumes it). 1) A group that couldn't accept an afterlife. Verse 29 seems to argue against this. 2) A group that believed the resurrection had already occurred. 3) A group that couldn't accept the resurrection of a *body*. This is so stressed in vv. 35–58 that one could scarcely mistake it. Thus, I will adopt the third view, though the second view is certainly compatible.

62. Isaiah 53:5; The use of Passover harkens back to the exodus, where liberation from captivity was the working out of God's divine plan for reconciliation.

63. The confirmation of actual physical death, asserted in all three of the Synoptic parallels: Mark 8:31; Matt 16:21; Luke 9:22. Simply, this was death for sin, and in order to abolish all sin from his creation, God had to come and abolish death itself in his person. The empty tomb casts light over the shadow of the cross.

64. The verb in "he has been raised" is a perfect passive. Fee, *1 Corinthians*, 726, points out that it means "[Jesus] was both raised and still lives."

the third day. What follows (vv. 5–7) is a list of witnesses to the resurrected Christ with Christ's appearance to Paul at the end of the list (vv. 8–11).

15:12–34

The *refutatio*[65] rhetorical phrase in verse 12 continues Paul's previous arguments. Since Christ's resurrection has been preached, why do they disbelieve? Verses 13–14 assert the futility of Paul's proclamation and indeed his entire mission to the Gentiles. Death, then, has not been defeated. For Paul, according to Thiselton, "Christ is the paradigm case of resurrection."[66] Thiselton's statement aptly sums up Paul's central message here.

In verse 15 Paul asserts that he and the apostles would be guilty of misrepresenting (*pseudomartyres* or being "false witnesses") God if God did not raise Christ[67] from the dead. The Corinthians accepted the death and burial of Christ, but the resurrection of the dead was a stumbling block. Verse 17 underscores the futility of such a belief, which if true means that humanity is to be pitied, everyone remaining in their sin. Paul intensifies the problem in verse 18: what about the dead? There is no hope for them, and if this life is all there is, we are worth pitying. They died; that's it.[68]

According to Paul, the "denial of the resurrection is the denial of the future."[69] So says Thiselton, "Sleep (v18) is a word pregnant with the promise of future awakening at the dawn of a new day."[70] Sleep indicates a sense of timelessness, for when one sleeps, time becomes irrelevant. Michael Gorman states, "Paul clearly believed that," if Christ is risen, "this state of sleep is temporary."[71] Because of these misconceptions about the resurrection, he

---

65. Thiselton, *1 Corinthians: A Shorter Exegetical & Pastoral Commentary*, 264.

66. Ibid., 265.

67. The definite article adds to Christ, indicating his Messiahship. So Fee, *1 Corinthians*, 742.

68. For Paul, here at least, one wonders about what he thought of the human soul. Most curiously, he simply says that they have "perished." That's it. Without resurrection, they would still be dead. He doesn't speculate of an intermediate state, nor does he argue for a tortured existence somewhere beneath the earth. The dead are dead, and that is that. However, for Paul, that is an unacceptable answer for those who died and live in Christ, and he will debunk it with passion.

69. Fee, *1 Corinthians*, 744.

70. Thiselton, *1 Corinthians: A Shorter Exegetical & Pastoral Commentary*, 267. This statement is also congruent with the concept of 'eternal time' when one sleeps. Time becomes timeless.

71. Gorman, *Reading Paul*, 175.

turns to the positive claims in verse 20,[72] asserting the reality of Christ's resurrection, the *"aparche"* (first fruits)[73] of those who have died. They are reaped, pulled out of the earth again, showing faithfulness to the creation narratives in Genesis 1–2. Verse 21 says the sin of the first human brought corruption and death, but the resurrection of the dead has also come through a human being. Verse 22 contains the famous text, "for[74] as all die in Adam, so all will be made alive in Christ." Those who sleep and live "in Christ"[75] will rise. Death is universal and unable to be resisted; to accept the universal offer of Christ requires faith and belief, freely offered.[76] Christ reverses the Adamic curse of death upon the human race. Furthermore, Christ is claimed as the first fruits in himself, and then those who belong to him (v. 23) when the Second Advent occurs.[77] The *"telos"* (end; v. 24) indicates that the eschaton has commenced, when Christ hands back the kingdom to God the Father, but only after he has put all his enemies under his feet.[78]

The end entails two facets of summation: the reign of Christ and return of the kingdom back to God, and the destruction of everything opposed to them. Chief among these enemies is death, which is "destroyed." Johnson suggests that the use of *"katargeo"*[79] (destroyed) in verse 26 means

72. As Thiselton, *1 Corinthians: A Shorter Exegetical & Pastoral Commentary*, 268, notes, "*Confirmatio*" occupies vv. 20–28.

73. The emphasis on "first fruits" regarding the "entire batch" is found in Rom 11:16, where if a part is holy, then the whole body is holy. See also Deuteronomy 26:1–11. First fruits may indicate harvest, which would reap "eternal life" (Gal 6:7–8).

74. The explanatory *"gar."*

75. A difficulty for universalism: "in Christ" is a corporate term reserved for believers and those who exercise faith (John 8:30–31; Acts 10:43; Rom 3:22; 4:17; especially in 1 Cor 1:21; 14:22; 15:11).

76. The Christian hope is that all would come to repentance in Christ, and join all things in being reconciled to God. To hope for this is not only mandated, it is to join God's heart as he wishes that none would perish (2 Pet 3:9).

77. The *"hotan"* clause specifies that this is an unknown future event. Paul isn't putting a timetable on Christ, but is speaking forth what will happen, not when it will.

78. LXX: Psalm 8:6; 110:1 (an allusion). See also Heb 2:9.

79. Thiselton, *1 Corinthians: A Shorter Exegetical & Pastoral Commentary*, 270, states, "The strong, emphatic word annihilate (vv. 24, 26) takes up the use of the same word in 1:28 and especially 2:6 (cf. 6:13; 13:8, 10, 11). See also *BDAG*, s.v. "καταργέω": 1) To cause something to be unproductive. While not inconceivable, this doesn't have the explanatory power and the depth of Paul's eschatological vision. 2) To cause something to lose its power or effectiveness. This is the definition Johnson and MacDonald take, but the use of the term in context simply suggests the nullification of the Law (Eph 2:15; Rom 3:31), and is thus simply an end to the Law. 3) To cause something to come to an end to be no longer in existence. The persuasive power of this is where Bauer places 1 Cor 15:24 & 26, it fits the permanent abolition of all things opposed to God, and more

"make/render ineffective."[80] While this isn't inconceivable, I would suggest "*katargeo*" in verses 24 and 26 more likely means "to abolish" or to "to be put out of existence, annihilated," a translation for which Anthony Thiselton argues.[81] This last enemy is annihilated *because* it is put beneath Christ's feet. To be put beneath the feet of another is to symbolize the defeat of an army or king (Ps 110:2, 5–6).[82] I. Howard Marshall states, "Therefore . . . the destruction of death includes the destruction of those who have died."[83] Paul includes a wide range of nouns to describe judgment as utter destruction.[84] Throughout 1 Corinthians, Paul never speaks to the resurrection fate of those not "in Christ."[85] According to Gordon Fee, "death is the final enemy. At its destruction true meaningfulness is given to life itself. As long as people die, God's own sovereign purposes are not yet fully realized."[86] Christ subjects himself to God the Father (v. 27) so that God may be all in all. The purpose of Christ's earthly subjection is to subsume death *through* his humiliation on the cross and his obedience unto death (Phil 2:5–11). Thiselton states, "In the Bible, by contrast, death is viewed as a disruption of life that, apart from resurrection, reduces the totality of the self as a psychosomatic unity. In this sense it is an enemy associated with fallenness, sin, and divine judgment."[87]

An obscure reference to baptism on behalf of the dead aside (v. 29),[88] it is possible that the Corinthians were struggling with an issue similar to

---

powerfully that once God is all in all, there is no room in existence for death.

80. Johnson, *1 Corinthians*, 292; MacDonald, *The Evangelical Universalist*, 89.

81. Thiselton, *1 Corinthians: A Shorter Exegetical & Pastoral Commentary*, 270.

82. "The Lord is at your right hand; he will shatter kings on the day of his wrath. He will execute judgment among the nations, filling them with corpses; he will shatter heads over the wide earth" (Ps 110:5–6); the language is remarkable similar to Isaiah 66:15, 24.

83. Marshall, "The New Testament Does Not Teach Universal Salvation," 61.

84. Ellis, *Christ and the Future in New Testament History*, 193 n. 65–69, n. 65, 66. These nouns include "*apoleia*" (annihilation; Rom 9:22; Phil 1:28; 3:19; 2 Thess 2:3) and "*olethros*" (destruction; 1 Thess 5:3; 2 Thess 1:9; 1 Tim 6:9).

85. Bassler, *Navigating Paul*, 91: "As in 1 Thessalonians, the fate of nonbelievers is not in view." This speaks as regards resurrection. Presumably, either they aren't raised at all, or they are included in the destruction of death. This is ambiguous and requires more detail than I can offer. It is also possible that Paul simply didn't consider their fate.

86. Fee, *1 Corinthians*, 757.

87. Thiselton, *1 Corinthians: A Shorter Exegetical & Pastoral Commentary*, 271.

88. Witherington, *Conflict and Community in Corinth*, 305, notes, "Verse 29 probably refers to Corinthian Christians who are being baptized for other Christian loved ones who have died without baptism." It isn't clear that Paul embraces the idea for the dead; he merely comments on it.

one that the Thessalonians dealt with. Both resurrection texts (1 Cor 15 and 1 Thess 4:13-18) deal with the issue of the dearly departed and the nature of resurrection, but 1 Corinthians is by far the more comprehensive text. However, in 1 Corinthians the boast of Jesus Christ is meant as vindication of Paul's actions (vv. 30-31). Paul assumes the historicity of the resurrection here. Why would he bother with beastly opponents in Ephesus if he didn't believe in the resurrection? (v. 33a). Why, for example, would we not "eat and drink" if "for tomorrow we die?" The futility of life is summed up perfectly: bad influences corrupt, and won't result in knowledge of God but rather shame (vv. 33-34). Life spent in pursuit of empty pleasures is futile and meaningless.[89] Relational, social and ecclesiological ethics matter in the eschaton.

15:35-57

After this, though, Paul anticipates the counter argument: "but someone will ask, "How are the dead raised? With what kind of body do they come?" (v. 35). Paul responds that what is sown must die before it can be harvested, or reaped (v. 36), suggesting a clear anthropological principle: human beings, like seeds, are not naturally immortal.[90] The fact that the seed and the body die are implied parallels. F. F. Bruce notes as well that "Paul evidently could not contemplate immortality apart from resurrection; for him a body of some kind was essential to personality."[91] Alan Padgett mentions,

> A seed is planted, and has one kind of body, but after it dies it grows into a different body, the body of the plant. God has given the plant a different substance or body than the seed had, one that is fitted for its new environment. There is also continuity between seed and the plant that grows from it. This parallel is similar to what he wants to say about our mortal bodies and the new resurrection body. In both cases, there is continuity and difference.[92]

---

89. Thiselton and Johnson suggest that Paul is loosely paraphrasing Isa 22:13 (LXX). See Thiselton, *1 Corinthians*, 276; Johnson, *1 Corinthians*, 298.

90. Marshall, "The New Testament Does Not Teach Universal Salvation," 58; Hughes, *The True Image*; Cullmann, *The Immortality of the Soul or Resurrection of the Dead?*; Scott, "Immortality," 431-42. Indeed, if immortality must be sought (Rom 2:7) from the only God who is immortal (1 Tim 1:10; 6:16), then immortality is not unified with human anthropology and we do not have such a natural trait.

91. Bruce, "Paul on Immortality."

92. Padgett, "The Body in Resurrection: Science and Scripture on the 'Spiritual Body' (1 Cor 15:35-58)," 155-63, 159.

Paul's emphasis now turns to the practical outworking of this resurrection; that is, how does this affect us at our most basic level—our bodies? Verses 35–38 assert that God will give the seed that is planted a body appropriate to it, and this analogy hints at the kind of body Christians will have in the future. Resurrection means to "rise," and what is raised is something that was dead. The use of the expression "what is sown" in verses 36–37 implies that something must die in order for life to bloom, whether it be a new body or the beginnings of an orchard. Verses 39–41 speak of different kinds of bodies.[93] So it is with the resurrection of the dead. What makes planets, animals and stars different from humans is something quite clear: God didn't breathe the breath of life into them. There is a different intimacy shared by the Creator with human beings.

In verses 42–43 the perishable body that is sown in dishonor and weakness will be raised in imperishability, in glory, and in power. Thus, the premise of the entire argument in 1 Corinthinians 15 is that the resurrection will be "of the body"[94] and not the return of an immaterial soul to a body. Paul then continues to argue strongly in favor of the resurrection of the physical body in verse 44. Joel Green says two things about this section of the text: "one, there is continuity between this life (present/worldly) and eternal life with God. Two, the present body is unfit for eternal life, given the frailties and limitation."[95] As Udo Schnelle says, Paul is stressing "God's ability to create various earthly as well as heavenly bodies, in order to illustrate again the creator-power of God, which is the guarantee of creation and the maintenance of the individual *doxa-* body."[96] Paul begins with Adam (v. 45) who became a "living being"[97] and Christ who became a "life-giving spirit." This "*soma pneumatikon*" is referred to as "spiritual" because is reflects "a

---

93. In the creation accounts, YHWH is distinguished from creation, yet is intimately involved in his world. To create humanity from his creation signifies the complexities involved in our relationship to creation. Therefore, as we return to where we came, so we can be re-created from the same place. If we even want to press this further, Wisdom 1:15 says that "righteousness is immortal." So when Paul may speak of those in Christ as being "righteous" then this verse has special significance.

94. Indeed, the Old Testament view of the body is both multifaceted and wondrous: Lev 13; Ps 44:25; Isa 66:14; Hag 2:13. The emphasis on purity, as well as the remarkable distinction of death and life within the revelation of God in the New Testament: Mark 12:27; Matt 22:32; Luke 20:38.

95. Green, *Body, Soul, and Human Life*, 173.

96. Schnelle, *The Human Condition*, 42–43.

97. Withering, *Conflict and Community in Corinth*, 309, suggests here "*Psyche* is decidedly this-worldly, of the earth. It is not an immaterial soul or spirit." He also points out on the same page that, "in Paul's view, the truly 'spiritual' person is ultimately one who has the resurrection body."

moral distinction between a life led by the Holy Spirit and one controlled by sinful desires."[98] Paul is making a distinction between the "man from dust" and the "man from heaven" (vv. 47–48),[99] which may echo Genesis 1:26–27. Adam was mortal, from dust and returned to dust.[100] Just as we are like Adam, so too will we bear the image of Jesus, the man of heaven. Padgett concurs, stating "When dealing with the stuff of the heavens, Paul notes that the stars even differ from one another in their "glory" or brightness, giving off different amounts of light. The main point is clear: God has created different types of bodies, or material objects, and not all bodies are alike in their substance and function. Each is fitted for the realm in which it exists."[101]

Paul confirms this assertion that "neither flesh nor blood," which is perishable, can inherit the kingdom of God (v. 50). Immortality is not a natural human property; it is a future reality that comes with the kingdom of God. Immortality and resurrection are, thus, linked together. Resurrection establishes a continued relationship between God and human beings. We are raised up by God, and because of our resurrection, we live forever in worshipful community with God. To be liberated from the exile of death is to be brought back into the presence of the God of the living. The Old Testament emphasis on worship of YHWH comes full circle here. However, we must be fitted for immortality in resurrection, and that fitting is the mystery that Paul expounds.[102] Hence, the statement "we will not all fall asleep, but we will all be changed."[103] Verse 51 indicates a transition from that which is

---

98. Bacchiocchi, *Immortality or Resurrection?* 265. See also Thiselton, *1 Corinthians*, 268–69.

99. Green, *Body, Soul, and Human Life*, 175, makes a distinction between "physical" and "spiritual" body, suggesting that the first body is subject to decay, and the second body is suited for the life to come.

100. Thiselton, *1 Corinthians*, 286: "The Greek uses pronouns denoting 'of such a quality' to convey the point that the old humanity is characterized by old-Adam qualities; the new humanity is characterized by new-Adam qualities."

101. Padgett, "The Body in Resurrection," 160.

102. Gorman, *Reading Paul*, 167–79.

103. Another issue to consider against the mainstream view of hell and universalism: they both must posit that all people are made "alive in Christ." In other words, immortality and eternal life are universal; the one difference is where and how you spend eternity. The biggest problem with this is not only the corporate nature of salvation, but also that Paul viewed the body as undergoing change and this is surely positive. The universalist has a stronger case in that one could argue that this change is positive and all are reconciled to God. However, since Paul has already asserted, "every enemy has been destroyed" including death, this leaves no one outside of God's redemptive scope. If this text teaches universal immortality, it logically follows that this is a universalist text.

perishable to resurrection imperishability (v. 52). For this perishable body[104] must put on imperishability, and this mortal body must put on immortality (v. 53).[105] Christ, according to Paul, *is* eternal life, that which can no longer die, that which cannot decay or be corrupted. Thiselton says

> The contrast between "perishable" and "imperishable" denotes not a static contrast between the mortal and immortal, but one between a life that stagnates into death, and a life that is rejuvenated with increasing "power." This life takes the form, as it were, of an increasing crescendo, as it moves from glory to glory, to match the dynamic nature of the living God.[106]

The summation of all things for Paul is that "death has been swallowed up in victory" (v. 55). It is abolished from God's eternal kingdom. Death is finished. The rhetorical question "where, O Death is your victory and your sting" answers itself. This question is expressed in the present tense,[107] which indicates that Paul believed that this victory was already set in motion. The sting of death begun in the Garden (Gen 3:3) is healed.[108] Thiselton sums up: "For Christ himself has absorbed in his own person the sting and the poison of death."[109] The sting of death is sin, and the Law has been, like death, abolished. Paul's doxology (v. 57) highlights the ecstasy that he feels, and further emphasizes the perfect victory of God over sin and death. In the words of Jürgen Moltmann, "Resurrection life is not a further life after death, whether in the soul or the spirit, in children or in reputation; it means the annihilation of death in the victory of the new, eternal life."[110] The emphasis on bodily resurrection highlights the love of God towards creation. That which was created is still loved by God, from creation to fall to eschaton and beyond.

---

104. Origen of Alexandria (who quotes vv. 53–56): "When [Paul] speaks of 'this corruption' and 'this mortal,' with the air of one who is as it were touching and displaying something, to what else can it apply except bodily matter? This matter of the body, then, which now is corruptible, shall put on incorruptibility when a perfect soul, instructed in the doctrines of incorruption, has begun to use it." *On First Principles*, 2.3.2.

105. Bruce, *Paul, Apostle of the Heart Set Free*, 309: "According to Paul, the dead—that is to say, the dead in Christ, who alone of the dead come into his purview here—will rise in bodies which are not liable to corruption, while the living will exchange mortality for immortality."

106. Thiselton, *The Living Paul*, 143.

107. Fee, *1 Corinthians*, 804.

108. Fudge, "The Final End of the Wicked," 32.

109. Thiselton, *1 Corinthians*, 289.

110. Moltmann, *The Crucified God*, 170.

This God, from the second he began to express relationship via physical creativity, has always had dirt beneath his fingernails.

CONCLUSION

Paul believed that the greatest threat to human life was the universal knowledge, reality and destiny of death. Death is and was and will be systemic, the ultimate equalizer of all mortals, removing the living, placing them in the ground where they return to nothing. Yet, in the end, Paul believed in something far greater than death: resurrection. Because Paul believed in the bodily resurrection of Jesus, he had great hope that Jesus could remember him. Because the body of the Son of God was resurrected, so it could be with the human person. Matter is redeemed, not rejected. Death is undone. Men and women are reborn in the image of God, not left to rot. In the end, death is consumed in the resurrected body of the risen Christ, who remembers us from on high and breathes the spirit of life back into us. As YHWH turned his face back to Hannah in 1 Samuel 1:19, so YHWH turns his face to those who have gone into death—a death he knows all too well. Despite this, we are not forgotten. We will all fall into sleep but we will be awakened again. In the end, death is annihilated in the very being of the Triune God, whose resurrection gives breath to all of his new creation.

In the end of all things, death ultimately dies.

9

Tempest Theophany, Cosmic Conflagration, and the Vanished Vanquished
Toward a Trinitarian Framework for Immortality and Annihilation

— PETER GRICE —

Peter Grice is founder of Rethinking Heaven, which explores new creation theology, and Rethinking Hell, which explores conditional immortality via a global network of evangelical scholars, teachers, and laypeople. He introduces the Rethinking Hell project and the present-day evangelical debate that spurred its inception in his contribution to the book Rethinking Hell: Readings in Evangelical Conditionalism. *He also contributed a chapter on reason and Christian faith to the book* True Reason: Confronting the Irrationality of the New Atheism, *and directs ministry efforts in the areas of discipleship and worldview. He lives in Brisbane, Australia with his wife Anchalee and son Lewis.*

Peter originally presented an early version of the following paper at the Rethinking Hell conference, 2014.

The following study situates the biblical doctrine of annihilation within a much broader theological worldview. Contours of a biblical framework for annihilation are identified[1] utilizing 1 Corinthians

---

1. It is not my intention to mount a rigorous argument for the model, due to limitations of space. Instead, it emerges in sketch form from various observations and recommendations. There is solid justification in the biblical texts cited, however, which invites

15 as a narrative lens, Psalm 8:6 and Romans 2:7 as paradigmatic keys, and *glory*, *image*, and *temple* as primary controlling motifs. This orientation sets anthropology within its larger frame of soteriology and cosmic redemption, opening up themes of transformation and participation through the powerful operations of the triune God. It is hoped that this general outline stimulates further work in extending the exegetical groundwork laid by Edward Fudge and others,[2] in pursuit of a robust and broadly evangelical theology of conditional immortality.

THE GOSPEL AND THE FRAMING QUESTION

One of the great gospel statements appears, by way of reminder, in 1 Corinthians 15. The apostle Paul points to the bedrock of the death of Jesus Christ for our sins and his victorious return to life, witnessed by many (vv. 1–11), and deftly refutes twin follies in this regard (vv. 12–34). On the one hand, if Jesus didn't rise from the grave, then neither will believers; on the other, since he did rise, they should not be so foolish as to deny their own resurrection. In this way, Paul frames his unfolding discourse around the central themes of life and death, with resurrection as the logical hinge upon which these turn. Paul limits his treatment to a "resurrection of life" (John 5:29b),[3] given that he is reiterating the good news to those being saved (vv. 1–2), and so we must look elsewhere to discover a resurrection of the unjust to shame and condemnation (John 5:28–29; Dan 12:2; Acts 24:15). A postmortem fate for the unsaved may still be apprehended through this passage via theological import, in that it gives explicit treatment of the qualities which distinguish the resurrections, as we will see. In any case, Paul's explicit gospel frame is aptly summarized by saying that Jesus Christ "abolished death and brought life and immortality to light through the gospel" (2 Tim 1:10). These are matters of "first importance," as the very foundation of the "eternal gospel" delivered to believers "once for all" (1 Cor 15:3; Rev 14:6; Jude 3).

After establishing the foundation, Paul abruptly scolds readers with "You foolish person!" simply for asking what seems to us a commendable question—"How are the dead raised? With what kind of body do they come?" (v. 35). It appears as if matters of anthropology (as constitution) are of secondary importance for the apostle within his more redemptive-historical frame. Here, soteriology embodies first-order theological truths

---

further investigation.

2. Fudge, *The Fire that Consumes* (2011). See also the collection of writings in Date, Stump, & Anderson, *Rethinking Hell*.

3. Quient, "Paul and the Particularity of Resurrection."

by thrusting such questions of mechanics into the background, disclosing the telos or significance of facts and events in light of God's works and ultimate purpose. Paul apparently expects his readers to have the necessary prior theological knowledge for naturally resolving such questions. His explanation to follow (vv. 35–58) compels us to recover that background via notions of *glory* (vv. 40–43) and *honor* (v. 43a), as the right framework or metanarrative for grasping their appropriation here. The fact that glory and honor are significant in the New Testament, beyond their familiar ascription sense in contexts of praise and doxology, may be seen through a cursory glance at several verses.

For Paul, three terms in concert—"glory, honor and immortality"—are sufficient to envision resurrected life in the eschaton (Rom 2:7). "Eternal glory" aptly describes that final reality, which will eclipse things merely "temporary" (2 Cor 4:17–18 NIV). So central is the notion of glory that the gospel itself is labeled "the gospel of the glory of Christ" and "the gospel of the glory of the blessed God" (1 Tim 1:11). Honor is likewise of ultimate significance, with its counterpart of shame characterizing the fate of the unsaved in the definitive resurrection text of the Old Testament (Dan 12:12). Indeed, "their glory is in their shame," writes Paul about those whose "destiny is destruction" (Phil 3:19 NIV; cf. Hos 4:7; Hab 2:16). Even those destined for glory have bodies presently "sown in dishonor" (1 Cor 15:43). Jesus himself was "crowned with glory and honor" in the course of "bringing many sons to glory," and he is "not ashamed to call them brothers" (Heb 2:9–11). But whoever is not so glorified as a son and brother, "of him will the Son of Man be ashamed when he comes in his glory" (Luke 9:26). In our exploration of these two terms, we will uncover connections to the third component in Romans 2:7, immortality, which also features in Paul's conclusion in 1 Corinthians 15:50–58, making Romans 2:7 something of an interpretive key. Establishing an anthropological-soteriological function for all three components will help to clarify these important secondary matters of the gospel according to Paul, and in turn yield certain implications for the fate of the unsaved.

Regarding the foolishness of denying a future resurrection even for the saved (1 Cor 15:12–19), it's not clear whether some at Corinth were instead emphasizing a disembodied postmortem existence, as was common in their culture, but for Paul the denial was tantamount to jettisoning the future altogether. In that hypothetical case, he speaks of the consolation of "hope in this life only" because those "who have fallen asleep in Christ have perished" (vv. 18, 19). If the dead are not raised, the peculiar practice of being baptized for the dead would be pointless, as would risking life and limb for the gospel, "for tomorrow we die" (vv. 29, 32). The logical structure of the argument is plain: if there is no resurrection, then death really is the end and only "this life" matters.

Whether this corrective took hold in Corinth historically is uncertain, but after so many centuries, regrettably, Christians are yet to resolve issues surrounding Justin Martyr's related provocation: "For if you have fallen in with some who are called Christians . . . who say there is no resurrection of the dead, and that their souls, when they die, are taken to heaven; do not imagine that they are Christians."[4] We have certainly resolved today that the dead are raised, with bodily resurrection being an orthodox tenet, but our disputes about constitution and any postmortem existence in the interval between death and resurrection (the so-called "intermediate state") have become intractable. Martin Luther attempted at least to ignite this discussion in his day, urging that the papal doctrine of an inherently immortal soul be consigned to the "endless monstrosities in the Roman dunghill," but this was soon quelled by a response from John Calvin.[5]

This is still controversial terrain for evangelical Christians in particular, to whom the Rethinking Hell organization is tasked with commending the biblical doctrine of conditional immortality, which likewise can be controversial. When paired with a physicalist anthropology, conditionalism does emerge very naturally, making advancing them together legitimate in principle.[6] Yet given that some leading evangelical conditionalists have been dualists, such as John Stott and P. E. Hughes,[7] the choice must be considered discretionary.[8] We may concur with Edward Fudge that these matters are secondary for conditionalism and may be adjourned,[9] yet exactly how they can be disentangled or held in tension remains to be more fully explained. In the framework here presented, conditional immortality is derived in a manner which should not need to solicit questions of constitution and in-

---

4. *Dialogue with Trypho*, 80:9; ANF 1:239.

5. Luther, "Assertio Omnium Articulorum M. Lutheri per Bullam Leonis X. Novissimam Damnatorum," article 27, 131–32. Also see Calvin, "*Psychopannychia*," 454–455.

6. A notable example of this integration is found in Froom, *The Conditionalist Faith of our Fathers*, 1965–66.

7. For example, Hughes, *The True Image*, 400, writes that "in the biblical purview human nature is always seen as integrally compounded of both the spiritual and the bodily . . . man is essentially a corporeal-spiritual entity."

8. Indeed, Rethinking Hell has made the discretionary nature of this subject its formal position and recommendation, in Rethinking Hell, *Statement on Evangelical Conditionalism*.

9. Fudge, *The Fire That Consumes* (2011), 322: "I do not take a hard stand on the intermediate state . . . one can hold that the believer is either awake or asleep between temporal death and the resurrection, while insisting on the final extinction of the perpetually unrepentant as the Biblical view."

termediate persistence. Specifically, in that dualism should be constrained by biblical language and cosmology, to insist that a return to "life" occurs with bodily resurrection. The dead are not the living, so death must negate the idea of continuing to live. If there is a form of continued existence, it must be considered non-normative subsistence, compatible with the designation "sleeping."[10]

Conditionalists of all stripes should reject the platonic and traditionalist definition of death as "separation," if what is meant by that includes mere "physical death" as the separation of soul from body (rather than person from life), where the locus of personhood and life is exclusively with the disembodied soul. It should be noted in passing that this scenario is commonly propped up by a dichotomy of so-called "physical" and "spiritual" deaths, which we are free to reject in favor of a single concept. Additionally, we must reject all claims which imply that death isn't an imposter and violent enemy which must be overcome by resurrection, leading to everlasting life (1 Cor 15:26; 50-57). Framing mortality and immortality in light of eternity, as a question of ultimate persistence, and not merely in terms of some form of continuance past death, means that we must rely on special revelation about God's intentions in the end (e.g., Matt 10:28). The impetus for doing so, explored below, comes from seeing that life should be understood in its cosmological and creational context.

Since these kinds of constraints emerge from biblical cosmology, it is not essential to adopt physicalism in order to challenge platonic assumptions about life and the universe. The current framework is therefore complementary, permitting a healthy agnosticism in this area, or independent commitment to either dualism or physicalism with their entailments for an intermediate state. It might even be preferred, since it is thereby streamlined for adoption within evangelicalism.

HOLISTIC ESCHATOLOGY: CREATION RENEWED

Richard Bauckham has identified a number of emerging focal points in eschatology, following the towering influence of Jürgen Moltmann. One area of burgeoning interest is that of *theosis* or *christosis*, which speaks to participation in the life of God (John 1:4, 5:26, 6:53; Eph 4:18; Col 3:3-4; 2 Pet 1:3-4), and is addressed further below. Bauckham sees as especially significant questions of "continuity and discontinuity in the concept of new

---

10. This is supplied by biblical language (e.g., Dan 12:2; Luke 8:52; Acts 13:36; 1 Cor 15:18, 20). It functions as a logical constraint, and need not entail what is pejoratively called "soul sleep."

creation," which we will also explore below in relation to annihilation, and a "renewed theological appreciation for the bodiliness of Jesus' resurrection" in connection to eschatology. In all likelihood, he suggests, the study of eschatology will continue in the direction of "a holistic vision of redemption and transfiguration for the whole of God's creation" which resists "the dualism of matter and spirit" that has "all too often abstracted the soul from the body, the individual from the human community, and human history from the rest of creation." The "rejection of these Platonic and Cartesian dualisms is widely shared by other contemporary theologians," in contrast to "a model in which the soul's destiny is to realize its immortality through escape from material creation."[11] Moltmann himself was insistent in this regard: "Christian eschatology must be broadened out into cosmic eschatology, for otherwise it becomes a Gnostic doctrine of redemption, and is bound to teach, no longer the redemption of the world but a redemption from the world, no longer the redemption of the body but a deliverance of the soul from the body."[12]

In an important recent book, *A New Heaven and a New Earth*,[13] J. Richard Middleton follows theologians such as Albert Wolters and N. T. Wright in making accessible this biblical metanarrative of the flourishing of earthly life from creation to eschaton, and defending a vision where the heavens and earth are renewed instead of annihilated. Stephens likewise denies cosmic annihilation after a comprehensive study of Revelation in conjunction with other key texts, concluding from Romans 8:19–22 alone that "Paul does not conceive of the destruction of the present world, and its replacement with another, so much as the eschatological redemption and transformation of the present creation," since the passage "clearly and unambiguously testifies to material continuity between present and future." The passage

> sees the glorious future of creation as coincidental with, or better still, *contingent upon* the future glorification of believing humanity. In this respect, Paul appears to be embracing the Jewish tradition of humanity as creation's leader and steward (Gen 1:26, 28; Ps 8:6), its principal actor if you will, through whom creation will be lead either to ruin or restoration.[14]

In this way, holistic eschatology supplies an important constraint of future space as being all-encompassing, with some continuity of the present

11. Bauckham, "Emerging Issues in Eschatology in the Twenty-First Century," 672–73.
12. Moltmann, *The Coming of God*, 259.
13. Middleton, *A New Heaven and a New Earth*.
14. Stephens, *Annihilation or Renewal?* 123.

creation into the future order. Bifurcated space, with eternally separated dualisms (whether heaven and earth, or heaven and hell), is rejected. Consequently, both the saved and the unsaved are resurrected bodily into an earthly space which is physical at the very least.[15]

HEBRAIC COSMOLOGY: GLORY AND TEMPLE

First Corinthians 15:24–28 and 35–49 (including v. 45 with Paul's gloss of Genesis 2:7), likewise point us back to Hebrew cosmology in conjunction with human destiny, in what may be respectively termed its *temple* and *glory* aspects. Ancient Hebrew cosmology, as indeed biblical cosmology, is an integrated whole comprised of qualitative structural divisions, such that glory and temple often intersect. Paul emphasizes the qualitative aspect in verses 35–49, in terms of the variegated display of glory within the plenitude of created being, but also includes the principal structural division of heaven and earth in verse 40. In so doing, he distinguishes heavenly from earthly glory, with special attention to the various luminous glories of the heavenly bodies, and the differing bodies of flesh among mankind and the animals. The concept of glory is rich and malleable, but at its core indicates an essential weightiness of being (whether of living beings or objects), which may manifest outwardly in expressions of beauty and dignity of form (such as gemstones, temples, or seraphim), nobility of character, breadth of dominion, and richness of status or possession. A notable example of the latter kind of glory is the status and virtual co-regency obtained by Joseph as manager of Pharaoh's house and "ruler over all the land of Egypt" (Gen 45:13, 8), which amplifies the very first occasion of the term in Genesis 31:1 (כָּבוֹד; δόξα LXX), where the wealth gained by Jacob for his own household before leaving Laban had come largely through managerial competence and divine blessing in animal husbandry (Gen 30:30–43; 31:8–12). But the highest level of glory is that which radiates as a literal effulgence, just as the shepherds saw "the glory of the Lord" surrounding the angels proclaiming Christ's birth; as Peter witnessed Christ's majestic radiance at Christ's transfiguration; and as believers also "shall see him as he is" at the "appearing of the glory" of the Savior when he comes "to be marveled at," being himself the very "radiance of the glory of God."[16] Paul thus draws on the full spectrum of expression of this concept, in conveying the relative dignity

---

15. Differences are presented in 1 Corinthians 15:35–55, and also captured in N. T. Wright's term "transphysicality," applicable to redeemed bodies and to consummated creation. See Wright, *Resurrection of the Son of God*, 606.

16. Luke 2:9; 2 Pet 1:16–17; 1 John 3:2; Titus 2:13; 2 Thess 1:10; Heb 1:3.

and beauty of different created forms. In terms of the cosmic whole, just as "the heavens declare the glory of God," so also "the whole earth is full of his glory" (Ps 19:1; Isa 6:3).

But some glory fades, fleetingly, while other glory is perpetual. Jesus compared Solomon's kingly glory to that of the lilies, and the clothing of mere grass "which is alive in the field today, and tomorrow is thrown into the oven," in the context of concerns for one's own quality, preservation and "span of life" (Luke 12:13–34). The axis here is that of duration in time: God values and sustains created life, and wills to give those who "seek his kingdom" that everlasting treasure which "never fails" nor is destroyed (vv. 31–33). First Timothy 6:11–19 contains echoes of this passage (vv. 17–19), extolling a God who "gives life to all things . . . who alone has immortality, who dwells in unapproachable light." In this context, those in the present age must "take hold of the eternal life" and "take hold of that which is truly life" by living rightly as a "good foundation for the future" (vv. 11–12, 17–19). James 1:9–12 also contains echoes, where those who receive the "crown of life" will not wither away. First Peter 1:22–25 does too, being grounded in Isaiah 40:8 and context, which also declares that "the glory of the Lord shall be revealed, and all flesh shall see it together" (Isa 40:5; cf. 1 Pet 1:7c). Finally, Psalm 103:14–17 indicates that while "we are dust" with days like the grass, those who fear the Lord receive his love "from everlasting to everlasting."

Irenaeus, drawing upon language from Psalm 21:4–5 which speaks of kingly exaltation in terms of "length of days forever and ever" and the king's great glory with "splendor and majesty" bestowed upon him, writes of the "grandeur" of heavenly bodies with their source and duration arising from the will of God. With a reference to Genesis 2:7, he states that even the human soul does not possess life in itself, but partakes in the life bestowed by God.[17] Elsewhere, Irenaeus emphasizes messianic aspects of Psalm 21, saying that since Jesus rose and "appeared no more" (that is, no more on earth, for he ascended to heaven), this shows that he "was to remain immortal. . . . For He received both *life*, that He should rise, and *length of days for ever and ever*, that He should be incorruptible."[18] The impartation of exalted, bodily life to a dead man was unthinkable to some among Paul's audience in Athens, though he made every effort to situate his gospel within its essential context of Hebraic cosmology and relational anthropology (Acts 24–29). That the Creator of life and "Lord of heaven and earth does not dwell in temples made by man" nor is attended by "human hands," also situates this

---

17. *Against Heresies*, 2.34.2; *ANF* 1:411.
18. Irenaeus, *The Demonstration of the Apostolic Preaching* (chap. 72), 133.

address within Scripture's temple motifs. The theme of idolatrous worship in Athens indicating an exchange of God's glory for images made by human hands and imagination also connects this passage with Romans 1:22-25, where "the glory of the immortal God" is exchanged for "images resembling mortal man" and other creatures (v. 21).

Doubtless, the glory of God means more than immortality or everlastingness, and the glory of mortal creatures is not merely about their finite duration. Nonetheless, varying degrees of persistence is an aspect of glory that is frequently overlooked. In Job 29:20 it is youthful vigor and vitality. In Psalm 89, the suffering servant experiences both debasement of glory (vv. 39, 44; his crown and throne are cast to the dust and his splendor ceases) and also exaltation of glory, resulting in his throne and "offspring" being established forever, "as the days of the heavens . . . as long as the sun before me. Like the moon it shall be established forever" (vv. 29, 36-37). He is made "the firstborn, the highest of the kings of the earth" while all are blessed "who walk, O Lord, in the light of your face. . . . For you are the glory of their strength" (vv. 27, 15, 17; cf. Col 1:15b). After associating the ideas of glory and duration in 1 Corinthians, Paul writes again in poetic fashion of an "eternal weight of glory beyond all comparison" and of the "permanent glory" of "beholding the glory of the Lord" under the new covenant, which eclipses that glory which faded from the face of Moses (2 Cor 4:17; 3:7-18).

This association between *glory* and *life*, especially everlasting life over against that which ends, is worked through 1 Corinthians 15 in terms of life, death, resurrection, perishability/imperishability and mortality/immortality, as well as the expression of victory over death. Paul makes the same connections in Romans 8:

> If the Spirit of him who raised Jesus from the dead dwells in you, he who raised Christ Jesus from the dead will also give life to your mortal bodies . . . that we may also be glorified with him . . . with the glory that is to be revealed to us. For the creation waits with eager longing for the revealing of the sons of God . . . the creation itself will be set free from its bondage to corruption and obtain the freedom of the glory of the children of God [who are waiting] eagerly for adoption as sons, the redemption of our bodies [and are being] conformed to the image of his Son," [finally to be found] glorified (Rom 8:11, 17-30)

Hence, "we all, with unveiled face, beholding the glory of the Lord, are being transformed into the same image from one degree of glory to another" (2 Cor 3:18). This important association of *image* with *glory* will be developed below.

The second dimension of Hebrew cosmology explored here is the cosmic temple motif, being a spatial-ethical category, and seen to be invoked by Paul in 1 Corinthians 15:24–28 on at least three accounts. First, by referencing the full cosmic scope of "all in all" and "all things"; second, by referencing fallen cosmic powers ("every rule and every authority and power . . . all enemies"); third, in respect of the heavenly kingdom reign of Christ progressively subduing earthly enemies "under his feet." Passages like Daniel 2:31–45 and Daniel 7 are in play as background knowledge, where in the first case, Nebuchadnezzar was called "the king of kings, to whom the God of heaven has given the kingdom, the power, and the might, and the glory, and into whose hand he has given, wherever they dwell, the children of man, the beasts of the field, and the birds of the heavens, making you rule over them all," yet in the future "the God of heaven will set up a kingdom that shall never be destroyed . . . and it shall stand forever" (Dan 2:37, 38, 44); such that in Daniel 7 this "dominion and glory and a kingdom" is given to the Son of Man, as a conquering and everlasting kingdom (Dan 7:14; cf. vv. 18, 26–27). But it is the explicit reference to Psalm 8:6, by which Paul most directly invokes the vertical structure in the cosmic temple, in terms of mankind's dominion within creation by putting "all things under his feet." Paul is referring to the feet of the messianic Son of Man (Ps 8:4), pivoting on the dual meaning of "son of man" between humanity and its exalted representative, Israel's Messiah.

The temporary earthly subordination of the divine son, who is "the brightness of his glory, and the express image of his person" yet was "born in the likeness of men" (Heb 1:3a KJV; Phil 2:6–11), and his subsequent exaltation to heavenly glory and conquering dominion, is captured in Psalm 110 using the metaphor of hands and feet. Although heaven is God's throne and the earth is his footstool, and all things are made by his hands (Isa 66:1–2; cf. Ps 8:3), astonishingly, to the Son of Man it was said, "Sit at my right hand, until I make your enemies your footstool" and "The Lord sends forth from Zion your mighty scepter. Rule in the midst of your enemies! . . . The Lord is at your right hand" (Ps 110:1–2, 5). As Hebrews 2 develops the theme, he is seen as "the firstborn into the world" who has "inherited" a more excellent status than the angels and "become" superior to them—in fact, they worship him! (vv. 4, 6)—by being "crowned with glory and honor" (v. 9). While Psalm 8:3–8 is actually a contemplation of the exalted status of mankind's role within the cosmic temple as the *imago Dei*, who would image forth divine qualities in stewardship over earthly creation (see Genesis 1:20–31, especially the mandate in verses 26–28 to exercise dominion by subduing the earth and flourishing in it), nonetheless, the author of Hebrews fully exploits the aforementioned ambiguity of "son of man," as well as a providential rendering of the Septuagint as "for a little while lower than the angels" (Heb 2:7–9; cf. Ps 8:5–6).

If the same temporary exaltation might also apply to mankind (that is, exalted within the earthly sphere), then it would seem to imply a subsequent fall from grace, a forfeit or debasement of this status of "glory and honor."[19] Indeed, the song of creation in Psalm 104 has many echoes of Psalm 8 and allusions to the original creation, yet no sign of mankind being exalted among other creatures. Instead, humans are presented as one among many mortal creatures for whom, "when you take away their breath, they die and return to their dust" (v. 29). Middleton has contrasted these two psalms, noting that they both

> envision the world as God's temple or sanctuary, consisting in the bipartite heaven and earth. . . . YHWH enthroned in heaven (corresponding to the holy of holies of the earthly tabernacle or the Jerusalem temple), from which God rules the earth and is responsive to the needs of creatures. . . . All the earth is holy ground or sacred space, intimately connected with heaven, the seat of God's throne.[20]

Within that space, a kind of liturgical worship emerges—what Calvin called "the theatre of the divine glory"[21]—as each created thing glorifies God simply by fulfilling its assigned function: "Just as lions, mountains, and stars praise God simply by being lions, mountains, and stars, so humans exalt their creator simply by being human, engaging in ordinary productive activities, rooted in the communal vocation of working of the ground, and thereby developing cultural patterns of life that glorify God."[22] This interconnectedness of terrestrial life, and the privileged role of human beings within it, is both rich and complex in its developed potentials:

> Whereas Psalm 104 and Genesis 2 focus on agriculture, Psalm 108 foregrounds animal husbandry as the basic human task in God's world. Humans are crowned with royal dignity and granted authority or dominion over various realms of animal

---

19. Consider the sudden shame of Genesis 3:7 in relation to the curses of 3:14–19, in light of the stewardship mandate as an honorable, functional expression of the *imago Dei* which had now been compromised.

20. Middleton, "The Role of Human Beings in the Cosmic Temple," 47, 48, 51.

21. Calvin, *Commentaries on the Epistle of Paul the Apostle to the Hebrews*, 266: "Correctly then is this world called the mirror of divinity . . . the faithful, to whom he has given eyes, see sparks of his glory, as it were, glittering in every created thing. The world was no doubt made, that it might be the theatre of the divine glory."

22. Middleton, "The Role of Human Beings in the Cosmic Temple," 51.

> life—land, air, and water. . . . The domestication of animals is here regarded as a task of great dignity and privilege. . . . By its emphasis on agriculture and animal husbandry, which are the basis for human societal organization, Genesis 1 ultimately envisions the development of all aspects of culture, technology, and civilization. Humans are to accomplish this development as God's representatives . . . exercising power to transform the earthly environment into a complex sociocultural world that glorifies the creator (the so-called cultural mandate) is thus a holy task, a sacred calling, in which the human race as God's image on earth manifests something of the creator's own lordship over the cosmos. . . . By our faithful representation of God, who is enthroned in the heavens, we extend the presence of the divine king of creation even to the earth, to prepare the earth for God's full—eschatological—presence, the day when God will fill all things. Then (when God fully indwells the earthly realm) the cosmic temple will have been brought to its intended destiny.[23]

The song of creation ends on a sour note, however: "Let sinners be consumed from the earth, and let the wicked be no more!" (Ps 104:35). Humans fail in their creational responsibilities. Instead of being wise and faithful stewards, we become foolish and self-serving. Among the many dimensions to the fallout, the failure to domesticate animals results in an escalating dominion of wild and ravenous beasts: an important but neglected theme running through Isaiah, which depicts Israel and the other nations falling

> under the particular curse of being overrun by wild beasts. This curse establishes that they have failed in their ability to carry out the basic task given to humanity after creation (Gen 1:28). The answer to this problem can be nothing less than a new humanity and a renewal of creation. . . . It is through Israel that the nations will be blessed with a new age that will include the ability to carry out the creation mandate.[24]

In light of the view that Israel represents a new humanity, the realization that the tabernacle not only symbolizes a cosmic temple in miniature, but also functions as an inaugurated new creation, is profound:

> At this small, lonely place in the midst of the chaos of the wilderness, a new creation comes into being. In the midst of disorder there is order. The tabernacle is the world order as God intended writ small in Israel. The priests of the sanctuary going

---

23. Middleton, *A New Heaven and a New Earth*, 42–43, 49.
24. Wenkel, "Wild Beasts in the Prophecy of Isaiah," 263.

about their appointed courses is like everything in creation performing its liturgical service—the sun, the trees, human beings. The people of Israel carefully encamped around the tabernacle in their midst constitutes the beginnings of God's bringing creation back to what it was originally intended to be. The tabernacle is a realization of God's created order in history; both reflect the glory of God in their midst. Moreover, this microcosm of creation is the beginning of a macrocosmic effort on God's part. In and through this people, God is on the move to a new creation for all. God's presence in the tabernacle is a statement about God's intended presence in the entire world. The glory manifest there is to stream out into the larger world. The shining of Moses' face in the wake of the experience of the divine glory . . . is to become characteristic of Israel as a whole, a radiating out into the larger world of those glorious effects of God's dwelling among Israel . . . mediating this glory to the entire cosmos.[25]

The calling of all creation, then, is a sacred one: to glorify God with every expression of its being. The fact that human beings have not faithfully exhibited God's glory and honor within the cosmic temple, and that this also introduces corruption into the earthly realm (Gen 3:14–19; Rom 8:18–23), means that such corruption as finally remains must be expunged.

JUDGMENT THEOPHANY: GLORY AND TEMPEST

> Suddenly, in an instant, the Lord Almighty will come with thunder and earthquake and great noise, with windstorm and tempest and flames of a devouring fire.
> —Isaiah 29:5–6

Theophanies (appearances of God) bear great significance for eschatology. Among the various types of theophany, the storm or tempest motif is dominant and dramatic. The tempest theophany is typified in passages such as Exodus 19:16–19, Judges 5:4–5, Psalms 18:7–15, Ezekiel 1:4–28, and Habakkuk 3:3–15. Characterized by a cluster of natural, elemental phenomena associated with extreme weather, YHWH's presence would be heralded by thick cloud, whirlwind, fire, lightning, thunder, rain, hail, and even ground-based effects such as scorching, melting, and quaking. God was not to be mistaken for an ancient Near East storm god, however, in terms of being directly identified with the elements. Rather, as the almighty Creator whose

---

25. Fretheim, *Exodus, Interpretation*, 271–72.

nature is as invisible, incorporeal, and pervasive as the wind, he is also capable of incorporating, coalescing as storms do, dramatically intensifying and manifesting his awesome presence. When the Lord passed by Elijah, he was not "in" the powerful wind, earthquake, or fire, in the sense of being identified with them (1 Kgs 19:11–12). When the Lord's glory appeared to the congregation of Israel in the wilderness, it appeared *within* a cloud (Exod 16:10), just as the Lord later called to Moses from "the midst" of the dark cloud atop Sinai (Exod 24:16), and he was able to enter (v. 18). This was "the glory of the Lord" which appeared "like a devouring fire" (Exod 24:17). In Psalm 18:7–15, the Lord was roused from his heavenly temple (v. 6), whereupon the earth quaked, smoke issued from his nostrils and "devouring fire" came from his mouth. He flashed forth lightning, sent hailstones and coals of fire, and covered himself with thick clouds. In the juxtaposition of light and dark storm elements, the cloud functions as an outer covering or veil, while God's brilliant presence is more closely identified with manifestations of fire and lightning from within: "His brightness was like the light; rays flashed from his hand; and there he veiled his power" (Hab 3:4). Even today, the familiar image of crepuscular rays penetrating a darkened cloud evokes God's glory, shining down from the heavens.

Storms can bring either blessing or curse: "The tempest comes out from its chamber, the cold from the driving winds. . . . He brings the clouds to punish people, or to water his earth and show his love." (Job 37:9, 13, NIV). In a similar way, a tempest theophany can both save and destroy, as if God's very holiness were decisively erupting in a moment of judgment or ethical crisis. As God's chosen people, Israel were saved by the manifestation of a pillar of cloud and of fire, "by war, by mighty hand and an outstretched arm" (Deut 4:34). To be rescued in this way by YHWH as mighty warrior, simultaneously signifies the destruction of God's enemies. When God speaks to Job in thunderous voice "out of the storm" adorned with "glory and splendor," he declares that his own arm and hand can save—by unleashing furious wrath to "crush the wicked where they stand" (Job 40:6–14, NIV). He can "cause his majestic voice to be heard and the descending blow of his arm to be seen, in furious anger and a flame of devouring fire, with a cloudburst and storm and hailstones" (Isa 30:30). Regarding the twin functions of such manifestations, Middleton observes: "Fire as lightning explains why the blazing glory of God is often combined with the darkness of clouds in biblical theophanies; both lightning/fire and clouds/darkness are phenomena associated with thunderstorms, by which God's dangerous holiness is visibly and tangibly expressed."[26]

---

26. Middleton, *A New Heaven and a New Earth*, 113.

The fact that God's *holy* presence is the source of such manifestations resulting in life-or-death ordeals, is elucidated by the paradox of the burning bush theophany. The bush was aflame with God's manifest presence, yet not being consumed because that place was designated "holy ground." Neither could a mere man come too close, for the same reason (Exod 3:2–6). Yet the righteous will be protected from being consumed even in other contexts, as one in theophanic appearance "like a son of the gods" protected the faithful in the fiery furnace (Dan 3:25), who effectively "quenched the power of fire" (Heb 11:34a). The wrong approach to God's holy presence, however, spells disaster. As Nadab and Abihu approached without authorization, "fire came out from before the Lord and consumed them" (Lev 10:1–2). When "the glory of the Lord" appeared before the assembly to "make known who is his, and who is holy, and who will be allowed to approach him; the one whom he will choose he will allow to approach him," it did not go well for the Sons of Korah, and "fire came out from the Lord and consumed the two hundred fifty men offering the incense" (Num 16:19, 5, 35, NRSV). In the destruction of Sodom and Gomorrah, the Lord sent down fire and sulphur from himself: "from the Lord out of heaven" (Gen 19:24). "The fire of God fell from heaven" in Job 1:16 and falls on the armies of Gog and Magog in Revelation 20:9. It comes down to consume men (2 Kgs 1:10; cf. Luke 9:54) and sacrifices (1 Kgs 18:38; 1 Chr 21:26). At the dedication of Solomon's temple, fire from heaven consumed the offerings, and commensurate with this the glory of the lord descended to fill the temple (2 Chr 7:1–3).

In terms of the overall theophanic glory motif, the redemptive trajectory is toward glory filling the whole earth in the eschaton: "the Lord will be your everlasting light, and your God will be your glory" (Isa 60:19; cf. Rev 22:5). God's glory ultimately cannot be contained, because the whole cosmos is his temple: "Thus says the Lord: 'Heaven is my throne, and the earth is my footstool; what is the house that you would build for me, and what is the place of my rest?' . . . the time is coming to gather all nations and tongues. And they shall come and shall see my glory" (Isa 66:1, 18). This spells certain doom for God's enemies, but prior to that encounter, there is a way to avoid being consumed.

CONSUMMATED ANTHROPOLOGY: DUST AND GLORY

> Just as we have borne the image of the man of dust,
> we shall also bear the image of the man of heaven.
> —1 Corinthians 15:49

In 1 Corinthians 15:21–23 and 42–50, Paul structures his argument around two contrasting humanities, or corporate groups, with a present-past human order under the headship of Adam, and a present-future order participating in Christ as the "last Adam" and "second man." Regarding the first, "by a man came death," which involves a "natural body" characterized by perishability and dishonor. As already noted, verse 45 contains a gloss of Genesis 2:7, the moment when God breathed life into Adam. He is "from the earth, a man of dust," as also are "those who are of the dust," speaking of all humanity, who have "borne the image of the man of dust" (vv. 45, 47–49). Those now "who belong to Christ" are exempted, since to them comes the resurrection of the dead in glorious, imperishable, powerful spiritual bodies. Unlike the man of dust, this man is from heaven, as also are "those who are of heaven" who "shall also bear the image of the man of heaven" (vv. 21–23; 42–44; 47–49). This pivoting on the concept of bearing one or the other image, thrusts us back to the concept of Adam's failure in terms of faithfully bearing God's image.

Curiously, Genesis 5:1–3 juxtaposes the creation of mankind in God's likeness, with the statement that Adam, in reference to Seth, "fathered a son in his own likeness, after his image." Luke's genealogy of Christ seems to pick up on this in making Seth "the son of Adam, the son of God" (Luke 3:38). Ortlund notes a traditional lack of attention to this connection, ruling out the interpretation that it merely signifies the transmission of the *imago Dei*. Instead, he concludes, it seems to invite a comparison between creation and procreation, between being created in God's image and being God's children, which would still be consistent with common interpretations of the image.[27] Although the *imago Dei* concept suggests that humanity is like God, Paul seems to have demoted Adam from any exalted position that this might imply—like Psalm 89:39's imagery of the crown defiled by the dust. It follows from this that to bear the image of the last Adam is instead to be like Christ, "the image of the invisible God, the firstborn of all creation" (Col 1:15).

Latham suggests that 1 Corinthians 15:45b contains an allusion to Ezekiel 37 (which describes a "life-giving spirit" in the context of a vision in which the dead are resurrected), while verse 49 alludes to Gen 1:27–28 and Gen 5:3, which indicates that "just as Adam passed on his image to his son and all those who followed after him, so Christ is passing on his image to all those who come after him. . . . The image of Christ is the perfect image of God that perfectly displays the glory of God, fulfilling the original intention of the image. . . . Thus, by his resurrection and his status as the life-giving

---

27. Ortlund, "Image of Adam, Son of God."

spirit, Christ is able to pass on his image to believers who are being transformed 'in the image of its Creator' (Col 3:10)." With this notion of newly minted Christians echoing the moment of Adam's creation, incorporated into Ezekiel's vision of the resurrected bones, Paul's use of the OT in verses 44–49 "links together soteriological, anthropological and eschatological concerns. Fallen man is being remade in the image of Christ, who is the image of God . . . upholding the pattern of the new humanity . . . pointing to Christ in his resurrection as the goal of what God is doing in redemptive history."[28]

Second Corinthians 4:4–6 gives us another grand relation between original creation and Christ via the concept of image, relating "the light of the gospel of the glory of Christ, who is the image of God" back to that glorious light shining out of primal darkness, with this same Creator shining "in our hearts to give the light of the knowledge of the glory of God in the face of Jesus Christ." P. E. Hughes agrees with this reckoning:

> [T]he doctrine of man (anthropology) can be truly apprehended only in the light of the doctrine of Christ (christology). Not only the destiny but also the origin of man involves a profound relationship with the Second Person of the Holy Trinity. . . . Of fundamental importance in the explanation of our subject is the understanding that *the Image of God* as itself designating, ontologically, the eternal Son, and the understanding of man as by creation constituted in or after that image, by sin fallen away from that image, and by redemption reconstituted in that image. Thus perceived, the divine purpose of creation is grounded in the Son, and what was begun in the Son is also completed in the Son. It follows that conformity to the image of God is essentially Christoformity.[29]

A fine litmus test of such a perspective should be whether or not it is found in Romans. Blackwell has investigated the meaning of glory (δόξα) in Romans, in order to interpret the important text, Romans 3:23 ("for all have sinned and fall short of the glory of God"), in conjunction with other important texts like Romans 1:23 (cf. Jer 2:11; Rom 1:18–25; Acts 17:22–34) and Romans 2:7. He identifies the majority usage in Romans as ontological, and assigns "compelling weight" to the evidence that Romans 3:23 is an "ontological statement related to incorruption and life," a conclusion regarded as "almost certain."[30] God's glory means honor and incorruption,

---

28. Latham, "The Use of the Old Testament in 1 Corinthians 15:44–49," 19, 21.
29. Hughes, *The True Image*, viii, ix.
30. Blackwell, "Immortal Glory and the Problem of Death in Romans 3.23," 300.

such that humanity's problem is "mortality and shame as the result of sin."[31] The gospel truth being presented in this verse is that "lack of glory signifies the condition of corruption and mortality.... Paul associates universal sin with universal mortality."[32] It may be the case that a traditional theme of Adam's loss of glory stands in the background, but the explicit claim is that humans lack God's own glory, so that "the future experience of glory is not a return to Adam's glory but a participation in God's glory through Christ" as developed in Romans 8:17–30.[33] In the various ontological contexts of δόξα in Romans, it "represents God's state of being and stands as the culmination of human soteriology, as believers are conformed to the image of Christ in their resurrection by agency of the Spirit" and functions thematically "as the culmination of the life of the new age described throughout the letter (e.g., 1.17; 5.21; 6.23; 8.10–11). While 'life' may only denote physical resurrection or moral enablement, glory incorporates new life as well as the additional nuance of elevated status."[34]

The confluence of glorified qualities and ontological life (against the backdrop of mortality) has important implications for conditional immortality, as it distinguishes two fundamentally different kinds of resurrection: that of "glory and honor and immortality" (Rom 2:7), and the converse, a resurrection of mortality and shame. Full justification is God's remedy for this condition (Rom 3:24), which

> leads to glorification, which is a life of incorruption.... Thus, the righteousness-glory association provides further evidence that Paul understands justification as the means to rectifying human mortality arising from sin, as well as rectifying the broken relationship arising from guilt and characterized by shame. This speaks against separating participationist and forensic categories but unites them in the act of setting believers right, which brings new life. Like righteousness, glory is a relational and ontological term ... through the agency of Christ and the Spirit ... believers, while maintaining the creator-creature distinction, participate in the divine attributes of incorruption and holiness. Believers do not become gods themselves, but rather they become like God with a participation in him, such that they reflect divine attributes.[35]

---

31. Ibid., 285.
32. Ibid., 300.
33. Ibid., 291.
34. Ibid., 296–97.
35. Ibid., 303–4. Of further relevance to our study is Blackwell's note on page 302 that while his focus is on anthropology, one might equally focus on glory as the

These explorations open up the prospect of *theosis*, with new creation humanity in some sense becoming "partakers of the divine nature" (2 Pet 1:4) and the fellowship of the holy Trinity. Evangelicals are rightly cautious in this area, not wanting to erode the Creator-creature distinction (Rom 1:23; Acts 17:24, 25). With all the important caveats, exploring the topic is here recommended for its potential insights for conditionalist theology. Reformed theologian T. F. Torrance commended theosis in his writings, which is ably presented today by Ben C. Blackwell, Donald Fairbairn and Michael Gorman, among others.[36] Blackwell and Miller write that theosis—which they carefully qualify as an "attributive" rather than "essential" participation in the divine nature—is a "theologically integrative perspective, bringing together Christology and Pneumatology, protology and eschatology, soteriology and ecclesiology."[37] Opening up Christological and Trinitarian vistas for the study of anthropology, they suggest, makes it "not merely about determining the constitution of humans—sorting out the existence and relationship of constitutive parts like soul and body—but should just as much be focused on the divine telos or intention for humans and how humans are constituted through relationship with God."[38] That constitution issues in a holistic "restoration of the image of God culminating in resurrection" and complete "incorruption through participation in God's own incorrupt life," seen as "participation in divine glory," exemplified at Christ's transfiguration.[39]

In the context of the cosmos as God's temple-kingdom, with humans created to manage the affairs of the terrestrial sphere as exalted stewards or vice-regents, yet also in the new humanity as priests (1 Pet 2:9; cf. Exod 19:6), Hebrews 3:1–6 is significant for tracking with the biblical metanarrative. Jesus, appointed by God as both "apostle and high priest," was "faithful in all God's house" like Moses before him (vv. 1–2). But whereas Moses was faithful "as a servant," Jesus "is faithful over God's house as a son. And we are his house . . ." (vv. 5–6). Jesus is worthy of more glory than Moses since the son in a household is greater than a servant, and to the degree in which the builder of a house has "much more glory" and "more honor than the house itself" (v. 3).[40]

---

mediation of God's presence in light of Old Testament motifs, such that "we cannot simply disaggregate Adam and Temple themes in the letter, and particularly in 1:23."

36. Blackwell, *Christosis*. Fairbairn, *Life in the Trinity*. Gorman, *Inhabiting the Cruciform God*.

37. Blackwell and Miller, "Theosis and Theological Anthropology," 303.

38. Ibid., 304.

39. Ibid.

40. While the passage stops short of referencing the cosmos itself as God's house, or

The role of Christ as faithful son in God's household makes sense here of Paul's language of adoption of human beings by God (Rom 8:15, 23; Gal 4:5; Eph 1:5). Without minimizing the intimate familial relationships involved in this adoption, which evokes other designations such as "children" and "brothers," there remains a lived-out expression of that glory and honor which attends the functioning of a household. This is why the Creator, "in bringing many sons to glory" (Heb 2:10) crowned the obedient Son of Man with the "glory and honor" and dominion given to mankind in the beginning (Heb 2:6–9; cf. Ps 8:4–8; Gen 1:26–28). Although believers were once "separated from Christ," they have now been reconciled to God "in one body through the cross" (Eph 2:16), so that they are fully-fledged "members of the household of God" (v. 19). This is not based in the covenant marked by a circumcision "made in the flesh by hands" (v. 11), but is "a holy temple in the Lord" not made with hands, "a dwelling place for God by the Spirit" (vv. 21, 22). As a living, breathing house, all the adopted children of God "are his workmanship, created in Christ Jesus for good works, which God prepared beforehand, that we should walk in them" (v. 10).

These newly created are called "*neos anthropos*" in Colossians 3:10, with the sense of being brand new in time, while in Ephesians the term is "*kainos anthropos*," which indicates newness of kind to supersede the old. Out of the two terms for "new," *kainos* is dominant and most closely associated with eschatology, as in the many references to things being made new in the book of Revelation. "If anyone is in Christ, he is a new (*kainos*) creation. The old has passed away; behold, the new has come" (2 Cor 5:17). Even in Colossians 3:10, the reference is quickly followed by a compound of this term such that what is brand new is actively "being renewed (*anakainoo*) in knowledge after the image of its creator." This development isn't passive for the new human, but occurs through the strivings of faith in a fallen world, being "rich in good works" in the present age "as a good foundation for the future" (1 Tim 6:17–19), and in the training of godliness, which "holds promise for the present life and also for the life to come" (1 Tim 4:7, 8).

This more nuanced view on the role of good works as a function of the new humanity, helps unlock meaning from Romans 2:6–10. On the one hand, the "self-seeking" disobey God and face his wrath as a result of their evil works (v. 8, 9), while on the other, those who "seek glory and honor and immortality" will receive "eternal life" and "glory and honor and peace" (vv. 7, 10). This latter class are described as "everyone who does good," and the ones who patiently persist in "well-doing" (vv. 7, 10). Dryden has

---

household, there is an analogy made between the "all things" of creation where God is the builder, and the house of God rendered as the people of God (vv. 3–6).

proposed a new category of "onto-ethical" rhetoric, examples of which are the themes of light and darkness in John. Applied to this passage, it yields a works-oriented realized eschatology, which

> reduces the distance between eternal life as gift and reward because it defines the fruits of the gift as a proleptic participation in the reward.... Using the category of onto-ethical immortality we have come to see how Paul affirms and defines proper Christian motivations for good works as something integral to the gospel. Understanding the commensurability afforded by the participatory images of "glory, honor, and immortality" effectively closes the distance between salvation understood as gift and reward.[41]

Unrestricted by a purely forensic frame, good works are no longer an individual affair. Gombis argues that the household codes in Ephesians 5:22—6:9 and elsewhere constitute a manifesto for the internal life of new creation communities. The old and new humanities (Eph 2:15; 4:24) are "not to be understood as two natures that co-exist within individuals, but rather as two cosmic realms . . . against a Jewish apocalyptic world view, an essential part of which was a temporal dualism," or in other words, a present evil age which would suddenly end, and a coming golden age of righteousness which would endure forever.[42] "In the thought world of Ephesians, the eschatological new age has dawned with the death and resurrection of Christ (Eph 1:20–23) so that it exists in the midst of the old creation ruled by the evil powers."[43] Since Christ has triumphed over the powers and authorities of the present age, who had "held people captive in death through transgressions and sins" he has achieved peace and obtained cosmic supremacy in the heavenly places (Eph 2:5–7). As conquering sovereign, he therefore "has the right to build his temple, which stands as a lasting monument to triumph (Eph 2:20–22)."[44]

Jesus disclosed the shift between a physical temple and a spiritual temple by referring to his own body as a temple which would be destroyed and raised up, after having cleansed the physical temple of corrupt administrations (John 2:14–22; Mark 14:58). He also spoke of this shift to the Samaritan woman, in saying that God would not be worshipped in Jerusalem but in "spirit and truth," and by a probable allusion to Ezekiel's vision of a spring of living water flowing from the temple (John 4:7–24; cf. Ezek

41. Dryden, "Immortality in Romans 2:6–11," 309–10.
42. Gombis, "A Radically New Humanity," 318 n. 10.
43. Ibid.
44. Ibid., 319.

47:1–12; Zech 14:8; Jer 2:13; 17:13). John 7:37–39 discloses that when Jesus also proclaimed this publicly, teaching that water would flow from the heart, he referred to the coming Spirit to be received by believers. The indwelling Holy Spirit is what makes the body of Christians a temple (1 Cor 3:16; 6:19), who together are becoming "a holy temple in the Lord ... being built together into a dwelling place for God by the Spirit" (Eph 2:19–22)—a "spiritual house" (1 Pet 2:5) and very "temple of the living God" (2 Cor 6:16–18; cf. Ezek 37:26–27; Isa 52:11; Lev 26:12). The goal of such spiritual development is to be presented "blameless before the presence of his glory," both individually, and corporately as Jesus will "present the church to himself in splendor" (Jude 1:24; Eph 5:27). Thus, the new covenant of the heart may be viewed for the individual as a microcosm of the temple of the new covenant community (Rev 21:9, 10), which itself will inhabit the cosmic temple as it pertains to the coming order of glorious renewal (Rev 21:5, 22).

The final displacement of the present evil order is not gradual, however, but climaxes at a definitive time at the end of the age (Acts 1:6, 7; 2 Pet 3:9). In light of the apocalyptic nature of the parousia on the final day, and its association with manifest glory, Guthrie has highlighted the necessity of individual transformation.[45] In other words, when "he appears we shall be like him, because we shall see him as he is" (1 John 3:2), and this Savior we wait for "will transform our lowly body to be like his glorious body, by the power that enables him even to subject all things to himself" (Phil 3:21). So, what it means to "be conformed to the image of his Son" (Rom 8:29) is a transformation into his glory, both ethically and somatically, as we, "beholding the glory of the Lord, are being transformed into the same image from one degree of glory to another" (2 Cor 3:18).

Ortlund provides an essential key to this by locating glorification this side of the eschaton, as the final link in the "golden chain" of salvation given in Romans 8:30. His "inaugurated glorification" model associates glorification in verse 30 with conformity to the image of the Son in verse 29, being mutually interpreting due to "the close link throughout Paul's letters between glory-language and image-language."[46] The close correlation between image and glory is most explicit in 1 Corinthians 11:7, he notes, where man is called "the image and glory of God," and further on in 1 Corinthians 15:40–49, in "the most eschatologically charged chapter in the NT, image and glory are closely correlated at length."[47] While not denying future glorification (Phil 3:20–21), Ortlund identifies 1 Peter 5:1 as especially realized,

---

45. Guthrie, "Transformation and the Parousia."
46. Ortlund, "Inaugurated Glorification," 116–17.
47. Ibid., 118.

with Peter himself "a partaker in the glory that is going to be revealed."[48] He concludes

> The future consummation of this glorification, as with adoption and justification, is the full-blown, public, vindicating manifestation through bodily resurrection. . . . The reality of glorification, according to Rom 8:29–30, is accomplished; the open manifestation is yet to be revealed. The eschaton has arrived, and glorification with it. The divine image, manifest supremely in Christ, has been restored. . . . We have become human again.[49]

IRRECONCILABLE KINGDOMS: DARKNESS AND LIGHT

Having by this point covered a range of intertwined themes, including life, death, resurrection, temple, new creation, image, glory, and transformation, we will now briefly consider the theme of life in relation to the kingdoms of darkness and light, before finally resolving on the implications for final annihilation.

Ephesians and Colossians together, as parallel texts, set forth God's grand unfolding purposes in terms of transformation through cosmic conquest. Ephesians summarizes this "plan for the fullness of time" as a goal of cosmic scope, "to unite all things in him, things in heaven and things on earth," which occurs through a program of reconciliation wrought by Christ's death on the cross (Eph 1:10; cf. Col 1:20). Colossians summarizes the same mystery for the individual, calling it "Christ in you, the hope of glory" (Col 1:27). This future hope is elaborated by saying, "When Christ who is your life appears, then you also will appear with him in glory" (Col 3:4).

What does it mean for Christ to be the life of a believer? In contrast, "the rest of mankind" are "alienated from the life of God," being dubbed "sons of disobedience" and "children of wrath" (Eph 2:2–3; 4:18). Believers, then, are rescued out of this "domain of darkness and transferred to the kingdom" of the Lord Jesus Christ, having been "qualified . . . to share in the inheritance of the saints of light" (Col 1:12–13) through "adoption as sons" (Eph 1:5). The essential qualification for this redemptive reconciliation is forgiveness of sins (Eph 1:7; Col 1:14; 2:13). Being formerly dead in sin (Eph 2:1, 5; Col 2:13), the transformation then follows a cruciform logic. With

---

48. Ibid., 123.
49. Ibid., 132–33.

Christ, believers have "died to the elemental spirits of the world" (Col 2:20; cf. Rom 6:2 "died to sin"), and having so died, are then "made alive together with him" (Col 2:13; cf. Phil 3:10–11). This participation means that "your life is hidden with Christ in God" (Col 3:3) and "you are no longer strangers and aliens, but you are fellow citizens with the saints and members of the household of God" (Eph 2:19).

The reason that Christ would not die again is that "death no longer has dominion over him" (Rom 6:9), which exposes the cosmic dimensions of the victory of the cross. Accordingly, by his death he destroyed "the one who has the power of death, that is, the devil" and liberated many from a lifelong "fear of death" (Heb 2:14–15). Satan is "the prince of the power of the air," who governs the corrupt "cosmic powers over this present darkness . . . the spiritual forces of evil in the heavenly places" (Eph 2:2; 6:12). When Jesus spoke of his imminent death, he said "now will the ruler of this world be cast out" (John 12:31–33). When challenged with the objection, "the Christ remains forever," he replied, "The light is among you for a little while longer. . . . While you have the light, believe in the light, that you may become sons of light" (John 12:34–36).

The program of rescue from the present evil age and transfer into the kingdom of light continues (Gal 1:4; Col 1:13), but not into the age to come, since as we've seen, it is determinative of transformation and the particular kind of resurrection, with respect to either a glorious or shameful presentation to the Son of God.

COSMIC CONFLAGRATION: ANNIHILATION AS SHAMEFUL DISINHERITANCE

The above framing supplies understandings which converge on a shameful final annihilation in terms of what Middleton called "cosmic disinheritance"[50] and Irenaeus described as forfeit of "existence and continuance."[51] Our remaining task is to verify this against some of the primary texts on final punishment.

Notably, the elusive text of Isaiah 33:14 is now elucidated. It has always been a candidate source text for the eternal fire concept of the New Testament, for it says, "The sinners in Zion are afraid; trembling has seized the godless: 'Who among us can dwell with the consuming fire? Who among us can dwell with everlasting burnings?'"[52] This climax occurs because

---

50. Middleton, *A New Heaven and a New Earth*, 207
51. *Against Heresies*, 2.34.3; *ANF* 1:411.
52. Targum Jonathan interprets the two designations of fire differently. The

the Lord, who "dwells on high," is arising in theophanic glory, coming to destroy his enemies who "will be as if burned to lime, like thorns cut down, that are burned in the fire," and to "fill Zion with justice and righteousness" (Isa 33:1–13; cf. 2 Pet 2:6; Mal 4:1–3; Isa 24:6; 66:1–5, 14, 24). After the righteous "dwell on the heights" and find refuge, they "will see no more the insolent people," but will instead "behold Zion," that holy city which is "an immovable tent," and the sins of those "who dwell there" will be forgiven (Isa 33:16–24). This is the eschatological city which "cannot be shaken" because it has everlasting "foundations" (Isa 33:20; cf. Heb 11:10; 12:22, 28). The tabernacling or dwelling motif is clear, as is the related purging of any sinners in the same domain.

In Hebrews 9–12, the logic of cosmos and temple conspire to yield the same kind of scenario. We are told that Jesus appeared "at the end of the ages" to purify and sanctify his people, securing for them an "eternal redemption" for "the promised eternal inheritance" in the final age. He offered himself as a living sacrifice to open the way and enter into the holy places in heaven, which is not yet opened on earth since the first section of the tabernacle "is symbolic for the present age" (Heb 9:8–26). There is a discernible vertical ascent motif here, but also a temple access motif which applies to humans as "those who draw near" to God, such that without a sacrifice for sins, there is "a fearful expectation of judgment, and a fury of fire that will consume the adversaries" (Heb 9:24; 10:12, 13; 10:1, 27). "For our God is a consuming fire" is the awesome conclusion to Hebrews 12:18–29 where this theme is continued, where the Sinai theophany is invoked: "For you have not come to what may be touched, a blazing fire and darkness and gloom and a tempest" (v. 18). It is critical to notice the association here between "what may be touched" and the idea of the present physical order, which includes both things "of this creation" and things "made with hands" (Heb 9:11; cf. 24; 2 Cor 5:1–4). This helps us to appreciate the time axis in Hebrews 12:25–29 with respect to the separation of things continuing on from things passing away. The point is that the first time around at Mt. Sinai, the earth was shaken and many died, but there will be another episode when both the earth and the heavens are violently shaken by God's mighty presence resulting in "the removal of things that are shaken—that is, things that have been made—in order that the things that cannot be shaken may remain" (v. 27). That this cataclysmic shift between the ages is a global conflagration of God's theophanic fire is discernible here in Hebrews, but

---

"consuming fire" is seen as that of the theophanic Shekinah glory, while the "everlasting burnings" are seen as those of Gehenna, adjacent to Zion (see Matt 10:28; Mark 9:47–48; cf. Isa 66:24). In this paper these are not significantly distinct, as Gehenna is shown to be generated by a destruction theophany.

is complemented by 2 Peter 2–3 where it is more explicit. Other important passages to connect to the world-shaking theme of Hebrews 12 and the glorious temple-city—which will remain in the new heavens and earth, while former things pass away—are Haggai 2,[53] Isaiah 60 (especially vv. 1–3, 11, 19) and Revelation 21 (also Isa 65:17; 66:22–24).

Second Peter 2 and 3 are about the shift of the ages, and a final judgment by fire. Reading 2 Peter 2:6 and Jude 7 in light of each other (2 Pet 2:1—3:3 runs parallel to Jude 4–18) yields the truth that the inhabitants of Sodom and Gomorrah serve as an example, by being burned to ashes, of "those who suffer the punishment of eternal fire," which is "what is going to happen to the ungodly." Jesus taught exactly the same thing: "on the day when Lot went out from Sodom, fire and sulfur rained from heaven and destroyed them all—so will it be on the day when the Son of Man is revealed" (Luke 17:29–30). Moreover, 2 Peter 3:7–13 echoes the narrative tradition of Sodom and Gomorrah,[54] which has the implication that Jesus' direct application can be applied: "Remember Lot's wife. Whoever seeks to preserve his life will lose it, but whoever loses his life will keep it" (Luke 17:32–33). That is to say, when 2 Peter 3:6 and 9 speak of perishing, as those in Noah's Flood, when it occurs next time by fire (2 Pet 3:7, 12), what is in view is that those who cling to the present sinful world, like Lot's wife did, will die. There was "a flood upon the world of the ungodly" and "the world that then existed was deluged with water and perished," and so, in parallel, there was also at Sodom a destructive fire as "an example of what is going to happen to the ungodly" which will be globalized, as "the heavens and earth that now exist are stored up for fire, being kept until the day of judgment and destruction of the ungodly" (2 Pet 2:5, 6; 3:6, 7). Just like Noah and Lot were rescued and continued on, so too the righteous will continue into the new creation where only righteousness dwells (2 Pet 3:13).

This final destruction also occurs prior to the completed vision of the new creation in Revelation 21. Revelation 19:11–16 describes Jesus as a warring judge, whose "eyes are like a flame of fire" (cf. Rev 1:12–16) and who wears "a robe dipped in blood" from treading on "the winepress of the fury of the wrath of God," the blood flowing from striking down the nations with a sharp sword "from his mouth." Isaiah 63:1–6 confirms that his garments are blood-spattered, as if by treading grapes, "I trampled down the peoples in my anger; I made them drunk in my wrath, and I poured out their lifeblood on the earth." Revelation 14:14–20 contains the same motif, where

---

53. Haggai 2:6 is quoted in Hebrews 12:26. For reasons to consider Haggai 2:6–9's intent as eschatological, see Kessler, "The Shaking of the Nations."

54. Juza, "Echoes of Sodom and Gomorrah on the Day of the Lord."

the winepress "outside the city" may be a reference to Gehenna as a fiery lake, if the wrathful wine of this passage interprets that of 14:10. Jeremiah 25:27–33 not only prophesies the same thing in terms of a theophanic judgment "against all the inhabitants of the earth," but also connects the winepress motif with the Gehenna motif, in describing all "the wicked" slain by the sword, and a "great tempest" of wrath resulting in "those pierced by the Lord on that day" being strewn across the earth, as "dung on the surface of the ground." This is the same result as in Isaiah 66:24, which Jesus identifies with Gehenna. Isaiah 66:1–2 and verses 18–19 confirm our framing: the Lord is arising from his heavenly throne, and coming to his earthly footstool, which his own hands have made. Therefore, no one can build him a house, but he will gather all nations to witness his glory. But "the Lord is coming with fire . . . he will bring down his anger with fury, and his rebuke with flames of fire. For with fire and with his sword the Lord will execute judgment on all people, and many will be those slain by the Lord" (Isa 66:14, 15).

Isaiah 30:27–33 prophetically defines Gehenna "in the day of the great slaughter" as that place kindled by "the breath of the Lord, like a stream of sulfur," whose "breath is like an overflowing stream that reaches up to the neck." He "comes from afar, burning with his anger, and in thick rising smoke; his lips are full of fury, and his tongue is like a devouring fire." With "furious anger and a flame of devouring fire," he will "sift the nations with the sieve of destruction." As Topheth ("place of burning") writ large, Gehenna will one day be called "the Valley of Slaughter," where the dead bodies will be food for birds and beasts, "and none will frighten them away" (Jer 7:30–34, 19:2–6; cf. 2 Kgs 23:10; 2 Chr 28:3, 33:6). This is the same theme of undying scavengers in Isaiah 66:24, and also points to the great feast of flesh in Revelation 19:17–21.

Gehenna therefore is a destruction theophany, when the Lord returns to vanquish his enemies by sword and by fire, as "a curse devours the earth, and its inhabitants suffer for their guilt; therefore the inhabitants of the earth are scorched, and few men are left" (Isa 24:6; cf. Ps 21:8–10). As the present heavens and earth vanish like smoke and wear out like a garment, "they who dwell in it will die in like manner, but my salvation will be forever" (Isa 51:6). The vanquished wicked of the earth will "vanish like water that runs away" when God judges the earth (Ps 58:7–11). This global-scale event we identify with "the day of judgment and destruction of the ungodly" of 2 Peter 3:7.

The parousia is likewise located on that unique day, and may be understood as a theophany of glory and destruction. Key signifiers of such are the notions of destruction from God's mighty presence, involving glory and fire, issuing forth as breath. According to 2 Thessalonians 1–2, on the day of the Lord, before believers are all gathered to him, he will "destroy with the breath of his mouth" the lawless one who had taken his seat in the temple of God, "annihilating him by the manifestation of his coming," while those sanctified by the Spirit will "obtain the glory of our Lord Jesus Christ" (2 Thess 2:1–4, 8, 13–14 NRSV). Those who are "considered worthy of the kingdom of God" will receive vindication "when the Lord Jesus is revealed from heaven with his mighty angels in flaming fire, inflicting vengeance" on the disobedient, who "will suffer the punishment of eternal destruction, away from the presence of the Lord and the glory of his might, when he comes on that day to be glorified in his saints, and to be marveled at among all who have believed" (2 Thess 1:5–10).[55] This passage may be associated with the "eternal punishment" of "eternal fire" in Matthew 25:31–46, on account of their similarities and their location at the same event (2 Thess 1:7, 10; cf. Matt 25:31).

Jesus spoke of the same ones "considered worthy to attain to that age and to the resurrection of the dead" who "cannot die anymore." They are not "sons of this age," but rather "sons of God . . . sons of the resurrection" (Luke 20:34–36). They also "shall never die," shall "not die," and shall "live forever" (John 11:26; 6:50, 58). Having obtained "a better resurrection" (Heb 11:35, NASB), like Christ they will "never die again" because they participate "in a resurrection like his" (Rom 6:5, 9; Phil 3:10, 11). That the resurrection here is not simply an event, but an age—to which only some belong—implies that the rest are judged unworthy of that future time. Unlike those who can enter the promised inheritance, they *can* die, *shall* die again (Matt 10:28; cf. Rev 21:8), and *shall not* live forever in the eschatological kingdom. Jesus taught that these are "sons of the evil one," who at the end of the present age will be gathered like weeds to be "burned with fire." His mighty angels will "gather out of his kingdom all causes of sin and all law-breakers" after separating the righteous from the evil, who will be thrown into "the fiery furnace," after which "the righteous will shine like the sun in the kingdom of their father" (Matt 13:37–43, 49–50). This last statement invokes Daniel 12:3, following the resurrection text of verse 2, saying that the righteous

---

55. Many who maintain an eternally conscious Hell claim that 2 Thessalonians 1:9 describes being separated from God's presence. However, our theophanic destruction reading is well-established, since "from the presence of the Lord" may be considered idiomatic due to an identical wording in Acts 3:20, and since Isaiah 2 appears to be the source text, in that "from the presence of the Lord and the glory of His power" ("ἀπὸ προσώπου τοῦ κυρίου καὶ ἀπὸ τῆς δόξης τῆς ἰσχύος αὐτοῦ") is virtually identical in the LXX to "from before the terror of the Lord, and from the splendor of his majesty" ("ἀπὸ προσώπου τοῦ φόβου κυρίου καὶ ἀπὸ τῆς δόξης τῆς ἰσχύος αὐτοῦ") which is repeated in Isaiah 2:10, 19, 21 (cf. Rev 6:15–16).

"shall shine like the brightness of the sky above . . . like the stars forever and ever." As we have seen, this idea evokes heavenly glory, and suggests a blessed life characterized by honor and glory, which requires transformation into glorified, incorruptible, immortal form.

CONCLUSION

Themes of *glory*, *image* and *temple* are critically important for discerning the biblical metanarrative and for the gospel itself, in conjunction with *honor* and *immortality* (Rom 2:7). In conquering *death* and bringing *life* and *immortality* to light, Jesus triumphed over the kingdom of darkness and the corrupt powers of the present evil age (2 Tim 1:10; Col 2:15; Heb 2:14). As Son of Man he lived faithfully and obediently to the point of death, being crowned therefore with glory and honor, which human beings made in God's image were always meant to display (Phil 2:5–10; Heb 2:5–10; cf. Ps 8:5–8; Gen 1:26–28). Exalted then to heaven, the Son reclaimed the distinct glory he shared with the Father from the beginning, and now reigns over the earth cleansing the cosmic temple until he has put all enemies "under his feet" (John 17:5; 1 Cor 15:24–28). Since his kingdom is imperishable, those who inherit it must be clothed in imperishability and immortality, being transformed and glorified by the power of the Holy Spirit, created anew in the image of the man from heaven (1 Cor 15:42–55; Rom 8:9–11, 18–30; 2 Cor 3:18). By this means they are qualified to participate in the resurrection of everlasting life, while others are disqualified after a resurrection of condemnation (John 5:21–29), characterized variously by the fires of theophanic destruction. This is a disqualification from future reality (annihilation), given the all-pervasive nature of the cosmic temple, and of righteousness within it once purged of evil. Finally, with all dividing walls in the cosmic temple dissolved, heaven and earth are intermingled, and God tabernacles with humankind, for in the New Jerusalem the "temple is the Lord God the Almighty and the Lamb . . . the glory of God gives it light" while the "glory and honor of the nations" is brought in as tribute (Rev 21:3, 22–27). This establishes a vision of the song of redeemed creation in full symphonic worship, functioning harmoniously as God intended, when the whole earth is filled with the knowledge of God's glory (Hab 2:14; cf. Isa 6:3; 11:9).

10

Divine Sovereignty in the Punishment of the Wicked

— Adam Murrell —

Adam Murrell is founder and CEO of Ichthus Publications, a company that specializes in Christian classic reprints and offers publishing services free of charge. He also serves as President of Redeeming Grace Ministries, a non-profit organization which promotes Christ-centered education to pastors and congregations around the world, with a view to starting a local Bible Institute for serious students who cannot afford a first-rate education. Adam is a graduate of Columbia College and Liberty Baptist Theological Seminary, a member of the Evangelical Philosophical Society, and writes on topics such as ecclesiastical history, Reformed theology, and worldviews. He has authored eight books including Training Young Hearts for Christ, Reclaiming Reason, *and* Essential Church History. *He lives in Pennsylvania with his wife, Laura, and four children.*

For more than three decades Edward Fudge has played a leading role in mediating to the English-speaking evangelical world a renewal of interest in the doctrine of conditional immortality. In his seminal book, *The Fire That Consumes*, Fudge invited us to ask ourselves if we could read the familiar passages on hell better, more in tune with what the ancient writers intended and without Neoplatonic presuppositions. Supposing we fine-tuned our understanding a bit, adjusted our thinking here and there, would the passages on hell reveal a different story? The answer for Fudge was a resounding *yes*, and his thoughtful and compelling scholarship revealed a completely different picture of hell than the one envisioned by Dante Alighieri and engrained in much of modern-day evangelicalism.[1]

While Fudge's labors resulted in a focused exegetical response to the traditional theology of hell by providing a thoughtful and compelling case for the irreversible destruction of the wicked, some still point out the need for closer examination of his conclusions in broader, more comprehensive terms and implications, especially in its relationship to the doctrine of God. Such inquiries are certainly important, and I believe doing exactly as some have urged will only strengthen the cause of conditionalism.

To that end, this contribution explores the relationship of God's power as it relates to the punishment of the finally impenitent by asking us to fundamentally reconsider *sovereignty* in light of personal eschatology. In that quest, would we be willing to set aside years of traditions, prejudices, and presuppositions to confront the biblical teaching of sovereignty afresh? Would we be willing to approach the subject as if we were encountering the biblical matter for the first time, to listen to what the Scriptures are trying to tell us in a consistent and rational manner? If so, a "Damascus Road" experience, one that is dramatic, unexpected, shocking, but refreshing, will certainly emerge, and we will realize that God will *truly* be victorious over sin in a real and palpable way.

For centuries Christians have been offered an inadequate explanation of the nature and duration of final punishment. They have been given a theology of hell that cedes God's sovereignty to the created order and portrays his actions in judgment as anything but sovereign or complete. Its advocates passed down this perennial teaching from generation to generation while ignoring an alternative reading that weaves together the reality of sovereignty and the reality of punishment in a way that makes better use of the biblical text and normal sense of human language. It is this alternative explanation, I believe, that marks the only approach in which Christians can be wholly consistent and radically biblical in espousing a theology of hell. The challenge before us now is whether or not we are willing to carry on the legacy of "reformed and always in need of being reformed according to Scripture."

---

1. For a helpful introduction to the development of hell throughout the church age, see Baker, *Razing Hell*, Part 1.

THE BIBLE AS WITNESS TO THE SOVEREIGNTY OF GOD

"O Lord, you are great, mighty, majestic, magnificent, glorious, and sovereign over all the sky and earth! You have dominion and exalt yourself as the ruler of all" (1 Chr 29:11). So read the words of the Chronicler who expressed an incontrovertible truth about YHWH's power—that God is "sovereign over all." The theme of divine *sovereignty* is certainly familiar to Christian worshipers and enjoys universal approbation as a fundamental truth about the nature of God. We assert this reality every time we recite any of the three ecumenical creeds (the Apostles' Creed, the Nicene Creed, and the so-called Athanasian Creed) by affirming God as the "Almighty."[2]

The normal meaning of *sovereignty*—also called *omnipotence*—is that YHWH, the living God, is the undisputed Ruler who has absolute power over his creation to do what he wills according to his good pleasure (Ps 22:28; Isa 46:9–10). Nothing stands in his way, nothing thwarts his ways or disrupts his dealings. God is never defeated, dethroned, dissatisfied, or disappointed since "all things" that transpire in time are part and parcel of *his* divine plan.

Indeed, the Bible overwhelmingly reveals a sovereign God who proactively governs his creation, weaving threads of God's omnipotence throughout the entire canon of Scripture. Sovereignty as a natural attribute of YHWH finds illustration, for instance, in the prayer of Jehoshaphat: "O Lord God of our ancestors, you are the God who lives in heaven and rules over all the kingdoms of the nations. You possess strength and power; no one can stand against you" (2 Chr 20:6).[3] Job responded to God by saying, "I know that you can do all things; no purpose of yours can be thwarted" (Job 42:2). Elsewhere, the psalmist declared: "Our God is in the heaven! He does whatever he pleases" (Ps 115:3). The prophet recorded YHWH making this declaration: "Remember what I accomplished in antiquity! Truly I am God, I have no peer; I am God, and there is none like me, who announces the end

---

2. The Apostles' Creed begins with the affirmation: "I believe in God, the Father *Almighty* . . . ." Similarly, the Nicene Creed opens thusly: "I believe in one God, the Father *Almighty* . . . ." The Athanasian Creed reads in part: "So likewise the Father is almighty, the Son almighty, and the Holy Ghost almighty. And yet they are not three Almighties, but one Almighty."

3. For the purpose of this contribution, I am following the classification of attributes as set forth by William G. T. Shedd in chapter 5, "Divine Attributes," of his *Dogmatic Theology*, vol. 1; see also Berkhof, *Systematic Theology*, 55–56. One helpful summation of *attribute* by Shedd is to say, "Attributes are essential qualities of God." A. W. Tozer simply stated an attribute is "something true about God." See his *Knowledge of the Holy*, 18–22. See also, Erickson, *Christian Theology*, 292–93.

from the beginning and reveals beforehand what has not yet occurred, who says, 'My plan will be realized, I will accomplish what I desire'" (Isa 46:9–10). And, "Whose command was ever fulfilled unless the Lord decreed it?" (Lam 3:37). God alone establishes the mightiest rulers and greatest nations (Ps 22:28) and even determines the length of one's days (Ps 139:16). The virgin Mary summed it up in the Magnificat by exclaiming, "Nothing will be impossible with God" (Luke 1:37). Such is but a small sampling of the power of Almighty God.

All of these pronouncements of inherent sovereignty are simply a way of saying that with such majestic power naturally arise the *privilege* and the *ability* to do with the created order whatever pleases God, according to his divine prerogative.[4] The Westminster Confession of Faith captures the essence of this sentiment in saying, "He is the alone fountain of all being, of whom, through whom, and to whom are all things; and has most sovereign dominion over them, to do by them, for them, or upon them whatsoever Himself pleases" (WCF 2.2).

What pleases God (and what logically flows from his nature) is to remain intimately connected with his creation, sustaining, maintaining, and fashioning all that unfolds, working the means in the "present age" to achieve the desired end in the "age to come"—and all for his glory. God's control extends to every aspect of life, as he governs and superintends all that transpires from the greatest events in earthly kingdoms[5] to the so-called coincidental happenings;[6] from the righteous deeds of mankind[7] and opprobrious actions of the wicked[8] to the actions of the spirit world[9] and habits of the animal kingdom.[10] Nothing remains beyond his control or out of reach.[11] There are no hurricanes that strike, no wars waged, no murders perpetrated, or no diseases that afflict apart from the decree of Almighty God. Only two possible choices exist for Christians: either God rules over

---

4. I must also stress here God's actions are not arbitrary or capricious. God's actions naturally flow from his nature which is to say he is radically loving and perfectly good so his actions will reflect that truth about him.

5. Isa 45:1–4.

6. Prov 16:33.

7. John 15:16; Eph 2:10; Phil 2:12–13.

8. Gen 45:5; 50:20; Exod 4:21; Judg 14:1–4; Ps 76:10; Prov 16:4; 21:1; Isa 44:28; Amos 3:6; Acts 2:22–23; 4:27–28.

9. 1 Sam 16:14–16; 1 Kgs 22:19–23; 1 Chr 21:1; 2 Sam 24:1; Pss 103:20–21; 104:4.

10. Num 22:28; 1 Kgs 17:4; Ps 29:9; Jer 8:7; Ezek 32:4; Dan 6:22.

11. For a helpful listing of biblical verses on the sovereignty of God, see "Is God sovereign over every single event that takes place on earth?" at http://www.monergism.com/thethreshold/articles/onsite/qna/godsovereign.html.

his creation, or his creation rules over him. Either God accomplishes his will, or his will is thwarted by forces outside his control (to which God attempts to respond appropriately). God either controls his creation down to the smallest particle, or he is subordinate (in some respect) to the created order. This is simply the logical outworking of affirming the sovereignty of God.[12]

Simply put, if God's power and might were somehow subordinated to any part of the created order, then YHWH, the living God would no longer be the "Almighty, the King of kings and Lord of lords." Sovereignty, therefore, is not something that can be diminished or increased. Rather, it is a glorious truth about the very character of God in every realm of all his dominions; sovereignty is what God *is* in the totality of his Being and addresses how he operates. Thus, any concomitant doctrine must be reconciled with this truth of divine sovereignty.

WHAT ABOUT EVIL?

In writing to the church at Rome, the apostle Paul provided comfort to Christians by pointing out the sovereignty of God in working together "all things" (Rom 8:28). Echoing this same truth on a different occasion, Paul again pointed out how God "accomplishes all things according to the counsel of his will" (Eph 1:11). The words and meaning here are unmistakable in that the Almighty works out *everything* according to his will. Every event, every detail, every contingency is under the control of the living God. If it were not so, then the apostle's message of hope and encouragement would provide little meaning or afford little comfort. But Paul directed his readers to this foundational truth about the nature of God as the basis of his confidence. The apostle wrote reassuringly that God's divine plan *is* continuously working out exactly as he intends, including life's most excruciating problem—evil, both *natural* (disease, plagues, hurricanes, and so on) and *moral* (murder, lying, stealing, and so on).

Most, if not all, non-Christian religions explain this apparent contradiction by postulating a concept of dualism, explaining that good and evil dwell in incongruity, are constantly engaged in warfare for supremacy. But espousing dualism, in any form or variation, is antithetical to the whole testimony of Scripture. The God of Abraham, Isaac, and Jacob is not engaged

---

12. This perspective is not uniquely confined to the Reformed tradition—though it is most ardently stressed therein—but is essential to Christian theism for rational coherence. For a defense of this thesis, see Sproul, *Chosen By God*, 23–28. Also, Sproul, *Truths We Confess*, 75–82.

in an epic struggle with a rival divine vying for supremacy; there is no nefarious Spirit thwarting God's will. "The Lord has established his throne in the heaven; his kingdom extends over everything" (Ps 103:19). The very nature of God's attribute, the essence of his sovereignty precludes even the possibility of a competing being or force. "I am the one who forms light and creates darkness; the one who brings about peace and creates calamity. I am the Lord, who accomplishes all these things" (Isa 45:7). Even human experiences with evil are not outside of God's sovereign control, otherwise they would not be a present reality, as Joseph affirmed to his brothers (Gen 50:20). If we conclude that God is unaware of evil or that evil is unknown to God, then I believe we are justified to conclude that God cannot, in any rational or meaningful sense, provide absolute assurance of victory over evil or be in control of all earthly events.[13] Likewise, if our theology guides us to the conclusion God cannot forever eradicate sin and evil, if our doctrines subordinate God's power to any part of the created order in this life or the one to come, then his sovereignty is limited at that point—and we can no longer say he is "sovereign over all."

Are we willing to affirm that God does as he pleases, everywhere, always, and forever? Are we willing to acknowledge there is nothing outside of his divine sphere of influence, and that there is no higher authority to which God turns in order to carry out his will? If so, we must be prepared to accept the implications wherever they may logically lead. After all, the Bible clearly reveals that God is sovereign *in* creation and *over* creation, *in* redemption and salvation and *over* redemption and salvation, *in* dealing with sin and evil and *over* sin and evil. Nothing is outside of God's sphere of power or influence and nothing stands in his way to accomplish his goal of ultimate victory against the finally impenitent.

SIN AND DIVINE PUNISHMENT

Because God is sovereign and exercises absolute control over the created order, he promises just judgment, rewarding righteousness and punishing evil. This is how a just judge operates. God's justice, therefore, is said to be both *remunerative* and *distributive*, remunerating good deeds and distributing

---

13. I recognize that Open Theists and Molinists, among others, have crafted an apologetic for this very issue (which I find very unconvincing and at tension with the doctrine of God), but, coming from a Reformed tradition and writing to those Traditionalists of the same persuasion, this argument stands—and so, too, do the conclusions that logically follow from affirming it, as I shall point out later on in the chapter.

punishment for sin.[14] On the one hand, God promises blessings for obeying his commands (Deut 28:1–6), while promising punishment for evil, on the other hand (Deut 28:15–19). Just as sure as the promise of receiving a blessing is, the promise of enduring divine wrath remains a certainty. "You will be cursed," the Lord promises unrepentant evildoers. This vow is not merely an idle threat in which the Lord boasts about distributing justice beyond what he is capable.

If God were unable or unwilling to punish sin, he would not be *sovereign* or *just*. And if he were neither the former nor the latter, he would not be God, because God must *always* act in harmony with his own nature. In other words, the wicked shall not prevail in perpetuity because of who God is. They will see a day of reckoning in which their unrighteous works will be exposed, and they will be held accountable. The wicked, despite ephemeral confident feelings of self-assurance or security, shall not prevail in perpetuity. Evil is limited for a season, the wicked's sin and activities are always temporary. "Evil men will soon disappear; you will stare at the spot where they once were, but they will be gone" (Ps 37:10). The days of the wicked, of mere mortals, are numbered; they will disappear and will forever be forgotten (Ps 103:15–16), will be cut off and will be no more (Prov 2:21–22; 10:25; 12:7; 24:15–20).

Ought we then to be worried that God is somehow unable to justly repay evil for evil as he says? Did the biblical writers speak out of turn when recording sinners would receive a just punishment for their impenitence? Should we be led to believe, from the testimony of Scripture, that God tries his best to punish but is never satisfactorily able to do so? Not at all. God patiently waits while mankind continues in sin. But once sin has a reached a certain tipping point, once the full measure of wickedness is attained, God's justice will be brought to bear (Gen 15:16, 1 Thess 2:16). The biblical narrative provides this sobering and certain warning that the ungodly will not go unpunished, their evil deeds will provoke divine wrath and discipline. The day of reckoning is a guarantee; YHWH will not allow the wicked to go unpunished (Nah 1:3).

Divine wrath will someday be poured out upon the denizens of hell without any restraint or moderation of degree; his anger will burst forth in fierceness of anger, with nothing to alleviate his wrath as sinners experience the full measure of his fury (Rev 14:11; 19:11–16). A proper and just punishment is a certainty since, after all, God "cannot deny himself" (2 Tim 2:13). But given the power of God to exercise sovereign punishment toward the denizens of hell, we have to ask ourselves at this point how the traditional

---

14. See Sproul, *The Character of God*, 114–17.

theology of hell can reconcile eternal consciousness with an all-powerful act of discipline, since that divine punishment is never efficacious.

Would human sovereignty or justice be served if the hangman's noose never broke the subject's neck, the electricity surging through the body never killed the condemned prisoner, or the lethal injection never properly resulted in the condemned's organs failing? The answer of course is a resounding *no*. When the neck does not break, when the electricity does not kill, or when the toxins do not destroy, it is considered by any measurable standard to be a failure and additional processes must be implemented to produce the desired result *of death*. It is the extinguishing of life, the removal of the condemned from the life of the living that marks the success of the punishment.

Yet this is precisely where the traditional theology of hell takes us. Traditionalism has bequeathed us an ineffectual divine executioner who is unable "to destroy the soul" as Jesus warned (Matt 10:28), unable to produce a punishment that satisfies wrath for sin, vindicates justice, and fulfills the solemn pronouncement that the "payoff of sin is death" (Rom 6:23). The conclusion is obvious: the sovereignty of God has reached its limit at the outskirts of hell.

IN WHAT SENSE SOVEREIGN?

We are now approaching the heart of the purpose in this contribution, which is to suggest that we have inappropriately moderated the sovereignty of God in the enactment of divine punishment. The historical position, one could plausibly argue, has unwittingly drowned out a very important message of Christ *as* Conqueror against evil, Executor of wrath, and Vindicator of justice. While on the one hand, the traditional position properly affirms Jesus as the conquering hero, on the other hand, his triumph is never realized in the sense that evil—that which God harbors an infinite hatred toward—is never eradicated. Sin is never properly dealt with in the whole divine scheme. Eternity cannot in any meaningful sense be called a place of complete victory and glorious triumph. It is, instead, a realm in which evil is relegated to a small dimension to continue in perpetuity in its own right. This is the palpable problem with the traditional teaching on hell, full as it is of important truths and supple understanding of the nefariousness of sin. But the problem is exposed most clearly in that the traditional theology of hell does not go *far enough* in maintaining the fullness of God.

Embracing the traditional teaching on hell moves us toward the understanding that God is either incapable or indisposed to reconcile all things fully unto himself, even though he claimed that he would do so eventually. The Bible reveals a picture of Jesus as the Warrior-Judge who rides victorious against sin and evil and wears the blood-stained robe of his enemies who have been crushed under his triumphant might (Rev 19:13–16). But traditionalism has fashioned a Judge who cannot seem to execute judgment to perfection in the sense that even under the strain of the full measure of sovereign wrath, the vessels fitted to destruction are never actually subjugated, sorrowful, destroyed, or redeemed.[15] These inhabitants of hell are sentient beings who are purposefully preserved to live an eternally lawless existence in order for YHWH to award a proper punishment and to expose his on-going rage against sin and sinners.[16] Yet somehow, we are assured, this manifests God's almighty power, even though there is never any resolution or redemptive purpose.

The problem becomes all the more acute when we realize that our tradition has for years forced us to accept this conclusion as the consequence of assuming unbiblical anthropological presuppositions about nature of the soul. Accepting this assumption about the soul leads us to embrace a position whereby we exchanged a Victor *over* evil for a suitor *against* evil. We have created a Judge who immortalizes prisoners of war and their rampant immorality in an eternal but fledgling attempt to propitiate wrath and vindicate justice—but is forever unsuccessful. In what context can anyone even remotely begin to assert this vision rightly supports the biblical definition of sovereignty or victory over sin?

The untenable implications of this view of personal eschatology for divine sovereignty are obvious. Hell is not simply a place of punishment, though it surely encompasses pain and misery; it is instead, at worst, a vivid picture that reminds the redeemed saints of heaven there is in YHWH a dearth of power unable to effect appropriate justice, an incapacity to satisfy divine wrath, and a powerlessness to eradicate evil.[17] It is ultimately this

---

15. It is worth questioning here how we are to believe that a finite creature could withstand an infinite amount of wrath. Indeed, there would inevitably come a point in which the finite succumbs to the infinite.

16. Some traditionalists have argued that God must forever display his wrath in order to expose the fullness of his attributes. But I do not see any inherent deficiencies in God's nature that compel him to preserve evil for the sole purpose of somehow exposing a "better" understanding of God—as if there is some deficiency inherent in his glory that necessitates this. Moreover, it does not logically follow that God *must* forever demonstrate wrath, because there was never wrath to demonstrate prior to creation, yet "eternity past" in which God eternally dwelled was still perfect and needed no demonstration of wrath.

17. See Edwards, *The Wrath of the Almighty*, 356, for a traditionalist's viewpoint of divine justice in light of unending torment. I respond simply by pointing out that there

point, one could properly argue, which serves as the Achilles's heel to the traditional theology of hell. Years of tradition, intentionally or not, have made it easy to gloss over the plain teaching of so many clear passages that assert divine omnipotence and promise a renewed world in God actually is exhaustively victorious. Let us not close our eyes to this tension any more, but hear afresh the words of the apostle Paul who, borrowing the language from Psalm 110, wrote forcefully and compellingly about Christ's ultimate victory that we cannot overlook its implications:

> Then comes the end, when he hands over the kingdom to God the Father, when he has brought to an end all rule and all authority and power. For he must reign until he has put all his enemies under his feet. The last enemy to be eliminated is death. For *he has put everything in subjection under his feet.* But when it says "everything" has been put in subjection, it is clear that this does not include the one who put everything in subjection to him. And when all things are subjected to him, then the Son himself will be subjected to the one who subjected everything to him, so that God may be all in all (1 Cor 15:24–28).

Here we gather from his writings that the apostle Paul anticipates an eschatological consummation of all things in the "age to come," a time when the created order and all the inhabitants thereof will be restored to their true condition, to a peaceful state wherein peace, justice, and healing are to be ushered in and all enemies of Christ are forever eliminated.[18] Only after this seminal moment, though, once *all* things are brought into unfettered subjection to Christ, once all earthly potentates lay down the offices which they are filling, only then will the reigns of sovereignty be returned to the Father "so that God may be all in all." One can plainly see that Paul does not say a *few* things, *some* things, or even *most* things will be conquered. Instead, the apostle says *all* created things must be brought into subjection unto Christ *before* the great divine transfer of power is consummated, before the Son subjects himself to the Father (v. 28). There is no sense here in which Paul anticipates a kingdom of righteousness shared with sin and brokenness, even if that evil resides in a different dimension. The vision for Paul is such that God's kingdom is brought to its completion and fullness under the sovereignty of the Father, as he reigns in his majesty and dominion. God's chief purpose of rescuing a decaying world will eventually come

---

is no meaningful sense in which justice or victory is accomplished if God is not efficacious in his punitive endeavors.

18. For an understanding of the nature of God's kingdom, see specifically Wright, *How God Became King*, 42–46.

to fruition, but only after absolute subjection is completed. There is no room in the language of the apostle to suggest evil cohabitates with righteousness. Instead, subjection is wrought upon all things under the headship of Jesus.

Yet it seems this promise of complete subjection and restoration is bifurcated by the traditional view of hell when carried to its logical terminus. What I mean by that is simply, within the traditional framework of hell as eternal torment exists two eternal kingdoms: the kingdom of God and, to a lesser extent, the kingdom of Satan, each with their respective limits. Certainly God is the more powerful in that he sets the boundaries of the satanic kingdom, but the necessity of a perpetual satanic realm (as postulated by the traditionalist position) exposes, at some level and to varying degrees, the impotency of God's sovereignty over his creation *at this point*.

We see this most clearly in the sense that God *must* forever immortalize evil and those who continue to pursue it, he *must* make room for evil in his righteous kingdom so that he may inflict torment upon sinners as ongoing punishment in an unsuccessful bid to satisfy his wrath and reclaim justice. This is quite a different picture than the one portrayed most often in traditionalism, but it is the dark side of hell, the inevitable end to which traditionalism brings us. God's exercise in divine punishment is not actually vindicating his justice and propitiating his wrath, but is instead an abortive *attempt* to vindicate justice and propitiate wrath. To declare that hell is a place of unending torment is to declare, even if tacitly, a limit upon God's ability to appropriately administer a divine punishment *worthy enough* for the crime committed. Yet God does not say he will *try* to avenge evil-doers; he indicates retribution *is* a guarantee. "'Vengeance is mine; I will repay,' says the Lord" (Rom 12:19). How can God make such a claim if he can never appropriate an "eye for an eye?" Instead, we would have to conclude God repays only "a nail for an eye," "a finger for an eye," or some other *unequal* payment.

By this, the traditional view of hell grants to finite creatures power too great. After all, created beings can only commit *finite* acts since they are *finite* creatures. Otherwise, how could a sovereign God empower rational creatures with power so great so as to commit sins for which he cannot also adequately punish?[19] Would not that then mean he is no longer sovereign over all? Essentially the traditional view compels us to believe that God endows his creation with the power to commit acts so egregious that

---

19. I can anticipate some here arguing from the standpoint that eternal torment is a sufficient punishment against an "infinite God." But that simply will not do, because the act of punishing never abates since the goal of obtaining justice is never obtained and turning away wrath is never satisfied. Thus God's purpose and intention are persistently thwarted.

even he himself can never appropriately compensate the evil-doer for his wicked deeds. Yet such rationale would imply that evil is a force greater than which even God himself can appropriately respond. Try as he might and surely will—because his nature demands it—God is unable to respond to the problem of evil since sin and evil will eternally endure. I grant that such a statement sounds nearly blasphemous, even heretical, but the logic behind the teaching inevitably leads to this unbiblical conclusion: God cannot respond sufficiently to evil. It is this necessary and logical conclusion of the traditional doctrine of hell that I wholeheartedly reject.

Imagine, for a moment, the implications. What we are asked to believe is that God's kingdom is forever constrained by the sphere of the kingdom of Satan in which evil dwells persistently. Vast portions of the universe are not his own; they are controlled by an opposing and foreign power. Satan's kingdom and all the denizens thereof are imprisoned in a domain in which they cannot perish but neither can they (nor will they) bow the knee to Christ. Their every word, thought, and deed are at enmity with God. There will exist for all eternity a sphere that has *not* been restored, has *not* been reconciled, has *not* been subjugated, has *not* been vindicated, and has *not* been adequately punished. The immortal followers of the Wicked One never cease doing evil, are utterly incapable of obeying God, thus securing for all eternity the reality that evil always keeps up with, if not outpaces, righteousness. Whether or not the traditionalist maintains evil is preserved by the sustaining hand of God or out of eternal necessity matters little. In either scenario, it would seem that God's sovereignty is limited in such a way that whatever punishment is inflicted upon the wicked pales in relation to the extent of injury caused. Here we find the apex of dualistic teaching: God's infinite being empowers finite creatures with the ability to cause him infinite injury, necessitating infinite torment against the wicked by God in an unsuccessful quest for justice. The flames of hell are forever burning since God's wrath is never satisfied, God's justice is never vindicated.[20] Good versus evil forever dueling, without end. Amen.

If traditionalism is to be embraced, we must believe that God for all eternity pursues justice but is powerless to vindicate it. Herein traditionalism has revived the ancient Greek mythological figure Erinyes who pursues

---

20. This problem becomes even more acute for those within the Reformed tradition, because now we have to admit that God ordained his own inability to adequately punish sin, ordained his eternal hatred in that sin and evil reside within a perfect world. Essentially, God ordained his own perpetual unhappiness and anger, which supposedly brings him the most glory. Common sense would indicate it is the exact opposite in that reconciliation would logically bring the most glory.

her victim, but without the power to destroy.[21] But is that anemic portrayal of the Divine true sovereignty? I do not believe it is; nor do I see that portrait painted in the pages of Scripture. That is not the God of the Bible. If we affirm God will punish, he must, in remaining consistent with his nature, punish in a way that manifests his sovereign power *over* sin, destroying that which he abhors and that which stands in stark contrast to his very essence.

GOD'S PROMISE OF RESTORATION

This entire contribution has been about absolute sovereignty, reclaiming something true about God that has minimized throughout the centuries. Where our theology reduces God and subordinates his power it is to be jettisoned, even our most cherished doctrines if they do not permit us to declare the truth about God as forcefully or consistently as the Bible makes clear we must. Sovereignty is a requirement about God and sovereignty must be retained for theological balance and consistency. Whether we are talking about creation, salvation, administration, or punishment, there is nothing YHWH cannot do consistent with his nature. God is sovereign in the exercise of his mercy, sovereign in the exercise of his love, sovereign in the exercise of his grace, sovereign in creation, sovereign in saving a people for his own glorification. In short, God is *always* successful in the exercise of all his endeavors, which is why it seems contrary to reason to believe God is never completely successful in pursuit of divine justice. Yet that is what we *must* believe if the traditional view of hell is to be embraced. We are told that God pursues justice but is unable to obtain it—which is a clear limitation to the sovereign power of God.

Beyond that, consider another conceptual problem with the traditional theology of hell, namely, that evil, as opprobrious as it is in this age, has yet to reach its pinnacle. We must wait for the age to come in which the hideous deformity and blackness of sin and evil will finally reach their zenith. We can say this confidently, because the entire population of hell, all the unrighteous who were ever created, are doing nothing but sinning and rebelling against their Maker. Within that wicked realm we call *hell*, nothing but sin abounds. Compare that to our world today where at least God's restraining hand is present. Our present age, as evil as it is, will seem a veritable Garden of Eden to the future age. Silly, yes, a bit. But, instead of reconciling all things to himself, God will someday effect a world in which the apex of evil, sin, and misery is finally realized. All that is evil, all that which *ought not* to be, is to be forever enshrined, though he abhors it with

21. Hudson, *Debt and Grace*, 96.

an everlasting hatred. This, the traditionalist position assures us, is the height of sovereignty, the manifestation of sovereign wrath against sin and evil. Yet the alternative view seems more in tune with reason and Scripture. God *is able* to acclaim justice, he *is able* to vindicate his holiness, he *is able* to propitiate his wrath—and he *is able* to so do because he is sovereign over all things, including the punishment of the finally impenitent. But these truths have no coherent or rational meaning in the traditional theology of hell.

Only death, destruction, and perishing—in its most forceful and primary sense—maintains the sovereignty of God in the administration of his just judgment. Only death cuts off the power of persistent transgression against God. Uncreating that which is created is the ultimate demonstration of sovereignty, a prospect that eases the tension between the traditional teaching on hell and the apostolic hope and the biblical promises to restore the creation to its rightful state, to usher in the kingdom in which the Judge of the world is ruling sovereignly, so that God may be all in all. Only one teaching consistently permits this eschatological reality.[22]

Finally, God need not annihilate his sovereignty in order to attain justice. A manifestation of omnipotence that vindicates justice and satisfies divine wrath is witnessed consistently only in the form of "terminal punishment" in which all that *ought not* to be is forever removed from the land of the living. Objections to the removal of sin and evil and all that stands in contrast to God for all eternity can be responded to by this one simple question: is God so powerful that he is able to create beings with the capacity to harm him, so great indeed that even he is unable to punish them justly?

---

22. I anticipate some might borrow the argument from sovereignty to argue in favor of universalism by insisting that God's sovereignty would be enhanced even more so by melting away all sin and evil and bringing all impenitent beings to himself. While that challenge will certainty not be adequately addressed in the span of a footnote, suffice it to say that my main point was in saying that what God intends to do, he does so efficaciously and perfectly. If God punishes, for instance, he does so in a way that is consistent with his nature (sovereignly) and the end result will be exactly as he intends, which is victory *over* sin—not merely the preservation of sin in failed attempts to satisfy his wrath against sin or anemic attempts at justice. Also, those of the Reformed tradition will answer the question of salvation radically different from those of an Arminian understanding of anthropology and soteriology. Reformed believers understand the condition of mankind is such that only those God chooses to rescue from the bondage to sin will be saved from the wrath to come. Thus, it is not our argument that God pleads with humans to repent; instead, we affirm that God rescues a people who are known only to him for purposes that glorify him. If God were willing that all mankind without exclusion would be saved, then we know it is within his power to do so. Indeed, God is sovereign enough to do that. But the question before us now is whether or not the Bible reveals that picture. So, arguments for universalism from God's sovereignty cannot be made unless it is first demonstrated the Reformed understanding of sin and salvation are incorrect.

The only biblical and coherent answer we can provide is this: only if God were to stop being God.

Part 3

BIBLICAL EXEGESIS

11

The Punishment of the Wicked in Isaiah 66:24

— Claude Mariottini —

Claude Mariottini has been Professor of Old Testament at Northern Baptist Seminary since 1988. Born in Brazil, he graduated from California Baptist College (BA), Golden Gate Baptist Seminary (MDiv), and The Southern Baptist Seminary (PhD), and has done additional graduate work at the Graduate Theological Union. Mariottini is the author of Rereading the Biblical Text, *as well as commentaries on Deuteronomy, 1 and 2 Chronicles, and 1 and 2 Kings. He has published more than 200 articles and book reviews in English, Spanish, and Russian, which have featured in* The Anchor Bible Dictionary, The Mercer Dictionary of the Bible, The Holman Bible Dictionary, Jewish Bible Quarterly, Perspectives in Religious Studies, The Expository Times, *and more.*

In his book *The Fire that Consumes*, Edward Fudge said that Isaiah 66:24 "is one of the most quoted biblical passages related to the topic of final punishment. It is also one of the most neglected."[1] The importance of Isaiah 66:24 to the proper understanding of the judgment of the wicked is seen in the fact that references to Isaiah 66:24 appear thirty-four times in Fudge's book. Fudge's study of Isaiah 66:24 presents a comprehensive exegesis of this important text. The purpose of the present study is to build on Fudge's exegesis and look at the structure of Isaiah 66 and the historical context of the message of Trito-Isaiah. I am grateful for the invitation to contribute this study to a book dedicated to Edward Fudge. I consider him to be a good friend. He is also a committed Christian and scholar whose

1. Fudge, *The Fire that Consumes* (2011), 75.

work expresses his deep commitment to the proper understanding of the biblical text.

THE STRUCTURE OF ISAIAH 66

There are two major views among evangelical Christians about the composition and authorship of the book of Isaiah. Those who accept a single author for the book argue that it is the work of Isaiah, the prophet who lived in Jerusalem in the eighth century BCE. Under this view, the oracles in Isaiah 40–66 are God's revelation to Isaiah of events that will happen hundreds and thousands of years in the future.

Those who argue for more than one author divide the book of Isaiah into three sections. Isaiah 1–39 is the work of the prophet Isaiah, a man who lived in Jerusalem in the eighth century BCE. He is also known as First Isaiah. Isaiah 40–55 was written during the exile and is the work of an unknown prophet also known as Deutero-Isaiah. Isaiah 56–66 is the work of Trito-Isaiah, a prophet who lived in Jerusalem among the Jews who returned from Babylon after Cyrus's decree in 538 BCE, the first year of his reign.[2]

Isaiah 66 is the work of Trito-Isaiah, probably a disciple of Second Isaiah, and should be interpreted in the context of the post-exilic community before and after the rebuilding of the temple in the days of Haggai and Zechariah.[3] The oracles of Trito-Isaiah are related to the restoration of the nation after the return from the Babylonian exile.[4] The final chapter of the book of Isaiah has a structure similar to chapter 1. The words and imagery found in chapter 66 reveal that the author was deliberately using the words of the prophet Isaiah to convey the same message to his post-exilic community. The language Trito-Isaiah used in chapter 66 to describe the punishment of the wicked in his days is very similar to the language used by Isaiah in the first chapter of his book to describe Yahweh's punishment of the citizens of Judah in the eighth century BCE who had violated the Mosaic covenant. It is evident that the writer of Isaiah 66 was familiar with Isaiah 1. The structure, language, and imagery of both chapters are almost identical. The language and the depiction of the judgment have much in common in both chapters. By drawing on the initial chapter of Isaiah, the author of chapter 66 closes the book and provides an inclusio that serves to demonstrate that there is a unity in the message of the book.

---

2. Bright, *A History of Israel*, 361.
3. Ibid., 369–70.
4. Ackroyd, *Exile and Restoration*, 229.

The verbal and structural similarities between chapters 1 and 66 are intentional. They serve as an inclusio to the book as a whole and an indication of its theological unity. These similarities also provide an affirmation that Yahweh fulfills his promise to deal with those who rebel against him. In his study on the compilation of the book of Isaiah, Liebreich lists twenty verbal correspondences between chapter 1 and chapter 66. These verbal correspondences reflect the intention of the final redactor of the book of Isaiah to express a unity in the message and theology of the book.[5]

A comparison of the structure of Isaiah 1:2—2:4 and Isaiah 66 also reveals that these chapters form an inclusio for the book as a whole:[6]

Chapter 1	Chapter 66
"have rebelled against me" (1:2)[A]	"have rebelled against me" (66:24)
Condemnation of the cult (1:10–14)	Condemnation of the cult (66:1–3a)
Call for repentance (1:16–18)	Judgment on the unrepentant (66:3b–4)
Blessing for obedience (1:19)	Comfort for the obedient (66:5)
Promise of judgment (1:20)	Anticipation of judgment (66:6)
Zion personified as a woman (1:21–26)	Zion personified as a woman (66:7–13)
Blessings and judgment (1:27–28)	Blessings and judgment (66:14–16)
Condemnation of the garden (1:29)	Condemnation of the garden (66:17)
The gathering of the nations (2:2–4)	The gathering of the nations (66:18–23)
Judgment by fire (1:31a)	Judgment by fire (66:16)
Judgment by unquenched fire (1:31b)	Judgment by unquenched fire (66:24b)

A. Unless otherwise noted, all Scripture quotations are taken from the New Revised Standard Version (NRSV).

The purpose for the similar structure between Isaiah 1 and Isaiah 66 is to provide a closure for the book. This means that, according to Trito-Isaiah, those in his day who rebelled against Yahweh will be judged in the same way the people who rebelled against Yahweh in the days of Isaiah were judged.

The book of Isaiah begins with Yahweh addressing those who "have rebelled against me" (Isa 1:2). The chapter describes the rebellion of Yahweh's children followed by a call to repentance. If the people refuse to repent they will be judged and be destroyed by the sword (Isa 1:20). Those who forsake the Lord (Isa 1:28) shall be destroyed with a fire that no one can quench

5. Liebreich, "The Compilation of the Book of Isaiah," 276–77.
6. This comparison between Isaiah 1:2—2:4 and Isaiah 66 is based on the work of Tomasino, "Isaiah 1.1—2.4 and 63–66, and the Composition of the Isaianic Corpus," 81–98.

(Isa 1:31). The book of Isaiah ends with Yahweh addressing "the people who have rebelled against me" (Isa 66:24). The use of *pāshaʻ bî* ("who have rebelled against me") in 1:2 and 66:24 indicates that these two verses form an inclusio for the book of Isaiah. "The rebels of the first verse of the book are dealt with once and for all in its final verse."[7] This inclusio demonstrates that the rebels and the wicked in Isaiah 1 and 66 refer to people in Israel "who by their actions are hindering YHWH's purposes for Zion to be 'the city of righteousness' to which the nations 'stream.'"[8] Thus, the judgment of the wicked becomes necessary so that Yahweh's work in the world can be accomplished. With the destruction of the wicked, they will no longer be there to disrupt God's work in the world and dishonor God by their behavior.[9]

THE HISTORICAL BACKGROUND OF ISAIAH 66

The correct exegesis of Isaiah 66:24 begins with the proper understanding of the historical context of the words of Trito-Isaiah. Some writers interpret Isaiah 66:24 as dealing with the destruction of sinners at the end of the age. However, such an interpretation removes the prophet's words from his historical context.

The historical background of Trito-Isaiah's message can clearly be understood from his words in verse 1. Scholars disagree with the historical situation that gave rise to Trito-Isaiah's criticism of the people in the post-exilic Jewish community. Smart asserts that Isaiah 66:1–6 reflects the prophet's objection to the rebuilding of the second temple in Jerusalem. According to Smart, Trito-Isaiah opposed Haggai's message that the rebuilding of the temple would renew God's favor upon the nation and would usher a time of great prosperity upon the land.[10] The same position is taken by Hanson who sees Isaiah 66:1–4 as a polemic against the temple and its ritual, which Trito-Isaiah and his followers considered an abomination against Yahweh.[11]

It is possible that the post-exilic community was divided over the importance of rebuilding the temple. However, a reference to the temple in verse 6 and the mention of people worshiping Yahweh in the temple in verse 23 seems to indicate that the prophet is not rejecting the temple or the worship of God that happens there. Trito-Isaiah's oracle is a polemic against cultic abuses. The prophet begins his oracle (Isa 66:1) by rebuking

---

7. Tomasino, "Isaiah 1.1—2.4 and 63–66," 86.
8. Olley, "'No Peace' in a Book of Consolation," 364.
9. Ibid., 369.
10. Smart, "A New Interpretation of Isaiah lxvi. 1–6."
11. Hanson, *The People Called*, 253–64.

the people in the post-exilic community who place their confidence in the temple, in the same way Jeremiah rebuked his contemporaries for their reliance on the temple. Mere reliance on the temple is not a guarantee of God's blessings upon the community. The prophet is also condemning the syncretistic practices of those who worshiped Yahweh in the temple.

Isaiah 66 speaks of two distinct groups who are clearly identified by the way they relate to Yahweh. They are the wicked who reject Yahweh and the faithful servants of Yahweh who are persecuted because of their commitment to be obedient to his words. The first group is composed of people who did what was evil in the sight of Yahweh, who rejected and corrupted the worship of God by their syncretistic practices. These were people who rebelled against Yahweh, who took delight in their own abomination, and chose not to please the Lord. These people are hostile to the servants of Yahweh because they are faithful to his laws. In his identification of those who rebelled against Yahweh, the prophet mentioned their false worship and some of their corrupt practices. The prophet accused them of killing people, of making pagan sacrifices that included breaking the necks of dogs, of offering swine's blood, and of worshiping idols (Isa 66:3). The unfaithful Jews criticized by Trito-Isaiah committed religious rituals that were condemned by the laws of Moses. These people sanctified and purified themselves and then went into the gardens and there ate the flesh of pigs, vermin, and rodents (Isa 66:17). Their behavior was an abomination to Yahweh. The prophet calls these unfaithful Jews those who "have chosen their own ways, and in their abominations they take delight" (Isa 66:3). These syncretistic practices were a flagrant violation of the Mosaic Law. Because of their unfaithfulness, Yahweh will judge them and will "bring upon them what they fear" (Isa 66:4).

The second group was the faithful servants of Yahweh. These faithful servants had three characteristics that set them apart from those who rejected Yahweh. They were humble, contrite in spirit, and they trembled at God's word (Isa 66:2). Those "who tremble at his word" (Isa 66:2, 5) are the pious people in Israel. They are the faithful followers of God, those who keep his commandments. Those who tremble at God's word shall be rewarded: "You shall see, and your heart shall rejoice; your bodies shall flourish like the grass; and it shall be known that the hand of the Lord is with his servants" (Isa 66:14). In order to assure them, Trito-Isaiah provides an eschatological view of the day when Yahweh will come to judge the nations and restore the true worship of God in the temple. It is a symbolic picture of the future.[12] The faithful people took comfort in the view that one day God would come

---

12. Fudge, "The Final End of the Wicked," 35.

to judge the world and vindicate their faith. In that glorious day, the faithful followers of God will participate in the blessings of the new age and what the Lord will do for Jerusalem (Isa 66:18–23). On that day, sinners will be destroyed by the devouring fire of a holy God (Isa 66:24).

According to Trito-Isaiah, there was an antagonism between the faithful people who served the Lord, "those who tremble at his word," and the people who rebelled against him. The animosity between the two groups is clearly expressed in verse 5: "Your brethren who hate you and cast you out for my name's sake" (RSV). These contending people were members of the same worshiping community. The faithful followers of Yahweh were rejected and criticized by the people who rebelled against God because they criticized their abominable practices. For this reason, they were thrown out of the temple and forbidden to worship there. The unfaithful Jews were scoffing at those who faithfully served the Lord. It is because of their attitude toward the faithful people that they were to be put to shame. The judgment against the evildoers will come from the temple, from where the Lord will bring retribution against them: "Listen, an uproar from the city! A voice from the temple! The voice of the Lord, dealing retribution to his enemies" (Isa 66:6). The reference to a voice coming from the temple indicates that the time for the oracle is after 516 BCE when the temple was already rebuilt.

Those who rejected the Lord have become his enemies. God's enemies will suffer a horrible judgment for "his indignation is against his enemies" (Isa 66:14; cf. Isa 1:24). Who are these enemies of God? Some scholars have identified them with the unfaithful followers of Yahweh mentioned in Isaiah 59:18: "According to their deeds, so will he repay; wrath to his adversaries, requital to his enemies; to the coastlands he will render requital." Others have identified the enemies with the pagan nations and the divine judgment with God's judgment upon the nations at the end of time: "The clamor will resound to the ends of the earth, for the Lord has an indictment against the nations; he is entering into judgment with all flesh, and the guilty he will put to the sword, says the Lord" (Jer 25:31). However, the context of Isaiah 66 is not the end of time or the judgment of the nations. Rather, Trito-Isaiah is referring to a group of people in his own day who opposed the faithful people who worshiped the Lord.

The punishment of those who rejected the Lord was to be a horrible judgment for "his indignation is against his enemies" (Isa 66:14). The prophet describes in vivid imagery the divine judgment of those who reject God. The theophany of Yahweh will be accompanied by fire, the agent of divine judgment. He will execute his anger with flames of fire. Yahweh will also come as a warrior and his sword will slay his enemies: "For the Lord will come in fire, and his chariots like the whirlwind, to pay back his anger in fury, and his rebuke in flames of fire. For by fire will the Lord execute judgment, and by his sword, on all flesh; and those slain by the Lord shall be many" (Isa 66:15–16).

These rebellious Israelites "have chosen their own ways" (Isa 66:3), so Yahweh "will choose their punishments" (Isa 66:4 NAS). Israel's punishment comes in the form of military war against Israel. According to the prophets of Israel, Yahweh, as a divine warrior,[13] fights against his own people.[14] In Isaiah 66:15–16 Yahweh is portrayed as the divine warrior who comes to defend his faithful followers and bring a severe punishment on those who have become his enemies. The war imagery is conveyed by the mention of "his chariots" (v. 15) and "his sword" (v. 16). Yahweh's name appears four times in this section to emphasize that the judgment is his work. The word "fire" appears three times to underscore the severity of the punishment. Judgment by fire also occurs in 66:24. Thus, the prophet emphasizes that Yahweh will come in anger and fury to rebuke the rebellious people and to execute judgment on his enemies.

The reference to people being killed by the word "sword" (66:16) seems to indicate that the judgment will come by means of a war. As a result of the battle, many people will be killed and their bodies will be left unburied. As the dead corpses begin to decompose, the putrefied bodies will generate worms. The bodies then will be burned to minimize the odor and to minimize the spread of diseases.

Isaiah 66:24 describes the result of God's judgment upon the wicked: "And they shall go out and look at the dead bodies of the people who have rebelled against me; for their worm shall not die, their fire shall not be quenched, and they shall be an abhorrence to all flesh" (Isa 66:24). The subjects of the divine punishment are not the nations, but the people in Israel who were in rebellion against Yahweh. The word *happōshʿim* ("the ones who rebelled," Isa 66:24) refers to unfaithful Jews (Isa 1:28, 46:8, 48:8). In his study on the punishment of the wicked, Olley concludes: "As there are many other links between chs. 1 and 66, it would seem most natural (*pace* some late Jewish interpretation) that in lxvi 24 reference is not to 'the nations' but

---

13. On Yahweh as a divine warrior, cf. Longman III and Reid, *God Is a Warrior*, and Nysse, "Yahweh is a Warrior."

14. On Yahweh's war against Israel, cf. Preuss, *Old Testament Theology*, 1:137.

to people in Israel/Jerusalem who persist in their rebellion."[15] According to Olley, the judgment upon the rebellious Jews came because they treated the message of comfort, forgiveness, and restoration lightly.

The words of the prophet should not be understood to refer to God's judgment upon the wicked at the end of history, the time after Christ returns to judge the living and the dead. In fact, Christopher R. Seitz has pointed out the similarity between Isaiah 66:24 and the decimation of the Assyrian army. He wrote, "The language is arguably influenced by Isaiah 36–37 and the description of the Assyrian defeat, which has here become a type of all national and internal rebellion."[16]

Rather, Isaiah 66:24 talks about people who lived in Trito-Isaiah's time, people who committed abominations and rejected Yahweh. Their bodies, infested with worms will be on display so that everyone could look at their bodies burning in the fire and see the terrible judgment of God upon those who rejected him. Nowhere in Isaiah 66:24 is the prophet saying that the dead people are suffering conscious unending torment. Rather, the prophet is referring to the total destruction of the people who rebelled against God. The burning fire is completely destroying the corpses of the dead. They are not being tormented. They do not feel any pain because they are all dead.

In his description of God's judgment upon the wicked, the prophet said that the fire would not be quenched until it consumed their bodies. He also said that those who trembled at God's word, the people who remained faithful to God, would go out and look at the bodies of the wicked in the place where their bodies were burning. The people who left Jerusalem could see the bodies of the wicked being burned in the fire, and the fire would not go out until all the corpses were consumed. Trito-Isaiah was not referring to an eternal fire, because eventually that fire would stop burning after the corpses were completely consumed.

This is also Jerome's view on the fire that shall not be quenched. Jerome (347–420), in his commentary on the book of Isaiah refers to the fire and the worm in Isaiah 66:24 as not being eternal. He wrote, "The fire, like the worm, must also be understood to burn as long as it has material with which the voracious flame is fed."[17]

Cyril of Alexandria (376–444) also does not take the fires of Isaiah 66:24 to be eternal. Speaking about the misfortunes that fell upon the Jewish people at the hands of the Romans, Cyril wrote: "Yet this is what perhaps

---

15. Olley, "'No Peace' in a Book of Consolation," 360.

16. Seitz, "Isaiah 40–66," 549. Fudge, *The Fire that Consumes* (2011), 78, also notes the similarity between Isaiah 37:36 and Isaiah 66:24.

17. Jerome's words are quoted in Elliot, *Isaiah 40–66*, 291.

is meant when it says, 'Their worm will not die nor the fire go out.' Some, however, want to refer these words concerning them to the time of the end of the age."[18]

Isaiah 66:23 speaks of the community of faithful who will come to the temple to worship the Lord every new moon and every Sabbath. As they leave Jerusalem and return to their homes, the worshipers see with their own eyes the dead bodies of the rebels who suffered the divine punishment in the same way the Israelites saw the dead bodies of Assyrian soldiers who were struck by the angel of the Lord (2 Kgs 19:35). The vision of the corpses burning and left exposed shall be abhorrent to everyone. When the worshipers left the temple and came to the place where the dead were, they did not see live people who were suffering, but corpses (*pegarim*) which were burning. In his study of the Hebrew word for corpse, *peger*, Hamilton wrote, "*peger* refers to the corpse of men, never of animals (except Gen 15:11), and not just the body immediately after death, but the corpse in which decay and stench have started (Isa 34:3)."[19]

In his study on the compilation of the book of Isaiah, Liebreich emphasized the importance of the expression "no one to quench" in Isaiah 1:31 and "shall not be quenched" in Isaiah 66:24. He said that the use of these two expressions represent a conscious effort to link the end of the book with its beginning.[20] Both chapters use the same word to describe the evildoers: those who "have rebelled against me." Both chapters use the same manner to describe the punishment upon the wicked: punishment by fire. Both chapters use the same way to describe the totality and the finality of the punishment: no one will be able to quench the fire.

People who see in Isaiah's words the triumph of Christianity and the appropriate punishment of the enemies of God[21] take the words of Isaiah out of the historical context in which they were proclaimed. The prophet is not referring to a time in the future when the kingdom of God will be established on earth. Nor is the prophet referring to the consummation of worldly affairs. Rather, Trito-Isaiah is dealing with issues that arose in Jerusalem after the remnant of Judah returned from its exile in Babylon.

---

18. Cyril's words are quoted in ibid., 291.
19. Hamilton, "*peger*," 2:715.
20. Liebreich, "The Compilation of the Book of Isaiah," 277.
21. Barnes, *Isaiah*, 445.

THE PLACE OF JUDGMENT

The prophet does not mention the place where these dead bodies are. He said that the corpses of the wicked are destroyed by fire outside Jerusalem in the presence of the righteous.[22] It is in the book of 1 Enoch 27 where the unfaithful Jews are tortured in the presence of the righteous in the "accursed valley."[23] According to the book of Enoch, the accursed valley is the second compartment of Sheol where sinners who have died without receiving the retribution for their sins will be punished. According to Russell, this is the first reference to hell in the apocalyptic literature. Eventually, this accursed valley became identified with the Valley of Hinnom.[24] It is for this reason that commentators identify the place mentioned in Isaiah 66:24 with the valley of Hinnom, the place which became known as Gehenna.

According to Jeremiah, the valley of Hinnom was the place where children were offered to Moloch and human sacrifices were made: "And they go on building the high place of Topheth, which is in the valley of the son of Hinnom, to burn their sons and their daughters in the fire" (Jer 7:31). The Topheth was probably the hearth or the furnace where the children were burned.[25]

Jeremiah says that when Jerusalem is conquered, the name of the place where human sacrifices is made will change: "Therefore, the days are surely coming, says the Lord, when it will no more be called Topheth, or the valley of the son of Hinnom, but the valley of Slaughter: for they will bury in Topheth until there is no more room. The corpses of this people will be food for the birds of the air, and for the animals of the earth; and no one will frighten them away" (Jer 7:32-33). The Babylonians will kill so many people in Jerusalem that the bodies of dead will not receive proper burial and will become food for the birds and other animals.

In another passage (Jer 19:1-13), Jeremiah gathers a group of elders and senior priests and takes them to the valley of Hinnom to be witnesses of what Yahweh will do to that place in the near future. Jeremiah proclaims that when Jerusalem falls to Nebuchadnezzar, king of Babylon, the place will become known as the valley of Slaughter because so many people will die in the invasion that bodies will be left unburied and people will be buried in that accursed place. He said, "I will make void the plans of Judah and Jerusalem, and will make them fall by the sword before their enemies, and

---

22. Russell, *The Method and Message*, 188.
23. Charles, *The Book of Enoch*, 52.
24. Russell, *The Method and Message*, 365.
25. The Mosaic Law prohibits child sacrifice, cf. Lev 18:21; 20:2-5; Deut 12:31; 18:10.

by the hand of those who seek their life. I will give their dead bodies for food to the birds of the air and to the wild animals of the earth" (Jer 19:6–7). Jeremiah's words are almost identical to the words of judgment against the unfaithful Jews described by Trito-Isaiah.

The word Gehenna comes from the Hebrew *gê' hinnōm*, "the valley of Hinnom." The valley of Hinnom was the place outside the walls of Jerusalem where human sacrifices were offered to Molech, the Ammonite god (Jer 7:31–33). The Topheth, the place where the sacrifices were made, was desecrated by Josiah "so that no one would make a son or a daughter pass through fire as an offering to Molech" (2 Kgs 23:10). "The valley also served for the incineration of the city's refuse and for dumping of animal carcasses and the bodies of criminals."[26] In post-exilic literature Gehenna became the place where the wicked are punished, although such a view does not appear in the Old Testament. According to Jeremiah, when Yahweh comes to judge his unfaithful people, the place will no longer be called Topheth or the valley of the son of Hinnom, "but the valley of Slaughter: for they will bury in Topheth until there is no more room" (Jer 7:32). This is what happened in Isaiah 66:24. The valley of Hinnom became the valley of Slaughter because those slain by the Lord were many (Isa 66:16). The only difference between the words of Jeremiah and the words of Isaiah is that Jeremiah said that some of the dead would be buried in Topheth while Isaiah said that the corpses of the slain were left unburied.

Isaiah 66:24 becomes the basis for the Jewish concept of Gehenna and the Christian view of hell as the place of everlasting punishment for the wicked. Jesus spoke of Gehenna as a place of destruction: "Do not fear those who kill the body but cannot kill the soul; rather fear him who can destroy both soul and body in hell [*Gehenna*]" (Mat 10:28). It is ironic that, according to Jeremiah, when Jerusalem is restored, the valley of Hinnom, the place that became known as the place of suffering and eternal punishment will become a holy place to Yahweh: "The whole valley of the dead bodies and the ashes, and all the fields as far as the Wadi Kidron, to the corner of the Horse Gate toward the east, shall be sacred to the Lord" (Jer 31:40). The valley that was defiled by human sacrifice and was the site of dead bodies left unburied will become "holy unto the Lord." On that day, the valley of Hinnom, the Gehenna of the New Testament, will "no longer exist as an affront to Yahweh."[27]

---

26. Werblowsky and Wigoder, "Geihinnom," 285.
27. Allen, *Jeremiah*, 359.

ISAIAH 66:24 IN MARK 9:48

According to Mark 9:44, 46, Jesus also used the words of Trito-Isaiah to refer to the punishment of the wicked. However, both verses are omitted in the best Greek ancient manuscripts. Several modern translations omit Mark 9:44, 46. The following translations omit these two verses in Mark: The New Revised Standard Version (NRSV), the Revised Standard Version (RSV), The Better Bible in English (BBE), The Complete Jewish Bible (CJB), The English Standard Version (ESV), The New American Bible (NAB), The New Jerusalem Bible (NJB), The Today New International Version (TNIV), The Good News Bible (GNB), and the Common English Bible (CEB).

In Mark 9:48 Jesus refers to the words of Isaiah 66:24 and mentions the undying worm and unquenchable fire as the punishment of the wicked in hell. The question is whether the reference to the undying worm and unquenchable fire should be taken literally since these words appear in a context that is highly symbolic, where Jesus speaks about cutting off one's hand, amputating one's foot, and plucking out one's eye.

The apocalyptic movement of post-exilic Judaism applied the text of Isaiah 66:24 to the punishment of the wicked. The book of Judith, a Jewish didactic fiction written in the first century BCE, equates fire and worms with endless weeping and pain: "Woe to the nations that rise up against my people! The Lord Almighty will take vengeance on them in the day of judgment; he will send fire and worms into their flesh; they shall weep in pain forever" (Jdt 16:17). This view is also present in other post-exilic and apocalyptic writings (see Sir 7:17). The church adopted the Jewish apocalyptic view that the undying worm and unquenchable fire are the agents that will contribute to eternal torment of the wicked in hell.

The interpretation of Isaiah 66:24 found in Jewish apocalyptic literature differs from the views of Trito-Isaiah. According to Trito-Isaiah, the reference to the fire that cannot be quenched does not refer to the fire of hell but to a real, historical judgment of the enemies of God. In his discussion of the use of Isaiah 66:24 in Mark 9:48, Marcus writes that the text in Isaiah "did not originally refer to hellfire but to a this-worldly judgment on the enemies of Israel."[28]

It is doubtful that Jesus' view on the future punishment of the wicked in Mark 9:48 is based on a Jewish novel or on the speculative apocalyptic writings of post-exilic Judaism since the concept of endless torment is not found in the Old Testament. Jesus' view of the punishment of the wicked in Mark 9:48 is consistent with the teachings of the Old Testament as expressed

---

28. Marcus, *Mark 8–16*, 697.

in the oracles of Trito-Isaiah. Trito-Isaiah's view of the punishment of the wicked is total death, not endless torment.

CONCLUSION

The punishment of the wicked mentioned in Isaiah 66:24 does not refer to the judgment of the nations that will occur after the return of Christ. The words of the prophet are addressed to a group of rebellious Jews who lived in Jerusalem in the post-exilic community. Because of their syncretistic practices, the prophet announced their punishment, which will happen when Yahweh comes to vindicate his faithful followers. On that day, the unfaithful Jews will be severely punished. They will die by the sword; their bodies will be left unburied and eventually set afire until they are completely destroyed. There is no mention of conscious torment in Isaiah 66:24 because the bodies being burned are the bodies of dead people.

When the prophet Isaiah spoke of what God was going to do against the mighty Assyrian army in the days of Hezekiah, the rebellious people of Judah were terrified: "The sinners in Zion are afraid; trembling has seized the godless: 'Who among us can live with the devouring fire? Who among us can live with everlasting flames?'" (Isa 33:14). Yahweh is the devouring fire because he is a holy God. Thus, those who turn away from Yahweh to serve other gods or who rebel against his word will face the severe judgment of God, for godless people "cannot dwell or abide in the presence of the Deity (cf. Isa 66:24)."[29]

---

29. Watts, *Isaiah 1–33*, 427.

12

Death, Eternal Life, and Judgment in the Gospel and Epistles of John

— Kim Papaioannou —

Kim Papaioannou was born and grew up in Greece. He holds a Bachelor's (1989) and Master's (1991) degree in Religion, from Newbold College, England, and a PhD in theology from the University of Durham (2005). His area of interest is the New Testament and Second Temple Judaism. He has served as pastor for fourteen years and as university professor for four, and enjoys writing on matters of faith and biblical exposition both academically and for a broader Christian audience. Kim is married to Esther, an educator (MA in Education), and God has blessed them with four wonderful children.

Eschatological judgment and the fate of the wicked play a prominent role in the Synoptic Gospels, Matthew, Mark, and Luke. Passages like the parable of the Rich Man and Lazarus (Luke 16:19–31), the parable of the Last Judgment (Matt 25:31–46), statements on Gehenna (e.g., Matt 5:22, 29, 30; 10:28; Mark 9:43–48; Luke 12:4–5), images of eschatological fire (e.g., Matt 3:10), among others, have attracted considerable attention in the ongoing discussion as to what exactly hell entails.[1] The Gospel of John,

---

1. E.g., Fudge, *The Fire that Consumes* (2011), 116–28, 148–54; Froom, *The Conditionalist Faith of Our Fathers*, 1:234–51, 286–304, 388–403; Morey, *Death and the Afterlife*; Papaioannou, *The Geography of Hell in the Teaching of Jesus*; Crockett and Gundry, *Four Views on Hell*; Morgan and Peterson, *Hell Under Fire*.

by contrast, has little to say on these issues and has been largely overlooked in the discussion. The same holds true even more of John's three epistles.

But that is not to say that these writings are silent. While detailed descriptions are lacking, John's vocabulary of life and death as well as incidental statements point to a very coherent outlook and one that is at variance with views of hell as a place of everlasting torment.

Discussions on the nature of the final judgment need to move beyond select proof-text passages to include other more obscure and incidental references. To that effect, a discussion of eschatological judgment in the non-apocalyptic writings of John aims to contribute. While the material is not abundant, it is weighty and can contribute to the bigger picture.

An understanding of the nature of the final judgment can be informed by a study on the nature of death. This is especially so for John who uses similar language to describe both death and the result of the final judgment. As such, this study will begin with a discussion of death before it moves on to a discussion of the final fate of the righteous and the wicked.

From this study the book of Revelation has been excluded and the reason is not its disputed authorship. While some doubt that John wrote Revelation, there is a strong voice, especially in the evangelical community that upholds Johannine authorship. The reason Revelation is excluded is that it has such a strong interest in eschatological judgment and such an abundance of relevant material, that it deserves and has received numerous studies on its own right. To try to treat it in the limited confines of this study would not do it justice. We will therefore focus only on the Gospel and his three epistles.

This study will be divided into three parts. First, John's depiction of death will be discussed; second, a few comments on eternal life will be made; third, texts that touch on the fate of the wicked will be tackled.

DEATH AND RESURRECTION

For John death is a state of no consciousness, a time of waiting until the resurrection. This becomes evident in the vocabulary he uses. There are a number of relevant words.

The main word is *thanatos*, which is used eight times in John's Gospel and six times in his epistles. The word can be used either of the temporal death that all humans die, righteous or wicked, or of eschatological death, which applies only to the wicked.[2] Revelation follows a similar pattern

2. E.g., John 11:4, 13 for a temporal use; 5:24, 8:51 for an eschatological use. See *LSJ*, s.v. "θάνατος."

whereby eschatological death is called the "second" death to distinguish it from the "first" temporal death (Rev 2:11; 20:14; 21:8). Of the fourteen uses in the Gospel and the epistles, eight have an eschatological application. Of the remaining six, four times *thanatos* is used in a temporal sense, and twice with reference to the death of Jesus.

The cognate verb *apothnēskō* appears twenty-eight times in the Gospel and none in the epistles, seventeen times of temporal death, four times of the death of Jesus, twice of eschatological death and three times in a context that can be either temporal or eschatological.

The interplay between temporal and eschatological death is important in understanding the nature of the final judgment and will be discussed in more detail below. For now we need only to make a few observations on the use of *thanatos/apothnēskō* in the temporal sphere.

Temporal death causes intense human sorrow and a sense of loss. This comes out most clearly in the raising of Lazarus where the noun and verb appear nine times in a temporal sense. When the disciples hear that Lazarus has died, Thomas expresses the desire to "die with him"[3] (John 11:16). The death also causes intense sadness to Martha and Mary, Lazarus's sisters. They weep (11:31, 33) with such intensity that Jesus is "deeply moved" and "greatly troubled" (11:33). Both Martha and Mary express their disappointment that Jesus did not come earlier, for had he, their brother would not have died (11:21, 32).[4] Such sorrow would seem unjustified had the sisters believed that Lazarus had gone to be with God.

When Jesus mentions to Martha the promise of the resurrection, Martha replies, "I know that he will rise again in the resurrection on the last day" (John 11:24). Martha did not anticipate any continued, blissful or dull existence at death, but only at the resurrection on the "last day."

Jesus in turn replies: "I am the resurrection and the life. Whoever believes in me, though he die, yet shall he live" (John 11:25). Two things are worth pointing out here. In the first clause Jesus binds together the concepts of resurrection and life. In other words, there is no life after death apart from resurrection. In the second clause Jesus indicates that this resurrection life will be received in the future, "yet shall he live."

John 11:26 seems to undermine what has just been noted by stating that whoever believes "shall never die." This statement is not intended to imply continued existence after death, but is an assurance that temporal death will be reversed. Wengst observes: "In both instances (v. 25 and v. 26) physical death is in focus. This death is not ignored but it is denied that it has

---

3. All Bible references from the ESV unless otherwise noted.
4. Cf. Bruner, *The Gospel of John*, 665.

ultimate significance, that it has the last word." He warns that Jesus words must not be placed antithetically to the promise of life at the resurrection.[5]

Apart from the words *thanatos/apothnēskō*, John also uses the verb *koimaomai*, "to sleep" (John 11:11). The comparison of death to sleep is very common in both the Old and New Testaments (e.g., 1 Kgs 2:10; 11:43; Job 3:13; Matt 27:52; Acts 7:60; 13:36; 1 Cor 7:39; 11:30; 1 Thess 4:13–17). The symbolism grew out of the obvious similarities between the two states—the body in lying position, the lack of communication with the environment, the appearance of lifelessness in the sleeping person.

It could also reflect the biblical belief in the resurrection. Just like a person who is asleep will at some point wake up, likewise all the dead will one day be resurrected, some to eternal life and others to judgment (John 5:28–29). It is worth noting in this respect that while John uses the vocabulary of sleep in relation to the first death, he never does so in relation to the second, eschatological death, since there will be no resurrection from the second death.

The comparison of death to sleep has long been used as evidence that at death there is no consciousness.[6] Just as there is no consciousness in sleep, likewise there is no consciousness in death: "For the living know that they will die, but the dead know nothing. . . . Their love and their hate and their envy have already perished, and forever they have no more share in all that is done under the sun" (Eccl. 9:5–6).

Others counter argue that the sleep in question affects only the body; that a person has a distinct entity within, an immortal soul, which escapes the body and goes to God if the person was righteous, or elsewhere if not. The metaphor of sleep therefore, they argue, only applies to the body.

This objection is negated in the writings of John by two facts. First, though the Greek word *psuchē*, "soul" can have a variety of shades of meaning,[7] in the Gospel and epistles of John it refers almost exclusively to biological life. For example, "the good shepherd lays down his life [*psuchē*] for the sheep" (John 10:11). It never refers to an immortal, intelligent entity that exists apart from the body and escapes the body at death

Second, John has a distinctly monist view of human existence; in other words man is one indivisible entity, not a combination of two, body and

---

5. Wengst, *Das Johannesevangelium*, 26, as cited in Bruner, 672. Schnelle, *Theology of the New Testament*, 745, writes: "No text in the Johannine writings states that believers are already raised from the dead. The Johannine concept of life does not exclude the reality of physical death."

6. Froom, *Conditionalist Faith*, 79–82.

7. *LSJ*, s.v. "ψυχή."

soul. This is evident in the way he refers to death and the tomb whereby he indicates that whole persons die and stay in the tomb:

> "Sir, come down before *my child* dies" (john 4:49).
>
> "Your fathers ate the manna in the wilderness, and *they* died" (John 6:49).
>
> Then Jesus told them plainly, "*Lazarus* has died" (John 11:14).
>
> "An hour is coming when *all who are in the tombs* will hear his voice" (John 5:28).
>
> He called *Lazarus* out of the tomb (John 12:17).

In these texts (among many) it is evident that what dies is a person, not the body of a person as supposedly distinct from the soul. And what lies in the tomb is the dead person, not the dead person's body as supposedly distinct from the soul.

This is also evident in the language of the resurrection. John in common with other biblical writers uses four key words to describe resurrection: the verb *egeirō* and the cognate noun *egersis;* and the verb *anistēmi* and the cognate noun *anastasis*. *Egeirō* means "to raise up" and can be used either of a raising from the dead, or simply of a raising from a lying position.[8] The cognate noun *egersis* appears only once in the New Testament (Matt 27:53) of the resurrection of Jesus and implies someone who stands up. *Anistēmi* and *anastasis* are compound words made up of the preposition *ana*, "again" and the word "to stand," giving the meaning, "to stand again."[9] This is exactly the meaning of "resurrect."

The language of resurrection clearly draws from the position of a person in life and death. In life a person stands, walks, runs, moves around. In death a person is placed in a prone position. At resurrection the person is made to stand again into the full vigor of life.

Just like with death and the tomb, resurrection also involves the whole person:

> "Do not marvel at this, for an hour is coming when *all who are in the tombs* will hear his voice and come out, those who have done good to the resurrection of life, and those who have done evil to the resurrection of judgment" (John 5:28–29).
>
> "Everyone who looks on the Son and believes in him should have eternal life, and *I will raise him up* on the last day" (John 6:40).

---

8. *LSJ*, s.v. "ἐγείρω."
9. *LSJ*, s.v. "ἀνίστημι" and "ἀνάστασις."

> *Lazarus* . . . *whom* Jesus had raised from the dead (John 12:1)
>
> He called *Lazarus* out of the tomb and raised *him* from the dead (John 12:17).
>
> *Jesus* was revealed to the disciples after *he* was raised from the dead (John 21:14).

More texts could be cited. But this sample is enough to indicate that in John's (and Jesus') view, resurrection involves the whole person, not a constituent part.

Of special interest is John 5:21: "For as the Father raises the dead and gives them life, so also the Son gives life to whom he will." In this text resurrection is tied to the act of "giving life." The Greek word for "give life" is *zōopoiō*, a compound word made up of *zōē*, "life," and *poieō*, to "make" or "create."[10]

The point is that at resurrection the Father and the Son don't just give life, but create life for the person who is raised, they make a person who has no life come alive. The implication is that before this act of resurrection, the person had no life.

Two last words pertinent to John's view of death is the verb *apollumi*, "to kill, destroy, lose" and the cognate noun *apōleia*, "loss, destruction, ruin."[11] The words, like *thanatos* but unlike *koimaomai*, can be used in both temporal and eschatological contexts, both of this life and of the final judgment. They are used of both humans and inanimate things.

I have elsewhere discussed *apollumi* and *apōleia* at length as they appear in the Synoptic Gospels and concluded that when used of eschatological judgment they imply death and destruction.[12] Their use in John is not dissimilar. They indicate loss when relating to inanimate things and death, the end of life when used of persons.

In John 6:12, after feeding the 5,000, Jesus commands that all leftovers be gathered so that "nothing may be lost," i.e., thrown away or wasted. In 6:27 he encourages his audience not to labor for the food that "perishes" but for the food that remains for eternity. In 10:10 Jesus warns that the thief only comes to steal "kill and destroy" and contrasts this with himself who came to give life in abundance.

In 11:50 Caiaphas declares that "it is better for you that one man should die [*apothnēskō*] for the people, not that the whole nation should perish [*apollumi*]." There is an obvious parallel between the words "die" and

---

10. *LSJ*, s.v. "ζωοποιέω."
11. *LSJ*, s.v. "ἀπόλλυμι" and "ἀπώλεια."
12. Papaioannou, *The Geography of Hell*, 52–56.

"perish." In 12:25 the person who "loves his life loses it [*apollumi*]" so that "he will keep it for eternal life." To lose one's life does not mean to move into another state of living existence but to be in a state without life, to cease to live. In 2 John 1:8 the apostle warns believers: "Watch yourselves, so that you may not lose what we have worked for." Clearly what is earned but wasted and lost is not had anymore.

In all these instances clear and complete loss is in view, whether of food that goes bad and is thrown away, or of life which is juxtaposed with death. There is no indication of another form of living existence between death and resurrection. It is this understanding of death that prompts Jesus to promise: "And if I go and prepare a place for you, I will come again and will take you to myself, that where I am you may be also" (John 14:2). The fact that Jesus will have to "come gain" to earth to "take" his people so that they can be with him indicates that between death and the resurrection at his coming, they are not in heaven, but on earth, awaiting his return asleep in the ground (cf. 1 Thess 4:17: "and so [at the parousia] we will always be with the Lord)."

We have looked at the vocabulary of John that relates to death and resurrection. We noted that the metaphor of sleep is used only of temporal death, the so-called "first" death that all humans die. By contrast, *thanatos* and *apollumi/apōleia* can be used of either temporal or eschatological death.

The language of death and resurrection apply to whole persons not just to the body. Life ceases at death and resumes at resurrection.

ETERNAL LIFE

We will now examine briefly the concept of eternal life. The key terms John uses to refer to the reward of the righteous are the noun *zōē*, "life," and the cognate verb *zaō*, "to live."[13]

Sometimes eternal life is referred to as a future reality, as one would expect, to be inherited at the end of the age. For example, in speaking of the resurrection Jesus declares that the righteous in their tombs will hear his voice and come out "to the resurrection of life" (John 5:29). Similarly, in John 3:16 he declares, "For God so loved the world, that he gave his only Son, that whoever believes in him should not perish but have eternal life." In the first instance eternal life is clearly future since it is tied to the resurrection; in the second it seems to be future since it is contrasted to eschatological "perishing."

---

13. *LSJ*, s.v. "ζωή" and "ζάω."

At other times, however, eternal life is something the believer already experiences in the present. "Truly, truly, I say to you, whoever hears my word and believes him who sent me has eternal life. He does not come into judgment, but has passed from death to life" (John 5:24). And, "We know that we have passed out of death into life" (1 John 3:14).

This future/present conflict is well brought out in John 3:36: "Whoever believes in the Son has eternal life [present tense]; whoever does not obey the Son shall not see life [future tense], but the wrath of God remains on him." In this text not only present and future tenses are juxtaposed, but life is contrasted to God's wrath that will fall upon sin. And while the wrath is usually an eschatological reality that will fall on the Day of Judgment, here it appears to already hang over the heads of unrepentant sinners.

The idea that both eternal life and wrath are present realities may help explain each other. Sinners are not experiencing now the eschatological wrath of God, neither were they doing so in the time of Jesus. Conversely, believers have not begun to live eternally. They are as much subject to temporal death as sinners are. Jesus himself said as much: "I am the resurrection and the life. Whoever believes in me, though he die, yet shall he live" (John 11:25).

It seems therefore that for John the current dimensions of eternal life and wrath are not existential but legal.[14] In other words, the believer does not experience eternal life in the present but rather receives the assurance of eternal life that will become a reality in the future. Likewise, the unrepentant sinner does not experience the eschatological wrath of God in the present, but nonetheless wrath is looming over his head, and its appearance is certain. It is as good as a done deal, so to speak. There is a certainty and assurance about both life eternal and wrath in the present, even though these will be experienced in the future: "Truly, truly, I say to you, whoever hears my word and believes him who sent me has eternal life. He does not come into judgment, but has passed from death to life" (John 5:24).

But despite this present dimension of life and wrath, John is clear that existentially both will be experienced in the judgment, after the resurrection: "Do not marvel at this, for an hour is coming when all who are in the tombs will hear his voice and come out, those who have done good to the

---

14. Bruce, *The Gospel of John*, 131, notes: "The believer does not need to wait for the last day to hear the judge's favourable verdict; it has been pronounced already.... This anticipation of a favourable verdict and resurrection life sums up what in more recent times we have come to call 'realized eschatology.'" See also Schnelle, *Theology of the New Testament*, 741-46.

resurrection of life, and those who have done evil to the resurrection of judgment" (John 5:28–29).[15]

Likewise in John 14:19 Jesus declares: "Yet a little while and the world will see me no more, but you will see me. Because I live, you also will live." Here Jesus declares three things. First, after his ascent, "the world," i.e., those who did not believe in him, would not see him again, at least not as a compassionate Savior but perhaps only as judge. Second, Jesus "lives"; he has eternal life in and of himself. Third, and in contrast to the world, by virtue of the fact that they have attached themselves to Jesus who "lives," his followers will themselves "live" in the future—Greek *zēsete*, future tense of *zaō*.

Summing up this section, in the Gospel of John and the epistles, eternal life is both a present and future reality. In the present assurance is given, in the future eternal life becomes an existential reality.

ESCHATOLOGICAL JUDGMENT

We now come to the key section of this short study, a discussion of eschatological judgment and especially its outcome. Before we examine pertinent texts, it is important to begin with a note on John's overall use of language in relation to judgment.

It was noted above and will be seen in the discussion below that the vocabulary of judgment that John utilizes is similar to what he uses for temporal death, namely *thanatos/apothnēskō* and *apōleia/apollumi*. This in itself is very important, for it implies a parallel between the temporal, first death, and the second, eschatological death. In other words, if temporal death propels a person into another form of existence of torment, then something similar would be expected to hold true after the day of judgment. Conversely, if at death a person ceases to live, then the use of similar language would suggest the same fate for unbelievers after the day of judgment. Similar language would suggest a similar fate.

Since nowhere in their descriptions of death do the gospel and the epistles of John speak of torment of any kind, we should beware of assuming everlasting torment after the Judgment. Since John uses the language of death both for temporal and eschatological death, we should consider that eschatological death is death, not torment.

Having made this initial note on John's vocabulary we can now explore relevant texts. John does not describe the final judgment in detail.

---

15. Moloney, *The Gospel of John*, 180, calls this eschatological resurrection, "traditional Jewish and Christian eschatological expectations." Cf. Carson, *The Gospel according to John*, 258.

But there are numerous statements that shed light on it. These are mostly juxtapositions where the fate of the righteous is juxtaposed with the stated or assumed fate of the wicked.

Eternal Life Contrasted with Death or the Absence of Life

The most common juxtaposition in John is between eternal life on the one hand and death on the other. In John 5:24 Jesus declares: "Truly, truly, I say to you, whoever hears my word and believes him who sent me has eternal life. He does not come into judgment, but has passed from death [*thanatos*] to life." And again in 1 John 3:14: "We know that we have passed out of death [*thanatos*] into life."

The death in view here is not the first, temporal death, for all persons irrespective of whether they believe in him suffer this death. The death from which the believer is released is the second death. If the believer will not face the second death, but has passed from death to life, it follows that the unbeliever will suffer the second death. So the punishment of the sinner is the second death.

In John 6:49–51 Jesus compares the exodus generation that ate the manna that God provided but nonetheless died (*apothnēskō*), with those who eat "the bread of life" that "comes down from heaven" (6:48, 50) who will receive life and live forever.[16] The juxtaposition between eternal life and death is clear.

The interesting point is that the exodus generation suffered the first, temporal death,[17] whereas when Jesus talks of life, he is talking of eternal life. So in a sense, Jesus contrasts the first temporal death, with the second, eschatological, eternal life. Is this a valid contrast? It is, since in John similar language is used of both the temporal and eschatological realm. The second death is a replication of the first, but without the prospect of a resurrection.

In John 6:53–54, Jesus returns to the contrast of life and death: "Truly, truly, I say to you, unless you eat the flesh of the Son of Man and drink his

---

16. Bruce, *The Gospel of John*, 158, surprisingly understands the life in view as a "spiritual life . . . safeguarded from the menace of death." But in the same page and in relation to 6:27 he speaks of "eternal life." This may give the mistaken impression that Jesus is speaking of two lives, a spiritual one that is present now and will not be touched by death, and eternal life which will be received at the end of the age. But this is not so. The life Jesus gives is one, eternal life, received by faith now and in reality at the end of the age.

17. Cf. Bruce, *The Gospel of John*, 157, who points out that though the generation in the wilderness ate the bread of heaven, that bread could not impart eternal life and so those who ate it died. Cf. Carson, *The Gospel according to John*, 294.

blood, you have no life in you. Whoever feeds on my flesh and drinks my blood has eternal life, and I will raise him up on the last day."

Three things are evident here. First, the believer has eternal life. Second, while the certainty of eternal life is received now, the reality of eternal life will be manifested when Jesus will raise the believer "on the last day,"[18] as was discussed already in the previous section. Third, by contrast to the believer, the person who does not believe will not receive life; he will instead die.

In John 6:63, Jesus declares that "it is the Spirit who gives life [*zōopoieō*]." As noted earlier, *zōopoieō* implies not simply a restoration of life, but creating life, bringing life to something or someone that does not have it. As such, the reference here could be either to the new birth, in the sense that when a believer is born again, he/she comes alive in a spiritual sense (cf. John 3:5), or it could be a reference to the resurrection of the dead at the end of the age (cf. Rom 8:11 where the Holy Spirit raised Jesus from the dead); or both experiences could be in view. If an eschatological application is in view here, then it follows that the unbeliever who will not be made alive by the Spirit, will be without life, dead.

In John 8:51, Jesus declares: "if anyone keeps my word, he will never see death [*thanatos*]." Clearly it is from the second death that believers escape, since the first death comes to all. The implication of the words of this text is that those who do not keep his word, will die the second death. That will be their fate.

In John 11:26, Jesus makes the same point in discussing death and resurrection with Martha: "everyone who lives and believes in me shall never die [*apothnēskō*]." But he explains what this means in the following words: "I am the resurrection and the life. Whoever believes in me, though he die [*apothnēskō*], yet shall he live" (11:25). The believer will indeed taste death, but only the temporal, first death. Jesus will raise him in the day of the resurrection since he is the "resurrection and the life." Again, since it is only those who believe in him that will "yet . . . live" it follows that those who fail to believe will not live.

In 1 John 3:15, John declares, "Everyone who hates his brother is a murderer, and you know that no murderer has eternal life abiding in him." The Greek for "murderer" is *anthrōpoktonos*, literally, a person who kills a person. So a person who removes the life of another person, will in turn not

---

18. Barrett, *Essays on John*, 43: "The eater still has to be raised up at the last day." Carson, *The Gospel according to John*, 297, observes that partaking of the flesh and blood of Jesus does not "immediately confer resurrection/immortality." These will be offered at the end of the age.

have life abiding in him. The point will come and life will be removed and the murdered will in turn die, not just temporarily, but eschatologically.

In 1 John 5:12 we read, "Whoever has the Son has life; whoever does not have the Son of God does not have life." Here John is obviously speaking of eternal life, since all, wicked and righteous alike, live now. The fate of the wicked then is absence of life.

In 1 John 5:16–17, John writes: "If anyone sees his brother committing a sin not leading to death [*thanatos*], he shall ask, and God will give him life—to those who commit sins that do not lead to death [*thanatos*]. There is sin that leads to death [*thanatos*]; I do not say that one should pray for that. All wrongdoing is sin, but there is sin that does not lead to death [*thanatos*]."

We will not go into a discussion of what kind of sins John has in mind. That is a separate study in itself. What is important for our purposes is his mention of death. Which death does John have in mind here? It is unlikely that he is talking of temporal death, since some of the weighty sins in the eyes of God like those mentioned by Paul in Galatians 5:19–21 would not cause death in this life. Clearly, John has the second death in mind. So in these two verse he describes the fate of the sinner by four times using the word "death."

Finally, in John 17:2, Jesus declares that the Father has given him authority "to give eternal life to all" whom the Father has given him. While Jesus does not state what will happen to the rest, the implication is that they will not receive eternal life.

Eternal Life Contrasted with *Apollumi*

In addition to the contrast between eternal life and eschatological death, in John we find a related contrast between eternal life and the verb *apollumi*. The verb is common also in the Synoptic Gospels in contexts of eschatological judgment. It has caused some confusion among commentators because it can carry two different meanings, "to lose," or "to destroy, kill." I have discussed this verb at length elsewhere.[19] When used in the context of judgment, the meaning is usually "to destroy" if the verb is in active voice or "to perish" if it is in passive voice.

In John's Gospel five texts are pertinent. The first and most famous is John 3:16: "For God so loved the world, that he gave his only Son, that whoever believes in him should not perish [*apollumi*—passive form] but have eternal life." The meaning here is fairly self-evident. "Perish" is almost

---

19. Papaioannou, *The Geography of Hell*, 52–56.

a synonym of "die."[20] Bruce notes that "to perish" is the alternative to having eternal life, and compares with 8:24 where "those who refuse to believe in Jesus will 'die in their sins.'"[21] Similarly, Carson notes: "the alternative [to eternal life] is to perish (cf. also 10:28), to lose one's life (12:25), to be doomed to destruction (17:12, cognate with 'to perish'). There is no third option."[22] So again, as we saw in several texts above, what we see here is a contrast between life and death. Clearly no everlasting torment can fit in any form or shape in this description.

In John 10:10 Jesus contrasts himself to a thief: "The thief comes only to steal and kill [*thuō*] and destroy [*apollumi*—active form]. I came that they may have life and have it abundantly." At first sight, an eschatological application is not immediately discernible; Jesus seems to be talking of every day realities. Nonetheless, eschatology lurks in the background. The "abundant life" for the believer may begin here and now, but in its fullness can only refer to eternal life. Likewise, the fact that Jesus uses two near synonyms, "kill and destroy" to characterize the work of the thief, could suggest that he is not only thinking of everyday realities but eternal ones. If that is the case, then the hendiadys "kill and destroy" is an emphatic way to underline the fact that those who attach themselves to the "thief" (Satan?)[23] will surely lose their life for eternity.

Jesus expands on this metaphor through another, by stating that he is the good shepherd who is willing to sacrifice his life for his sheep (John 10:11). By contrast, the hireling leaves the sheep and the wolves attack them (John 10:12). As the good shepherd Jesus gives his sheep "eternal life, and they will never perish [*apollumi*—passive voice]" (John 10:28). The eschatological dimension is clearer here. Jesus does not just give "abundant life" as in John 10:10, but "eternal life." By contrast, the sheep that do not recognize him as their shepherd will "perish."[24]

In John 6:39 *apollumi* seems to imply loss more than destruction or perishing: "And this is the will of him who sent me, that I should lose

---

20. Bruner, *The Gospel of John*, 203, who seems to believe in hell, takes an interesting and evidently self-contradicting approach to this text. On the one hand he translates *apollumi* as destruction and notes, "there is a danger of destruction." Yet, this destruction he understands not as real destruction but as "a life that is wasted" and "goes to hell."

21. Bruce, *The Gospel of John*, 90.

22. Carson, *The Gospel according to John*, 206.

23. For Moloney, *The Gospel of John*, 303, the "thiefs" and "robbers" of John 10:8 and 10:10 are the Jewish leaders who came before Jesus and rejected Jesus.

24. Moloney, *The Gospel of John*, 315, understand the perishing in question to mean "death." He notes: "an unwillingness to respond . . . will lead the Jews to death."

[*apollumi*] nothing of all that he has given me, but raise it up on the last day." This verse is unusual in that it uses the words "nothing" and "it," instead of "no-one" and "he/she" giving perhaps the impression that it is referring to objects rather than persons. However, the fact that it mentions resurrection "on the last day" is clear enough indication that persons are in view.[25]

What does "lose" imply here? Based on the use of the word alone we cannot be sure. The context however suggests "death" since it is contrasted with the resurrection in the last day. Therefore this verse divides people into two groups: those who will be raised in the last day (to life), and those who will be lost. To be lost therefore means to not partake of the resurrection of life.

Verse 40 throws additional light: "For this is the will of my Father, that everyone who looks on the Son and believes in him should have eternal life, and I will raise him up on the last day." So the person who believes receives eternal life and is resurrected to that effect, whereas the unbeliever does not.

The contrast between eternal life and the verb *apollumi* therefore also fits better a view of the final judgment where the result for the wicked is death and destruction rather than torment. Of the texts discussed above, this is clearly the case in John 3:16, 10:10, 10:28 and 6:39–40, and, though less clear, also seems to fit better in 6:27.

Other Images and Motifs

In addition to the juxtapositions between eternal life and death, and eternal life and *apollumi*, there are a few other pertinent texts that need to be explored if we are to build a fuller and more complete picture of eschatological judgment in John's Gospel and epistles.

Perhaps the most telling is the metaphor of the vine in John 15:1–8. Jesus compares himself to the true vine, while the disciples are the branches. Whoever abides in him will bring much fruit. But whoever does not abide in him will not bring forth fruit.

What will happen to those who do not bear fruit? In verse 2, Jesus gives the answer. Branches that bear no fruit "[the Father] takes away," meaning he will cut them off. Moloney writes: The Father destroys the branch that bears no fruit by separating it from the vine."[26] Then in verse 6 Jesus makes

---

25. Bruce, *The Gospel of John*, 154, is of the opinion that the neuter "all" (Greek *pan*) though impersonal, "speaks of the sum-total of his [Jesus'] people."

26. Moloney, *The Gospel of John*, 420. He adds: "Jesus is the lifegiving vine, but it is the Father who promotes growth and decides on the destruction of the unfruitful branches."

an even stronger statement: "If anyone does not abide in me he is thrown away like a branch and withers; and the branches are gathered, thrown into the fire, and burned."

The idea of the sinner as a fruitless plant that is thrown into the fire has strong counterparts in the other gospels. In Matthew 3:10, after comparing the Pharisees to a "brood of vipers" (v. 7), lacking in repentance (v. 8), John the Baptist declares: "Even now the axe is laid to the root of the tree. Every tree therefore that does not bear good fruit is cut down and thrown into the fire" (cf. Luke 3:9). Jesus expresses an identical sentiment in Matthew 7:19: "Every tree that does not bear good fruit is cut down and thrown into the fire." In Luke 13:7 and 9, the fate of a vine tree that does not produce fruit after repeated effort and care, is to be cut because it uses up the ground.

In Matthew 3:12, sinners are compared to chaff that is burnt with "unquenchable fire." "Unquenchable" does not mean a fire that will never go out, but rather a fire that is of such intensity that it cannot be quenched.[27]

In the natural realm when trees and plants that are no longer useful are thrown into the fire, they are certainly not thrown there to be tormented. They are thrown there either to be gotten rid of, or even to provide fuel. The casting into the fire is not an act of vengeance of any kind, but rather a cleansing process. Since the plants are no longer useful, they need not occupy space any more, or "use up the ground" as Jesus said.

The use of such metaphors for the spiritual realm indicates that something similar holds true here as well. Sinners are humans created by God just as much as believers are, God's children by creation. The final judgment must be God's most difficult act. To suggest that God would torment his children does not make sense. Rather, since he cannot give them the gift of eternal life since they have clung on to sin, the least painful and most fair action would be to remove them from the scene, much like a farmer removes through fire a tree that despite intense care refuses to bear any fruit.

In John 6:27, we have another metaphor for eternal realities. Shortly after the miracle of the feeding of the 5,000, the crowds seek Jesus to forcibly make him king (v. 15) because they have been fed out of nothing (v. 26).[28] A

---

27. Papaioannou, *The Geography of Hell*, 34. The Greek for "unquenchable" is *asbeston*, a compound word made up of the negating *a-* and the verb *sbennumi*, "to extinguish" or "put out." It implies the fire that cannot be put out. It concerns the intensity not the duration of the fire, and there is no intimation that the fire will not or cannot go out on its own once it has done its work and its fuel has been used up. Compare with Mark 9:48, a fire that "is not quenched." The force of the English "unquenchable" is similar.

28. Carson, *The Gospel according to John*, 284, draws a parallel with the women at the well in Samaria (John 4:15) who likewise wanted the water Jesus had to offer so that she would not make repeated trips to the well.

king who could thus feed multitudes would surely be able to eliminate hunger and poverty from among his people. As such, in their eyes, Jesus would be an ideal king. Jesus rebukes them for their focus on the material and instead declares: "Do not labor for the food that perishes [*apollumi*], but for the food that endures to eternal life, which the Son of Man will give to you."

Here Jesus compares two foods, physical food that perishes and spiritual food that leads to eternal life. The implication is fairly obvious. Those who eat only the perishable food will themselves perish. Those who eat of the food that leads to eternal life, will inherit eternal life. So there is an implied parallel between the fate of the food and the fate of the person who eats it. Food that has perished will be thrown into a garbage heap, and possibly burnt or buried so as not to pollute the environment through its foul smell. In that sense, the fate of the perishable food is similar to the fruitless tree.

Of interest is that the word for "perish" here is the verb *apollumi* already discussed above, and which was noted, implies death/destruction. It is usually used of persons, not inanimate objects like food.[29] Perhaps it is used here intentionally to tie the fate of the perishable food with the fate of the sinner who will likewise perish.

The Final Judgment as Exclusion

In the Synoptic Gospels one of the most prominent motifs in relation to eschatological judgment is that of the outer darkness where there will be weeping and gnashing of teeth. Though often understood as a description of the sufferings of the torments of hell, a study of the vocabulary and context indicated that the outer darkness is the darkness outside a banqueting hall which in the contexts in question is a symbol of the kingdom. So to be in the outer darkness is to be excluded from the kingdom. Likewise, the weeping and gnashing of teeth are not descriptions of torment but of sadness (weeping) and anger (gnashing of teeth) of the ones left outside who thought they would be inside. So the whole description is not one of torment but of the sadness of the loss of the kingdom. It is language of exclusion.[30]

John does not mention the outer darkness or the weeping and gnashing of teeth, but twice he describes the kingdom in terms of exclusion and loss.

---

29. Of ninety occurrences of *apollumi* in the New Testament, seventy-nine times it refers to humans or parts of the human body, or other living beings, and eleven times to inanimate things.

30. Papaioannou, *The Geography of Hell*, 177–233.

In the first, in John 3:3 Jesus declares to Nicodemus: "Truly, truly, I say to you, unless one is born again he cannot see the kingdom of God."[31] In the second, John 3:5, again in the context of the discussion with Nicodemus, he repeats: "Truly, truly, I say to you, unless one is born of water and the Spirit, he cannot enter the kingdom of God."[32]

In the same context Jesus spoke of judgment in terms of "perishing" (John 3:16) as discussed above. Putting the whole picture together it seems that those who fail to exercise faith fail to enter the kingdom and end up perishing. Yet, the sad point is not so much that they perish, but that they have failed to receive the Spirit, be born again, and therefore see/enter the kingdom. The fact that they lose out on the kingdom is much worse than what they suffer. In that context, eschatological judgment is more about the sadness of the loss of the kingdom and less about the punishment, death.

SYNOPSIS AND CONCLUSION

This study looked at the themes of death, eternal life, and the final judgment in John's Gospel and epistles. With regards to eternal life, it appears both as a present reality, and as a future one to be inherited on the resurrection day. Eternal life in the present appears primarily as a judicial reality, the certainty that a person who believes now in the present receives the certainty of eternal life. As an existential reality, eternal life is yet future.

With regards to temporal death, we noted that in these writings death is the absence of life. At death life ceases, and resumes again at the resurrection.

With regards to the fate of the wicked we noted that John uses similar vocabulary to describe their fate as he does to describe temporal death. This alone would suggest a parallel in nature between temporal death and the final fate of the wicked. An examination of a long string of relevant texts

---

31. The kingdom of God is a very prominent motif in the Synoptic Gospels and draws from the Old Testament concept of God as Sovereign (cf. e.g., Bruce, *The Gospel of John*, 82–83; Carson, *The Gospel according to John*, 188; Exod 15:18; Ps 103:19; Matt 12:28; 21:23; Mark 1:15; 4:26). In John the kingdom of God appears only twice (3:3 and 3:5) but the expression "eternal life" is closely related (see Bruner, *The Gospel of John*, 199–200). According to Bruce, *The Gospel of John*, 83, "to 'see the kingdom of God'" means to have a share in the final consummation of God's kingly rule, participation in the age to come.

32. Carson, *The Gospel according to John*, 188: "To a Jew with the background and convictions of Nicodemus, 'to see the kingdom of God' was to participate in the kingdom at the end of the age, to experience eternal, resurrection life."

indicated that this is indeed the case. The fate of the wicked is never described in terms of torment but in terms of death, perishing, and the absence of life.

Perhaps the whole study can be summarized in the well-known and beautiful if sober words of Paul: "for the wages of sin is death, but the free gift of God is eternal life in Christ Jesus our Lord" (Rom 6:23).

13

Hades in Revelation

— ROGER HARPER —

The Reverend Roger Harper is an Anglican vicar who studied at the University of Cambridge (French and Russian) and St. John's College, Nottingham (Theology). He is also the author of The Lie of Hell, *which Edward Fudge has called "a stimulating and nuanced form of conditional immortality likely to invigorate Bible students of all persuasions."*

Roger originally presented the following paper at the Rethinking Hell conference, 2014.

METHOD

When doing biblical theology, where do we begin? Some scholars begin with Genesis or with the Old Testament as a whole. This approach follows a simple logic, to start with the first page of the Bible. The Bible, though, is a library and it is not good practice to begin at the first entry in the library catalogue. Deeming the oldest understandings the most important is an assumption that sits uneasily with Jesus saying, "You have heard it said . . . but I say to you . . . ." Why begin with an understanding that may be contradicted later? For Christians, Jesus is the foundation and cornerstone, the place to begin building.

Biblical theology is like piecing together a jigsaw. The Bible is a wonderful collection of books which together contain a large number of jigsaw pieces. If we want a true picture of something, we take all the relevant pieces from all the books and join them together. Edward Fudge used the jigsaw metaphor:

> Biblical theology uses biblical data to paint a picture until it runs out of data. Systematic theology uses biblical data like jigsaw puzzle pieces to create a picture it already had, sometimes inventing data to fill in for missing pieces. Historical theology arranges these puzzles from through the centuries to show how they developed.[1]

Fudge here points out the danger of starting with a picture we already have rather than with the pieces we are given. We need to see the biblical data as jigsaw pieces with existing colors and shapes which make only one fully coherent picture rather than as a supply of materials from which we can make a range of pictures. The biblical jigsaw pieces have to fit together naturally. Most of us have had the frustration of "knowing" that a jigsaw piece fits in a particular place in a jigsaw, only to find that it does not slot into place easily. We are tempted to force the piece into the place we think it has to go.

Some people have a picture of hell as everlasting torment. This is a common picture, painted in lurid colors, which most of us have been given. We then take the biblical pieces with the word "destruction" and twist, mangle, or even chop these pieces to make them fit. As Fudge has demonstrated conclusively ultimate destruction cannot be made to fit with eternal torment. The jigsaw pieces themselves show us, when we look at them as objectively, that the picture of hell as eternal torment is not the biblical picture.

Jigsaw pieces can also be put to one side and not used. Revelation 1:18 is a jigsaw piece which has been put to one side both by traditionalists and conditionalists. John MacArthur quotes many verses in his sermon, "The Truth about Hell," but does not mention this verse. Fudge quotes many verses in *Hell: A Final Word*, but not this one. It is hard to find a single writer on the biblical understanding of hell who has given a significant place to this text. All the jigsaw pieces need to be seen for what they are, looked at carefully and fitted in smoothly. All the jigsaw pieces are useful for making the full picture.[2] With which jigsaw pieces do we begin? The edge pieces are identified first. The corner pieces are put into place first. For Christians Jesus is the cornerstone and foundation. The words of Jesus, the stories by Jesus and about Jesus, are given to us as the place where we start.

If in doing biblical theology we begin with Genesis we may well find that we are using inside pieces as corner pieces, creating a more or less false

1. Fudge, *Gracemail*, June 4, 2014.
2. 2 Tim 3:16.

picture. Or, changing to a building metaphor, we may find that we are using roofing materials as foundation stones, to create a structure which does not properly hold together and can be unsafe. If we begin with Jesus we know that we are beginning with the given corner pieces, creating a true picture, building from the foundation stones, a structure which will last. Starting with Jesus may lead us to: "You have been given this picture . . . , but I am showing you . . . ." The picture we see as we piece the jigsaw together may not cohere with the picture we already have in mind. The film *Hell and Mr. Fudge* shows the slow and painful process of fundamental picture-changing. We need to be continually open to this process, to the possibility of rethinking again.

Nowadays there is debate as to how much any of us can look objectively, how much we can see what we are not in some way already looking for. It is useful to be aware of our own prior assumptions. The advances of science show us, however, that we can come to see a clearer picture than the one we've been handed, whether it is a picture of the sun at the center of our solar system, a picture of light travelling, or of subatomic particles. Contemporary Christians who seek to have their understanding shaped by the Bible, can also come to see in the Bible fresh insights that paint a clearer and more complete picture than we've inherited or have pieced together hitherto.

REVELATION 1:18

> Do not be afraid; I am the first and the last, and the living one.
> I was dead, and see, I am alive forever and ever; and I have the keys of Death and of Hades.

These words are not only the first mention of "Hades" in the book of Revelation, but they are, as all words of Jesus, a corner piece to the jigsaw, part of the foundation and cornerstone of our understanding of what happens to the unrighteous after death. For this paper I follow the common Christian understanding that these words are from Jesus, rather than only from John the writer. Indeed, these words communicated to John by Jesus after his death and resurrection were written down much sooner than any of the words of Jesus in the Gospels, so, in this way, we can be more certain that these are the words of Jesus. We note, too, that these words are not figurative; this is not language in which what is said represents something else. Later in the book of Revelation the Lamb represents Jesus; here Jesus speaks as himself. Jesus is truly alive. When he says that he was dead, he refers to his actual death on the cross. When he says that he is alive, he refers to his actual resurrection. It is right also to understand that when Jesus talks of death and Hades, these are not metaphors but realities. Here we have cornerstone insight into the reality of death and Hades.

No Fear

Jesus begins by saying, "Do not be afraid." These words apply to all that follows. If anything we say about these verses actually causes or increases fear, it is not a true understanding of this corner piece of the jigsaw. All our understanding of these words of Jesus and what follows from them must lessen fear.

Free Access

"I have the keys," says Jesus. Having keys means having the right of entry and exit, having free access, for oneself and for others. A prison chaplain has keys, can go in and out of any part of the prison. The chaplain can take prisoners with them from one part to another. Jesus has the keys; Jesus has the right of entry and exit for himself and whoever is with him.

What is Hades?

"I have the keys of Death and of Hades," says Jesus. What or where is Hades? This is a key question (pun intended). To answer it we need to look at other places where Jesus uses the name Hades:

> "And you, Capernaum, will you be exalted to heaven? No, you will be brought down to Hades. For if the deeds of power done in you had been done in Sodom, it would have remained until this day." (Matt 11:23 / Luke 10:15)

> "And I tell you, you are Peter, and on this rock I will build my church, and the gates of Hades will not prevail against it." (Matt 16:18)

> "In Hades, where he was being tormented, he looked up and saw Abraham far away with Lazarus by his side. He called out, 'Father Abraham, have mercy on me, and send Lazarus to dip the tip of his finger in water and cool my tongue; for I am in agony in these flames.' But Abraham said, 'Child, remember

that during your lifetime you received your good things, and Lazarus in like manner evil things; but now he is comforted here, and you are in agony. Besides all this, between you and us a great chasm has been fixed, so that those who might want to pass from here to you cannot do so, and no one can cross from there to us.'" (Luke 16:23–26)

As these texts show, Hades is mentioned in parable and outside parable. Hades is not just a fictional place in parable, any more than Jerusalem and Jericho are fictional places in parable. It is right to assume that the place Jesus talked of but did not describe outside of the parable is the same place that Jesus described a little more in the parable, and that these descriptions, albeit somewhat poetic, convey important truths about the place Hades. From the teaching of Jesus above, we see that Hades is a place to which people, especially those who reject Jesus or reject compassion for the poor, are brought down after death; it is an unwelcome place, a place of suffering.

Hades in Luke 16

It has been argued, however, that we can learn nothing about Jesus' understanding of Hades from the parable of the Rich Man and Lazarus. Gregory Crofford, for instance, recently stated that "Jesus' story is a cautionary tale meant for this life and is not a road map to the next."[3] Kim Papaioannou also argued extensively along these lines.[4] The argument of Crofford and Papaioannou is that parables contain only one point of teaching and that the existence of other similar stories at the time of Jesus casts doubt on the extent to which Jesus intended to convey information about Hades. (Papaioannou does, however, argue that Jesus made two points in the parable: Care for the poor now, and don't trust stories which purport to give insight into life after death.)[5]

There is not space here to give a detailed examination of the parable of the Rich Man and Lazarus, but the headings of a counter-argument to Crofford and Papaioannou are as follows:

Parables can contain more than one truth, especially if they are closely related: "Care for the poor now, so that you don't suffer in future," can easily be understood to be the dual message of this parable. This meaning is consistent with the message of other warning parables. The Wise and Foolish Virgins teaches, "Make sure you have extra oil now so that you are not shut

3. Crofford, *The Dark Side of Destiny*, 24.
4. Papaioannou, *The Geography of Hell*.
5. Ibid., 134–35.

out in the end." The Prodigal Son teaches, "Welcome those whom the Father welcomes, so that you do not shut yourself out of the celebration." Jesus specifically names the dwelling place of the rich man beyond death "Hades." He could have constructed a story with a more metaphorical location, as he did in other parables.

Jesus aimed his teaching only at those with ears to hear rather than those with prior theological or cultural knowledge. These "simple" people would assume that he was indeed giving insight into the nature of the place he had spoken of on other occasions to be as real as Capernaum. If Jesus had spoken of Hades knowing that many people would indeed draw unwarranted conclusions about that place, he would have been issuing a severe empty threat. It is inconsistent for Christians to see Jesus as an issuer of empty threats or warnings.

Jesus also taught on another occasion a very similar truth to the picture of Hades contained in the parable:

> "There will be weeping and gnashing of teeth when you see Abraham and Isaac and Jacob and all the prophets in the kingdom of God, and you yourselves thrown out." (Luke 13:28)

> "I tell you, many will come from east and west and will eat with Abraham and Isaac and Jacob in the kingdom of heaven, while the heirs of the kingdom will be thrown into the outer darkness, where there will be weeping and gnashing of teeth." (Matt 8:11–12)

This, too, was not an empty warning but a real warning of a real Hades similar to that contained in the parable of the rich man and Lazarus.

Hades Distinct from Gehenna

Hades is one of two words used by Jesus to describe the fate of the wicked after death; the other is Gehenna. Bible translations have hidden the difference for centuries, using the same word, "hell" in English, for both Hades and Gehenna. Even before vernacular translations, from the time of the Latin Bible, it was very widely assumed that Hades and Gehenna are the same place. When Jesus says that he has the keys of Hades, is this another way of saying that he has the keys to Gehenna? Edward Fudge has written, particularly recently, that hell is Gehenna, the eschatological consuming fire.[6] This implies that Hades is not hell. But the Hades texts have always

---

6. Fudge, *Hell: A Final Word*, 21.

been seen as part of the one jigsaw picture of hell. We conditionalists need to make sure that our understanding includes the Hades texts as well as the Gehenna texts or we will not be seeing the full picture.

Reasons for thinking that Hades and Gehenna are different are as follows:

Different names usually refer to different places.

There are some differences in meaning associated with the two different words. Hades is described as a place for people, Gehenna as the place for the devil and his angels. Hades is a place people go down to after death. Gehenna is a place into which the devil, his angels, and some people, are thrown after the final judgment. Hades is a place of darkness. Gehenna is a place of fire. Fire and darkness do not normally coexist.

The understanding of two consecutive places for the unrighteous after death is consistent with the understanding of two places for the righteous after death: paradise and the new heaven/earth.[7]

If Hades and Gehenna are the same place to which Jesus has the keys, then Jesus has the keys to the eternal fire where people are consumed like chaff. How does that make us "not fear?" Chaff burns so quickly and irrevocably that there can be no escape. Jesus having the keys of Gehenna makes no difference to the awful reality of Gehenna, in no way diminishes our fear of Gehenna. Jesus having the keys of Gehenna makes no sense.

If Hades and Gehenna are the same place, Jesus has radically changed his teaching. In Matthew 10:28 Jesus says, "Fear him who has power to destroy soul and body in Gehenna." In Revelation 1:18 Jesus says, "Do not fear . . . I have the keys of Death and Hades." Jesus is the same yesterday, today and forever, and we cannot understand him as telling us to fear and then not to fear the same place. If Hades and Gehenna are distinct, it makes sense to fear him who has power over one, and not fear him who has power over the other.

These are strong indications that Hades and Gehenna are not the same place. Another indication is to come as we look further in Revelation. For now, distinctness is a good working hypothesis.

From the teaching of Jesus we understand that Hades is a place to which people, especially those who reject Jesus or reject compassion for the poor, are brought down after death; an unwelcome place, a place of suffering and a place distinct from Gehenna. Jesus has the keys to this place.

---

7. Wright, *Surprised by Hope*.

Hades is Sheol. Soul Sleep?

Another important insight about Hades comes from Acts.

> "Fellow Israelites, I may say to you confidently of our ancestor David that he both died and was buried, and his tomb is with us to this day. Since he was a prophet, he knew that God had sworn with an oath to him that he would put one of his descendants on his throne. Foreseeing this, David spoke of the resurrection of the Messiah, saying, 'He was not abandoned to Hades, nor did his flesh experience corruption.'" (Acts 2:29–31)

Here Peter, speaking on the day of Pentecost, quotes Psalm 16, using Hades as a translation of the Old Testament word "Sheol." Sheol was the most common Old Testament word for the general abode of the dead. According to Acts 2, Hades is synonymous with Sheol. The most common understanding of Sheol was that it is a place of half-life, of very limited consciousness, or "soul sleep." If we begin our thinking about Sheol/Hades with Jesus, we see first that Hades is a place for the unrighteous and then that Hades is a place for all people. From this we can understand that all people are unrighteous, all have sinned and fallen short of the glory of God, or that Hades contains both parts for general humanity and parts for the particularly unrighteous. (Jesus talked of an "outer darkness" which could imply also an "inner darkness.") However for those who start with the Old Testament understanding of Sheol, it is common to argue that Sheol/Hades is a place of "soul sleep" and that Jesus' mention of conscious torment, as in the parable of the Rich Man and Lazarus, is hyperbole. We have already seen that there are good reasons to understand the description of Hades in the parable of the Rich Man and Lazarus not as hyperbole, but as conveying information, albeit in somewhat poetic form, about Hades. The rich man in Hades is not in a state of soul sleep, but is feeling, thinking, talking and even arguing.

It is important also to ask how Jesus having the keys of Hades would diminish fear, if Hades is soul sleep. If people die physically and are then in suspended animation until the resurrection and final judgment, Jesus can use his keys to look at these people but his presence would make no difference them. But Jesus having the keys of Hades can make a difference to people in conscious affliction. Jesus can visit them and they can be conscious of his presence. Jesus has the power also to use his keys to release them from Hades. This is indeed an antidote to fear. If Hades is not soul sleep but conscious affliction, it is indeed a place to fear, and knowing that Jesus has the keys diminishes that fear.

Implications of "I have the keys of death and Hades."

Jesus says, "I have the keys." The normal understanding of "the keys" *is all the keys* to every part of Hades. Jesus does not say, "I have keys to Hades," which could mean that he has some keys and not others. He does not say, "I have keys to some parts of Hades." Jesus has the full set of keys to every part of Hades, not only the parts containing the people from before the flood, not only the parts inhabited by the patriarchs, not only to a kind of antechamber. Jesus has the keys to every corner of Hades, giving him access to every soul in Hades.

Jesus says, "I have the keys." As he speaks, he still has, still holds, the keys. Jesus did not say, "I have had the keys and have no more use for them." Jesus did not use his keys once to release only a few people. Jesus did not use his keys once to release all people, opening the gates of Hades once and for all so that all are free to leave. The keys to Hades are a permanent possession of Jesus. Jesus holds the keys so that he can continue to use them.

Jesus saying that he has the keys is therefore one indication that he continues to use them, or at least has the possibility of using them. Other indications that Jesus uses his keys are his choosing to broadcast his key-holding and in the claim that his key-holding diminishes our fear. If Jesus does not use his keys, he is saying, "I have the keys. I just want you to know. I never use them, but they're a great symbol of the full reach of my authority." In this case, Jesus having the keys makes no difference to anybody, and certainly does not lessen their fear. It would instead make them more afraid of Jesus, as they understand that he has the ability to release them and others, but chooses not to use this power. Jesus having the keys of Hades and not using them is inconsistent with his character. Jesus said that he came to seek and to save the lost. Unlocking people from Hades is consistent with the character and mission of Jesus and is a clear antidote to fear. Hence Jesus declaring that he has the keys of Hades is should be taken as indicating that he continues to use these keys.

In the parable of the Rich Man and Hades, the rich man is told that a great chasm has been fixed between Hades and "the bosom of Abraham," which no one can cross. This could be an indication that Jesus cannot use the keys of Hades. We need, though, to be careful not to take the words spoken by a character in a parable as the direct words of Jesus. In the parable Abraham explains about the chasm. This is the understanding of Abraham, not necessarily that of Jesus. Abraham was the great father-figure and great man of faith. He was not, however, a great conveyor of God's truth, not a prophet, nor a law-giver. Abraham's words express the common traditional Jewish understanding, which contain a good deal of truth, but are not authoritative for all time. Jesus' own words indicate that, since his death and resurrection, he has ability to bridge the chasm. It remains true that no ordinary human, such as Lazarus, has the ability to cross the chasm, to come to people in Hades. Jesus, however, the one who uniquely has died and has risen, who is now uniquely alive for ever, does have the ability to cross the chasm, an ability which he expresses in a different picture, that of having the keys of Hades.

Another verse which has been used to argue against Jesus using his keys to Hades is Hebrews 9:27: "it is appointed for mortals to die once, and after that the judgment." Several scholars have, however, pointed out that the writer to the Hebrews says nothing about how soon judgment follows death. The writer to the Hebrews here asserts that there is no opportunity to return to this life after death. The writer does not deny the possibility of Jesus reaching someone between their one death and their final judgment.

There are no other clear indications in the rest of Scripture that Jesus, who has the keys of Hades, does not or cannot use them. This post-mortem salvation by Jesus has not been generally understood by Christians, and, indeed, has been deemed unbiblical by many. It has been argued that the onus is on those who propound post-mortem salvation to provide biblical justification. This exposition of Revelation 1:18 shows the required biblical justification and more will follow in this paper. The onus is now on those who dispute post-mortem salvation by Jesus to provide biblical justification for their view.

Conclusions from Revelation 1:17–18

The following, then, comprise a corner piece of the jigsaw puzzle which needs to be primary in our consideration:

- Hades is distinct from Gehenna
- Hades is before the final judgment
- Hades is a place of affliction for the callous and those who reject Jesus before the final judgment
- Hades can therefore be understood as a remand prison for those awaiting judgment
- Hades is open to Jesus who has the keys of Hades, and is likely to use these keys as God Saving
- All people in Hades have the potential to be released, saved, by Jesus but for this they need the specific intervention of the key-holder

REVELATION 6:7–8

> When He opened the fourth seal, I heard the voice of the fourth living creature call out, "Come!"
> I looked and there was a pale green horse! Its rider's name was Death, and Hades followed with him; they were given authority over a fourth of the earth, to kill with sword, famine, and pestilence, and by the wild animals of the earth.

Hades follows death. Death sweeps people into Hades. Who decides how many people they can imprison? The Lamb, Jesus. He has the keys. He decides who goes in. We see here that Jesus uses his keys to unlock Hades so that a limited number of people, determined by Jesus, enter Hades. This shows that Jesus does use his keys. In this instance, though, there is no antidote to fear, but rather a strengthening of the potential to fear Jesus.

REVELATION 20:11–15

> Then I saw a great white throne and the one who sat on it; the earth and the heaven fled from his presence, and no place was found for them. And I saw the dead, great and small, standing before the throne, and books were opened. Also another book was opened, the book of life. And the dead were judged according to their works, as recorded in the books. And the sea gave up the dead that were in it, Death and Hades gave up the dead that were in them, and all were judged according to what they had done.
> Then Death and Hades were thrown into the lake of fire. This is the second death, the lake of fire; and anyone whose name was not found written in the book of life was thrown into the lake of fire.

At the final judgment, Hades is emptied. This confirms the understanding of Hades as a remand prison for people pending the final judgment. Once the judgment has begun, there is no further use for the remand prison. Hades is then thrown in the lake of fire. The lake of fire is understood, especially by conditionalists, as Gehenna. Hades is thrown into Gehenna. This confirms the understanding that Hades and Gehenna are not the same place. Hades and Gehenna are separate, distinct places. It is not even that the one place named Hades before the final judgment is named Gehenna after it, for this is inconsistent with the picture in Revelation 20. Hades is one place, which is thrown into another place, the lake of fire, Gehenna. Death is also thrown in the lake of fire and is no more. We know that death is the last enemy to be destroyed.[8] Death is not eternal. Hades, the partner of Death whose ultimate fate is the same as Death's, is not eternal.

We know also from these verses and from the following chapters that the ultimate fate of the unrighteous after the final judgment is to be thrown into the lake of fire, Gehenna. The unrepentant wicked will be destroyed, taken out of life, outside the heavenly Jerusalem where there is no life at all. The unrighteous will ultimately be removed from the life-giving, luminous, presence of the Lamb.[9] After the final judgment the righteous will enjoy the presence of the Lamb, will live in his light, in his city. The unrighteous will have none of these benefits.

REVELATION 14:9–11

> Then another angel, a third, followed them, crying with a loud voice, "Those who worship the beast and its image, and receive a mark on their foreheads or on their hands, they will also drink the wine of God's wrath, poured unmixed into the cup of his anger, and they will be tormented with fire and sulfur in the presence of the holy angels and in the presence of the Lamb. And the smoke of their torment goes up for ever and ever. There is no rest day or night for those who worship the beast and its image and for anyone who receives the mark of its name."

These verses have been a main proof text for hell as eternal torment. If Hades and Gehenna are the same place, both are places of torment forever and ever. But Hades and Gehenna are not the same place. This has been established conclusively. The place described in Revelation 14 must therefore be either Hades or Gehenna. Which place are these verses describing?

A key distinction between Hades and Gehenna is that one is in use before the final judgment and the other after. Is the place of torment described in Revelation 14 before or after the final judgment? Further on in Revelation 14, John looks again and sees more of the same series of visions. In verse 14 he sees one like the Son of Man, seated on a white cloud with a crown on his head and a sharp sickle in his hand. He is told that now is the time to use his sickle. He uses his sickle to reap the earth. This is a picture of the second

---

8. 1 Cor 15:26.
9. Rev 21:8, 27; 22:15.

coming and final judgment echoing other descriptions of the same event.[10] In the sequence of the vision in Revelation 14, the place of torment is before the final judgment. Therefore it is good to start with the hypothesis that this is Hades and to see if this hypothesis fits.

The most striking element of the description in Revelation 14:10 is the phrase "in the presence of the holy angels and of the Lamb." These words have sometimes been taken to mean "in the sight of the angels and the enthroned Jesus," but this interpretation goes against the actual words of the text. There is no hint that Jesus is watching from afar. Those in torment are in the presence of Jesus. He is simply with them. We know from Revelation 20 and the following chapters that after the final judgment, in Gehenna, the unrighteous will be excluded from the presence of Jesus. Therefore, the place of torment in Revelation 14 cannot be after the final judgment. This place must be Hades.

Ralph Bowles, as a conditionalist, has argued rather that Revelation 14:9–11 describes Gehenna, with the smoke going up being the residue of ultimate destruction. He bases his argument on seeing Hebrew parallelism in Revelation 14:9–11.[11] He does not, however, show how the holy angels and the Lamb can be present in Gehenna. Revelation 20–22 show clearly that after the final judgment the wicked are excluded from the presence of the Lamb. Revelation 14:9–11 cannot therefore be a description of Gehenna. "Torment" translates the Greek word βασανισμός. This derives from the same word βάσανος used in the parable of the Rich Man and Lazarus (Luke 16:28) to describe torment specifically in Hades. Those tormented have "no rest day or night" (Rev 14:11). After the final judgment, day and night will be no more as the Lamb will be the continual light.[12] Therefore, those not resting "day or night" are before the final judgment, in Hades not Gehenna.

One objection to the designation of Hades is that the smoke of the torment in Revelation 14 is described as going up "forever and ever." Looking more closely at the Greek text, we see that "forever and ever" is not the best translation. The common phrase translated "forever and ever" is, literally, "to the ages of ages." The expression here, without the definite article, is unique in the New Testament. It has been assumed that the omission of the "the" makes no difference to the meaning. But there could be a considerable difference in meaning. The smoke of torment would more closely be translated as going up "for ages and ages." "For ages and ages" means "a very, very long time," but is significantly different from "forever and ever." This

10. Mark 13:26–27; 14:62; Acts 1:11; Dan 7:13.
11. Bowles, "Does Revelation 14:11 Teach Eternal Torment?"
12. Rev 22:5.

alternative translation is consistent with the place being Hades as indicated strongly in other parts of the text.

Hence there is good clear evidence to conclude that Revelation 14:9–11 describes or refers to Hades, not Gehenna. Revelation 14:9–11 therefore adds to our knowledge of Hades: Hades is a place of God's wrath. In Hades God hands people over to suffer what they have inflicted on others.[13] Hades gives people a foretaste of the consuming fire. Fire and sulfur are the chief agents of the destruction of Gehenna, as prefigured in the destruction of Sodom and Gomorrah. In Revelation 14:9–11 the same agents have a different effect, causing torment rather than destruction. This can be understood as a severe warning to the unrepentant wicked. They feel powerfully something of the force of the ultimate punishment for which they are heading, of the ultimate destruction to which they are on the road. Hades continues "for ages and ages," but is not eternal. In Hades the wicked are "in the presence of the holy angels and of the Lamb." The Lamb is Jesus. How has Jesus come to be present in Hades? He has used his keys. Revelation 14:9–11 confirms that Jesus not only has the keys of Hades, he uses them, so that he can be present with the people there. Here, too, there is no indication that Jesus is only present with some people in some parts of Hades. All those in Hades are in the presence of the holy angels and of the Lamb.

The Lamb in Revelation is the one looking as though slain.[14] The Lamb is not a victorious conqueror resplendent in armor. The Lamb is wounded, drained, apparently lifeless. This Lamb is present with people in Hades. The Lamb is with the afflicted as one also afflicted, sharing their experience. The Lamb brings compassion; he suffers with. He is with the tormented as one who has himself been tormented, inviting from them a response of compassion. The Lamb is also preeminently the Lamb of God who takes away the sin of the world.[15] The Lamb is Jesus, whose name means "God Saving," whose purpose is to seek and save the lost. The holy angels are also defined in the book of Hebrews as "spirits in the divine service, sent to serve for the sake of those who are to inherit salvation."[16] Their purpose is akin to the purpose of Jesus, to save people for the Father. The angels are mentioned first, probably because they are seen, noticed, first. Revelation 14:9–11 indicates therefore that the purpose of Jesus being with people in Hades is not to judge them or to confirm their fate but to save them. Jesus uses his keys to continue to seek and to save the lost, in Hades.

13. Pss 7:12–16; 9:15–16.
14. Rev 5:6.
15. John 1:29.
16. Heb 1:14.

BIBLICAL CONCLUSIONS

- Hades is distinct from Gehenna.
- Hades is before the final judgment.
- Hades is a place of affliction for the callous and those who reject Jesus before the final judgment.
- Hades can therefore be understood as a remand prison for those awaiting judgment.
- Hades is open to Jesus who has the keys of Hades, and uses these keys as God Saving. Jesus enters Hades firstly, with his angels, to be alongside those in Hades. Jesus is also able to release people from Hades.
- All people in Hades have the potential to be released, saved, by Jesus, but for this they need the specific intervention of the key-holder.

These conclusions are significantly different from the usual teaching of the church.

REASON, TRADITION, AND EXPERIENCE

Logical Consistency with a God of Love

Reason says that there must be consistency between the character of God as revealed by Jesus and the actions of the same God. The character of God is love: he is patient, kind, slow to anger, faithful and consistent, desiring that everyone be saved. The action of tormenting for eternity is logically inconsistent with the character of love. This inconsistency has been argued strongly by conditionalists and others. Consuming fire, effective immediately after death, is less inconsistent, less cruel, but still mostly inconsistent with a God who is love as Jesus and the Bible show us love. The condemnation of most of humanity to destruction after death is not consistent with a powerful and loving God. Such an action is more consistent with a callous destroyer, as pitiless as a volcano. If the doctrine of eternal torment had not been taught, the doctrine of consuming fire, effective at death, would have appeared more clearly to be logically inconsistent with the God of love.

The doctrine of death as the final chance shows a God who gives some people many easy opportunities to turn to Jesus and be saved, some people only very limited opportunities, and some people no opportunity at all. This is inconsistent with a God of love and faithful consistency. To put the same argument the other way, God's revealed character leads logically to the understanding that final destruction must be preceded by people being given many good opportunities to repent. In this life many people are given no or few such opportunities. Therefore the opportunities must be given beyond this life. "Optimal grace" is the name that Jerry Walls has given to this rational argument.[17] If God isn't concerned to give people a really good opportunity to turn to him, then he's not Love; he's not the Shepherd who leaves ninety-nine to search for the one; he's not the God and Father of Jesus. Walls argues that the post-mortem opportunity comes in purgatory, a place of sanctification—based on Catholic theology—rather than in Hades, a place of repentance—based on Scripture. This is an important difference, but separate to the logical argument of optimal grace.

In the movie *Hell and Mr. Fudge*, the young Edward is much distressed by the question of the eternal fate of his young friend, Davey, who died in a car crash. "Where is Davey?" is his anguished cry. The answer of traditionalism is that Davey is either in or inexorably on his way to eternal torment. This makes no sense to the young Edward and gives him no hope. The answer of conditionalism is that Davey is inexorably on his way to irreversible destruction. This too gives no hope for Davey and thus makes no sense to those with a simple belief in the God of Love revealed by Jesus. A more logical, more hopeful answer is that Davey is in the remand prison of Hades to which Jesus has and uses the keys.

Logical Consistency of Punishment

Reason demands consistency between the punishment decreed by God to be applied by people toward one another and the punishment applied by God toward people. Punishment decreed by God to be applied by people is inherently proportional, punishment fitting the crime. Eternal torment as the punishment applied by God on all unrepentant people is logically inconsistent with punishment fitting the crime decreed by God to be applied by people. This has been argued strongly by conditionalists and others. Consuming fire, effective immediately after death, applied by God on all unrepentant people, is also in no way proportional punishment. Some conditionalists argue that prior to destruction there will also be "blows" administered, many or few. These blows are, however a minor matter; the outcome, the essential punishment of destruction, is the same for everyone. This is not logically consistent with the proportional justice of God as revealed by Jesus and Scripture.

---

17. Walls, *Purgatory*, 129.

Hades preceding final judgment and ultimate destruction is essentially proportional. The torments or afflictions of Hades are closely related to the pain which the unrepentant have inflicted on others. In Hades people are handed over to "the receiving end" of the sin of which they have previously been on "the giving end." This handing over to the effects of sin committed is consistent with the proportionality of punishment decreed by God to be applied by people and therefore, logically, more likely to be true.

Logical Consistency with God's Desire that People Repent and Be Saved

The conditionalist Gregory Crofford argues, "Does purgatory or any idea that promises second chances after death discourage obedience to God in the present? As long as we think that we are guaranteed a second chance to make things right with God, we are likely to procrastinate, counting on that final opportunity."[18] Crofford effectively claims that there is inconsistency between God's aim of bringing people to repentance and salvation in this life and a declaration that people can come to repentance and salvation beyond this life. Crofford focuses exclusively on one aspect of Hades, that Jesus has and uses the keys to give people a "second chance." The other aspect of Hades is that it is a place of torment or affliction, which is to be strenuously avoided. If both elements are stressed, there is both clear motivation to "make things right with God" and an avoidance of despair about those who did not "make things right with God" in this life.

For some people, even many, a chief prospect of eternal life is to continue, or to enjoy again, loving relationships with those close to them. These people will be motivated to "put things right with God" at least partly to secure these eternal human relationships. If they understand that there is no possibility of them ever having a relationship with a deceased beloved who died without "putting things right with God," this will be a serious disincentive to their own "putting things right with God." Without the incentive of avoiding severe affliction in Hades, the prospect of destruction is also a very weak motivator to "put things right with God." The prospect of dying and then ceasing to exist holds no fear for many people. Straight conditionalism makes it seem that we can be as selfish as we like and when we die, we will simply know nothing, feel nothing. There may be a short uncomfortable time, but the essence will be that we cease to exist. If, on the other hand, without repentance, we are afflicted in Hades, for ages and ages, no one will knowingly choose such affliction even for a short while. Thinking of Hades

---

18. Crofford, *The Dark Side of Destiny*, 25.

is very different, more sobering, than thinking that when we die we sleep until we cease to exist.

It is important to keep together the hard truth of Hades with the good news that Jesus has the keys. The hard truth is the truth of justice. The good news is the truth of mercy. Jesus shows that Micah was right: God does justice and loves mercy. Mercy is a stronger, more central, part of the character of God. Therefore, giving people good opportunities to repent is more important to God than a possible danger of incentivizing procrastination. Destruction preceded by Hades is more consistent with God's aim of bringing people to repentance and salvation than destruction preceded by soul sleep, which is the most common understanding of conditionalism.

The Shoulders of Giants

The logic of post-mortem repentance has been argued by others, including:
- Edward White in *Life in Christ* (1846)
- J. A. MacCulloch in *The Harrowing of Hell* (1930)
- C. S. Lewis in *The Great Divorce* (1946)
- John Sanders in *No Other Name* (1994); Sanders quotes Joseph Leckie from the early twentieth century, as well as Gabriel Fackre and George Lindbeck from the 1980s
- Clark Pinnock in *A Wideness in God's Mercy* (1992)
- Donald Bloesch in *The Last Things* (2004)
- Andrei A. Buckareff and Allen Plug, and Stephen T. Davis, in *The Problem of Hell* (2010)
- Jerry Walls in *Purgatory: The Logic of Total Transformation* (2012); Walls quotes O. A. Curtis from the early twentieth century, P. T. Forsyth from 1948, W. Willimon from 2008, and Karl Rahner from 1983
- Stephen Jonathan in *Grace Beyond the Grave* (2014)

The most notable of these writers is C. S. Lewis. *The Great Divorce* depicts a bus which takes people from hell to the outskirts of heaven. Some people make the difficult journey further into heaven. Some return to hell on the same bus. *The Great Divorce* is Lewis's last work dealing with hell, closest to his final word. Also notable is Jerry Walls as a leading traditionalist. The understanding of Hades as a place of torment, from which Jesus can and does save people preceding Gehenna the place of ultimate destruction, has the potential to unite traditionalists and conditionalists. Even theologians who are drawn strongly to universalism may also agree to this understanding. An understanding which unites previously divided Christians is more likely to be true, as well being very welcome for the well-being of the church.

Logical Consistency with Scripture

Gregory Crofford also argues, in common with other conditionalists, "Though there may be an intermediate state, we have no indication anywhere in the New Testament that during this period there will be a second chance."[19] Even those who have argued for such a second chance have stated that the biblical basis is weak. However the teachings that Jesus holds the keys of Hades and that the Lamb is present with souls in Hades are clear indications that he continues to seek and save in Hades. Jesus also implied that there is repentance after death for every sin except blasphemy against the Holy Spirit (Luke 12:10). Paul wrote that death, and therefore the place of the dead, Hades, cannot separate us from the love of God (Rom 8:38), and that Jesus has taken captive the captivity of the lower parts of the earth (Eph 4:8–9). The lower parts of the earth are Hades, a place of captivity. Authority over this place is now in the hands of Jesus who holds the keys. Peter wrote of the gospel having been proclaimed to the dead (1 Pet 4:6). The writer of Psalm 139 wrote clearly of God's presence in Sheol. The biblical basis for post mortem repentance is not weak. The biblical basis, together with the logical consistency with more general revealed biblical truth, constitutes a strong case for post mortem repentance.

Tradition

Christian tradition contains the strong, widespread, and largely forgotten understanding of the harrowing of hell: Jesus rescuing people from hell. Until about the fourteenth century, the harrowing of hell was taught in paintings, Mystery Plays, and hymns. These are direct depictions of Jesus using his keys of Hades, albeit without the biblical distinction between Hades and Gehenna. The most famous painting is the Anastasis fresco in the Chora, Istanbul. There are also modern representations of the Harrowing. Peter Howson, a contemporary English artist, has produced a series of "Hades" paintings of people in torment in the presence of the crucified Jesus, of the Lamb.

---

19. Crofford, *The Dark Side of Destiny*, 26.

The Lichfield Mysteries is a modern re-enactment of medieval plays using authentic medieval texts. In one play, Jesus approaches hell and commands it to open its gates that he may enter and bring peace and bliss to those trapped inside, and unite them with himself. The hymn "Ye choirs of new Jerusalem" was written by St. Fulbert, who died in 1028. In it the Lion of Judah crushes the serpent's head and ransoms the dead from the clutches of hell. "O come, O come, Emmanuel," written in the twelfth or thirteenth century, entreats the Rod of Jesse to free his people from the tyranny of Satan and from the depths of hell. A more recent and striking depiction of hell is in the well-known "Guide me O Thou Great Redeemer" by W. Williams (1717–91), in which death and hell are said to be destroyed. Countless Christians, including theologians, have sung these words with faith. They are consistent with a belief in Hades as the intermediate state which is ultimately destroyed by Jesus, and whose power is undermined by the Jesus who holds the keys. They are, on the other hand, inconsistent with either traditionalism or conditionalism without Hades.

Even Charles Wesley at least implied that Jesus has power over hell, over the devils in hell, power to change hell into heaven, power to break the chains of those imprisoned in hell, having vanquished the power of Satan:

> Jesus! The Name high over all,
> In hell or earth or sky;
> Angels and men before it fall,
> And devils fear and fly.
> Jesus! The Name to sinners dear,
> The Name to sinners giv'n;
> It scatters all their guilty fear,
> It turns their hell to Heav'n.
> Jesus! The prisoner's fetters breaks,
> And bruises Satan's head;
> Power into strengthless souls it speaks,
> And life into the dead. (1749)

Wesley's words apply more logically to Hades than to the traditional hell.

Christian tradition contains a strong, neglected, witness to Jesus having and using the keys of Hades.

Experience

Christian experience includes the testimony of people who believe they have been rescued from hell or Hades. Experience, particularly experience which seems to be a result of the work of the Holy Spirit, such as Peter's experience of a vision of a sheet full of animals, is widely commended as a potentially useful contribution to Christian understanding. Edward Fudge recently commended such experience as part of theology in his preface to Gregory Crofford's *The Dark Side of Destiny*.

The increased awareness of incidences of resuscitation, partly through the advances of modern medicine and partly through modern widespread dissemination in the media, conveys evidence of life beyond death in "near-death experiences" (NDEs). Theologians, however, including conditionalists, have held back from examining such evidence. Among conditionalists this could be an *a priori* presumption that those who are destroyed, or are in soul sleep before destruction, cannot be resuscitated, and that therefore all Christian NDEs of hell or Hades bear no relation to reality. With the strong indications from Scripture, reason, and tradition that Jesus having and using the keys of Hades is a reality, we do well to examine at least some such NDEs to see if there is any coherence.

The experiences of Howard Storm and of George Ritchie are particularly relevant, among others. Storm's experience, at a time when he had no biblical or theological understanding, was of "gnashing teeth in outer darkness," from which Jesus rescued him.[20] Ritchie's experience, which he never in any way connected with Revelation 14:9–11, was of seeing souls in ongoing torment "being attended, watched over, ministered to" by angels and by Jesus.[21]

Further NDEs are reviewed in my book, *The Lie of Hell*, and at roger-harper.wordpress.com.

CONCLUSIONS

The unrepentant wicked will suffer after this life. Before they are judged, the wicked are held in a horrendous remand prison, Hades, which is to be avoided at all cost. Jesus has the keys to this prison, and uses them. He continues, after death, to be the one who seeks and saves the lost, until the final judgment and the ultimate annihilation of the wicked. This is the truth of Hades as shown by the book of Revelation, confirmed elsewhere in Scripture, confirmed by reason, tradition, and experience. It is time the church believed this, taught this, preached this, lived by this, and repented for previously hiding or denying this truth.

---

20. Storm, *My Descent into Death*, 28.
21. Ritchie, *Return from Tomorrow*, 66.

Part 4

HISTORY AND POLEMICS

14

Eternal Punishment in First-Century Jewish Thought

— David Instone-Brewer —

David Instone-Brewer (B.D. hons, Cardiff University; PhD, University of Cambridge) is a Baptist minister and was seconded to the academic world at Tyndale House, Cambridge, where he currently serves as Senior Research Fellow in Rabbinics and the New Testament. He researches mainly rabbinic Judaism in New Testament times, and develops electronic resources for biblical studies.

BACKGROUND TO JESUS' TEACHING

This paper looks mainly at extra-biblical sources, not in order to find answers about the Christian doctrine on hell, but to discover the questions which New Testament authors were answering. The aim is not to discover the beliefs of NT authors, but to know what beliefs influenced their hearers and readers. This will help us understand the influences that NT authors were addressing and how they expected their hearers and listeners to understand the vocabulary they used.

We can safely assume that they were aiming to communicate accurately to the audience of their time, so they had to interact with ideas of the time and use vocabulary in the sense in which it was understood at the time. If they used words or concepts that were in wide circulation, such as Gehenna or punishment by fire, they knew that their contemporaries already had an idea of what these words meant. If the meaning they wished to convey was different, they would have to make this clear. Therefore, if they did not indicate that they were using these terms with a different meaning, then we can assume (like their audience would have) that they used these terms with the same meaning as their contemporaries.

We also need to know what questions were being debated at the time. Anyone walking into a conversation knows the dangers of misunderstanding what they hear. We can be misled by hearing an answer without knowing the question, or by hearing only one speaker in a phone conversation. The NT represents a response to questions and convictions that are found in extra-biblical literature.

To a modern reader, the Jesus traditions in the Gospels present a confusing and contradictory depiction of hell. Jesus appears to emphasize the horror of eternal penalties in hell without relating this to God's love, which he apparently also emphasizes. At a rough count, the four Gospel writers devote sixty-six verses specifically to Jesus' teaching on the love of God and forty-five verses specifically to Jesus' teaching on hell. Given this combination, we would expect Jesus to emphasize that punishment for evil is linked to God's love though his justice. Although we do find occasional teaching on the justice of hell, most of Jesus' emphases concern the horror of hell, and the fact that even Jews can go there.

The details about hell in the gospels also appear contradictory. Punishment is described as consisting in torment by maggots,[1] fire and (paradoxically) darkness,[2] and it is likened to the valley of Gehenna—a place for burning rubbish outside Jerusalem.[3] These instruments of torture are said to be "eternal," and one verse says that the punishment of hell is as eternal as the reward of the saints.[4] However, punishment is also described as destruction—Greek *apollumi*, usually translated "destroy" or "perish"—in all four Gospels.[5]

This paper will find that most of the vocabulary used by Jesus was already in wide use before the first century—as noted in varying detail in previous studies. The major part of this paper will look at the debate about hell within Judaism during the early first century, which has not previously been investigated thoroughly. The data is sparse, but the various sources are in agreement. We find that Jesus' teaching concentrates on two issues in particular that Jews were in disagreement about: whether any Jews will go to

1. Isa 66:24; cf. Mark 9:48.
2. Matt 25:30, 41.
3. Matt 5:22, 29, 30; 10:28; 18:9; 23:15, 33; Mark 9:43, 45, 47; Luke 12:5.
4. Matt 25:46.
5. Matt 10:28; Mark 12:19; Luke 13:3; John 3:16.

hell, and whether anyone can be reprieved from hell after being sufficiently punished.

APOCALYPTIC JUDAISM

Dating sources is difficult, but by scholarly consensus the following come from the material which can be dated before the first century. We must always be aware that Christian editors may have inserted details because, apart from the few fragments preserved at Qumran, we rely on late copies.

First Enoch

The books that make up 1 Enoch contain several references to hell. Qumran contained fragments from an estimated fifteen separate copies of 1 Enoch. This large number of duplicate copies suggest that the book was widely circulated and well known at the time.

Some of the references to hell occur in Book 2 (chapters 37–71, "the Similitudes"), which some scholars regard as originating later than the NT and perhaps influenced by Christian thought. However, there is now a growing consensus that it is pre-Christian. The fact that no fragments were discovered at Qumran can be regarded as a coincidence with low statistical significance, and the Son of Man mentioned in this section would have been described differently if these passages had a Christian origin. Nevertheless, one should still be cautious about passages from this section.

Almost all the vocabulary and ideas about hell that are used by Jesus in the Gospels are already used by Enoch. He describes a place which is prepared for the Watchers (i.e., the angels who sinned in Gen 6:4) where human sinners are also sent:

- It is full of fire (10:13; 21:3, 7; 54:1; 91:9; 103:7; 108:4–5).
- It is dark, despite the fire (22:2; 103:7; 108:4, "something like an invisible cloud ... completely dark yet I could not see the flame"[6]).
- The fire is associated with torment (10:13, "into the bottom of the fire—and in torment"; cf. 108:5).
- The fire is destructive (10:13–15, "into the bottom of the fire ... they will burn and die ... destroy all the souls"; 91:9, "into the judgment

---

6. Unless otherwise indicated, all translations in this section ("Apocalyptic Judaism") are from Charlesworth, *Old Testament Pseudepigrapha*.

of fire, and perish"; 38:5–6, "shall perish . . . their life is annihilated," though fire is not mentioned here).

- The inhabitants will suffer torment and pain (10:13; 21:10; 22:11; 103:10; 108:5).
- Torment and destruction can both occur to the same persons (10:13–16; 103:10, "tortured and destroyed").
- The destruction is described as "to all generations" or "forever" (10:13; 91:9, "thrown into the judgment of fire, and perish . . . in the force of the eternal judgment").
- By contrast, the Watchers (i.e., fallen angels) are imprisoned forever, and not destroyed (10:13; 21:6, 10, "ten million years . . . detained here forever").
- It is in a valley or abyss (10:13; 27:1; 54:1, 5).
- The name "Gehenna" is not used.
- Worms (i.e., maggots) are mentioned once (46:4–6, though this may have been subject to Christian editing).[7]

A useful summary of all this is found in the following passage from the book of the Watchers which is generally dated to the second or third century BCE. The Watchers are imprisoned forever while the sons of the Watchers (who are half human) share the fate of other humans—i.e., torture followed by destruction—while the righteous experience eternal joy.

> In those days they will lead them [the sons of the Watchers] into the bottom of the fire—and in torment—in the prison (where) they will be locked up forever. And at the time when they will burn and die, those who collaborated with them will be bound together with them from henceforth unto the end of (all) generations. And destroy all the souls of pleasure and the children of the Watchers, for they have done injustice to man. Destroy injustice from the face of the earth. And every iniquitous deed will end, and the plant of righteousness and truth will appear forever and he will plant joy. (10:13–16)

---

7. First Enoch 46:4–6: "This Son of Man . . . shall loosen the reins of the strong and crush the teeth of the sinners. He shall depose the kings from their thrones and kingdoms. For they do not extol and glorify him, and neither do they obey him, the source of their kingship. The faces of the strong will be slapped and be filled with shame and gloom. Their dwelling places and their beds will be worms."

Sibylline Oracles

Books 3–5 of the Sibylline Oracles are pre-Christian Jewish works. Books 1–2 also appear to have pre-Christian Jewish origin, but have suffered a lot of Christian editing. Nevertheless they help to confirm that the Gospels are using terminology about hell that is already well-known.

- Tartarus, which is well-known in Greek mythology as a place of darkness,[8] is referred to by these Jewish authors (1.101; 2.303; 4.186).
- Gehenna is named; twice it is used alongside Tartarus (1.103; 2.292; 4.186).
- Hell is described as both full of darkness (2.292) and flames (1.103) and the two images are merged (4.43, "the gloom in fire").
- Gnashing of teeth is mentioned (2.305, 332), though this is in a section containing Christian editing (cf. 2.312, 344).

Many of these features are seen in the following significant passage that tells us their punishment is severe though proportional—it is three times what they deserve. (It should be noted that this passage has clearly suffered some Christian editing.)

> ... below dark, dank Tartarus. In places unholy they will repay threefold what evil deed they committed, burning in much fire. They will all gnash their teeth, wasting away with thirst and raging violence. They will call death fair, and it will evade them. No longer will death or night give these rest. Often they will request God, who rules on high, in vain, and then he will manifestly turn away his face from them. For he gave seven days of ages to erring men[9] for repentance through the intercession of the holy virgin.[10] (2.303–12)

---

8. Hesiod, *Theogony*, 736–39.

9. This may refer to the seven days during which the wicked see the rewards of the righteous before they go to hell. This is not described in detail until 4 Ezra 7:75–101 (a late first-century work), but Richard Bauckham conjectures that this was based on an earlier Jewish concept (Bauckham, "Early Jewish Visions of Hell," 361).

10. Terry, *Sibylline Oracles*, reads: "... repentance through signs by the hands of a virgin undefiled." This is less obviously Christian but it is nevertheless unlikely to be part of the Jewish original. Some regard this as part of a paraphrase of *The Apocalypse of Peter*—see Lightfoot, *The Sibylline Oracles*, 94–106. However, the similarities are few and consequently the direction of influence (if any) is difficult to decide, and there are many other closer parallels—see the list in Bremmer, "Tours of Hell," 311–13.

Jubilees and Judith

The Book of Jubilees (first–second centuries BCE) similarly describes the fate in Sheol as "darkness" (7.29) and destruction (7.28; 22.22–23), though this is also mixed with torment: "with devouring burning fire ... will be destroyed ... always be renewed with eternal reproach and execration and wrath and torment and indignation and plagues and sickness" (Jub. 36.10).[11]

Judith dates from the 1st or 2nd century BCE and is more interested in nationalistic fervor than theology. While decrying the enemies of Israel, Judith asserts:

> Woe to the nations that rise up against my people! The Lord Almighty will take vengeance on them in the day of judgment; he will send fire and worms into their flesh; they shall weep in pain forever. (Jdt 16:17, NRSV)

The word here translated "in pain" (ἐν αἰσθήσει from αἴσθησις) normally means "wisdom" or "understanding."[12] Older translators understood it here to mean "in feeling" (as in KJV and Douay). This was influenced by the Vulgate translation *sentiant* from which came the concept of eternal sentient suffering. However, "sentient weeping" does not make much sense, because what would be the point of punishment by non-sentient weeping? The Latin is presumably influenced by the normal LXX use of αἴσθησις to mean "knowledge" or "wisdom" (e.g., Prov 1:4, 7; Phil 1:9).

But in Greek literature αἴσθησις is commonly used for "perception"—i.e., the experiences of the senses.[13] The closest analogue in terms of grammar and context in the LXX is 1 Esdras 1:24 [22]: "[they] did wickedly against the Lord ... they grieved him *exceedingly*" (KJA); "... grieved the Lord *deeply*" (NRSV); "... they *conspicuously* grieved him" (NETS). Judith is therefore more likely to be referring to the degree of weeping or the sensations such as pain that cause the weeping rather than the concept that someone is "sentient" while weeping.

---

11. Partly preserved at Qumran on 4Q223_224 f2ii:52—iii:1.

12. E.g., "for they [the false gods] have no *sense*" (Letter of Jeremiah 1:41 NRSV); "filled with the spirit of *wisdom* and perception" (Exod 28:3 Brenton); "piety toward God is the beginning of *discernment*" (Prov 1:7 LXA).

13. *LSJ*, s.v. "αἴσθησις."

Common Features in Intertestamental Literature

We can see that the images and concepts of hell in early Jewish sources are virtually uniform, despite the wide range of this literature. Jubilees comes from a very conservative Jewish group with a particular emphasis on Bible chronology; Enoch from an apocalyptic group which introduces fantastic visions of underground and celestial geography; and the authors of Sibylline oracles are happy to integrate Greek ideas in order to communicate to Hellenized Jews. Despite this variety of origins, they all agree that:

- Hell is a place of both flames and darkness.
- In hell both torment and destruction are experienced.
- A variety of names are used: Sheol, Gehenna, Tartarus, the Valley.
- Sinners are punished for eternity and the righteous are rewarded for eternity.

This consensus is very significant, because it is difficult to infer these details from the Old Testament, even from the text which inspired them most at the end of Isaiah:

> For as the new heavens and the new earth, which I will make, shall remain before me, says the Lord; so shall your descendants and your name remain. From new moon to new moon, and from sabbath to sabbath, all flesh shall come to worship before me, says the Lord. And they shall go out and look at the dead bodies of the people who have rebelled against me; for their worm shall not die, their fire shall not be quenched, and they shall be an abhorrence to all flesh. (Isa 66:22–24, NRSV)

The concepts found in intertestamental Judaism that are not explicit in the Hebrew scriptures include:

- Punishment will be eternal.
- The place of the dead is the mythical Tartarus and/or the physical valley of Hinnom (Gehenna).

This latter identification was a good match with the passage in Isaiah because it was close to Jerusalem (where Isaiah presumably envisioned they would come to worship God), and the physical location was literally characterized by fire and maggots.

QUMRAN JUDAISM

Although the above documents were found at Qumran in fragmentary form, these books did not represent the particular doctrines of this sect. Their distinctive doctrines are found particularly in the War Rule (1QM), Community Rule (1QS), Thanksgiving Hymn (1QHa) and Damascus Document (CD), along with and their commentaries and worship documents (the Pesherim and Hodayot) though these latter two do not specifically refer to hell. All of these were written before the first century CE.

These documents mirror most of the beliefs about hell found in other Jewish literature of the time:

- Hell is a place of burning (CD 2.5; 1QM 14:17–18; 1QS 2:7, 15; 4:13; 1QHa 4:25, 19; 4Q174 f1_3ii:1).

- At the same time it is a place of darkness (1QM 14:17, "fire burning in the dark places of the damned";[14] 1QS 2:8, "eternal flame, surrounded by utter darkness"; 4:13; 4Q287 f6:4; 4Q418 f69ii:7). This is especially significant at Qumran because their enemies are called the Children of Darkness (e.g., 1QS 1:10).

- Being in hell presumably involves torment, but there is no specific reference to this, except that the angels will afflict them (1QS 4:12).

- The result of being in hell is eternal destruction. (CD 2:6; 1QS 2:15; 4:14; 5:13; 1QHa 14:21–22, "a fire which burns up all the men of guilt completely"; 4Q174 f1_3ii:1–2, "consuming fire and destroying all the children of Belial"; 4Q287 f6:6,9; 4Q286 f7ii:10; 4Q418 f69ii:6,8; 4Q491 f1_3:4, "eternal annihilation"; 4Q496 f3:5).

A good summary is found near the start of the Community Rule. After an extended Aaronic blessing for the Sons of Light comes a reversal of it for the Sons of Darkness:

> May you be damned without mercy in return for your dark deeds, an object of wrath licked by eternal flame, surrounded by utter darkness. May God have no mercy upon you when you cry out, nor forgive so as to atone for your sins. May He lift up His furious countenance upon you for vengeance. May you never find peace through the appeal of any intercessor.... Damned be anyone initiated with unrepentant heart, who enters this Covenant, then sets up the stumbling block of his sin, so turning

---

14. Unless otherwise indicated, all translations of the Dead Sea Scrolls are from Wise, Abegg, and Cook, *Dead Sea Scrolls*.

apostate. . . . God's anger and zeal for His commandments shall burn against him for eternal destruction. (1QS 2:7–15)

The Qumran material takes for granted much that is found in intertestamental Jewish literature. They are keen to make two points: that hell is inescapable, and that fellow Jews can go to hell. There is a strong emphasis that hell results in complete and inescapable destruction "without remnant or rescue" (1QS 4:14) or "without remnant or forgiveness by the fierce anger of God for all eternity" (4Q287 f6:9; 4Q286 f7ii:10). It is not surprising that the Children of Darkness will go to hell, but we learn that hell is also for those who joined themselves to the Children of Light and then fell away (1QS 2:12–17). This means that the Qumran sect has no difficulty with the concept that fellow Jews or even former members of their elite sect will go to hell.

We find the reasons for these emphases when we look at rabbinic sources which take an opposite stance on these two issues. This suggests that the Qumran sect wishes to emphasize these points to counter the widespread rabbinic teaching.

RABBINIC SOURCES

Early first century rabbinic teaching is difficult isolate from the later sources.[15] When the dating of rabbinic material is taken seriously, there are very few traditions that we can safely use, especially in the area of theology. Written traditions from this time were concerned mainly with *halakhah*—i.e., discussions and rulings about how to obey the commandments. The discussions about everything else (normally referred to as *aggadah*) were not regarded as equally important and were not committed to a fixed form as early as *halakhah*.

This does not mean that we cannot know the theology of Jews from the early first century, but it does mean that it is difficult, and consequently many studies have neglected this area. This is typified by Fudge's *The Fire That Consumes*, which includes a very good survey of background literature, and a glance at the "Ancient Document Index" finds several columns of references to intertestamental literature, but there is only a single reference to rabbinic literature.

Halakhic literature has been found to be reliable with regard to the dates of attributions. That is, if it says that a certain rabbi said something,

15. Although "Rabbi" did not become an official and consistent title until after 70 CE, it is still a useful term for describing the beliefs of the precursors of these rabbis, as preserved in what is commonly called "Rabbinic" literature.

then it is most likely that he (or, occasionally, someone else from the same time period) did say it.[16] This is in contrast to aggadic literature such as the Midrashim and Targums, which may contain early traditions but they have been edited and re-attributed without concerns about preserving the exact original wording or source. We must therefore (regrettably) avoid the aggadic literature. However, halakhic literature often contains aggadic material, and we can find a few important traditions which give us insights into the rabbinic concepts of eschatological punishment. However, we cannot always trust the attributions of aggadic material even within halakhic literature, so we will need to justify the early origin of each of these traditions.

Mishnah is the earliest written compilation of halakhic traditions (completed about 200 CE) and Tosephta is a similar collection committed to writing about a century later. The Talmuds are halakhic commentaries on Mishnah and often contain first- or second-century material that was included in neither of the earlier collections—though these must be used with extra care. The oral traditions preserved in this literature were fixed and passed on verbatim, even when the words were no longer understood. For example, R. Joshua b Hananiah, at the start of the second century, passed on a tradition concerning cattle which are "*shelashit*" even though he did not know what this meant; someone else had to explain it (m.Par. 1.1).

Traditional Theology of Yohanan ben Zakkai

More than seventy passages in halakhic literature (i.e., Mishnah, Tosephta, and the Talmuds) refer to Gehenna, though only two of them include material which may arguably originate from the first century. However, this widespread use of the name "Gehenna" implies that such usage was already common by the time of Jesus. It is impossible to imagine that rabbinic terminology would have been so heavily influenced by Jesus or by the Sibylline Oracles, which are the only two surviving sources that use "Gehenna" before the first rabbinic source used this term. This is a salutary reminder that the precursors of rabbinic theology have been largely lost. Unlike apocalyptic Judaism and Christianity, their beliefs were not generally written down but were passed on in preaching and personal teaching. The following few surviving traditions represent scraps from a vast community of oral theologians.

---

16. Stemberger explains that named attributions are generally reliable. Even when they are inaccurate, they tend to point to the correct time period. This is the conclusion of Neusner's studies of extensive text units. See Strack and Stemberger, *Introduction to Talmud and Midrash*, 57.

The earliest rabbi who spoke about hell in a datable source is Yohanan ben Zakkai. The following tradition is a biographical story, so we should be initially dubious about its historical value. This form of tradition is more interested in storytelling than in accuracy, and like Christian hagiography, honorific stories about the rabbis were written long after their lifetime.

> And when R. Yohanan b. Zakkai fell ill, his disciples came in to pay a call on him. When he saw them, he began to cry. His disciples said to him, "Light of Israel! Pillar at the right hand! Mighty hammer! On what account are you crying?" He said to them, "If I were going to be brought before a mortal king, who is here today and tomorrow gone to the grave, who, should he be angry with me, will not be angry forever, and, if he should imprison me, will not imprison me forever, and if he should put me to death, whose sentence of death is not for eternity, and whom I can appease with the right words or bribe with money, even so, I should weep. But now that I am being brought before the King of kings of kings, the Holy One, blessed be he, who endures forever and ever, who, should he be angry with me, will be angry forever, and if he should imprison me, will imprison me forever, and if he should put me to death, whose sentence of death is for eternity, and whom I cannot appease with the right words or bribe with money, and not only so, but before me are two paths, one to the Garden of Eden and the other to Gehenna, and I do not know by which path I shall be brought, and should I not weep?" They said to him, "Our master, bless us." He said to them, "May it be God's will that the fear of Heaven be upon you as much as the fear of mortal man." His disciples said, "Just so much?" He said to them, "Would that it were that much." (b. Ber. 4:2, I.2)[17]

One reason for giving credence to this story is that Yohanan is expressing a theology that (as we will discover) was no longer normative when this story was recorded. After 70 CE it might well be regarded as heretical, though before 70 CE (i.e., during Yohanan's earlier career) it was an acceptable point of view that would have been regarded as traditional or already old-fashioned by most hearers.

He clearly believes that there are only two options: Gehenna or Paradise (the Garden of Eden). And he believes that he, a relatively good Jew, is not assured a place in Paradise. By the time the story is recorded (long after Yohanan's lifetime), Jews believed that they all went to heaven except for a few heinous sinners who couldn't really be regarded as within the covenant.

---

17. Neusner, *The Babylonian Talmud*.

That is why his disciples in this story express no real concern for Yohanan, and assumed he was merely being humble. Instead, this proof of his humility and holiness prompted them to ask him for a blessing. Therefore, although his theology had been superseded by the time this story was recorded, it was still acceptable to record it because it could be regarded as a sign of spectacular humility by Yohanan.

Therefore, it is likely that this story preserves the actual theology of Yohanan, but this has been subverted and transformed into a story of humility and a reminder to live in the constant fear of God. Yohanan, therefore, believed that God sent imperfect Jews to hell, forever—a view which most Jews even in his own time had already rejected.[18]

How Long Did Torment Last in Hell?

The tradition of Yohahan emphasizes the eternal nature of punishment in hell but does not tell us what this punishment consists of. Does this refer to eternal torment (as in later Christian interpretations of Judith 16:17) or eternal destruction with no chance of remission (as in all extant early non-rabbinic Jewish sources)?[19] The Yohanan tradition is unclear but other traditions give a clear indication that rabbinic teaching agreed with other Jewish sources in this regard.

A tradition by Akiba in the early second century is based on a received belief that torment lasts only twelve months before destruction in hell:

> Also he [Akiba] would list five things which [last for] twelve months:
>
> the judgment of the generation of the Flood is twelve months;
>
> the judgment of Job is twelve months;
>
> the judgment of the Egyptians is twelve months;
>
> the judgment of Gog and Magog in the time to come is twelve months;
>
> and the judgment of the wicked in Gehenna is twelve months,

---

18. We should not be confused by the beliefs of R. Yohanan in b.RH 16b-17a where he believes in the three groups referred to by Hillel & Shammai. "Yohanan" (without a patronym) in the Babylonian Talmud refers to a second generation Amora (i.e., late 3rd century), and not Yohanan b. Zakkai.

19. 1 En 10:13–15; 91:1; Jub 36:10; CD 2.6; 1QS 2.15; 4.14; 5.13; 1QHa 14.21; 4Q174 fl_3ii:1; 4Q287 f6:6, 9; 4Q286 f7ii:10; 4Q418 f69ii:6, 8; 4Q491 fl_3:4; 4Q496 f3:5.

as it is said, *It will be from one month until the same month [a year later]* (Isa 66:23). (Mishnah *Eduyyoth* 2.10)[20]

We should not conclude that the concept of punishment for twelve months originated with Akiba, because it is also found in earlier traditions (see below). Akiba is here attempting to find a scriptural foundation for this idea, and does so in two ways. First he connected it with other periods of twelve months which were concerned with judgment. Then secondly he used an exegesis based on Isaiah 66:23-24.

Isaiah said that at the end of time, people would come from all over the globe to see the dead corpses of God's enemies "From new moon to new moon, and from Sabbath to Sabbath" (Isa 66:23 NRSV). Akiba's reasoning was, presumably, that the population of the earth cannot turn up weekly or even monthly at Jerusalem, so this must mean "on one particular Sabbath or New Moon, and then the same one annually." He does not mention the problem that, according to this text, these corpses are not destroyed, but another exegete did deal with this, as we see next.

Other Commonly Accepted Beliefs about Hell

The foundational principle about hell was that "we" do not go there. For sects like those at Qumran, this meant none of their members would go to hell; but for mainstream Judaism this meant that no Jews would go to hell. This is stated bluntly in an early saying in Mishnah: "All Israelites have a share in the world to come" (m. San. 10.1). However, this is the start of a long section which lists and discusses the many exceptions to this general rule, because it is clear that even Jews sometimes deserve to go to hell. Conversely, all Gentiles were expected to go to hell, but some rabbis (such as Joshua ben Hananiah in the early second century) thought there were exceptions to this too.

The theology of hell is discussed much more fully in Tosephta than Mishnah. The traditions are helpfully grouped at Tosephta Sanhedrin 13.1-5. Most of this discussion cannot be dated in detail, but the logic shows us which layers come before others, and how they are related to those that can be dated. This allows us to identify the earliest layers and we will find that some portions originated in the early first century or earlier.

When both sides in a debate assume that the other holds certain beliefs, then those beliefs must already be fixed and generally accepted. So if

---

20. Unless otherwise indicated, all translations of the Mishnah are from Neusner, *Mishnah*.

(as in this debate) opposing second-century teachers both assume that a belief is generally held, it must date back to at least to the first century, though not necessarily before 70 CE. Theology changes slowly, though change can be prompted by a significant event such as the destruction of Jerusalem. However, when these common beliefs are held by people who taught both before and after this destruction (such as Yohanan ben Zakkai), or by conservatives who are famous for not changing their views (such as Eliezer ben Hyrcanus), or by those who did not survive the destruction (such as the Shammaites), we can assume these views also held sway before 70 CE.

The School Dispute in this section (t. San. 13.3) will be analyzed in more detail below and the others will be analyzed first. In the following, left-most aligned text indicates the likely earliest layer and indents indicate additions by succeeding editors, as discussed below:

> t. San. 13.1:
>
> Minors, children of the wicked of the Land [of Israel] have no portion in the world to come,
>
>> as it is said, *Behold, the day is coming, burning like a furnace, and all the proud, and all who do wickedly, shall be as stubble* (Mal 4:1)"—the words of Rabban Gamaliel [II].
>>
>> R. Joshua [b. Hananiah] says, "They come into the world to come. For later it says, *The Lord preserves the simple* (Ps 116:6), and further, *Hew down the tree and destroy it, nevertheless, leave the stump of the roots thereof in the earth* (Dan 4:23)."
>>
>> Said Rabban Gamaliel, "How shall I interpret, *He shall leave to them neither root nor branch*" (Mal 4:1)?
>>
>> [Joshua] said, "That the Omnipresent will not leave for them [the merit of a single] religious duty or the remnant of a religious duty, or for their fathers, for ever."
>
> t. San. 13.2:
>
>> Another interpretation: *Root*—this refers to the soul. And *branch*—this refers to the body.
>
> And the children of the wicked among the heathen will not live [in the world to come] nor be judged.
>
>> R. Eliezer [b. Hyrcanus] says, "None of the gentiles has a portion in the world to come, as it is said, *The wicked shall return to Sheol, all the gentiles who forget God* (Ps 9:17). The wicked

shall return to Sheol—these are the wicked Israelites. [*And all the gentiles who forget God*—these are the nations.]"

Said to him R. Joshua, "If it had been written, *The wicked shall return to Sheol, all the gentiles* and then said nothing further, I should have maintained as you do. Now that it is in fact written, *All the gentiles who forget God*, it indicates that there also are righteous people among the nations of the world, who do have a portion in the world to come."

t. San. 13.4:

The Israelites who sinned with their [own] bodies and gentiles who sinned with their [own] bodies go down to Gehenna and are judged there for twelve months.

And after twelve months their souls perish, their bodies are burned, Gehenna absorbs them, and they are turned into dirt. And the wind blows them and scatters them under the feet of the righteous, as it is written, *And you shall tread down the wicked, for they shall be dust under the soles of the feet of the righteous in the day that I do this, says the Lord of Hosts* (Mal 4:3).

t. San. 13.5:

But heretics, apostates, traitors, Epicureans, those who deny the Torah, those who separate from the ways of the community, those who deny the resurrection of the dead, and

whoever both sinned and caused the public to sin—for example, Jeroboam and Ahab,

and those who sent their arrows against the land of the living and stretched out their hands against the *lofty habitation* (Ps 49:14) [i.e., the temple],

Gehenna is locked behind them, and they are judged therein for all generations,

since it is said, *And they shall go forth and look at the corpses of the men who were transgressors against me. For their worm*

> *dies not, and their fire is not quenched. And they shall be an abhorring unto all flesh* (Isa 66:24).

> Sheol will waste away, but they will not waste away, for it is written, *and their form shall cause Sheol to waste away* (Ps 49:14).

>> What made this happen to them? Because they stretched out their hand against the *lofty habitation*, as it is said, *Because of his lofty habitation*, and lofty habitation refers only to the Temple, as it is said, *I have surely built you as a lofty habitation, a place for you to dwell in forever* (1 Kgs 8:13). (Tosephta Sanhedrin 13.1, 2, 4, 5)[21]

The indents indicate the growth of this tradition in at least three stages.[22] The earliest layer is coherent by itself, and its unity is indicated by a clear internal structure:

> Children of the wicked of the Land [of Israel] have no portion in the world to come,
> And the children of the wicked among the heathen will not live nor be judged.
> The Israelites who sinned with their [own] bodies
> and gentiles who sinned with their [own] bodies
> go down to Gehenna and are judged there for twelve months.
> For those who both sinned and caused the public to sin
> —for example, Jeroboam and Ahab—
> Gehenna is locked behind them, and they are judged therein
> for all generations.

The second layer includes sayings by some named scholars whose ministry spanned from about 80–120 CE. The existence of a third layer is revealed by comparing the tradition in 13.5 with a version preserved in the Babylonian Talmud (b. RH. 17a) which lacks the paragraph about the "lofty habitation," presumably because it was added later. This third layer concerns those who destroyed the temple—they were added to the list of the most heinous sinners.

The possible time period for the second layer spans from the late first to early second century. However, the most likely time period for the third layer is also the late first century (immediately after 70 CE) or possibly the

---

21. Unless otherwise indicated, all translations of the Tosephta are from Neusner, *Tosefta*.

22. Unfortunately there is not room in this paper to fully justify these conclusions about editing. More details will be available in a forthcoming volume of my *Traditions of the Rabbis in the Era of the New Testament*.

early second century. It is unlikely to originate after the Bar Kokhba revolt (132–36 CE) because the tradition identifies the destroyers of the temple (i.e., those who destroyed it at 70 CE), and not the destroyers of Jerusalem (in 136 CE). This means that the second layer must be dated at the early end of its possible range—at the end of the first century.

If the scholars in the second layer made their comments at the end of the first century, this means that the material they were commenting on must have been already fixed, and therefore originated in the early first century or earlier. It also means that doctrines which they assumed to be generally accepted must also date back to at least the early first century. This tell us that the following beliefs about hell were generally accepted before 70 CE:

- Only the utterly wicked of Israel will go to hell (13.1: at the end of the first century they debated if their underage children also shared this fate).
- Bodies and souls will be destroyed in hell (13.2: this was a later addition probably in the early second century, to counter Joshua's novel interpretation, but it would not be an effective counterargument if it wasn't recognized as a traditional belief).
- All Gentiles will go to hell (13.2: at the end of the first century they debated whether perhaps some were too good for hell).
- "Gehenna" is a designation for hell (13.3: to be discussed below).
- Evil Israelites and the Gentiles in hell will be burned to ash after twelve months of torment (13.4: not debated, but datable by the "lofty habitation" in 13.5).
- Corpses of heinous sinners will remain on view forever, as in Isaiah 66:24 (13.5: "lofty habitation" was added as a response to the destruction of 70 CE).

These beliefs cohere with those found in non-rabbinic Jewish writings that we looked at above. Both apocalyptic groups and the Qumran community assumed that anyone outside their group would go to hell, whether or not they were Jews—which is roughly equivalent to believing that the sinners of Israel go to hell as well as Gentiles. These groups also believed that the fire of hell would destroy those who went there.

The single novel element is the attempt to deal with the fact that Isaiah 66:24 describes corpses that are *not* destroyed. The earliest layer identifies an especially heinous group of sinners who "are judged for all generations." A later comment explains that their corpses are eternally preserved unlike the corpses of normal sinners that are burned to ash.

NEW RABBINIC THEOLOGY ABOUT A THIRD GROUP

The one aspect of hell that was not explored outside of rabbinic literature is the problem of those believers who are neither perfectly good nor perfectly evil. Sects like those at Qumran or those who wrote apocalyptic literature could assume that all their members were sufficiently perfect to warrant heaven, and they were happy to consign everyone else to hell.

The teachers in majority Judaism, however, could not come to this easy conclusion. Their congregations and followers included many ordinary fallible people who sincerely tried but failed to live out all the commandments. So they had to consider the fate of those who were not yet perfect. A debate about this is preserved in the School Disputes in Tosephta Sanhedrin 13.3.

The School Disputes is a list of about three hundred points of disagreement between the Schools of Hillel and Shammai who flourished in the early first century. The original list has not survived, but it is cited frequently, and the regularity of its form means that it is usually possible to identify elaborations or explanations that have been added later. One of these disputes concern who will go to hell, and for how long. In the following, left-most aligned text indicates the likely oldest layer (as analyzed later) and italics indicate citations of Scripture:

> The School of Shammai says:
>
>> There are three groups, one for *eternal life*, one for *shame and everlasting contempt* (Dan 12:2)—these are those who are completely evil.
>
> An intermediate group go down to Gehenna and scream and come up again and are healed,
>
>> as it is said: *"I will bring the third part through fire and will refine them as silver is refined and will test them as gold is tested, and they shall call on my name and I will be their God"* (Zech 13:9).
>
> And concerning them did Hannah say, *"The Lord kills and brings to life, brings down to Sheol and brings up"* (1 Sam 2:6).
>
> And the School of Hillel says: *"Great in mercy"* (Exod 34:6)—He inclines the decision toward mercy,
>
>> and concerning them David said: *"I am happy that the Lord has heard the sound of my prayer"* (Ps 116:1), and concerning them is said the entire passage. (Tosephta Sanhedrin 13.3)

The original tradition was as brief as possible in order to aid memorization. There was no need to include the Bible texts and their exegesis, because these could be regarded as implied and easy to remember. Prooftexts were later added to many of these disputes though it is likely that these were the actual proofs originally used by the Schools. We can conclude this because in many cases (as here) the Shammaite viewpoint is given a stronger foundation than the Hillelite one. It is unlikely that anyone would invent strong arguments in favor of the Shammaite position after 70 CE because the only rabbis who survived were Hillelites. All later rabbinic theology and practice was based on the opinions of Hillel, and the opinions of Shammai were preserved merely for historical interest, rather like the views of Marcion in Christianity. So it is unlikely that anyone would invent support for the Shammaite positions after their demise. Consequently it is also likely that the support given for the Hillelite position can also be traced back to the original Schools. However, the exegeses added to these texts were unlikely to have been remembered and recorded verbatim, in the way that the wording of the original summaries were remembered.

Because this is such an important passage, it is worth examining a very literal translation alongside the Hebrew. In the following (as previously), left-most aligned text indicates the earliest layer and italics indicates quotations from Scripture. Also, [brackets] mark unique sections in Zuckermandel (based mainly on the Erfurt MS) and {braces} indicate unique text at Mechon-Mamre.org (based mainly on the Vienna MS).[23]

The House of Shammai says:	בית שמאי אומרים
there are three groups	שלש[ה] כתות הן
one *for eternal life* to come	[אחת לחיי הע[ו]לם [הבא]
and one *for shame, for eternal contempt*	[ואחת לחרפות לדראון עולם]
The one *for eternal life*—	[אחת לחיי עולם]
these are the perfectly righteous.	[אלו צדיקים גמורים]
The one *for shame, for eternal contempt*—	[אחת לחרפות לדראון עולם]
these are the perfectly evil (Dan 12:2).	א{י}לו רשעים גמורים
The balanced of them go down	שקולין שבהן יורדין
to Gehenna and squeal	לגיהנן ומצ{ט}פצפין
and rise from there and are healed.	ועולין {הימנה} ומתרפאין
As it says (Zech 13:9):	שנאמר
I will bring the third through fire	והבאתי את השלישית באש
and refine them like silver is refined	{וצרפתים כצרף את הכסף}
and test them like gold is tested	{ובחנתים כבחון את הזהב}
They will call on my name	{הוא יקרא בשמי}

---

23. Zuckermandel and Liebermann, *Tosephta*; Mechon-Mamre.org accessed 23 May 2014.

and I will be God to them.	{ואני אהיה לו לאל}
And about them Hannah said (1 Sam 2:6):	ועליהן אמרה חנה
The Lord is killing and making alive	יי ממית ומחיה
bringing down to Sheol and he brings up.	{מוריד שאול ויעל}
And the House of Hillel says (Exod 34:6):	ובית הלל אומרים
And great in mercy.	ורב חסד
He inclines toward mercy.	מטה כלפי חסד
And about them he/David says (Ps 116:1):	ועליהן [הוא] א[ו]מר {דוד}
I love the Lord because he hears	אהבתי כי ישמע {יי}
and the whole passage speaks about them.	ועליהן נאמר}ה] כל הפרשה [כולה]

When analyzing this passage we have to bear in mind the extreme abbreviation used by rabbinic traditions. Originally they were preserved by the oral recitation of a community of scholars, so brevity was very important. The words were designed to remind the scholar about what they already knew, rather than communicate to someone who did not already know about the subject. When they were written down, explanations could be added, but this had to be done without changing the original words. These additions themselves were also very brief, and later editors commonly added further explanations to them.

In this passage we can see at least two further layers of editing. The original school dispute was:

> The School of Shammai says: The balanced of them go down to Gehenna and squeal and rise from there and are healed.
>
> The School of Hillel says: *And great in mercy*. He inclines towards mercy.

A later editor added the introduction about the other two groups and proof-texts from Zechariah 13:9, 1 Samuel 2:6, and Psalm 116:1.[24] This may have been done in two stages, because the passage would look well balanced and less confusing with only two texts and no introduction. In the following, the additions are indented:

> The School of Shammai says: The balanced of them go down to Gehenna and squeal and rise from there and are healed.

---

24. It is unlikely that the original Shammaite tradition included the proof-text from 1 Samuel 2:6, because R. Eliezer uses this same text at the start of the second century to argue the opposite—that that Korah will not be released from hell—without explaining why the Shammaite exegesis is wrong (see m. San.10.3). Equally, the tradition in t. San. 13.3 does not interact with Eliezer's use of the text. It is likely that they both arose independently, but the Shammaite use was little known till it was recorded here.

> And concerning them Hannah said (1 Sam 2:6): *The Lord is killing and making alive.*
>
> The School of Hillel says: *Great in mercy* (Exod 34:6)—He inclines towards mercy.
>
> And concerning them David says (Ps 116:1): *I love the Lord because he hears.*

These two original proof-texts are both cryptic, so we are not surprised that a third editor extended them further. He continued the first so that it included some more significant words: *"bringing down to Sheol and he brings up."* And he added a comment to the second: "The whole passage speaks about them." This tells the reader to examine the wider context of the words that are actually quoted:

> I love the Lord, because he has heard my voice and my supplications. . . . The snares of death encompassed me; the pangs of Sheol laid hold on me; I suffered distress and anguish. Then I called on the name of the Lord: "O Lord, I pray, save my life!" Gracious is the Lord, and righteous; our God is merciful . . . when I was brought low, he saved me. . . . For you have delivered my soul from death . . . I walk before the Lord in the land of the living. I kept my faith, even when I said, "I am greatly afflicted." (Ps 116, NRSV)

Even with these additions and explanations, it is still not clear what the exact distinction was between the two Schools. However we do know what united them because it is stated in the introduction which was added at the beginning of the Shammaite response:

> There are three groups: one *for eternal life* to come, and one *for shame, for eternal contempt*. The one *for eternal life*: these are the perfectly righteous. The one *for shame, for eternal contempt*: these are the perfectly evil.

Although this occurs immediately after "The School of Shammai says," it must nevertheless be regarded as an introduction to the views of both Schools, because it tells us there are three groups, but describes only the two groups found in Daniel 12:2. The summaries by both Schools, on the other hand, each give an opinion concerning a single group. We can safely conclude that both Schools agree about the first two groups, and they state only their differences, which concern the third group.

Therefore, both Schools believed that God's judgment would result in three groups: the absolutely good would go immediately to eternal life and those who were absolutely evil would go to eternal contempt, as stated in Daniel 12:2. However, many people were somewhere in the middle, and this third group had a different fate.

It is likely that this view, which was common to both of these schools, was the view held by the majority of Jews in the early first century. The leaders of the Schools of Hillel and Shammai were not many—on one occasion they all met in one room (m. Shab. 1.4)—but they had a huge influence. This influence was possibly exaggerated in the history of the survivors, because there were few or no survivors of any School except the Hillelites after 70 CE. However, even if there were other influential Schools at the time, it is likely that they held this same common view, because otherwise we would expect a defense against that other view too.[25]

The Sadducees, who rejected all ideas of resurrection, presumably had no belief in hell, but they had little influence on the people. We know this from the Gospel writers and Josephus (Acts 23:8; *Antiquities* 18:12–17; *Wars* 2:163–66) and the influence of rabbinic teaching is confirmed in excavations of normal houses of the time. These excavations reveal a widespread occurrence of stone vessels which is surprising, given their relative expense and weight compared to ceramic vessels. The only plausible explanation is the rabbinic insistence that stone vessels do not pass on impurity.[26] Similarly the discovery of immersion pools in the foundations of almost all excavated houses implies that households took seriously the rabbinic rules about daily immersion.

DISTINCTIVE BELIEFS OF THE HILLELITES

The tradition we examined above (t. San. 13.3) tells us very little about what the Hillelite view actually was. We know that the Shammaites believed the third group went down to hell for a while and then went to heaven. We might assume that they went to hell for a proportionate time, or that they

---

25. The Sadducean view was, of course different. But Pharisees tended to ignore Sadducees and other outside groups in their debates, rather like modern-day Protestants tend to ignore Catholic views when debating with each other.

26. Magen, *The Stone Vessel Industry*.

were tormented in a proportionate way while down there, though we do not know this.

The opposing Hillelite position is stated briefly and ambiguously, with a generalized reference to Psalm 116. This psalm includes phrases that might imply that the Psalmist went to hell and was released: "The snares of death encompassed me; the pangs of Sheol laid hold on me; I suffered distress and anguish . . . you have delivered my soul from death" (v. 3, 8).[27] On the other hand, the psalm might merely mean that he was rescued before going to hell: "For you have delivered my soul from death . . . I walk before the Lord in the land of the living" (v. 8-9).

Rabbis in later centuries were also confused by the ambiguity of the Hillelite response. Discussions in the fourth century concluded that Hillelites thought only the worst of this middle group went to hell, while the Shammaites thought that all of the middle group went to hell (b. RH. 17a). There is, however, an early tradition which helps to clear up this ambiguity and give us a clearer view of Hillelite beliefs.

Do the Middle Group Really Need to Go to Hell?

Yohanan ben Zakkai is regarded as the re-founder of Judaism after its near demise at 70 CE. Although he was keen to be regarded as someone who represented and interacted with all Judaism,[28] he was clearly a Hillelite. The form of Judaism that he re-established followed Hillelite rulings in almost every detail. This confirms later traditions which regarded him as a disciple of Hillel.

His theology of hell and judgment is found in a parable that is attributed to him. This parable is very similar to some parables Jesus told. In the following, italics indicate the details that are *not* found in related parables of Jesus.

> said R. Yohanan b. Zakkai, "The matter may be compared to the case of a king who invited his courtiers to a banquet, but he didn't set a time. The wise ones among them got themselves adorned and waited at the gate of the palace, *saying, 'Does the*

---

27. This is presumably Danby's conclusion because he says in *Tractate Sanhedrin*, 123, "see especially vv. 3-4."

28. For example, even in disputes between Pharisees and Sadducees he is keen to stand as an outsider, even if his conclusion sides with the Pharisees. Yohanan stood up against the Zealots (ARNb.31), pagan critics (y. San. 1.2-4, 19b-d), Sadducees (b.BB.115b-116a; b.Men.65ab), and both Pharisee and Sadducee (m. Yad. 4.6—though he finds a proof to bolster the Pharisee viewpoint).

palace lack anything?' [They can do it any time.] The foolish ones among them went about their work, *saying, 'So is there a banquet without a whole lot of preparation?'* Suddenly the king demanded the presence of his courtiers. The wise ones went right before him, adorned, but the fools went before him *filthy from their work.* The king received the wise ones pleasantly, but showed anger to the fools. He said, 'These, who adorned themselves for the banquet, will sit and eat and drink. Those, who didn't adorn themselves for the banquet, *will stand and look on.*'" (b. Shab. 153a)[29]

The similarity with parables of Jesus are striking, and far beyond a coincidence—especially the version in Matthew 22:2–15.[30] The following details are not found in that parable, though many are found in related parables:

- The king announces a banquet without setting a time so some get ready and some do not. This is close to the version in Luke 14:17, where the actual time is only announced later but none of the original invitees are ready.
- Those who are ready sit outside the door. This is close to the parable of the virgins who sat ready at the door of the wedding feast (Matt 25:1–13).
- Yohanan's two groups are called wise and foolish. This is also similar to wise and foolish virgins (Matt 25:1–13).
- The king announced the start without any warning. This kind of surprise is featured in various parables of Jesus (Luke 12:36, 39, 46; Matt 24:36, 43, 48; 25:13).
- Yohanan's badly-dressed guests have to stand and watch, but in Jesus' version he is thrown out. This is the only significant detail which is entirely unparalleled in Gospel records of Jesus' teaching.

We can find elements of this parable in several parables of Jesus. The foolish virgins were kept out a feast because they weren't ready (Matt 25:1–13); the householder who doesn't recognize his late guest and keeps his door shut (Luke 13:25–28); the Lukan parallel where the actual time is unknown until just before (Luke 14:16–24). We do not have a large body of parables by Yohanan, like we do for Jesus, so we do not know if these elements featured in his other parables.

---

29. Based on Neusner, *The Babylonian Talmud*.
30. In Luke 14:15–24 the story ends before the actual banquet.

The crux of both the parables of Yohanan and Matthew 22 lies in the badly-dressed guests. Among all the similarities between the parables of Jesus and Yohanan, this detail stands out starkly different. In Yohanan's version they are punished by being made to stand and watch while the well-dressed guests sit down and feast, but in Jesus' version he is thrown out. This is consistent with details in related parables: the late guest is told "I do not know where you are from" and is left outside; the foolish virgins arrive to find the door shut and they cannot enter (Matt 25:10–12); the guest in Luke's version of the banquet who "shall not taste of my dinner" are left outside. The implication in these parables is that those who do not enter the hall are going to hell: "into the darkness, where there will be weeping and gnashing of teeth" (Matt 22:13); "depart from Me, all you evildoers ... to weeping and gnashing of teeth (Luke 13:27–28); "I never knew you" (Matt 25:12; cf. Luke 13:27 in a similar context).

Yohanan's message is that Jews who are not ready for the day of judgment will find themselves in a second-rate heaven, where they will not fully enjoy the eschatological banquet along with the others. This coheres with the view of Yohanan that we saw before (in b. Ber. 28b) where he speaks about only two destinations—heaven or eternal hell. If the Hillelites believed that the middle group went to a second-rate heaven, then only the utterly evil will go to hell, and they will stay there.

This contrasted with the teaching of non-rabbinic Jews.

CONTRASTING RABBINIC THEOLOGY WITH QUMRAN AND THE GOSPELS

We have found many similarities between Judaism and the Gospels with regard to the theology of hell and the vocabulary used to express it. But we have also identified a rift in Jewish theology concerning those who are not utterly evil but are not good enough for heaven. The apocalyptic sects and the Qumran sect were not concerned about this group because they could assume that all of their members were worthy of heaven. But the theology of majority Judaism had to deal with the problem of "average" people who weren't evil though they didn't keep the Law perfectly.

The Shammaites concluded that this third middle group went to hell for a brief punishment and then went up to heaven. The Hillelites concluded that they went straight to heaven but didn't enjoy its full benefits, at least to start with.

Qumran Judaism

Qumran Judaism and the gospels both disagree with this novel teaching. They do so by emphasizing:

- There are only two groups at the judgment.
- Those who to go to hell cannot leave there.

At Qumran they divided humanity into the Sons of Light (themselves) and the Sons of Darkness (everyone else). At the start of the Community Rule, they describe the fate of all those who fail to keep their strict version of Judaism:

> The judgment of all who walk in such ways will be multiple afflictions at the hand of all the angels of perdition, everlasting damnation in the wrath of God's furious vengeance, never-ending terror and reproach for all eternity, with a shameful extinction in the fire of Hell's outer darkness. For all their eras, generation by generation, they will know doleful sorrow, bitter evil, and dark happenstance, until their utter destruction with neither remnant nor rescue. (1QS 4:12 14; duplicate at 4Q257 5:12–13, and the ending is similar to 4Q286 f7ii:10)

This emphasis concerning the two groups is unsurprising, given that this is sectarian literature. However the emphasis on the eternal nature of punishment in hell is unexpected, given the fact that they believe that punishment in hell results in destruction. It becomes more understandable when we realize that a large proportion of their rival Jews were teaching that most of those who go to hell will stay there for only a short period, and will soon be released to go to heaven. The Qumran Jews therefore emphasized that their punishment is:

- "everlasting ... never-ending ... for all eternity, with a shameful extinction ... for all their eras, generation by generation, ... until their utter destruction with neither remnant nor rescue." (1QS 4:12–14)
- "eternal destruction" (1QS 2:15)
- "eternal destruction with none spared" (1QS 5:13)
- "eternal annihilation" (4Q491 fl_3:4; 4Q496 f3:5)
- "[disgra]ces of destruction wi[thout remnant ... for all eternit]y. (4Q286 f7ii:7)
- "eternal destruction ... the children of evil will no longer exist" (4Q418 f69ii:4–8)

- "burn [the damned of Sh]eol, as an [eternal] burning" (1QM 14:18)

Gospel Traditions

There is no room in this paper to examine the Gospel traditions properly, except to confirm the same emphasis as found at Qumran. Jesus in the Gospels is concerned to deny the same two novel ideas by affirming: judgment results in only two groups; punishment in hell is eternal and not temporary.

A quick way to demonstrate the emphasis on the two groups at judgment, is to list those parables which hinge on this dualism:

- The closed door (Luke 13:22–30)
- The doorkeeper (Mark 13:33–37)
- The thief in the night (Matt 24:42–51)
- The unfaithful servants (Luke 12:32–48)
- The Sower and the Seeds (Mark 4:3–9; Matt 13:3–9; Luke 8:5–8)
- The Weeds in the Grain (Matt 13:24–30)
- The Net (Matt 13:47–50)
- The Barren Fig Tree (Luke 13:6–9)
- The Tree and its Fruits (Matt 7:16; Luke 6:43–49)
- The Weather Signs (Luke 12:54–56; cf. Matt 26:2–3; Mark 8:11–13)
- The Talents or Pounds (Matt 25:14–30; Luke 19:12–27)
- The Wicked Vinedressers (Matt 21:33–41; Mark 12:1–9; Luke 20:9–16)
- The Two Builders (Matt 7:24–27; Luke 6:47–49)
- The Ten Virgins (Matt 25:1–13)
- The Wedding Feast (Matt 22:1–10; Luke 14:16–24)
- The Wedding Garment (Matt 22:11–14)
- The Rich Man and Lazarus (Luke 16:19–31)
- The Prodigal Son (Luke 15:11–32)
- The Lost Coin (Luke 15:8–10)
- The Lost Sheep (Matt 28:12–14; Luke 15:4–7)
- The Sheep and the Goats (Matt 25:31–46)

These do not all equally emphasize judgment itself, but they indicate a constant emphasis in the Jesus traditions that you are either in or out, saved or lost, punished or rewarded, and there is no room for a middle third group.

The second emphasis, that the consequences of going to hell are eternal, can be appreciated by looking at every tradition concerning the fires of hell. Although there is only one verse where it unequivocally says that the punishment itself is eternal (Matt 25:41–46), more than half of the passages refer to the eternal nature of the flames.[31] One can, of course, quibble that the flames may be eternal but a person may only spend a short time there. However, if that was the intended meaning, what would be the point of mentioning that the flames are eternal? This detail is clearly stated in order to raise the level of threat, so the implication is that there is no escape.

Jesus therefore contradicts the new rabbinic theology of hell in the same way that Qumran does, and with very similar language. The Community Rule and War Rule are particularly concerned to emphasize that the fire burns forever in order to prove that the destruction is absolute. This is not a matter of burning away the bad bits in order to reveal the good. This burning leaves no remnant which can be redeemed for heaven. Jesus similarly speaks about hell as a final destination.

As well as contradicting the ideas of a third group, and the Shammaite idea that this third group may escape hell, Jesus also addresses the Hillelite idea that a third group may get into heaven by some subtle means.

The parallels between the parables of Jesus and Yohanan's parable of the surprise banquet are very striking. It is particularly significant that the one detail in Jesus' parables that consistently contradicts Yohanan is the fate of those who are foolish and badly dressed. This forms the climax and the main lesson in Yohanan's parable: be ready, or you may have a substandard position in heaven. Jesus appears to deliberately pick on this point in three similar parables: the foolish virgins are not let in; the late guests are not let in; the invited guests miss the banquet, and the badly dressed guest is thrown out. And in these parables the point is made stronger by references to hell such as "weeping and gnashing of teeth" (Matt 22:13; Luke 13:27–28).

Another emphasis in Jesus traditions that contradicts established rabbinic theology is that ordinary Jews can go to hell. A quick way to get a measure of this emphasis is to look at all the places where the Gospels mention Hades or Gehenna. Only a third of these texts refer to sinners going to hell, and two thirds refer to ordinary unrepentant Jews.[32] The Jews who are

---

31. Eternal or unquenchable flames are referred to in Matt 3:10–12; 18:8; 25:41–46; Mark 9:43; Luke 3:9–17. But this aspect of the flames is not mentioned in Matt 5:22; 7:11; 13:42, 50.

32. Sinners go to hell in Matt 5:22; 5:29–30; 18:9; Mark 9:43–45. But no specific sin

destined for hell, according to these passages, even include the better classes of society, like religious teachers and the rich (Matt 23:15, 33; Luke 16:23).

A final point of contrast with the rabbinic theology of hell lies in Jesus' attitude to the sins which deserve punishment in hell. In rabbinic theology only utterly evil Jews go to hell. In Jesus' theology the specific sins which are named as deserving hell include almost universal sins of unjustified anger (Matt 5:22) and lusts of the eye and hand (Matt 5:29–30; 18:9; Mark 9:43–45). In contrast, Jesus specifically welcomed gross sinners such as enemy collaborators and prostitutes so long as they repented. He regarded repentance as key to heaven instead of regarding sin as the key to hell (Matt 11:20–23; Luke 18:2–5).

This quick survey shows that Jesus criticized each aspect of rabbinic theology that departed from the traditional Jewish theology of hell that is found in non-rabbinic Jewish sources.

CONCLUSIONS

The theology of hell and the vocabulary used to discuss it in Jewish literature between the testaments is virtually identical to that found in the gospels. Hell is a place where evil people are punished by both torment and by destruction. It is a place of both fire and darkness. It is called variously Gehenna, Hades, Tartarus, and "the Valley."

Rabbinic literature indicates that the theology of hell was subject to debate and development during the early first century. The Pharisaic/rabbinic schools concluded that God's judgment would divide people into three groups: the good, the evil and the in-between. They agreed that this in-between group would go to heaven, but some of them (including Shammaites) thought they would visit hell for some punishment first. Others (including Hillelites) believed the in-between group would not fully enjoy the benefits of heaven, at least for some time.

The literature of Qumran and the Gospels both emphatically rejected these new ideas in the rabbinic theology of hell. Both sets of literature emphasized that there were only two groups at judgment day, and that the effects of hell are eternal because the destruction is utterly complete. The Gospels added a new teaching: that ordinary Jews can go to hell if they do not repent, and that even gross sinners can go to heaven if they repent.

The questions that Jesus' generation were asking were: do people remain in hell for eternity, and is there a third group of those who aren't evil enough for hell or good enough for heaven? The Gospels' emphasis on the

is referred to in Matt 10:28; 11:23; 23:15, 33; Luke 10:15; 12:5; 16:23.

two ways shows that Jesus rejected the concept of a third group and the idea that one could escape from hell. In one verse punishment is clearly stated as having eternal consequences (Matt 25:46) and other references to eternal features (such as "eternal flames") imply that punishment in hell has no end.

No one in Jesus' generation, as far as we know, was asking what hell was like, or where it was or what kind of punishment occurred there. They were all agreed that it was characterized by fire and darkness with pain of torment and eventual destruction. Contemporaries of the rabbis tended to emphasize the eternal consequences of hell more than others, in order to counter the idea that someone could visit hell for a short punishment.

Jesus used exactly the same terminology as his contemporaries, so we should assume that he meant the same thing that they did, except where he stated otherwise. This means the verse stating that "punishment" is eternal should be understood to mean that torment plus destruction is eternal—without any means of escape—because this is what his contemporaries meant when they used the same language.

The later church doctrine that this punishment consisted of eternal sentient torment resulted from the Vulgate translation of αἴσθησις as *sentiant*, though similar passages suggest the correct translation is: "they shall weep in pain forever" (Jdt 16:17 NRSV). This doctrine was inspired by a misunderstanding of "eternal punishment" which would have been understood by all first-century readers as a reference to torment followed by eternal destruction with no hope of redemption or resurrection.

Jesus did add one emphasis that is not seen in any contemporary Jewish literature: that ordinary Jews are liable for punishment in hell unless they repent and that even the worse sinner can escape hell by repentance. Therefore the unique emphasis of Jesus in the Gospels was that going to hell is determined not so much by the presence of sin but by the absence of repentance.

15

Important Forgotten History
The Roots of Opposition to Conditionalism

— JAMES KENNETH BRANDYBERRY —

Rev. James Kenneth Brandyberry is currently a seminary professor in Karachi, Pakistan, and holds the degrees of AA, DipTh, BS, MA, and DD. He has also taught in Bible colleges in both the United States and London, England. Jim pastored for several years and his wide range of speaking engagements throughout America, Asia, and Europe includes Harvard University and London's Metropolitan Tabernacle. He has been preaching since 1973 and was ordained in 1981.

James's article, "The Roots of Opposition to Conditionalism," originally appeared in volume 94 of Resurrection *magazine, and has been updated for inclusion in this volume.*

Innate immortality and acquired immortality have been engaged in a protracted struggle for dominance throughout most of the Christian centuries. At virtually no time has this been so true as it is in the present hour. A mere half century ago, a prominent conditionalist could write, "Recent decades have been marked by a ground swell of revolt against the traditional position. So conditionalism has steadily shifted from the defensive position of an ostracized view to a recognized school of Christian teaching in a vital field."[1]

The 1980s saw a remarkable rise in profile for the doctrine that immortality is bestowed. From *Eternity* magazine to *Christianity Today*, conditionalism has been given a hearing. Perhaps no factor has been as

1. Froom, *The Conditionalist Faith of Our Fathers*, 2:1045.

instrumental in this advance as the publication of *The Fire That Consumes* by Edward Fudge in 1982. Promoted by the Evangelical Book Club, this work has broadly influenced readers toward rethinking the subject of personal eschatology.[2]

The upswing continued and the decade closed with the public declaration for life only in Christ by eminent thinkers John Stott (*Evangelical Essentials*) and Philip Hughes (*The True Image*). The cumulative impact has, in a phrase, stopped theological traffic!

As expected, traditionalism has reacted, a few examples of which are chronicled here. The limitation of our subject prohibits us from enlarging on the polemic specifics involved. Suffice it to say that when innatism is held, its presuppositions determine the interpretation one puts on such phrases as "unquenchable fire" and the "undying worm" and mitigate against biblical usage and ordinary exegesis.[3]

CONTEMPORARY REACTIONS

The journal *Presbyterion* in its Spring 1990 issue contained a response by Robert L. Reymond to John Stott which is civil in its tone. Not all such rejoinders have been so gracious.

Robert Morey's 1985 book *Death and the Afterlife* begins its chapter on "Annihilationism" by credulously writing that conditional immortality was first advanced by Arnobius in about AD 300, a piece of historic revisionism few others would be academically willing to risk.[4] The author then proceeds to attempt to trash Arnobius in an *ad hominem* approach characteristic of the work in general. Similarly, Morey slights the ability as an historian of Leroy Edwin Froom, author of the *magnum opus*, *The Conditionalist Faith of Our Fathers*, because Froom doesn't hold the same perspective of Arnobius as did Phillip Schaff. Contrast that method with the position of the late Dr. Martyn Lloyd-Jones, who wrote of Froom's work, "This magnificent *Conditionalist Faith* volume is characterized by your customary careful scholarship" (book jacket).

---

2. Since the original publication of this article, Fudge's book has been published in two subsequent editions which have continued to widely impact the evangelical world.

3. By "innatism" is meant the view that the souls of all human beings are innately immortal, but the same is true of the presuppositions underlying the more nuanced form of traditionalism in which the souls of all human beings live forever, being granted immortality by God.

4. Morey, *Death and the Afterlife*, 199.

Virtually ignoring Fudge, Morey uniquely accuses conditionalist writers of "inadequate research" while exaggerating of himself that "our research has involved every conditionalist work, in or out of print, that is accessible today."[5] He further pompously declares, "We have consistently found that none of the annihilationists, Froom included, seem acquainted with the classic orthodox treatments of the subject."[6] That several conditionalists have closely critiqued Augustine and Calvin, among others, does not thus deter Morey from pronouncing the *argumentum ad ignorantium* censure on those differing from the traditional posture.

Still, Morey is mild in contrast with John Gerstner in his curiously titled *Repent or Perish*. This writer's theme is "non-existence is non-punishment." When referring to Philip Hughes's answer to the criticism that annihilation is "no punishment at all," he can only pen, "I won't even condescend to quote it."[7] A few citations from Gerstner exhibit what he *is* willing to impart:

- Of the Christian, he declaims, "If he loves God, he must love hell, too."[8]
- "... when a conservative believer attacks hell, he has ceased to be a conservative believer, if a believer at all."[9]
- "... Hell does not exist, according to John Stott."[10]
- "the only thing worse than hell is to deny hell ...."[11]
- The Bible "is out-Platoing Plato."[12]
- Conditionalists are "attempting to annihilate God."[13]
- "Probably ministers and other witnesses who do not believe [in Gerstner's version of hell] ... are going to hell daily by the tens if not hundreds. In comparison with such ministers, those who go to hell by the thousands will find hell 'tolerable.'"[14]

Surely this is not exactly what Jude had in mind when he spoke of the "defense of faith" (Jude 3).

---

5. Ibid., 205.
6. Ibid.
7. Gerstner, *Repent or Perish*, 57.
8. Ibid., 31.
9. Ibid., 32.
10. Ibid., 64.
11. Ibid., 66.
12. Ibid., 73–74.
13. Ibid., 185.
14. Ibid., 216.

It should be noted, however, that Gerstner does make concessions to conditionalist thought not often found in traditionalist writers:

- He rejects the argument for inherent immortality based on man's being created in the image of God.[15]
- He states that Christ did not literally "descend into hell."[16]
- Likewise, he grants, "It is possible that Constable [a notable nineteenth-century conditionalist] and others are quite correct in saying Paul used common language others used for extinction and did not use language they used for a period of suffering."[17]

Additionally, R. C. Sproul's July 1990 issue of *Table Talk* includes articles focusing on the nature of hell by five writers. Examples such as these, plus John Ankerberg's irresponsible labeling of conditional immortality as among the "doctrine of demons" at the "Evangelical Affirmations" gathering in 1989, point to one thing: A sore nerve has been pressed for those who would hold to Dante's type of hell.

What shall we say of this reaction? Chiefly this: it comes too late in the day to withstand the progress made in twentieth-century biblical exegesis and the overwhelming tide of increased understanding on the Bible's teaching of man and his destiny.

THE ROOTS OF MODERN OPPOSITION

Plato

From whence, then, come the problems of interpretation posed by "orthodoxy" as it speaks of death? A good starting place is with Plato in the fourth century BC. This pagan philosopher developed metaphysically and metaphorically the doctrine of the mystery religions in regarding the soul as intrinsically immortal and capable of an incorporeal existence after its separation from the body.[18] In contrast, the Apostle Paul made the resurrection of the dead the gateway to eternal life. Likewise, it may be said that the earliest Christian apologists "argued against a belief in the natural immortality of the soul" and saw that same doctrine as a "denial that any redemptive grace was necessary for man."[19]

---

15. Ibid., 48.
16. Ibid., 161.
17. Ibid., 164.
18. Moore, *Ancient Beliefs in the Immortality of the Soul*, 130.
19. Ibid., 74.

Soon, however, a megashift began to take place as Platonic thought came to exercise a direct and crucial influence upon Christian thought concerning death and beyond. Various writers have captured this as follows:

- "Undoubtedly, the strongest force working in favour of a general acceptance of the belief in natural immortality has been the dominant influence of Platonism in the earlier stages of the development of Christian doctrine."[20]

- "The controversy concerning human immortality commenced as early as the latter part of the second century, and was, as might be expected, considerably influenced by the philosophical notions of the time concerning the constitution of man."[21]

- "The notion about the separate state of the soul was an importation into Christianity of the old Greek philosophy. The departed *souls* of the early Christians were the *shades* of Homer and the Greeks."[22]

- "... early a majority of the Christians were Greeks or people more or less Hellenized in thought, so that Greek ideas were bound to assert themselves, especially the Platonic concept of the soul as an indestructible entity."[23]

- "The Hellenistic world had thoroughly assimilated the notions of a cosmic dualism which inevitably gave rise to the idea of a soul which is the immortal part of man and continues to exist in a disembodied state after it has been freed from the body. These ideas had come to be accepted almost without challenge in the Mediterranean basin."[24]

- "Many Christian writers of the second and third centuries wanted to show their pagan neighbors the reasonableness of the biblical faith. They wrapped their understanding of Scripture in the robes of philosophy, choosing from the vocabulary of worldly wisdom the words which sparkled and adorned it best."[25]

- "When the Apologists and early Fathers presented Christianity to the Greeks ... they appealed to the poets and philosophers and general tradition of Greek thought in support of belief in immortality."[26]

20. Joyce, "Annihilation," 545.
21. Ellis, *Bible vs. Tradition*, 293.
22. Ibid., 297–98.
23. Moore, *Ancient Beliefs in the Immortality of the Soul*, 71.
24. Gatch, *Death*, 50.
25. Fudge, *The Fire That Consumes* (1982), 66.
26. Brady, "Immortality," 347.

The conclusion, then, of Plato's *Phaedo* became the accepted tenet of the church and, given time, church creeds contained the formula of victorious Platonism. While valuing the religious function of philosophy, it nevertheless in this context must be asked as it was of old: "What indeed has Athens to do with Jerusalem?"[27]

Ante-Nicene Fathers

The concept of the innate immortality of the soul as a Christian doctrine does not make a distinct appearance in patristic literature until toward the close of the second century AD in the writings of Athenagoras of Alexandria (c. 127–90).[28] This Greek philosopher converted to Christianity and retained his Neoplatonic concept of the nature of man. His *Apology*, a philosophical defense of Christianity, spends much of its substance endeavoring to show to Roman Emperor Marcus Aurelius that Platonism and the religion of Christ are in fundamental accord. Other works, such as his *Treatise on the Resurrection*, are unchecked in employing immortal soul terminology.

Tertullian of Carthage (c. 160–240) pushed innatism forward with a power surpassing Athenagoras. One of the influential Latin Fathers, a cadre of thinkers who gave Western Christianity its theological foundation, Tertullian altered the sense of Scripture so as to interpret "'death' as *eternal misery*, 'destruction' and 'consume' as *pain* and *anguish*."[29] He goes beyond this devious treatment of the terminology of Scripture to give us such phrases as "perpetual life in hell" and "eternal killing." It should be noted that the considerable following the doctrine of ultimate reconciliation gained in the Ante-Nicene period is owed in no small part to a revolt against the eternal tormentism of Tertullian.

Still, as a late patristic voice, Lactantius of Nicomedia in Asia Minor (c. 250–330) addressed the Roman Emperor Constantine in the fourth century, vividly maintaining conditionalism.[30] And moving into the Nicene and post-Nicene periods, Athanasius, bishop of Alexandria (c. 297–373) and most prominent theologian of his generation, championed certain aspects of conditionalism. But as such, he was virtually the last man of renown in his era to do so.[31] The consuming fire gave way to the tormenting fire.

---

27. Tertullian, *The Prescription against Heretics*, 7.
28. Froom, *The Conditionalist Faith of Our Fathers*, 928–99.
29. Ibid., 951.
30. Ibid., 1052.
31. Ibid., 1066.

Augustine

Augustine (AD 354–430), bishop of Hippo, extended and augmented Tertullianism. For him, eternal loss of life was an eternal life of loss. Significantly, he had written a book giving sixteen reasons for the immortality of the soul before he became a Christian.[32] This Neoplatonism was never abandoned. His *City of God* is arguably the most elaborate philosophy of history ever attempted. In it, Book XXI contains twenty-seven short chapters regarding eternal punishment. Therein he answers pagan critics who reject his view of personal eschatology. His chief concern is final punishment in the form of eternal torment.

Largely, the subject is approached in a philosophical rather than scriptural discussion. Indeed, Augustine offered proofs of immortality which show him a debtor to the Platonic line. One involved borrowing "bodily from Plato's *Phaedo* and from Plotinus [the premier Neoplatonist] when he maintains that life and the soul are identical, whereas the body is animated not by itself but by its soul. The body, therefore, can die—that is, be deprived of life; but the soul, whose essence is life, cannot lose that essence, cannot lose itself, and therefore cannot die."[33]

Augustine's crucial role in the development of theology—his advocacy of eternal torment—tended to cause it to become the accepted doctrine of the church for the centuries that followed. His Platonic presupposition of the natural immortality of the soul erected a barrier to clear exegesis and consequently set a similar standard for most of Christendom. To this effect, one writer has commented:

> The evidence in the early Christian writers is clear that much confusion of thought prevailed until Augustine by his genius clarified Christian doctrine through the modified form of Neoplatonism. His system in no slight degree determined the course of thinking within the church on the question of immortality down to the latter part of the nineteenth century.[34]

THOMAS AQUINAS

Platonic influences and the growth of purgatorial doctrine tended to lead further away from conditionalist thought. The Middle Ages were therefore

---

32. Ibid., 1072–73.
33. Moore, *Ancient Beliefs in the Immortality of the Soul*, 122.
34. Ibid., 72.

characterized by this emphasis at the expense of a significant resurrection. Foremost in influence among those of that time was Thomas Aquinas (1225–74), whose dogmatic corpus, Thomism, is officially recognized as the foundation of Roman Catholic theology. His argument, briefly recapitulated, is remarkable:

> In theory it is possible that God should annihilate His creatures. ... As He brought them into existence under no compulsion, but by the act of His will, so might He by a similar free act reduce them again to nothingness.[35]

Though hence establishing Aristotelianism as the chief foundation of Christian philosophy, Thomas, in his eschatological doctrine, returned to Neoplatonic mysticism.[36] His *Summa Contra Gentiles* "leaves the impression of being primarily interested in the interim destiny of the soul, in its immediate individual judgment of which the general judgment is to him but a reaffirmation."[37]

Of Aquinas, it has been observed, "With Plato he had little direct acquaintance; but from St. Augustine he learnt of later Platonism."[38] The same writer continues, "It is sufficient to note that proof of the great influence of Thomas's work soon after his death is given by Dante's use of his philosophy and theology in his *Divine Comedy*."[39]

JOHN CALVIN

While rejecting the Roman Catholic distinctive of purgatory, Protestantism in the main took over this eschatology. Upon death, souls passed at once to heaven or hell. The resurrection remained an afterthought. Still, the Reformation had broken the fetters upon free speculation and conditional immortality once again was propounded and defended. Since those eventful days, there has been an almost unbroken and well-documented chain of conditionalist thought.

Martin Luther, for example, held at one point in his theological development that the notion that the soul is immortal is a "monstrous opinion" from the "Roman dunghills of decretals."[40] His views prompted no small

---

35. Joyce, "Annihilation," 547.
36. Moore, *Ancient Beliefs in the Immortality of the Soul*, 149.
37. Gatch, *Death*, 120.
38. Moore, *Ancient Beliefs in the Immortality of the Soul*, 138.
39. Ibid., 150.
40. Ellis, *Bible vs. Tradition*, 303.

dialogue with England's Thomas More, whose *Utopia* made public denial of the immortality of the soul punishable by death.[41]

It was, rather, John Calvin who "put the Protestant stamp of approval on the traditional understanding of souls and hell."[42] The power of his influence may be seen in the history of theology since.

The entry into France of certain Anabaptists hindered Calvin's own Reformation. The term "Anabaptist" ("rebaptizer") is a very general description which is applied to a wide diversity of Reformation Christians who rejected the state churches of Luther and Calvin. Wrote Edward Fudge:

> It is not surprising that these Anabaptists should be more open to new ideas—and to question the established doctrines of those around them. They stressed the authority of the Word of God apart from creeds and confessions of faith. They also championed the right of each individual to study the Scriptures himself, relying on the Holy Spirit alone for guidance and understanding.[43]

Calvin maintained that "the Anabaptists in general all hold that souls, being departed from the body, cease to live until the day of the resurrection."[44] Against this Calvin wrote a treatise entitled *Psychopannychia* in 1534, which, apart from his work on the "De Clementia" of Seneca, was the first of his writings. In it Calvin confesses to have never seen the tracts circulated by proponents of the view he opposes, but says he has "received some notes from a friend."[45]

Calvin's blusterous language against the Anabaptists is unrestrained; he calls them "babblers,"[46] "dregs,"[47] a "nefarious herd"[48] fraught with "insanity."[49] Weaknesses in the treatise are obvious, including a selective use of the church fathers, the synonymous use of the terms "soul" and "spirit," and, extraordinarily, deeming death the first resurrection of Revelation 20:6.[50]

---

41. Brady, "Immortality," 352.
42. Fudge, *The Fire That Consumes* (1982), 466.
43. Ibid., 71.
44. Calvin, *Treatises Against the Anabaptists*, 119.
45. Calvin, *Tracts Relating to the Reformation*, 414.
46. Ibid.
47. Ibid., 415.
48. Ibid., 416.
49. Ibid., 414.
50. Ibid., 446.

Of greater concern is Calvin's contention that, contrary to Isaiah's prophecy, Christ did not "pour out his soul unto death." To wit:

> Now, O dreamy sleepers, commune with your own hearts, and consider how Christ died. Did He sleep when He was working for your salvation? Not thus does He say of Himself, "As the Father hath life in himself, so hath he given the Son to have life in himself." (John 5:26.) How could He who has life in Himself lose it?[51]

Along the same lines, he says of Christ, "If He can die, our death is certain."[52] The implications for theology that arise from Calvin's statement are grave.

The Reformer of Geneva does show humor, it might be added, stating that the "Anabaptists . . . in the place of white robes, give souls pillows to sleep on."[53]

In the first book in its final form of Calvin's monumental *Institutes of the Christian Religion*, there is a lengthy discussion of the immortality of the soul and the commendation of Plato as a good teacher in this area of learning: "not only enjoyable, but also profitable."[54] So vehemently is he opposed to the "sleep of souls" that he holds Romanist John XXII's embrace of the position as proof of the fallibility of the papacy.[55]

Even Reformed scholars such as Hoekema and Ridderbos have called into question Calvin's biblicity in this area. No small wonder—do you hear the voice of Plato in this passage from Calvin?

> The body, which decays, weighs down the soul, and confining it within an earthly habitation, greatly limits its perceptions. If the body is the prison of the soul, if the earthly habitation is a kind of fetters, what is the state of the soul when set free from this prison, when loosed from these fetters? Is it not restored to itself, and as it were made complete, so that we may truly say, that all for which it gains is so much lost to the body? . . . For then the soul, having shaken off all kinds of pollution, is truly spiritual, so that it consents to the will of God, and is no longer subjected to the tyranny of the flesh; thus dwelling in tranquility, with all its thoughts fixed on God.[56]

---

51. Ibid., 436.
52. Ibid., 439.
53. Calvin, *Treatises Against the Anabaptists*, 127.
54. Calvin, *Institutes of the Christians Religion*, 193.
55. Gatch, *Death*, 119.
56. Calvin, *Tracts Relating to the Reformation*, 443–44.

Heinrich Quistorp is poignant in his analysis of Calvin, accusing Calvin of misidentifying the mortal body with sinful flesh, of conflating the "soul" and "spirit," and of thinking too lowly of the body.[57] Indeed, Quistorp thinks Calvin is guilty of "disesteeming the body altogether, literally making the soul into a substance independent of the body with a life and being of its own, and hence giving it immortal status," which Quistorp rejects as unbiblical.[58] Additionally,

> Quistorp observes Calvin's dependence on the early Fathers for his principal views and regrets that in this case the Reformer did not subject them to as thorough a scrutiny as he did in other matters. Quistorp also comments on Calvin's "horror of fanatical excesses" and thinks this horror made him too cautious in his eschatology.[59]

Regardless, as Calvin's passion on the issue of the soul outweighed such voices as Luther, William Tyndale, and the Anabaptists, his Augustinian view gained the ascendancy in steering the Reformation. To that effect, Edward Fudge has commented:

> When the Lutheran reformers failed to give vigorous support to psychopannychism, soul sleeping lost what small chance it might have had to be considered a debatable doctrine, a thing indifferent. Once it was identified solely with the Anabaptists, there was no hope for a hearing before respectable Protestants.[60]

For personal and historical reasons, then, Luther and Tyndale's influence was not determinative. Expressly, Calvin more than any one man "put the Protestant stamp of approval on the traditional understanding of souls and hell."[61]

CONCLUSION

And so, stamped with the approval of Athenagoras, Tertullian, Augustine, Thomas Aquinas, and John Calvin, the innatism of Plato has heavily impacted Christian thinking throughout most of church history. Opposition from outside the mainline in such groups as Anabaptists, Socinians, Adventists

---

57. Calvin, *Treatises Against the Anabaptists*, 33.
58. Ibid., 33–34.
59. Ibid., 34.
60. Fudge, *The Fire That Consumes* (1982), 72.
61. Ibid., 466.

and Jehovah's Witnesses "would only harden the established churches in the received interpretation and would effectively prevent any full-scale exegetical study of the subject in the same open-minded manner other important subjects might receive."[62]

That milieu has changed considerably, however, now well into the twenty-first century. Conditionalism's hermeneutical strength and historical support are rapidly being perceived and this trend is nowhere near cresting. The day of *small* things has become much bigger.

Is a theological reformation at hand? Will the names of such worthies as Froom and Fudge someday be heralded as twentieth-century reformers by a future evangelical consensus? We must wait and see. But, to be sure, "Nothing is more powerful than an idea whose time has come."

---

62. Ibid., 383.

16

Sic et Non
Traditionalism's Scandal

— Ronnie Demler —

Ronnie Demler is a contributor to the Rethinking Hell blog and podcast. He received his BA in Philosophy from Biola University (2003) and is currently earning his MA in Philosophy at Cal State Long Beach.

Ronnie originally presented the following polemic against the traditional view of final punishment at the Rethinking Hell conference, 2014, under the provocative title, "Persuasive or Evasive? Subtle and Not-So-Subtle Shifts in Traditionalist Dialectics."

For many conditionalists, the "aha moment" in their journey away from traditionalism is the realization that biblical descriptions of final punishment sound nothing like the descriptions often given by pastors and preachers. For example, how often have we heard evangelists proclaim that "everyone lives forever, the question is where?" But doesn't John 3:16 indicate that only believers will live forever, and that everyone else will perish?

Fair enough—the traditionalist might reply—but do the declarations of some modern evangelical preachers accurately represent traditionalism per se? In what follows I attempt to answer this question.

PART ONE

In the first part of this paper I will lay out five interrelated biblical affirmations. Each teaching will then be set in contrast to statements made by influential traditionalists over the centuries.

1. The Death of the Damned

Scripture teaches, quite plainly and explicitly, that the eschatological fate of the unrepentant is death:

- Romans 6:23: "For the wages of sin is death, but the free gift of God is eternal life in Christ Jesus our Lord."
- Romans 8:13: "For if you live according to the flesh you will die, but if by the Spirit you put to death the deeds of the body, you will live."[1]

The same idea is sometimes expressed indirectly, but no less clearly:

- John 6:50: "This is the bread that comes down from heaven, so that one may eat of it and not die."
- John 11:25–26: "I am the resurrection and the life. Whoever believes in me, though he die, yet shall he live, and everyone who lives and believes in me shall never die."

The obvious implication here is that those who do not partake of the bread from heaven and those who do not believe in Christ *will* die.

Traditionalists throughout history, on the other hand, have plainly and explicitly taught that the damned in hell will *never* die:

- Saint Anselm writes that the damned soul in hell will cry out: "Ah, poor me, poor me! And I want to die; but, dying and dying, still I cannot die."[2]
- John Gill asserts that "the soul in torment shall never die, or lose any of its powers and faculties."[3]
- Robert Murray M'Cheyne writes that, in hell: "Wicked men shall be cast away by themselves.—It is said, they shall wish to die, and shall not be able. They shall seek death, and death shall flee from them."[4]

---

1. Unless otherwise indicated, all Scripture quotations are from the ESV.
2. Anselm, "Fifth Meditation," 66.
3. Gill, "Mark 9."
4. Bonar, *Memoir and Remains of the Rev. Robert Murray M'Cheyne*, 423.

- John Wesley writes that after the resurrection, "neither the righteous nor the wicked were to die any more: their souls and bodies were no more to be separated."[5]
- Scottish divine and author John MacDuff writes: "[If we could] look into the lake of fire, and have a sight of the wretched beings who are there writhing in deathless agonies, we should bless the most miserable condition on earth, if it were only sweetened with the hope of escaping that place of torment!"[6]
- Scottish minister, John Willison writes: "Pray earnestly, that all your sins may die before you die; for if they die not before you, but outlive the dying body, they will live eternally to sting and torment the never-dying soul."[7]
- Evangelist Hyman Appelman, reflecting on how in this life we can escape pain through suicide, writes: "You can take poison; you can blow your brains out; you can hang yourself and believe you have left your difficulties behind. But there is no poison in Hell. There are no guns in Hell. There is no death in Hell."[8]
- Pastor Jerry Vines writes: "To go to into hell knowing you will never return is the tragedy of all tragedies. 'Let some air in.' No air is in hell. 'I need a drink of water.' No water is in hell. 'Turn on some light.' No light is in hell. 'Let me die.' No death occurs in hell."[9]

2. Only the Righteous Live Forever.

If it's true that the eschatological fate of the damned is death, then the obvious corollary is that the damned will not live forever. And Scripture affirms this repeatedly when it emphasizes that only the righteous will live forever:

- John 3:16: "For God so loved the world, that he gave his only Son, that whoever believes in him should not perish but have eternal life."
- John 3:36: "Whoever believes in the Son has eternal life; whoever does not obey the Son shall not see life, but the wrath of God remains on him."

---

5. Wesley, *Explanatory Notes upon the New Testament*, 758.
6. MacDuff, *The Footsteps of Jesus*, 103.
7. Willison, *The Whole Works of the Reverend and Learned Mr. John Willison*, 13–14.
8. Appelman. "Hell—What Is It?" 142.
9. Vines, "Sermon on John 3:16," 27–28.

- 1 John 2:17: "The world is passing away, and also its lusts; but the one who does the will of God lives forever." (NASB)

Traditionalists, however, have unapologetically taught that the inhabitants of hell will also live forever.

- George Whitefield writes that the person in hell will cry out, "I have in effect denied the Lord that bought me, and therefore justly am I now denied by him. But must I live for ever tormented in these flames?"[10]
- Charles Spurgeon writes: "Man was condemned to live forever in Hell."[11] In a different sermon he tells the unbeliever, "thou art a fallen creature, having only capacities to live here in sin, and to live for ever in torment."[12]
- Menno Simons writes: "Therefore, consider seriously the heartrending misery and wretchedness of their poor souls which must live forever, either in heaven or in hell."[13]
- C. S. Lewis writes: "Christianity asserts that every individual human being is going to live forever, and this must be either true or false."[14]
- American preacher and evangelist John Rice writes that: "the Bible carefully teaches that sinners must live on in torment forever beyond the judgment."[15]
- Pope John Paul II writes: "The images of hell that Sacred Scripture presents to us must be correctly interpreted. They show the complete frustration and emptiness of life without God."[16]
- John Piper writes: "You are not mere matter and energy. You are an embodied soul who will live forever in heaven or in hell . . . ."[17] In another publication he says: "If we will live forever in bliss or torment, then securing the one and escaping the other is more important than most of what we think about."[18]

---

10. Whitefield, *The Christian's Companion*, 170–71.
11. Spurgeon, *Sermons of the Rev. C. H. Spurgeon. 4th series*, 217.
12. Spurgeon, *The New Park Street Pulpit Sermons*, 22.
13. Simons, *The Complete Works of Menno Simons*, 273
14. Lewis, *Mere Christianity*, 74.
15. Rice, "Hell—What the Bible Says about It," 123.
16. Pope John Paul II, quoted in Haraburda, *Christian Controversies*, 291.
17. Piper, "Hijacking Your Brain Back from Porn."
18. Piper, *A Godward Life*, 207.

- John MacArthur writes: "The message of the Bible is that death does not end the existence of anyone, that every human being who has ever lived will live forever ... either in hell or in heaven, either in eternal death or eternal life. ... Not merely as a disembodied spirit, but every person will live forever in bodily form."[19]
- Robert Peterson, who is widely considered to be one of the most able contemporary defenders of traditionalism, writes the following: "Believers will enjoy the new heavens and the new earth, whereas the final destination of the unrepentant will be 'the lake that burns with fire and brimstone.' Evidently God does not view unbelievers' being eternally alive in the lake of fire as incompatible with His being 'all in all.'"[20] In a different article, he writes: "The picture of the righteous and unrighteous living forever in bliss and misery, respectively, does not fit either universalism or annihilationism."[21]
- Mark Driscoll, in a sermon, says: "God is an eternal God; a sin against him is an eternal act that requires an eternal consequence. And we are going to live eternally into the future—the question is where." Later in the same sermon he reiterates: "You are going to live forever, and it will be unceasing joy or unceasing anguish."[22]
- Finally, Billy Graham says that "[The soul] will never die, but will live forever in either Heaven or Hell."[23]

3. Only the Righteous Gain Immortality

In his writings, Saint Paul is emphatic that only believers are gifted with immortality through Christ:

- Romans 2:6–7: "[God] will render to each one according to his works: to those who by patience in well-doing seek for glory and honor and immortality, he will give eternal life."
- 2 Timothy 1:10: "[Christ Jesus] abolished death and brought life and immortality to light through the gospel."

---

19. MacArthur, "The Resurrection of Jesus Christ."
20. Peterson, "Does the Bible teach Annihilationism?" 25.
21. Peterson, "A Traditionalist Response to John Stott's Arguments for Annihilationism," 566.
22. Driscoll, "Part 68: Heaven and Hell."
23. Graham, *The Heaven Answer Book*, 75.

- 1 Corinthians 15:52–53 [speaking of the righteous]: "For the trumpet will sound, and the dead will be raised imperishable, and we shall be changed. For this perishable body must put on the imperishable, and this mortal body must put on immortality."

Despite this unambiguous teaching, Christians throughout history have frankly taught that the damned, both soul and resurrected body, will be immortal.

- Frederick Faber says: "But the indestructible immortality of a lost soul even in the tightest grasp of omnipotent anger this gives us another measure of the severity of God's punishments." And again: "These are but figures of the divine punishments. God can find unimaginable capabilities of pain in the immortal body, and yet more unimaginable capabilities in the soul."[24]
- Jonathan Edwards says: "The righteous are no more in the very words said to be immortal in happiness, than the wicked are said to be immortal in misery."[25]
- Edward Payson writes: "We shall only add, that, as after the resurrection, the bodies of the wicked will be immortal, they will be capable of enduring sufferings, which in this world would cause instant death."[26]
- Richard Baxter writes: "They knew it was an everlasting kingdom which they refused, and what wonder if they are everlastingly shut out of it. Their immortal souls were guilty of the trespass, and therefore must immortally suffer the pains."[27]
- Article thirty-seven of the Belgic Confession affirms that the wicked "shall be convicted by the testimony of their own consciences, and, being immortal, shall be tormented in that everlasting fire which is prepared for the devil and his angels."[28]
- C. S. Lewis writes: "There are no *ordinary* people. You have never talked to a mere mortal. Nations, cultures, arts, civilisations—these are mortal, and their life is to ours as the life of a gnat. But it is immortals whom we joke with, work with, marry, snub, and exploit—immortal horrors or everlasting splendors."[29]

---

24. Faber, *Notes on Doctrinal and Spiritual Subjects*, 187–89.
25. Edwards, "The Salvation of All Men Strictly Examined," 230.
26. Payson, *Sermons*, 481.
27. Baxter, *The Saints' Everlasting Rest*, 172–73.
28. Schaff, *The Creeds of Christendom*, 435.
29. Lewis, "The Weight of Glory," 46.

- Ligon Duncan writes: "Furthermore, one must begin to look at unbelievers with the same kind of pathos and compassion that Jesus and his disciples evinced when they contemplated an immortal soul and the reality of eternal darkness."[30]

Before moving on to affirmations four and five, one additional point should be made. If the damned are immortal and will live forever, then surely they have eternal life. Of course, very few traditionalists of note would ever say that or concede the point, given the theological and historical prominence of passages such as John 3:16. On a popular level, however, it's fairly easy to find Christians who affirm that both the saved and the damned have eternal life.

- The statement of faith of Calvary Chapel Deer Park includes the following: "We believe in the resurrection of both the saved and the lost. For those who are saved, life in heaven, and those who are lost, damnation and eternal life in hell."[31] I have found several other churches with the same phrase in their statements of faith.

- Adam Zens, who was interviewed by the Rethinking Hell podcast in 2012, says the following in a YouTube video where he defends traditionalism: "There are two choices: eternal life with god, eternal life apart from God. The Scriptures demonstrate that."[32]

- Occasionally, even respected evangelists and Bible teachers slip up and candidly express their beliefs. Chuck Swindoll writes: "Don't misunderstand. *Everybody* has eternal life because everyone has an eternal soul. The issue is not 'Do I have eternal life?' It is, rather, 'Where will I spend my eternal life?'"[33]

- Likewise, Billy Graham says: "And this life on earth is nothing compared to the everlasting life to come. . . . Where will you spend that life?"[34]

---

30. Duncan, "Speaking Seriously and Sensitively about Hell to the Sons of this Age and the Next."
31. Calvary Chapel Deer Park, "What We Believe."
32. Zens, "Closing Statement on Hell and Annihilation Debate."
33. Swindoll, *Growing Deep in the Christian Life*, 309.
34. Wright, "Billy Graham Talks about Eternal Life," 2.

4. The Destruction of the Damned

"Destruction" is among the most common ways for biblical authors to describe the fate of the damned. Here's a very small sample:

- Matthew 7:13: "Enter by the narrow gate. For the gate is wide and the way is easy that leads to destruction, and those who enter by it are many."
- Matthew 10:28: "And do not fear those who kill the body but cannot kill the soul. Rather fear him who can destroy both soul and body in hell."
- 2 Thessalonians 1:9: "They will suffer the punishment of eternal destruction, away from the presence of the Lord and from the glory of his might."
- 2 Peter 2:12: "But these, like irrational animals, creatures of instinct, born to be caught and destroyed, blaspheming about matters of which they are ignorant, will also be destroyed in their destruction."

And yet many traditionalists candidly affirm precisely the opposite:

- John Walvoord writes: "Those being resurrected from Hades and the grave will receive a body that can never be destroyed, but unlike the body of the righteous, it is a body that is still wicked, still in rebellion against God, and still deserving God's judgment."[35]
- Contemporary apologist J. Warner Wallace writes: "Orthodox Christianity has always maintained that Hell is a place where those who have rejected God will be left unforgiven in a state of eternal conscious torment. They will not be destroyed, but instead, will be left in a conscious state to experience the torment and anguish of their punishment forever."[36]
- Likewise, apologist Greg Koukl says that in hell: "men are not destroyed, they are in torment."[37]
- Robert Peterson writes that "hell is where 'the fire is not quenched.' This is a picture of everlasting suffering, not of destruction."[38]
- Evangelical philosopher J. P. Moreland writes: "If God is the source and preserver of values, and if persons have the high degree of intrinsic

---

35. Walvoord, *Major Bible Prophecies*, 410.
36. Wallace, "Is There an Eternal Conscious Hell?"
37. Koukl, "Hell, Yes!"
38. Peterson, "Does the Bible Teach Annihilationism?" 15.

value Christianity claims they have, then God is the preserver of persons. He would be wrong to destroy something of such value just because it has chosen a life it was not intended to live."[39]

- Frank Turek and Norman Geisler write: "Hell is real. In fact, Jesus spoke more of hell then he did of heaven. God will not annihilate unbelievers because he will not destroy creatures made in his own image."[40]
- Robert Thomas, New Testament professor at *The Master's Seminary* says: "Jesus described the fire as 'unquenchable' (Mark 9:43), as did John the Baptist (Matt 3:12; Luke 3:17). Jesus said it will be a fire that acts like salt, preserving rather than destroying...."[41]

The teaching that the damned will be destroyed is so explicit and so prevalent in Scripture that I think many traditionalists have been reluctant to say "the damned will never be destroyed" even if that's what they actually believe. But what often happens is they end up expressing just that, albeit in other ways. For instance, instead of saying that the damned will never be destroyed, they say that the damned are indestructible. Two examples:

- Fourth-century apologist Lactantius says: "For because [the wicked] have committed sins in their bodies, they will again be clothed with flesh, that they may make atonement in their bodies; and yet it will not be that flesh with which God clothed man, like this our earthly body, but indestructible, and abiding forever, that it may be able to hold out against tortures and everlasting fire."[42]
- Erwin Lutzer writes that "*Hell*, then, is the raw *soul* joined to an *indestructible* body, exposed to its own sin for eternity."[43]

Other traditionalists reveal their belief that the damned will not be destroyed by describing annihilationism—a view which they reject—using the language of destruction. That they frequently characterize annihilationism this way is somewhat incredible. For centuries, they have adamantly insisted that English Bibles' use of "destroy" to describe the fate of the lost is no evidence for annihilationism. But if that's the case, then why do these same traditionalists voluntarily and without qualification use "destroy" when describing annihilationism?

---

39. Moreland, *The God Question*, 240.
40. Geisler and Turek, *I Don't Have Enough Faith to Be an Atheist*, 386.
41. Thomas, "Jesus' View of Eternal Punishment," 167.
42. Lactantius, "The Divine Institutes," 217.
43. Lutzer, *One Minute After You Die*, 117.

- Christopher Morgan says that "Annihilationism is the belief that those who die apart from saving faith in Jesus Christ will be ultimately destroyed."[44]
- Albert Mohler writes: "The Socinians ... questioned the eternality of punishment in hell, teaching instead that the wicked would be destroyed in hell—a view that has come to be known as annihilationism."[45] And again, "[John] Wenham leaned toward the annihilationist view that unbelievers might be destroyed rather than endlessly tortured in hell."[46]
- J. I. Packer writes, "Furthermore, the theory of annihilationism, in which unbelievers are not tortured but destroyed in hell, must be read into the Bible."[47]
- Vernon McGee, in a sermon says: "[Hell is] not annihilation. Some of our cults like Jehovah's Witnesses, Seventh Day Adventism, they teach that the righteous will live forever but the wicked are just going to be destroyed and that ends it as far as they're concerned."[48]
- Randy Alcorn writes, "Another view [of annihilationism] states that unbelievers are destroyed not at death, but sometime later."[49]

5. The Consumption of the Damned

In Scripture, the ultimate fate of the unrepentant is sometimes likened to the burning up of weeds or chaff.

- Matthew 3:12: "[Christ's] winnowing fork is in His hand, and He will thoroughly clear His threshing floor; and He will gather His wheat into the barn, but He will burn up the chaff with unquenchable fire." (NASB)

- The author of Hebrews, without using the imagery of chaff or furnaces, plainly teaches that God's fire will consume his enemies: "For if we go on sinning deliberately after receiving the knowledge of the truth, there no longer remains a sacrifice for sins, but a fearful expectation of

---

44. Morgan, "Annihilationism: Will the Unsaved Be Punished Forever?" 196.
45. Mohler, "Is Hell for Real?" 13.
46. Ibid., 19.
47. Packer, "Does Everyone Go to Heaven?" 67.
48. McGee, "Hell—Fact or Fiction?"
49. Alcorn, *If God Is Good*, 313.

judgment, and a fury of fire that will consume the adversaries" (Heb 10:26–27).

Traditionalists throughout history have, again, flatly denied this plain biblical teaching:

- Cyril of Jerusalem writes: "but if a man is a sinner, he shall receive an eternal body, fitted to endure the penalties of sins, that he may burn eternally in fire, nor ever be consumed."[50]
- Thomas Aquinas, speaking of the lost, says: "Likewise they shall be passible, because they shall never deteriorate and, although burning eternally in fire, they shall never be consumed."[51]
- Richard Baxter warns: "Woe to the soul that is thus set up as a butt for the wrath of the Almighty to shoot at! and as a bush that must burn in the flames of his jealousy, and never be consumed!"[52]
- Jonathan Edwards says: "And here the bodies of all the wicked shall burn, and be tormented to all eternity, and never be consumed; and the wrath of God shall be poured out on their souls."[53]
- John Gill says: "So the fire of hell, as it will burn, torture, and distress rebellious sinners, it will preserve them in their beings; they shall not be consumed by it, but continued in it."[54]
- Charles Spurgeon says: "Your body will be prepared by God in such a way that it will burn forever without being consumed: it will lie, not as you consider, in a metaphorical fire, but in actual flame."[55]
- John MacArthur says: "Transcendent, eternal bodies, greater than anything we have on this earth, are going to be given to the damned so that they can suffer in those bodies forever.... With the present body, man couldn't endure hell. You ... the body that we have now, would be consumed in a moment. So as God fits the redeemed with new bodies for heaven, He fits the damned with new bodies for hell." Later in the same sermon he says: "in hell, the worms never die because the body, though it is continually being consumed, is never consumed."[56]

---

50. Cyril, "The Catechetical Lectures"; *NPNF* 7:139.
51. Aquinas, *The Catechetical Instructions of St. Thomas Aquinas*, Article 11.
52. Baxter, *The Saints' Everlasting Rest*, 168.
53. Edwards, "A History of the Work of Redemption," 504.
54. Gill, "Mark 9."
55. Spurgeon, *Sermons of the Rev. C. H. Spurgeon. 2nd series*, 275.
56. MacArthur, "The Furnace of Fire."

- This is somewhat curious because in a different sermon MacArthur criticizes Rob Bell, saying: "Just how serious is Rob Bell's heresy? It is not merely that he rejects what Jesus taught about hell; Bell rejects the God of Scripture. He deplores the idea of divine vengeance against sin. He cannot stand the plain meaning of texts like Hebrews 12:29: 'Our God is a consuming fire.'"[57]

- Robert Peterson concedes that there are five biblical texts which might reasonably be interpreted to teach annihilationism. After mentioning the first three passages he writes: "Hebrews also contains two texts that could be construed as teaching annihilationism: 'a raging fire that will consume the enemies of God' (Heb 10:2); 'our God is a consuming fire' (12:29). These five texts could possibly be so interpreted, but should they be? I must answer in the negative due to the Scriptural testimony that hell-fire speaks of the pain of the wicked, not their consumption."[58] If a passage which directly states the wicked will be consumed does not actually speak of the consumption of the wicked, it's unclear to me how biblical authors could ever communicate such a thing!

Additional Affirmations

In addition to these five affirmations, the same point can be made with other biblical phrases. For instance, "perishing" is a common way for English Bibles to describe the fate of the lost (e.g., John 3:16). And yet traditionalists maintain that the damned in hell are imperishable. Norman Geisler, for instance writes: "[The fire of hell] is *real* but not necessarily *physical* (at least not as we know it), because people will have imperishable physical bodies (John 5:28–29; Revelation 20:13–15), so normal fire would not affect them."[59]

Or consider Paul's teaching that the resurrection bodies of the *righteous* will be incorruptible. Traditionalists must maintain that the bodies of the damned are also incorruptible. Gerard Hopkins, for instance, writes: "No one in the body can suffer fire for very long, the frame is destroyed and the pain comes to an end; not so, unhappily, the pain that afflicts the indestructible mind, nor, after Judgment day, the incorruptible body."[60]

---

57. MacArthur, "Bell's Inferno."

58. Peterson, "A Traditionalist Response to John Stott's Arguments for Annihilationism," 558.

59. Geisler, *If God, Why Evil?* 104.

60. Hopkins, *The Sermons and Devotional Writings of Gerard Manley Hopkins*, 241.

I'll wrap up all this quoting with a few statements from Augustine, wherein he contravenes several of the above teachings in the span of a few sentences. Here we see that the venerable tradition of contradicting the plain pronouncements of Scripture goes back to at least the fifth century. In *The City of God* he writes: "As the soul too, is a proof that not everything which can suffer pain can also die, why then do they yet demand that we produce real examples to prove that it is not incredible that the bodies of men condemned to everlasting punishment may retain their soul in the fire, may burn *without being consumed*, and may suffer *without perishing*?"[61] Later on he concludes, "I have already sufficiently made out that animals can *live in the fire*, in burning *without being consumed*, in pain *without dying*, by a miracle of the most omnipotent Creator."[62]

Observations and Conclusion to Part One

Allow me to make three observations before looking at how some traditionalists respond to the challenge I just presented.

First, some readers may suspect that these five teachings are all more or less getting at the same thing, and that I spent a lot of time unnecessarily parsing it into five different categories. After all, if a person won't die, then isn't he immortal by definition? And if a person is immortal, then won't he live forever and never be destroyed? I think that's right; it's almost as if the biblical authors went out of their way to express the same idea in as many ways as possible, just so there would be no confusion later on. Unfortunately, it's also as if traditionalists got together at some point in history and said "OK guys, no matter what Scripture says about the fate of the damned, just assert the opposite!"

Second, as tedious as all that quoting may have been, I included less than half of the quotes I've compiled. That's just to say that these statements are ubiquitous in Christian literature, both historical and contemporary. The next time you read an article or hear a sermon about hell, be on the lookout and chances are you will encounter such statements.

Third, I want the reader to notice the breadth and diversity of personalities whom I've quoted. Included are church fathers, doctors of the church, medieval theologians, Protestants, Catholics, Puritans, Calvinists, Arminians, theologians, exegetes, apologists, pastors, preachers, evangelists, and missionaries. So what I've assembled is not a misrepresentation: this *is* traditionalism. Moreover, these are all people who ought to know better; I

---

61. Augustine, "The City of God," 21.4; *NPNF* 2:454; emphasis added.
62. Ibid. 21.9.2; *NPNF* 2:461; emphasis added.

included many of the biggest, most highly respected names of historic and contemporary Christianity. Further, many of the people I quoted are not only aware of conditionalism, but have argued against the view publicly in sermons, speeches, books, and other publications. One might think that their familiarity with the arguments conditionalists offer would prompt them to describe their own view in ways that do not leave it wide open to criticism, and yet they apparently can't help but to do otherwise.

It's hard to believe that anyone committed to the authority of Scripture can read what these traditionalists have said and not conclude that we've stumbled into a bit of a doctrinal scandal. I am aware of no other doctrine that's considered to be historically orthodox, whose adherents appear to contradict Scripture so brazenly and to such an extent. In part two, I'll examine how some traditionalists have attempted to resolve this apparent scandal.

PART TWO

As might be expected, traditionalists react to the implicit argument above in various ways. Some take a step back and realize that, at the very least, something fishy seems to be going on; when respected traditionalist theologians habitually repudiate plain biblical affirmations and employ biblical language when describing *conditionalism*, surely something is amiss! Unfortunately, many are unwilling to entertain the notion that traditionalism is simply at odds with Scripture and so dig in their heels and attempt a defense. I will evaluate four common responses.

1. Denial

One response is to simply deny that traditionalists have said things such as "everyone lives forever." In fact, it was my frustration with this response that inspired this project. In personal conversations and debates I would sometimes receive pushback after asserting things such as "traditionalism teaches that everyone has immortality" or "traditionalists deny that the damned will be destroyed." Accusations of "attacking a straw man" were not uncommon. Phil Fernandes for instance, in his debate with Chris Date, made just this claim; he accused Chris of misrepresenting traditionalism when he claimed that it affirms the immortality of the lost.[63] Hopefully what I've presented above shows conclusively that traditionalism is not being misrepresented.

2. Repudiation and Obfuscation

Others respond by repudiating what all these influential traditionalists have said. In fact, some have claimed that traditionalists of the past were just not careful—or even sloppy—to say things such as "the damned are immortal." This is somewhat curious because these people often scoff at the suggestion that these same traditionalists could have been wrong about the doctrine of hell for so long. Perhaps their exegesis was sloppy as well?

Whatever the case, the response usually goes something like this: "The biblical view is not that the damned will *live* forever, rather it's that they will *exist* forever." We see some traditionalist authors, for instance, being very mindful to not use the words "live," "life," or "alive" in reference to the damned (even though most of them eventually slip up and say it anyway when they're not being careful).

For example, here are two comments that were left on the Rethinking Hell blog:

- Commenter 1: "Being raised with a physical body that eternally endures the displeasure of God is not, on my reading of Scripture, a form of immortality. . . . To put it another way, unbelievers will not live forever. They will die forever."[64]

- Commenter 2: "I agree that the unbeliever does not 'live' forever. There is no living in hell or the [lake of fire]. Existence is a different distinction from 'living' 'life' or even being so called 'immortal.'"[65]

In a discussion on Facebook, evangelical philosopher and apologist William Lane Craig wrote the following:

> It seems to me that annihilationists mistakenly assume that death means the cessation of existence. *But while the denizens of hell do not have life in the biblical sense, they nevertheless do*

63. Rethinking Hell, "Chris Date and Phil Fernandes Debate Hell (HD)."

64. Peter G. [pseudonym], comment on Date, "Cross Purposes," comment posted August 26, 2012.

65. Breckmin [pseudonym], comment on Date, "Obfuscating Traditionalism," comment posted February 15, 2014.

exist. The difference between eternal life and eternal death is not a matter of prolongation of existence. Both the saved and the damned will exist forever but the one in a condition of everlasting life and the other in a condition of everlasting death.[66]

Unfortunately, this type of response is not limited to online comments. For instance, Kenneth Boa and Robert Bowman write, "In popular explanations of Hell, one often hears that people will live forever either in Heaven or Hell. This way of speaking of Hell is, we will argue, getting at something that is true but is not worded in the best way. Biblically speaking, the righteous will live forever in Heaven, but the wicked will not 'live' forever in Hell."[67]

Perhaps suspiciously, traditionalists will usually deny that the damned in hell are alive *only* when responding to conditionalist arguments. In other words, when conditionalism is not at the forefront of their attention, traditionalists are typically more than happy to explain that "everyone lives forever." This, of course, is exactly what we should expect because it's not for nothing that traditionalists have always affirmed that the damned are immortal and will live forever. Just consider the traditional conception of the inhabitants of hell: They're embodied; traditionalists typically define "death" as the *separation* of soul and body. They're animated; they are active and breathing and moving—they're not just lumps of inert matter such as clay or dust. Biblically, that means that they must have what's sometimes called the "breath of life." They're conscious; they can think; they can remember; they can feel pain and remorse; they can use all their senses; they can communicate; they can sin and do evil. These are clearly *living* human beings.

So "existence" does not sufficiently describe the fate of the damned, given traditionalism. Jonathan Edwards explains it well. He writes: "The wicked, in their punishment, are said to weep and wail, and gnash their teeth; *which implies not only real existence, but life*, knowledge, and activity, and that they are in a very sensible and exquisite manner affected with their punishment."[68] Augustine likewise points out the obvious fact that in order for something to feel pain, it must be alive: "For we cannot call it reasoning to make pain a presumption of death, while, in fact, it is rather a sign of life. For though it be a question whether that which suffers can continue to live

---

66. Craig, William Lane, comment on Facebook, March 3, 2013, online: https://www.facebook.com/rick.baskett/posts/363374160442747?comment_id=1806299; emphasis added.

67. Boa and Bowman, *Sense & Nonsense about Heaven & Hell*, 106. Notice the authors' curious use of scare quotes around "live." Traditionalists will sometimes put scare quotes around biblical phrases when speaking of the damned, indicating that something other than their normal use is intended.

68. Edwards, "The Eternity of Hell Torments," 270; emphasis added.

for ever, yet it is certain that everything which suffers pain does live, and that pain can exist only in a living subject."[69]

So it just won't do for traditionalists to change their vocabulary without changing their beliefs; simply replacing the word "life" with "existence" does not strike me as an honest effort to accurately communicate their view, but rather a transparent attempt to evade an uncomfortable challenge.

3. Paradox

Some traditionalists, even though they believe the damned are immortal and indestructible (and will therefore live forever and never die) have recognized that Scripture seems to indicate the opposite. Their response has been to simply affirm the contradiction, chalking it up to "paradox."

Henri Blocher, for instance, writes:

> One can sense a paradox in the concept of permanence in destruction which the Bible itself expresses when it speaks of "second death," "undying worm," and tradition sharpens, for example, in the words of Saint Gregory the Great: "a deathless death, and endless end, a ceaseless cessation, since the death lives, the end always begins, and cessation knows not how to cease."[70]

Paradoxical indeed—almost to the point of sounding like a Zen Buddhist *koan*![71] But this idea of a "deathless death" or "living death" is found often in the historical literature.

- Cardinal Newman writes: "God is in hell as well as in heaven, a thought which almost distracts the mind to think of. . . . Where life is, there is He; and though it be but the life of death—the living death of eternal torment—He is the principle of it."[72]

- Seventeenth-century German Catholic theologian, Martin of Cochem writes: "The existence of the damned is more like death than life; it is a living death, an everlasting, unlimited torture and misery."[73]

---

69. Augustine, "The City of God," 21.3; *NPNF* 2:453.

70. Blocher, "Everlasting Punishment and the Problem of Evil," 288.

71. Consider the following quotation attributed to seventh-century Zen Grand Master, Hui-Neng: "Annihilation is still not annihilated, and birth is said to be unborn." Hui-Neng, *The Sutra of Hui-Neng, Grand Master of Zen*, 69.

72. Newman, *Newman on the Bible*, 53.

73. Martin von Cochem, *The Four Last Things*, 135.

- John Boys, the seventeenth-century Dean of Canterbury writes: "[In Hell] all shall not be punished in the same degree, though in the same fire: all shall be burnt, yet none consumed." Then, quoting Saint Prosper and Saint Augustine, he writes, "In that unquenchable flame, 'Hell fires torment but do not consume the body; they punish, without destroying.' Prosper. Mors sine morte, finis sine fine, defectus sine defectu. 'Deathless death, endless end, destruction of the indestructible.' Aug."[74]

- Seventeenth-century cleric, Jeremy Taylor, known as "Shakespeare of Divines," writes the following:

  > After all this, there shall not want in hell the pains of death, which amongst human punishments is the greatest; that of hell is a living death. The death which men give, together with death, takes away the pain and sense of dying; but the eternal death of sinners is with sense; and by so much greater, as it hath more of life, recollecting within itself the worst of dying, which is to perish ; and the most intolerable of life, which is to suffer pain. In hell there shall be, unto the miserable, a death without death, and an end without end; for their death shall ever live, and their end shall never begin.[75]

- Johann Gerhard, seventeenth-century Lutheran theologian:

  > Severe indeed is their punishment on account of the bitter pain of the torments they shall suffer; severer still because of the diversity of these torments; but the thought that they shall last forever and ever with no diminution, no cessation, is the worst of all. That will be death without death, end without end, perishing without perishing; because that death is an ever living death; that end is a ceaseless beginning; and that perishing knows no perishing. Those poor lost souls shall seek for life and find it not; they "shall desire to die, and death shall flee from them"; and after a hundred thousand, thousand, thousand years they shall simply suffer renewed torments without end! The very thought of the endlessness of their pain will torment them more than the sense of eternal pain itself. What can be conceived of as more intolerable than thus to die that you are always living, and thus to live that you are always dying? That life will be lifeless, and

---

74. Boys, *An Exposition of the Several Offices*, 309.

75. Taylor, "Contemplations of the State of Man, in This Life and in That Which Is to Come," 1851.

that death will be deathless! If thou art life, why dost thou die, and if death, how dost thou always endure?[76]

I grant that this sort of paradoxical extravagance may strike some as profound, but notice how simple and straightforward the biblical passages are by comparison; the righteous live and the unrighteous die, period.

4. Equivocation

The best the traditionalist can do, I think, is to affirm that the damned will die in *one* sense of the word, but not die in another sense. That they will forever be alive in one sense, but not alive in another. That they are immortal in one sense, but not another. That they will be destroyed and consumed in one sense but not another. In other words, the traditionalist must argue that he is not contradicting Scripture; he is simply using words equivocally.[77]

Now that seems needlessly complicated, and again, this sort of ambiguity is not present in any judgment passage that I'm aware of. But I think this is the best stance that the traditionalist can take, and really the only plausible one. I sometimes refer to this position as "the final form of traditionalism" because in my interactions, I often witness traditionalists begin with one of the responses mentioned above, before finally settling on this stance.

So regarding the word "life," for instance, Charles Hodge takes this very approach. He writes, "The Scriptures everywhere recognize the distinction, in reference to men, between animal, intellectual, and spiritual life. A man may have the two former and be destitute of the latter."[78] In other words, in hell the damned may be physically alive but "spiritually" dead. There are several problems with this view, but I will only mention one here: When biblical authors speak of the death of the unrepentant, it's often clear that they don't have something like "spiritual death" in mind. Take John 11:25–26 for instance: Jesus says: "I am the resurrection and the life. Whoever believes in me, though he die, yet shall he live, and everyone who lives and believes in me shall never die." So what sort of death is being spoken of in the second clause? If we set aside our doctrinal presuppositions, there's no reason to think Jesus means literal, physical death in the first clause, but figurative, "spiritual" death in the next.

---

76. Gerhard, "The Eternity of Future Punishment," 294–95.

77. This may be what's going on in some of the "paradoxical" statements just cited; it's difficult to be certain.

78. Hodge, *Systematic Theology*, 873–74.

Regarding "immortality," contemporary traditionalists often rely on this same equivocation argument. They concede that Paul ascribes immortality only to the saved and that traditionalism ascribes immortality to all humans, saved and lost. But they insist that there's no genuine contradiction here because when Paul uses the word "immortality" he means something different from what people normally mean when they use the word "immortality." Doug Moo for instance argues:

> Does this mean, then, that Paul teaches "conditional immortality"? Yes and no. If we define "immortality" as Paul uses the terminology, then the answer is yes. But Paul's way of using the word is not the same as the way the word is usually used in theology. In this broader sphere the word usually has the sense of unending existence. Because Paul's focus is restricted, nothing in his letters denies the immortality of human beings in this broader sense.[79]

So what Moo and others are saying is that when Paul speaks of "immortality" he has in mind a particular *quality* of immortality, not immortality *per se* (that is, mere deathlessness or incorruptibility). In other words, while the damned are immortal in the normal sense of the word, they are not immortal in the "Pauline" sense.

Now it has to be pointed out that this move is simply unmotivated by the relevant texts themselves. There's no reason to think that Paul is using the Greek words for "immortality" in some qualified, idiosyncratic way. But this is the move that traditionalists *must* make, or else abandon traditionalism: if endless torment requires unconditional and universal immortality, but Paul teaches conditional immortality, then the doctrine of endless torment is false. That is, of course, unless Paul uses "immortality" to mean something other than what theologians mean when they use the same word. I grant that this may sound uncharitable but, by my lights, this is an ad hoc maneuver—and a rather desperate one at that—to avoid an unpleasant conclusion.

We see the same thing with words like "destroy" and "consume." In 2011, I debated this issue on Chris Date's Theopologetics podcast. During cross examinations, my opponent said: "I don't think that people could experience [burning] forever if they are consumed at some point." To which I enthusiastically agreed; if people are consumed, they can't experience being burned forever. I asked him if he therefore disagreed with Hebrews 10:27, which explicitly states that the damned *will* be consumed. Consider his response: "They will be consumed in the sense that that passage is describing

---

79. Moo, "Paul on Hell," 109.

and that sense is the sense that those people will be eternally tormented in hell. That's what that's a reference to, which is not the literal sense of 'consume.' I fully concede that point."[80]

Perhaps now it's clearer what I mean by ad hoc. "Consume" simply does not mean "eternally torment," and there is literally no contextual indication that this is what the author of Hebrews has in mind. But my opponent *had* to say that "consume" is not being used literally there—either that, or concede the debate, but of course that wasn't going to happen.

So it turns out that, even at its best, traditionalism is quite convoluted:

- Will the damned die? Well, yes and no.
- Do only the righteous live forever? Yes and no.
- Are only the righteous granted immortality? Yes in one sense, no in another.
- Will the damned be destroyed? In one way yes, in another way no.
- Will be they be consumed? Not literally, no. Perhaps figuratively?

And notice: Traditionalists can answer these questions in the negative only by denying that the biblical language is true in its literal, plain, ordinary sense. Likewise, they can answer these questions in the affirmative only by allowing the biblical language to be true in some extended, figurative, spiritual, or otherwise qualified sense.

One is left to wonder: If the biblical authors really *had* intended to communicate that the damned would *literally* be put to death, destroyed, and consumed, what else could they have said? And if biblical authors wanted to communicate that the damned would be immortal and live forever in the normal, literal sense, could they not have simply said so plainly? And yet we can scour Scripture and not come up with *one* passage that says "the damned are immortal" or "the unrepentant will never die."

This is how the debate must be framed. Those genuinely seeking truth on this matter need to recognize the unenviable position that contemporary traditionalists find themselves in. Traditionalism is far from the "face-value" interpretation of Scripture that it's often claimed to be.[81] We conditionalists bear no burden to show that words like "destroy," "death," and "consume"

---

80. Date, "Episode 65: Immortal."

81. For instance, Walvoord, "The Literal View," 27, writes, "If exegesis is the final factor, eternal punishment is the only proper conclusion; taken at its face value, the Bible teaches eternal punishment." Likewise, Morey, *Death and the Afterlife*, 21–22, writes: "The Bible was written to be understood by the normal person who would take the words of the Bible in their simplest and most natural meaning." And again: "We cannot accept the notions that the authors of Scripture were willfully deceptive in teaching the opposite of what their words imply."

mean "to annihilate" or "cease to exist"; traditionalists have already implicitly conceded that the common, plain, literal sense of those words entails our view. The burden lies squarely on traditionalists to show that a multitude of passages *must* be interpreted figuratively or spiritually and that their equivocal answers to the above questions are genuinely motivated by careful exegesis and not a pre-commitment to a particular theological tradition.

I think it's going to be a tough sell.

Part 5

THE ROAD AHEAD

17

The Future of Hell

— Glenn Peoples —

Glenn Peoples runs the popular New Zealand blog Right Reason and podcast Say Hello to My Little Friend. There and elsewhere he writes and speaks on theology and biblical studies, moral and social philosophy, and philosophy of religion. He completed undergraduate studies in Theology at the Bible College of New Zealand (now Laidlaw College), followed by an M.Th. and a PhD in Philosophy at the University of Otago. Peoples is the author of the article, "Fallacies in the Annihilationism Debate" (JETS 50.2), and of an introductory chapter in Rethinking Hell: Readings in Evangelical Conditionalism.

Glenn originally presented the following paper as a plenary speaker at the Rethinking Hell conference, 2014.

WHERE ARE WE NOW?

> We must all die; we are like water spilled on the ground, which cannot be gathered up again. (2 Sam 14:14)

The image of water spilled on the ground and which you cannot put back into the bucket is an effective one to illustrate something that cannot be undone. We have our own expressions for the same purpose: You cannot put the genie back in the bottle. You can't put toothpaste back into the tube. All of these images and others apply to the current state of the discussion on final punishment.

Whether you think it is for better or worse, everyone should be of one mind in saying that there is no undoing the change that has taken place within the evangelical world when it comes to the way that we think and talk about hell, due in no small part to the work of Edward Fudge, but also the work of a number of other evangelicals. The pitcher has been shattered; the silver cord has been cut; the water has been spilled. Use any metaphor you like. There is no going back. Our world is different. It is pointless (although that does not stop everyone) to try to proceed in the discussion as though we can serve up the same material in favor of the one view that everyone in our church community holds, cross our fingers and hope that it will have the same effect that it did a few generations ago. Those of us who think that conditional immortality represents the biblical perspective think that this is a change for the better.

From the vantage point of this new landscape in the discussion about the doctrine of eternal punishment, where do we go next? I am no prophet and the question of what the discussion will in fact look like in fifty years is somewhat beyond me. But I have some ideas about where I think we should try to take the discussion next. Of course Christians, be they conditionalists or not, are all on the same side in the war. With that in mind I ask the reader to understand the metaphor in context when I say that rather than offering a prediction, I want to offer some tactical advice in the war room.

LOWEST COMMON DENOMINATOR

Before I get to that advice, let me get something off my chest about where we are now, because I think it makes a difference in regard to what the future looks like.

A number of times I have been exasperated in discussions where my partner in dialogue realizes that I have thought about what they say but I just do not agree with his or her supposedly liberating or fresh perspective. The reply that they leave me with is something like: "Glenn, what's happened to you? You're willing to question and reject the mainstream evangelical view on hell, you're willing to question and reject the mainstream evangelical view of the soul, so why are you now stubbornly putting on the brakes on that critical thinking when it comes to this view that I'm trying to get you to accept on women in the church, or the Trinity, or vaccines, or Catholicism, or full preterism, or something else?"

Such comebacks reveal a line of thinking that worries me and which, I think, should worry us all: that we hold this view because we are the sort of people who give up mainstream views. That's just what we are like. Since we give up mainstream views and delight in going against the flow (a terrible misconception about what it means to think "critically"), why won't we give up the mainstream evangelical view on whatever the subject happens to be in the represent discussion? It worries me that people think that of me because it is frankly not true of me, but it also worries me for another reason, one that undermines the credibility of the "movement" towards conditional immortality. How many people have adopted our view because of the understandable thrill of parting with the mainstream and becoming part of the exclusive club of those "in the know," the "elect" of evangelical theology? Against some of my more opportunistic desires to be able to point to our numbers as evidence of a sea change in our favor, I respectfully request that if this describes you, you go back to where you came from. Do not return until and unless you can honestly justify the conditionalist view to yourself on biblical grounds. We do not need your support. We have that in Scripture.

I am going to make that most arrogant of comparisons by comparing us to Jesus, who had two very different approaches to the call that he gave to potential followers. On the one hand, his message sounds almost accommodating: Come to me if you are heavy laden and I will give you rest. My burden is light! But the truth is that Jesus spoke the words that people needed to hear. To those who were oppressed by the burdens laid upon them by others, the freedom an unburdened life to be found in Christ is just what they needed to know about. But to his disciples and to those who took themselves to be in the know, he said some very strong words.

After teaching them that nobody comes to him unless the Father draws him, that nobody can come to him unless it is granted by the Father, that everyone who has heard from the Father comes to Christ, that Jesus is the bread of life, and that by eating the bread of life we will not die like they did in the wilderness but we will have eternal life (John 6), some people left him. In response Jesus did not say, "Wait, I take it back! Maybe you can come to me even if the Father hasn't granted it—a little bit. Forget what I said about my flesh and blood if it offends you!" Instead, and perhaps unexpectedly, he turned to his disciples and said, "So, do you want to leave too?" Jesus welcomed everyone, but had some very direct words for those who wanted to conform the faith to their comfort.

This puts me in two minds about the attitude we should have to people who are coming into the conditionalist "camp" and those who will do so in future (I dislike the word "camp" because of its partisan overtones but it is convenient to speak that way). Of course we want Christians to embrace this truth, and the evidence that conditionalism is biblical is overwhelming.[1] But I'm the kind of stickler who cares how and why we embrace the truth.

---

1. Edward Fudge's work *The Fire That Consumes*, now in its third edition, continues to be the standard modern work on the subject. However, I summarize a biblical case for conditional immortality in Peoples, "Introduction to Evangelical Conditionalism."

I don't want you to embrace this view because you're into embracing the next big thing. If you do that, after you tire of this thing you will embrace the next thing, or God-forbid, what you perceive to be the easiest thing. I don't want you embrace it because of the thrill of going against the flow, because if I have my way, *this will become the flow*. As best I can tell, if the mainstream view on hell becomes one with the biblical view, conditionalism will be the mainstream view. What will you do then if going against the mainstream is your thing?

On to my advice, for what it is worth.

DO NOT REINVENT THE WHEEL

In the sciences, once discoveries have been made and demonstrated multiple times, the experiments stop and scientists move on to new ones, testing new hypotheses. What we have established then passes into our repository of knowledge. Anyone who today wrote a book arguing for the truth of what we now know about gravity or bacteria would be told by a prospective publisher: "Your evidence is very good, but this has already been done. There is simply no need for a book like this." He might still write an educational book that laid out all the facts for an uninitiated audience, or he might publicly respond to a quack who argued that the earth was flat (but his time would probably better be spent in other ways), but there is no point in him trying to establish from the ground up something when there is already a body of knowledge out there that lays this groundwork. Once all the work has been done to firmly establish a theory, scientists do not keep repeating that work. They appeal to it in their future work and build on it.

I sometimes wish that in the world of theology we treated knowledge in the same way. Often we do. But evangelicalism sometimes suffers from a sense of disconnection from historical discussions, and the discussion about hell is a prime example of this. Going forward in the discussion of conditionalism we need to get this right so that we make the most of the limited time that we have in this life.

I think very little of the "new atheist" movement, but there is something to learn from it. One of the things that I object to about the likes of Richard Dawkins or the late Christopher Hitchens is that they carried and carry out their vendetta against religion with a confidence that is unearned. They speak as though they had an authority earned by in-depth knowledge and insight, when in reality their would-be scathing attacks on religion are hollow precisely because they very often have only the slightest idea what they are talking about. But other atheists appreciate the confidence as something refreshing. On the whole, *The God Delusion* is one of the worst popular books on religious belief ever written, but a reviewer praised it, saying that reading it was like "coming up for air" because of its directness. There was no pussy-footing around. The author took something to be obvious and so he said that it is obvious. Those who appreciate such writing appreciate it for its frankness. I am glossing over some of the more obnoxious tendencies that such pieces of writing often include in order to make this point: If only the state of the evidence really were what these writers claimed it to be, their confidence would have been justified.

I am confident of the truth of what I see in Scripture about death and mortality being our lot for now, eternal life being found only in Christ. I'm confident of the solemn claim that God makes in his word that sinners will not stand in the judgment and that the road that seems right to man ends in death forever. And more relevantly in the evangelical milieu, I'm confident that Scripture teaches these things and to anybody who will listen I am prepared show them that it does, as Edward Fudge has done so ably. This, however, is an earned confidence. You are entitled to appeal to the things of which you are confident where that confidence is earned.

The most positive and frequent feedback that I get regarding anything that I have publicly said about the subject of hell has come to me because I wrote an "open letter to my traditionalist friends," publishing it online in June 2011. It is probably the most direct and confident thing that I have ever said on the subject. In it I candidly told the published defenders of the doctrine of eternal torment that:

> ... your endless stream of apologetics on behalf of your doctrine of eternal torment is very poorly argued, fallacious, tiresome, ineffective and even just lazy sometimes. That will appear very blunt. Those sound like insults to some people. But if they are true, then you are not helped by not being told these things. You need to hear them. There has to be a context in which you are willing to hear people tell you these things if they believe they're true.[2]

That letter was born out of a frustration on my part at those evangelical gatekeepers who continually raise the same bad objections to conditionalism time and time again, breaking every sensible rule in the book when it comes to biblical interpretation. They are doing something that would not be tolerated in other contexts, using methods of argument and biblical interpretation for which they would give their own students a failing grade in any other subject (or at least they would be justified in doing so).

2. Peoples, "An Open Letter to My Traditionalist Friends."

If people kept on saying, over and over again, that thunder comes from the clouds banging together (as I was once told as a child), would we feel compelled to continually make the case, from the ground up, for the existence of static electricity and lightning? Would that not simply be seen as a case of holding up scientific progress while we sink our time into re-hashing the basics? Would we not eventually be justified in simply stating in plain terms that such nonsense has no place in serious discussions about weather?

I frequently call to mind an article from 2006 where I looked at the many articles of Robert Peterson in which he makes the same arguments against conditionalism (I looked at other authors also) and I pointed out that in each case we are seeing the repetition of arguments that seek to cover old ground. These are objections that have been preempted and comprehensively addressed in the literature already. They constitute the reemergence of some basic mistakes in biblical interpretation. His reply to me, ironically, was that my argument does not advance the discussion. Quite right, but that was the point.

You don't have to re-cover the same ground as though it has been lost and we need to "reclaim" it every time somebody raises an objection—especially somebody who should know better. One of the worst things we could have done with the *Rethinking Hell* book project would be to write a whole new volume trying to show from the ground up that the Scripture teaches annihilationism. Indeed the book that we did create shows why that would have been a bad idea: just look at how many times this has already been done in all the works that we draw on! The case for conditionalism has been made, and made very well.

When your teachers or pastors throw out the same objection that every other objector has used—and they probably will—make it your business to make them aware that they are attempting to cover old ground. It is no different than a professor of theology who says "You know, I've just had a thought. How can Jesus be God is he's a man? Ridiculous!" True, that may be a thought worth having, but anybody in that position who didn't know how this thought had been responded to and who ran with that objection as something ground-breaking instead of addressing the existing explanations has not done their homework.

Those of us who have arrived at a conditionalist understanding of Scripture and who have spent a few years reading the objections as they appear are confident—rightly so, I maintain—that the case for the biblical basis of conditional immortality is decisive and the objections are without merit. Of course we should be willing to interact with new objections. Yes, we should gently and kindly help those who admit that this is unfamiliar territory. For that matter, be kind to everyone with whom you discuss this, but we need to develop a frankness with those in a position to know better or who act like they have settled the matter when they effectively try to drag us back into the courtroom to re-hear exactly the same case that we've made time and again. That is not, I think, how God would have us use the time that he has given us.

BUT . . . NOT TOO BOLD?

And here is my double-mindedness again.

There's a parallel between what we are seeing here in this changing outlook among evangelicals and the biblical distinction between this age and the age to come. Think of the era during which, among evangelicals, most in the mainstream were unfamiliar with the concept of annihilationism or conditional immortality—and hostile to it if they had heard of it, since it violated their tradition and represented a wholly unfamiliar way of thinking. Now think of an era when the majority of evangelicals are familiar with it and perhaps the better part of that majority are at least kindly disposed to it as a plausible scenario or better yet, persuaded that it is at least likely to be true.

Which era do we live in? Do we still live in the age of being considered borderline heretics or of begging for a seat at the table? Not as far as I can tell. We should not act as though we do. There are some who think of us that way, but in relative terms they are very few. In the early 1960s Joseph Arthur Baird was able to talk about the subject of the nature of eternal punishment as "this matter which is seldom examined except within highly conservative circles, and there so often uncritically."[3] Is that still so? Certainly not to the same extent. The door had been opened to a new kind of discussion, partly by the work of Henry Constable almost a century earlier, also by Edward White, and now by Joseph Baird's own work. But among evangelicals, annihilationism was a very dirty word still, if they knew the word at all.

What about now? Some things have happened since the sixties. Edward Fudge's work is one of them. So too is the acknowledgement, perhaps the "confession" or coming out of the closet of British evangelicals like John Stott—practically the Pope of evangelicalism for some time—or Michael Green or John Wenham, that they believe that this is what Scripture teaches, along with F. F. Bruce's kind words about the case for conditionalism. The acknowledgement of the weight and the visibility of the biblical evidence is becoming uncomfortably ubiquitous in the evangelical world.

---

3. Baird, *The Justice of God*, 228.

If I were a suspicious man, I might think that there is an invisible hand at work. But my confidence could be based on over-active optimism about where we are on that timeline. Maybe I am getting ahead of myself when I say that we do not have to make a ground-up case over and over again. We have—unambiguously, I think—passed the point where a large part of evangelical Christianity in the developed world, at least, knows that this is a live option. But how large is that number? And why would I ask?

Here is why I ask: We look back, some of us, with a sense of disbelief that any decent Christian man or woman could think that slavery was tolerable. But we should not do so. When you live in a world in which slavery is normal, and everything you are taught, you are taught by people who believe that slavery is acceptable, and you live in a social and economic environment that only exists because of slavery, you literally do not have the ability to think about slavery in the same way as somebody in the twentieth or twenty-first century who was born and raised in a society where slavery is illegal and universally regarded as repugnant. The reverse is also true—somebody born in today's world is literally unable to think like somebody from the old world.

This fact can be described in a number of ways, but one way is via the idea of plausibility structures. Because of many factors, some our own doing, others not, the mental book-spaces in the library of our mind are of a given size and shape. We have ways of thinking that are built up over time by our environment and by habit, and short of a miracle, these ways just cannot be torn down overnight—not without a mental breakdown. We should not want to do that to people.

For those who are in a position to hear it, then as I said earlier, we should take for granted what we are confident of and present it in a manner that conveys just that confidence. And, I say, in a missionary context, this is a perspective that we are entitled to offer as the biblical perspective without having to even suggest that it's just one of several possibilities. The Scripture teaches repeatedly and clearly that we are mortal and will disappear forever without saving grace. The evidence in the text is utterly overwhelming. The dogma of eternal torment is not biblical, not even close, and it is simply incredible that so many assume that it is, and think of those who deny this as the opponents of Scripture. Some can hear that, and they need to hear it. It will come perhaps as a surprise, but as a surprise to which they are able to be open. To anybody who is in that position, that is exactly what we must tell them without diluting the strength of that conviction one iota.

But culture and tradition are more powerful forces than a lot of people realize. Neuroscientists call these neural pathways that are forged through repetition. To suddenly rewire our thinking is no more possible than it is to rewrite the roadmap by changing all the roads in the city in a day. It's unlikely. God accommodates to us quite extraordinarily. He has spoken and still speaks to people in cultures and states of mind that must be so very prohibitive from a human point of view, but he speaks to people in ways that they can hear where they are at. Put another way, God is patient with us.

Were all of this not the case, we would be justified in thinking that the problem with evangelicals is either that they do not read the Bible or that they simply cannot read at all. The Bible clearly and repeatedly teaches the truth that we have given this cumbersome and unpleasant name "conditional immortality." If only they could read and read the Bible, they would know this. If only they had seen this verse or that verse, they would change their mind. Nonsense. That is the sort of naïve fundamentalist thinking that we combat every day.

We all read—not just through our own glasses that we can take off at will, but through our own eyes that we cannot swap out, but must change over time as old cells are replaced by new. When somebody doesn't hear you out, dismissing you in a way that you don't think is fair or open on the doctrine of hell, that evangelical centerpiece of times gone by, do not assume that it is only because they will not hear you. It may genuinely be that they cannot. That is what makes me double-minded about the sort of confidence we should have. We should simply and confidently declare that this is what Scripture declares to those who can hear it, not begging to be heard but proclaiming the truth of Scripture in an age where there really is no excuse among those who are ostensibly evangelical, critical, biblically literate, and open. But we also need to be realistic about the world we live in and the human condition.

I was intrigued to read recently of Martin Luther who, upon discovering the gospel of grace, that God saves us because of his grace, appropriated through faith, that he was slow to introduce it to his own parish. This is not because he was not confident that it was true, and it was not because he didn't think the idea was good for people, but because he was first a pastor and not just a scholar. He wanted people to take on board the idea that God does not accept us because we are good or clever or anything else in ourselves, but only because we place faith in Christ. What might happen, wondered Luther, if the church quickly embraced this understanding of divine grace and thought that God would more readily accept them because they did so? The theological reform would become self-defeating, because they would no longer act like people who believed that God accepted and saved them through faith alone.[4]

Perhaps this dual attitude of confidence and carefulness that we need going forward is nicely paralleled by the way that philosopher Alvin Plantinga describes the approach that he thinks scholars should have in the world of academia (as recalled by Tom Crisp, who sat in Plantinga's class):

> In professional philosophy, you'll find a sort of hierarchy or totem pole, a pecking order of power and influence. If you find yourself somewhere on that totem pole, my recommendation is that you go out of your way to be generous, kind, and helpful to those below you in the ordering, and that you attempt to be somewhat feisty to those above you.[5]

So maybe it's like this: When not involved in any controversy, what we have found in Scripture about life in Christ alone should be what we take to be normal—what we are justified in taking for granted. Any denial of the biblical teaching on conditional immortality is a deviation. If anyone says that man is, in truth, immortal, or that eternal life can be had outside of Christ, or that evil will always exist, or that anybody will suffer forever without end, we are right to treat that as aberrant theology in need of correction. In our conversations, in our writing, in our speaking and our preaching from Scripture, we do not have to rewrite this book. The Scripture is clear and a number of faithful expositors have shown this to be so, roundly addressing the familiar objections. It will still be useful to point out at times that this is what we are taking for granted so that nobody assumes that we mean to be interpreted in ways that we do not intend—by life we mean life, by death we mean death and so on.

When controversy arises, as it does from time to time, we need to think about how to proceed. Should these particular critics know better? Can we expect them to know better? What do they need? Is it just that they have not seen a biblical exposition of the subject? Are they able to hear us? Are we speaking to them or to their audience? Is this an instance in which a bit of feistiness is the right thing to offer? It sometimes is—sometimes we really ought to be showing the pubic that a certain familiar crowd of writers is being downright naughty, should know better and is breaking all the rules again (this is why I wrote my open letter). Our default position must be that we are entitled to take the stance of confidence in what Scripture so clearly teaches, but the way in which we minister must, perhaps to our own frustration, acknowledge these limitations.

4. This became clear to me when reading Payton, *Getting the Reformation Wrong*.
5. As quoted in Gorra, "Honoring Alving Plantinga."

EXPLORING THE IMPLICATIONS

Until now I have mostly been negative, talking about what we should not do, or else I've been somewhat vague: Be bold! But what should we do then? The obvious arguments have been made. Of course, don't forget them. Defend them when they are challenged. And of course continue to present the gospel to the world, which will mean revisiting what we say about divine justice and eternal life: eternal life is found only in Christ, the ark who saves us in the midst of the present order that is passing away. But the data required to justify—no, require—the move to a conditionalist perspective has been mined out of the rocks already. It's there for the taking. Instead of laying again the foundation, or being continually drawn in and tempted to play the defendant in yet another trial for the same crime where you have been repeatedly vindicated, we can move on to show the evangelical world—and perhaps ourselves—what things look like as we look at our faith with new eyes. How is our wider theology impacted by this understanding of eternal life?

We cannot assume that because we are conditionalists we will know what our beliefs imply. In the same way that we, or many of us, inherited the traditional view of hell, we also inherited our views on many other doctrinal matters. We did not systematically or carefully put our overall worldview together. We just ended up with it.

Sometimes those who oppose the conditionalist view are only too happy to help us see the implications—disastrous ones, they insist—of what we believe. We're destroying the Trinity. We're breaking up the hypostatic union and committing to Christological heresy. We're undermining missionary efforts, diminishing the urgency of the call to repent. I maintain that none of these charges is true. We are never so prone to imagine that a belief has disastrous consequences when we are already hostile to it, and the critics of conditional immortality are no exception. When we want our opponents' view to crash and burn, there is a perfectly natural temptation to take the shortest route to success, not exploring as carefully as we might the ways in which they might get out of what we think is a bind.

The remedy is that conditionalists need to explore these questions from within their own perspective. What does the world of systematic theology look like once we make the changes to the doctrines of eternal life and judgment that we maintain are mandated by Scripture? Earlier this year I was privileged to make a start on that in regard to Christology and the death of Christ in the forthcoming Ashgate research companion to theological anthropology.[6] It is interesting to see the very wide divergence of belief regarding the incarnation, for example, that evangelicals permit themselves and others to hold while claiming orthodoxy: from William Lane Craig's open acceptance of an Apollinarian view, where the divine logos put on a human body like a glove without any new human mind arising that wasn't already in the Logos from eternity,[7] right through to the other end of the spectrum where Millard Erickson wonders what might have happened had Jesus been about to sin—the answer being that the man Jesus of Nazareth would have lived on while the divine Son of God departed, a view called Nestorianism in which there are two persons.[8]

And yet, a conditionalist who follows the lead of numerous passages of Scripture and believes that Christ truly and fully died is deemed guilty of a sort of technical foul implying outright heresy. I have some sympathy for those who make this charge, but only some. Most evangelical specialists in Christology are probably not conditionalists and simply don't know what it is like to think about the death of Christ from a conditionalist point of view. Seeking out all the ways in which a person of a different perspective might respond is not necessarily easy.

The shortest way to describe one possibility that is compatible with conditionalism and also with the bare bones of orthodoxy is to say that the truly human and truly divine person Jesus of Nazareth truly died. Not his human nature or his divine nature alone, for these cannot be separated—but the person. Living and dying is what persons do. Is the Trinity therefore obliterated? Not if you believe in the doctrine of divine timelessness. The Logos, the second person of the Trinity, exists timelessly. Although it was true that at 3pm yesterday the divine Logos existed, it's not true that the divine Logos existed at 3pm yesterday, for his existence, at least according to the traditional doctrine of divine timelessness, is not spread over points in time. And so even if the incarnation of the Logos in Jesus had never taken place—if Jesus of Nazareth had no existence at all—the Trinity would be unaffected. Similarly, if the person of Jesus of Nazareth had truly and fully died—the Trinity is not affected, for nothing that happens in time can affect the timeless existence of God.

Obviously that extremely brief taste of an answer leaves much unsaid, and there are other possibilities to consider (this is just one, and it is the one

---

6. Peoples, "The Mortal God." While the essay focuses on theological anthropology (the doctrine of human nature) rather than the doctrine of final punishment, it nonetheless grapples with the issue of the death of Christ on the cross as a case of genuine death without survival.

7. Craig, *Philosophical Foundations*, 597–614.

8. Erickson, *The Word Became Flesh*, 563–64.

I currently think is most likely the correct way to make sense of things). My point in briefly re-telling it is just to illustrate the way that many facets of our faith need to be reexamined, not necessarily so that they can be reevaluated and possibly discarded (I never intended to, nor would I, discard the incarnation of God in Christ!), but so that we can take an inventory of what we now have. How do things now look, once we have changed a few parts of the whole? Instead of re-laying the foundation of our conditionalist views unnecessarily, we must take those views back to our faith more broadly and build a consistent biblical faith—rather than just being right about hell.

Traditionalists and their near-cousins can help us here. Evangelicals like Robert Peterson have taken the offensive on the question of the incarnation and the death of Christ (albeit very briefly), and Shawn Bawulski had something to say about it at the conference at which I originally delivered this paper. Whether we agree with them or not (I do not), we can certainly take guidance from the fact they have raised the issue. It should be addressed. And it is not the only issue of its kind.

Regardless of what we think of their merits, arguments from the seriousness of sin and the holiness of God have been raised a number of times, particular from, again, modern evangelicals, drawing on the likes of Jonathan Edwards. I am unmoved by the arguments, but they do suggest opportunities for us. Instead of sinking time into again making the case for conditionalism, how about we refer people to existing works on that subject and move forward to talk about, not a "conditionalist" view of sin or the holiness of God, as though we want to build a ghetto within the Christian world, but instead simply a re-visitation of the subject of sin and divine holiness? Not as a polemic against people who, I think, misapply these areas of theology in an effort to find holes in conditionalism, but just because the holiness of God and the seriousness of sin are genuinely important.

Instead of always, as people labelling ourselves as conditionalists, complaining that the traditional view makes God into a moral monster—although there is a place to say so—how about more positively directing our efforts into the wider subject of suffering and evil, where our understanding of the biblical picture of eternity provides a major part of the solution (instead of magnifying the problem, as I think the traditional view does)? This is, for example, how John Wenham became known as a conditionalist through his book *The Goodness of God*. Let's emulate that, not by writing about conditionalism, but by writing and talking about *everything*.

Let me put this differently. When we write about our faith, we do not endlessly and only say, "Jesus died for you, turn from sin, trust him and have eternal life," although we do say that. But we move on. We talk about loving each other, about doing justice, about missions, about various matters of doctrine and so on. The gospel has implications. So does conditionalism, which, if we're right, is a central feature of the gospel—God through Christ takes our death and gives us life so that we will not come to a final end.

If I get everything I want, there won't even be a conditionalist "movement" in a hundred years' time. It will be the new normal for evangelicals. In the new normal, we want the church to talk about something other than hell. Right now, that is the church we are working to build. This is part of the previous things that I've said about not reinventing the wheel. If we're not reinventing the wheel then what are we doing? When do we pass the point where we're beyond harping on about the basics?

Maybe in some parts of the church—I don't want to call them "unreached" because of the implications, but you know what I mean—the basics are still needed. Teach them about life being found only in Christ. But in our parts of the world where conditionalism is out there—it is on the table of discussion, it is regarded as plausible, it is becoming more widely accepted—I cannot see that more articles about how we know it's true are what is called for, or at least not often. Those are in the library now. We should regard that as having passed into the repository of knowledge to when we can refer people.

Instead, from the perspective we now inhabit, let's talk about the cross in its own right. Let's talk about mission because mission matters. Let's talk about holiness, about spirituality, about bioethics and the value of life, about suffering, about the value of the material world and the natural environment. If you particularly like talking about winning the battle or having a strategy (I don't especially), then let me put it still another way: We don't just want our agents in the discussion about hell, we want them everywhere.

SUMMARY

So. Where are we going? How should we go? For starters, at the risk of ruffling the feathers of some and being seen by others as Pharisaical, I want us to have a clean house. I don't think universalism is true, but I still feel bad for them over the fact that there are people joining them gleefully because they feel liberated by Rob Bell, and that is the name and approach with which they are now associated. I wish on their behalf that this were not so. And I don't want that for us either. Almost ironically, I want to discourage people from associating themselves with our view if they are people who love disagreeing with the establishment or who love chasing after the next thing or the perceived radical thing. In an almost Stoic fashion we need to say to people like that—I don't think you're ready. We can't stop them proclaiming any belief they like of course, but we've got to maintain integrity. It's not a race or a numbers game. I believe the Lord will win out in the end.

Secondly, see this movement in its historical context. The biblical foundation has been laid, and most competently laid. If we discover new material, great. But we don't need to cover the same ground again and again, in spite of the fact that so many traditionalists are doing just that. Have confidence in what we have seen in Scripture. You don't have to establish it again. There are times and places to do so, you understand, and we have to discern that. Answer those who ask. Defend the truth. But if we forever act like the doctrine of life in Christ alone needs a ground-up defense and we forever beg for it just to be heard, we're making the truth out to be precisely the outsider that we don't think it is or should be.

But thirdly, see this movement in it historical context in another way. No matter what we're talking about, we're talking about people situated within a particular culture, life and mind. Their problem isn't that they are evil or illiterate. No matter how confident we are entitled to be in what we've found in Scripture, and even when our view is held by the majority of evangelicals, should that ever happen, we still have to think and act pastorally and lovingly.

Fourthly and lastly as I said, we don't want to be stuck records. Each time I talk about theology with somebody who's a conditionalist, I don't want to hear again about how the doctrine of eternal torment is false. Let us mature. Not just as people but as a people. The gospel of God in Christ saving the world is at the center. We think that we've seen the way this biblical teaching works: Saving us from what? From sin and death. How? By becoming sin for us, by taking our burden and destroying it in his body through his death, rising again to give us eternal life. We must always remember and proclaim that. But don't stop there. As the writer of Hebrews said, go from milk to meat. The faith is a big place to explore with this insight we believe we've found, so we have our work cut out for us.

18

Doctrinal, Biblical, and Psychological Obstacles to Accepting Conditionalism
Successfully Rethinking Hell in a Small Christian Movement

— Douglas A. Jacoby —

Douglas A. Jacoby is a graduate of Duke University (History), Harvard Divinity School (New Testament), and Drew University (Ministry). After twenty years of full-time preaching, Douglas launched an independent Bible teaching ministry in 2003 and has served as an adjunct professor in the MA program in Bible and Theology at Lincoln Christian University. He has written two dozen books, including What's the Truth about Heaven and Hell? Sorting Out the Confusion about the Afterlife.

Douglas originally presented the following paper at the Rethinking Hell conference, 2014.

INTRODUCTION

Given its positive implications for divine mercy and proclaiming the gospel, one would think conditionalism would receive a hearty and global welcome. And yet conditionalism continues to encounter significant resistance among persons of faith. This study considers three clusters of impediments to the acceptance of conditionalism. A number of the obstacles are doctrinal—the effects of indoctrination. A handful are biblical—intrinsic to the text of Scripture. Many obstacles are psychological—and perhaps the most intractable. Mainstream denominations seldom embrace conditional immortality. Although increasing numbers of individuals within mainstream denominations are rethinking hell, better chances for large-scale doctrinal change may lie with independent Christian groups. In my experience as a member of a small Christian movement (approximately 105,000 members[1] in 160 nations), none of the doctrinal, biblical, or psychological obstacles has proved insurmountable. In fact, "terminal punishment" has won widespread acceptance. Rethinking hell has occurred not only at the grass roots, but also among the vast majority of leaders worldwide. The process serves as a possible model of how to bring about change—doctrinal or practical—in any committed Christian community. The story of why so many in my denomination have changed their minds has implications for Christian unity, communication, and humility.[2]

THE CORPORAL/CAPITAL PARADIGM

The term *"terminal punishment"* specifies a conditionalist understanding of divine judgment and hell. In contradistinction to the dominant medieval view of infinite torment, along with the view of several sects that teach that death entails extinction of the soul without punishment, the terminal view teaches that after a period of torment ("corporal punishment") suited to the individual, God destroys him/her ("capital punishment"). There is no need to quantify or qualify this torment (in terms of duration or degree), since any non-infinite duration of hell constitutes terminal punishment.

Traditional view:	(Infinite) Corporal punishment
Straight annihilationist view:	Capital punishment
Terminal view:	Corporal + capital punishment

Although technically unrelated to terminal punishment, it should be noted that the intermediate state of the dead precedes whatever judgment and consequences the Lord has assigned to us, based on our faith. This is in contrast to the position of most churches, who hold that one's eternal

---

1. Weekly attendance in early 2015 was 135,000.

2. Note that it is not the purpose of this chapter to prove terminal punishment. This I have attempted in a 1991 paper and, presenting further evidence, including opposing viewpoints, in a book on heaven and hell. See Jacoby, "Heaven and Hell"; *What Happens After We Die?*; and *What's the Truth about Heaven and Hell?*.

destiny, whether glory or gory, begins immediately upon death. In effect, not only does the traditional view require infinite punishment, but a hell beginning the very moment we die. Thus the traditional view errs on two counts.

THE RESTORATION MOVEMENT: ICOC

The ICOC provides a good case study of a group adopting conditionalism. The Restoration Movement (RM), originally an ecumenical fusion of Christ-followers serious about rejecting sectarianism and inauthentic Christian devotion, took root and grew on both sides of the Atlantic, particularly from the mid-nineteenth to the mid-twentieth century. The RM delighted in doctrinal discovery, and seems to have taken some pleasure in overthrowing sacred tradition. Despite its historical tendency towards legalism and division, the RM actually promulgated relatively few doctrinal tenets, ostensibly rejecting creeds, councils, and human traditions.[3]

From the days of its roots in Scotland (mid-seventeenth century), the RM exhibited four unifying characteristics: They are congregational autonomy, leadership by elders, believers' baptism (immersion), and weekly communion. Without a global headquarters, hierarchy or office of the inquisition, there was (and is) freedom. Theoretically, there is nothing keeping a congregation from embracing a particular view, just as nothing prevents it from rejecting it.

The Churches of Christ (COC), with one to two million members, were birthed by the RM, and the branch of the COC least indoctrinated in mainstream Protestant thinking may well be the International Churches of Christ (ICOC), membership about 105,000. Among the ICOC there is room for multiple understandings of hell—as long as one doesn't contradict the fundamental teaching of the last judgment, a doctrine that is non-negotiable in the Christian Churches and Churches of Christ.

---

3. Sadly, the RM eventually divided into three broad sections (each of which continued to form factions). To simplify, they were the Disciples of Christ (ultraliberal), Christian Churches (conservative though moderate), and Churches of Christ (ultraconservative). But even with various disputes and divisions in the past century, the number of semiofficial doctrines remains small in number—semiofficial because the Churches of Christ, like other restorationist movements, take pride in having "no creed but Christ" and "no book but the Bible."

RETHINKING HELL, 1984–2014

I first considered conditionalism thirty years ago, and share my story in hope that it may assist you in your own study and, hopefully, impact on others. I came to embrace terminal punishment during my early years on church staff in London. A small team of Americans and Britons planted the church in 1982. We were building our own teaching curriculum, and were not afraid to jettison the teachings or methods in which we had been trained. We were confident the Lord would teach us whatever we needed to know. These were heady times. But let me back up a bit.

Conditioning

I was confirmed as an Episcopalian in 1972. Interestingly, nothing we were required to learn in confirmation classes specified the duration or nature of final punishment. In 1976, through involvement on the fringes of the Charismatic Movement, I absorbed the traditional view of hell. Eternal torment was repeated so many times, I simply assumed it must be biblical. The lost would roast in hell for all time. And yet even though this was my view—and perhaps because this was my view—I seldom shared my Christian faith with others. But then I had not yet committed my life to Christ. That would happen only once I left home.

It was as a college student that I came into contact with the RM, specifically the COC. Here we were taught to question tradition—to be on the lookout for errors in biblical interpretation. A handful of the members in our local church held to the doctrine of the intermediate state of the dead (Sheol/Hades), which I never heard taught. I wasn't ready to embrace it anyway; it felt too contrived. Had I accepted the doctrine of the intermediate state, I might have come to accept terminal punishment more quickly, aware that the church's teaching on the postmortem state was off base.

Conditionalism

It was in 1984 that I was first exposed to conditionalism, through the writing of Edward Fudge. Initially, I felt my heart skip a beat. Later that same year, after my sister died (a seminal event in my faith journey), I began to open up theologically, rethinking several positions. I asked if I might present the terminal view in a London Church of Christ staff meeting. (I served on staff 1983–2003.) Permission was granted—provided I agreed to present "both sides." I taught both conditionalist and traditionalist views, without asking my twenty fellow ministers to come to a firm conclusion. For all of us, this was new territory. Incidentally, the thought that hell might not be a nonstop, infinite experience did nothing to lessen our evangelistic fervor. Over the following years I found myself unable to stop thinking about the issues.

In 1990 I shared my new thinking with the principal leaders in my own sphere of ministry: the British Isles, Nigeria, India, Australia, Southeast Asia, Scandinavia, and part of the United States. Of the dozen or so brothers in our discipleship group, only one opposed my teaching. All the others were in agreement. And so I began to write a paper titled "Terminal Punishment." I was captivated!

In 1991, and with the encouragement of my supervisors, I sent the paper to key leaders globally—to everyone in my denomination whose thinking I respected and who seemed to be a person of influence. Then in 1992 I was invited to make a presentation in Los Angeles to the main international leaders of the ICOC. Nearly all accepted terminal punishment (eleven out of twelve; the twelfth later joined our ranks). It has been gratifying to have the freedom to present a view of final judgment that sits well with my conscience and my interpretation of Scripture.

Although terminal punishment was never a central focus in my ministry, I continued to share my paper, to pen short articles on the topic, and weave my new perspective into the occasional workshops I was asked to lead on the afterlife. Finally, in 2013 I published *What's the Truth About Heaven & Hell*. As a result, I was invited to speak in the first *Rethinking Hell* conference in Houston, in 2014.

In short, I left traditionalism for terminal punishment, eventually becoming a change agent. Nor am I alone. In my own fellowship there are others who have written and taught the same. Fortunately, terminal punishment was well received virtually everywhere in the ICOC. That is, I am aware of only a few minute pockets where (often less biblically educated) leaders have been surprised that true Christians could espouse such a view. These hold-outs for traditionalism are becoming fewer and fewer.

OBSTACLES: DOCTRINAL, BIBLICAL, AND PSYCHOLOGICAL

Is the transition from tradition to terminal punishment an easy one? For some, it may be a quick and decisive move, yet for others the way forward is not so smooth. There are numerous obstacles—doctrinal, biblical, and psychological—that may prevent an individual, group, or movement from accepting terminal punishment. The obstacles considered below could be analyzed differently; in this section they are separated only for analytical purposes.

Doctrinal Hurdles / Indoctrination

Doctrinal hurdles are numerous. In most cases, people hold an opinion not because they arrived at it by conscious or studious effort, but because it was the opinion of their spiritual peers or superiors. Indoctrination may take place formally or informally. We shall note four examples: failure to appreciate the intermediate state; the notion that the human soul is immortal; the notion that offenses against an infinite being require infinite punishment; and belief in *two* eternal kingdoms.

Few Christian groups teach the intermediate state of the dead (*Sheol* in the Hebrew Old Testament, *Hades* in the Greek New Testament). Since they have been taught that we "die and go to heaven/hell" (against John 3:13; 5:25; Acts 2:34; 1 Cor 15:12–53), there is no room in their theology for the intermediate state. Or to look at it from the reverse angle: once willing to question the notion that the departed somehow bypass the resurrection of the dead and the judgment day, people might more easily realize that they have been misled concerning the afterlife. And since many reason that heaven/hell are entered immediately upon death, they conclude that God "leaves" the lost in hell for centuries or millennia—or forever.

Another doctrinal impediment is the Greek philosophical idea of the immortality of the soul. This idea was imported into Christianity in the second century, despite the scriptural teaching that only God and those to whom he grants it as a special gift are immortal (1 Tim 6:16; Rom 6:23; 1 Cor 15:53–54). Like Adam, separated from the Tree of Life (Gen 3:24), we mortals cannot live forever—at least not apart from Jesus Christ (John 3:16).

A third doctrinal obstacle, closely related to the second, is the common view that at the end of time there will be *two* eternal kingdoms, that of God and that of Satan. And yet 1 Corinthians 15:28 speaks of a time when God will be in all in all. Good will triumph; evil will be destroyed. Satan will be destroyed in the fire (Rev 20:10; see also 19:20). The devil is not immortal, nor does his dominion last forever. Yet this misguided doctrine naturally follows once Satan's immortality and infinite torment are granted. Biblical religion does not envision two eternal kingdoms; Satan will exist in the eternal future no more than we existed in the eternal past. Since he is one of God's creatures, the devil came into being. Satan and evil did not exist in the beginning, nor will they exist after the end.

We should also consider the late medieval view that an offense against an infinite being requires an infinite punishment. Anselm (eleventh century) argued that infinite punishment was required because of God's offended honor. Just as an offense against a nobleman was more serious than an offense against a commoner, an offense against God required the greatest punishment—an infinite one. Biblically speaking, Anselm's model is wrong. The degree of the offense is not rated by feudal thinking; with God there is no such favoritism (Exod 23:3; Lev 19:15; 24:19–22; Deut 1:16–17; Acts 10:34; Rom 2:11; Gal 2:6; Eph 6:9; Col 3:25; Jas 2:1, 9). The notion of infinite sin is also found in Thomas Aquinas (thirteenth century). Aquinas reasoned that at death the soul begins to suffer in hell, joined later by the body after the general resurrection. Another person of influence was Dante Alighieri (thirteenth–fourteenth centuries). His graphic descriptions of the pains of purgatory and hell in *The Divine Comedy* still haunt the modern mind.

Doctrinal confusion is often fossilized in creeds, which all too often serve as instruments of division. With prior allegiance to the views of historic Christian teachers or councils, new thoughts rank as infidelity. The creed becomes the yardstick against which doctrine is assessed, whereas in fact scripture alone should serve as the final norm for Christian teaching.

Biblical Challenges

A good number of scriptures are difficult to interpret. Once again, let's consider four examples: the difficulty of conceiving of eternity; mistranslations of words related to the afterlife; ambivalent passages; and widespread failure to train Bible readers in the interpretation of parables and apocalyptic. People prattle almost thoughtlessly about eternity, even as they comment casually on infinitude. Yet how can finite humans, lacking in knowledge, wisdom, and divine perspective, capture eternity in words (Eccl 3:11)? Whether in tightly reasoned theology or in the most sublime poetry, we simply cannot. Eternity is so far beyond us, "Even though a wise man claims to know, he cannot find out" (Eccl 8:17c).

Next, mistranslation may muddy the water. Few readers of Scripture are competent in the original Hebrew, Aramaic, and Greek, which means that they depend on translators to get it right. Alas, translators and translation committees stumble. The King James Version, to cite an example, inexcusably renders *Hades, Sheol,* and *Tartarus* as "hell"—a word which ought to translate only *Gehenna*. Their errors were recycled in multiple versions depending on the KJV. Take, for instance, Luke 16:23, where the original

NIV (1973) translated Hades as "hell," reinforcing the medieval impression that the departed wicked are already burning in hellfire.

Thirdly, ambivalent passages, especially when isolated from their immediate contexts, are easily pressed into service to support popular theological concepts. Let us return to Luke 16. Though the story contains echoes of the afterlife, this is not the point. The story appears in a chapter almost entirely focused on money matters. Apart from three verses, all of Luke 16 concentrates on proper and improper attitudes towards wealth: The parable of the shrewd Manager (verses 1–9), stewardship of earthly riches (verses 10–13), the Pharisees' love of money (verses 14–15), a few brief additional teachings (verses 16–18), and then our parable. Strikingly, early Christian writers did not understand the Hades of Luke 16 to be hell.[4] While Luke 16 is certainly suggestive of punishments and rewards in the afterlife, the purpose of the parable is not to describe them. Whatever may be said about Luke 16 goes double for the book of Revelation—which leads us to a fourth challenge of a biblical nature.

Understanding Revelation is challenging because of a widespread lack of training in the interpretation of apocalyptic, which is the genre of Revelation as well as of many Old Testament prophetic texts upon which Revelation is built. And yet at a much simpler level, Bible students suffer from a lack of understanding of context. For example, insentient corpses are being destroyed in Isaiah 66:24. As Jesus reminds us, the destruction of the wicked is certain. No one can survive unquenchable fire. There is no hint here of either the immortality of the soul or the infinite torment of the lost.

Psychological Factors

If only disagreement could always be resolved by opening the scriptures or through further study! Yet often the obstacle appears to be biblical or doctrinal, while the true core is psychological. We may not be aware of our own feelings, many of which connect with obstacles previously referenced. Feelings of "weirdness" are generated through the dissonance of the terminal view with traditional teaching. Conceiving of non-existence (the ultimate end of the lost) is mind-boggling. There is a natural tendency to feel anxiety when we are presented with menus of options—perhaps a reaction to relativism? And no doubt we usually prefer simple answers; at first blush, Terminal Punishment may seem complex.

Second, feelings are regenerated by way of reminder. The traditional view is frequently reinforced not only in churches, but also in the media

4. Take a look at the index of scriptures cited in the *Ante-Nicene Fathers*.

(cinema, novels, cartoons, etc.). Thus biases leaning towards eternal torment may be confirmed at the subconscious level. Third, traditionalism receives further impetus from evangelistic efforts, when there may be a motive for reinforcing fear of hell. Preaching hell gets results—so they have become convinced—and there is a fear of "backing off" lest other believers construe conditionalism as a license for immorality. Fourth, rejection by peers is a huge issue in the academy—sadly, among those who have the best tools (original languages, theological training, church history, and so forth) for getting at the truth and communicating it to the public (John 9:22; 12:42–43).

Fifth, younger people are more prone to derive a sense of empowerment by flaunting unconventional doctrines. As a young leader, I too often relied on the element of shock, novelty, or the implied threat of hell. As we grow older, we take less joy in judgmental behaviors and attitudes. Hopefully we're beginning to resemble the One who rejected meanness and manipulation—appealing to his listeners in love. Love takes no pleasure in evil, but rejoices in the truth (1 Cor 13:6). Sixth, we may reject terminal punishment because we feel guilty about sinners "getting off light"—heightened by suspicion that God is a deity of grim justice. We wouldn't want to be viewed as "soft on sin," and so we hold to the traditional doctrine. Or perhaps we feel guilty about not giving our whole heart to God, and accept eternal punishment out of an inverted sense of guilt. Some Christian preachers and teachers fear that their hearers may not take the word of God seriously if the consequences of rejecting it aren't "eternal" in the common medieval sense of the word (everlasting suffering).

There is a seventh psychological obstacle, perhaps especially a peril to believers who place a high premium on being "relatable" or minimizing offense. We may find repellent the idea that the Seventh-day Adventists, Jehovah's Witnesses, or Christadelphians might have it right. We do not want to be associated with them, and we fear we might jeopardize our chances of success if our doctrines match any of theirs. Our tendency to distance ourselves may easily prevent our giving alternate interpretations a fair hearing.

STRATEGY FOR EFFECTING CHANGE

I indicated that terminal punishment came to be accepted in large sections of my own denomination. How did this happen? Allow me to review my story (above). First, likeminded persons talked; they empowered one another. A paper was written and shared, first with fellow thinkers and writers who could be trusted to offer fair criticism. Then it was distributed to the highest level leaders in the denomination. I did not just send an email; I urgently presented my paper *in person*. I also followed up in private conversations. Once I realized that terminal punishment was not going to hurt the faith of others, or cause disunity, I shared it in ever wider circles. I wove it into biblical presentations touching on the afterlife. Momentum built. Later, I began to network with those outside my own denomination.

Such an approach can work for you as well. Begin with friends, then colleagues, then your leaders, both locally and globally. I would not insist that this is the only way to effect change. I only relate how things worked out in my own case. Putting it all together, here is an action plan for promoting terminal punishment:

- *Network.* Seek out like-minded persons—they may become your "support group"—and empower one another.
- *Organize your thoughts.* Write, making a strong biblical case. (An alternative would be to share someone else's material.)
- *Share the paper* with those in positions of influence in your church/fellowship.
- *Follow up* in private conversation.
- *Teach the intermediate state.* Begin with what happens after we die—the doctrine of the intermediate state of the dead may be easier to swallow than terminal punishment, and this may pave the way for a conditionalist understanding. Be sure to establish that no one is in heaven or hell yet (John 3:13; Acts 2:34; Matt 25:46).
- *Use the Scriptures.* Illustrate judiciously with the church fathers. Teach about parable and apocalyptic, as necessary.
- *Be realistic.* Accept that some will appreciate your efforts more than others. That's okay.

Lest I offer false hope for achieving unity around a common understanding of eternal punishment, let me stress the urgency of true discipleship on the part of our hearers. There should be little surprise that nominal Christians will tend to challenge new ideas and resist change—especially when going down a new path requires commitment. Those most open to new thoughts are those most open to following the truth, wherever the road may lead (John 7:16–17).

Why is it that dissonant ideas are welcome more in some places than others? First, those who live evangelistic lifestyles are more tuned in to the emotional stumbling blocks of Christianity. They are more familiar with the intellectual objections of unbelievers and skeptics, because they are in the fight and have to defend the faith on a regular basis (1 Pet 3:15–16). Moreover, groups less bound by creeds are more likely to consider alternate views. Furthermore, in fellowships where genuine discipleship is the norm, ideas may be communicated more safely. Interactions are less adversarial. When the author is known personally, it's harder to dismiss his/her position.

Today the overwhelming majority of senior leaders in the ICOC accept the terminal view (conditionalism).[5] Further, the majority of members believe in the biblical doctrine of the intermediate state of the dead. Yet neither is likely ever to become an official doctrine, nor is this necessarily desirable. The fundamentals of the faith (Eph 4:3–6) are central teachings. The issues dealt with in this chapter, like those addressed in the *festschrift* in which it is located, are peripheral to the central doctrines of Christianity. Agreement was achieved in the ICOC not because of convincing writing or unrelenting effort. The audience must be divinely prepared. Because of their prior commitment to truth, dialogue was fruitful, and change (rethinking hell) became a realistic possibility.

Is This Strategy Realistic?

Will this work? It *has* worked, at least in the case of the ICOC.[6] Moreover, terminal punishment never became a divisive issue in the ICOC. The closest we ever came to an incident was when one brother, hearing that my paper had been favorably received by the principal leaders (Los Angeles, 1992), assumed that new doctrine was being determined. In a movement that expects its members to study God's word on a daily basis, rejects the clergy-laity distinction, and is leery of doctrinal decrees, his anxiety was understandable. Yet a single conversation put that doubt to rest—with no further controversy to date (that was twenty-three years ago).

Of course resisting tradition is seldom easy. And in the case of infinite torment, the cumulative momentum of nearly two millennia of Christian interpretation is deeply felt. And yet I have found thousands of persons—including the vast majority of our principal leaders—who are on board with

---

5. Yet since terminal punishment is not viewed as a basic doctrine, and so is only occasionally discussed before baptism, many new Christians have not (yet) heard of it.

6. My denomination was something of a blank slate. Certainly there were elements from the COC, other denominations, various world religions and even skepticism—all sorts of persons have been won to Christ in the past few decades. And yet overall the ICOC has tended towards a naïve view of biblical interpretation. While this can feed into traditional interpretations, they have less force. Members do not feel obligated to support the status quo, and are more than willing to break with their peers over matters eschatological.

conditionalism. Nearly all the pushback I have received has been from persons outside my denomination, for instance when I have been on the radio, or when readers of my book on heaven and hell were offended that I had broken with tradition.

Once again, let me emphasize what I consider our greatest obstacle. Because the traditional doctrine of infinite torment has the weight of history on its side, it is perceived as *biblical*. The burden of proof, it is expected, falls on him who would challenge orthodoxy. Let us be prepared to do exactly that. And let us not underestimate the challenges facing us. The traditional view has reigned nearly supreme since the second century. This is the weightiest obstacle to the terminal view, and it could just as easily be slotted into the psychological category as into the biblical or doctrinal category. Yet where there is humility—when Christians are united in authentic faith—we have a superb chance of influencing the majority to rethink hell. In such conditions, a strategy like the one outlined above works!

ATTITUDE: GUARDING OUR SPIRIT

Do you like what you are reading? Are you comfortable with terminal punishment? Or are you disturbed that a challenge is being mounted to the dominant paradigm of judgment in the Christian world? However we feel about the prospect of the challenge to the traditional view of hell, it's vital that we have the right attitude. Accordingly, let us close with some practical advice for the heart.

- If terminal punishment is a new concept, *take your time*. We shouldn't embrace doctrine because it is appealing (any more than we should reject doctrine if it is appalling), but because it makes sense scripturally. Nothing should be rushed. Due diligence must be exercised in our own study, as well as in our communication of terminal punishment. Be patient; allow others time to think through the issues. It probably took *you* a while to change your mind. Your mind may still be developing, and we tend to be unaware of our inner mental processes.
- *Insist on authenticity.* No amount of grace can compel a hard or lazy heart to be receptive to the things of God. Those who wear the name of Christ simply must make time to meditate on the word, as well as to share the message with outsiders. Otherwise their spiritual growth will be stunted. Daily Bible reading empowers us to struggle with the tough issues. Just as vital, evangelism brings people into contact with multiple views, as well as with the emotional struggles of seekers trying to make sense of the gospel in light of eternal judgment. Outreach

also brings us into contact with the tensions and paradoxes of Scripture. Insist on authenticity—that those you seek to influence should be willing followers of Christ, and if they are not then any points you score in the discussion will be moot.

- When it comes to the weightiest doctrines, *strive for a sense of proportion*. Not all doctrines are equally weighty (Matt 22:37–40, 23:23). Although judgment is a basic teaching (Heb 6:2), the technical definition of "eternal" is not, and our view of hell must never be a "shibboleth" by which we label and exclude (Judg 12:6). And speaking of proportion, we will do well to watch our adverbs. I've noticed a weakness in my own writing. Whenever I make a weak point, or am overly eager to advance my cause, I am tempted to buttress my writing by adverbs like "clearly" or "obviously." If we have a truly biblical case, all we need do is present the scriptures and encourage readers to draw a conclusion. Sometimes adverbs serve as nothing more than indicators of the writer's insecurity, or of a weak case.

- *Don't look down on others.* Let us be gracious, not combative or condescending. Scorn is especially easy to rationalize when we know that our critics have not studied out the issues as well as we have. Theologian Helmut Thielicke put it well: "Disdain towards those lacking theological rigor is a real *spiritual disease.* It lies in the conflict between truth and love. This conflict is precisely *the* disease of theologians."[7] And there is an excellent reason we should be horrified if we look into our hearts and detect disdain towards our opponents. The same theologian continues, "I don't believe that God is a fussy faultfinder in dealing with theological ideas. He who provides forgiveness for a sinful life will be also surely be a generous judge of theological reflections."[8]

May this be the spirit that guides us in our inquiry, as well as in our outreach. The implications for Christian unity are obvious.

---

7. Thielicke, *A Little Exercise*, 7.
8. Ibid., 37.

19

The Offer of Life

Conditional Immortality in the Practice of Evangelism

— Ralph G. Bowles —

Ralph G. Bowles has served as a priest in the Anglican Church of Australia since 1979, ministering in parishes in Sydney and Brisbane, and for six years as a church health coach in the Anglican Church Southern Queensland. Shaped by the evangelical, Reformed tradition of the Anglican Church, he has received, among other degrees, a Bachelor's in Divinity from London University, and a Doctorate of Ministry from San Francisco Theological Seminary.
Ralph originally presented the following paper at the Rethinking Hell conference, 2014.

What is being offered in the Christian gospel? What also are the consequences of rejecting or refusing the offer contained in the good news of Jesus Christ? The evangelist must be clear on these matters, and should make them clear to the hearers. Since the doctrine of "hell" concerns the consequences of not accepting or participating in the salvation offered in the gospel of Jesus Christ, it is not therefore a minor doctrine of a secondary importance, a matter of indifference, which we can relegate to the optional category. The matter of final destiny cannot be left out of the Christian message without loss of integrity and clarity.

I was nurtured and formed as a Christian in the conservative evangelical tradition of the Anglican Church of Australia, an heir of the Protestant and evangelistic heritage of the English evangelical wing of my church. From my church and mentors, I imbibed the belief that final judgment for those outside of Christ's salvation will lead to a state of permanent, punitive separation from God, commonly called "hell."

Despite the fact that this belief in hell as an eternal conscious, ongoing judgment is deeply embedded in conservative evangelicalism, I noticed years ago that it was rarely enunciated in public in my part of the church. On one occasion, a non-churched person offered that she didn't like coming to churches because of "those hell-fire sermons condemning people." I said to her that I had hardly ever heard such a sermon myself, but it provoked me to think more about the place of "hell" in evangelical preaching and communication. Why do people (conservative evangelical preachers, for example) who fervently believe in the awesome reality of final judgment as personal eternal conscious separation from God and blessedness, fail to make this clear in their teaching and especially in their evangelism? Why don't they make their belief in this view of hell clear when they are summarizing the gospel and actually referring to final judgment? I found the same tendency to avoid the topic of hell or to speak of it in euphemistic code language in many popular evangelistic tracts and evangelistic presentations. I was aware of my own reticence in teaching about "hell" or explaining it clearly in evangelistic presentations. I would think about this matter from time to time, and studied the doctrine of hell again, reading classic texts and looking at the scriptural passages.

Then one day I came across Edward Fudge's book, *The Fire That Consumes*. I read it with great interest and was introduced to a way of looking at the topic of hell that was new to me. Fudge's work led me back to an intense study of the biblical passages. I was amazed to see how the key texts could be understood in a straightforward way—even the classic "eternal torment" proof-texts.[1] I adopted the conditionalist view and began to speak more plainly about these weighty matters of destiny in my teaching and evangelism. Finally, I had a gospel message that I could fully proclaim, serious in impact but without the problematic aspects of the traditional interpretation. I could talk to people about the consequences of being outside of salvation without euphemisms or evasion. God offers eternal life in Christ and through Christ; to reject the offer of salvation is to choose death in all its dimensions—loss of God now and forever, with loss of existence as a sad consequence. No one can live forever without God.

How does the conditional immortality interpretation of final divine judgment shape the practice of evangelism? I want to explore some ways in

---

1. See Bowles, "Does Revelation 14:11 Teach Eternal Torment?"

which conditionalism affects the evangelistic task.² I am not arguing here for the truth of the conditionalist view, but assuming it as a platform for evangelism and exploring the difference it can make.

DEFINITIONS

I understand *evangelism* as the activity of communicating "the good news that God has accomplished our salvation for us through Christ in order to bring us into a right relationship with him and eventually to destroy all the results of sin in the world."³ This "gospelling" can take many forms, since there are many motivational entry points for conveying the good news (*evangel*). Whatever pathway of communication is followed, there is a core of biblical truths that need to be covered: about God as Creator (where did we come from?); about the problem of sin (why did things go wrong?); about Christ's incarnation, substitution, and renewing of creation (what will put things right?); and about our response to God (how can I be put right?).⁴ The biblical storyline of creation-fall-redemption-renewal is the basic framework for evangelistic communication.

The evangelist will address the basic question: what is offered in the good news of Christ? There is an unavoidable corollary question too: what difference does it make if the gospel is received or rejected? The traditional view of hell (*eternal conscious punishment*) maintains that there will be a punitive separation of the impenitent from God and his blessings, in an ongoing existence for the purpose of this endless sentence. However it may be imagined, it is usually viewed as extremely unpleasant, a tormenting, endless punishing. It is punishment without prospect of reform, or an end to the sentence.

I understand "conditional immortality" to be the view that eternal life as enduring endless existence is found only with God as a blessed gift. Our present mortal existence is given by God with the invitation to fullness of eternal life promised through union with Christ. "No existence is possible for a being absolutely cut off from God, in whom all things consist," wrote E. Petavel.⁵ Divine judgment or accountability for human life is consistent with this view. The ultimate, eternal loss of life and God is indeed central to

---

2. For the sake of convenience, I will use the term "conditionalist evangelism" to denote some distinctive applications of this view on the practice of evangelism.

3. Keller, *Center Church*, 31.

4. Ibid., 33.

5. Pétavel-Olliff, *The Struggle for Eternal Life*, 65.

the judgment. Eternal life with God is the gift of God's grace, through the work of Jesus Christ.

CONDITIONALIST EVANGELISM

I will use "conditionalist evangelism" as a kind of shorthand for "evangelism shaped by conditional immortality positions." I acknowledge that there will be a range of views among conditionalists about some issues (such as theories of Christ's atonement; different understandings of the process of final judgment). Let me offer these five distinctive applications of conditionalism to the task of communicating the Christian gospel.

1. A Consistent and Confident Gospel

Conditionalist evangelism has a full, reasonable, and confident gospel proclamation.

There is a problem with the traditional view of hell as eternal conscious torment. It is a very unpleasant and severe doctrine, a fact admitted by many of its proponents. For this reason there is a tendency among adherents of the traditional view to avoid a clear statement of this teaching, leaving a vague presentation of the gospel. There can be a real vagueness about the consequences of rejecting Christ's salvation. It is hard to avoid the conclusion that hell as eternal conscious punishment is not confidently portrayed even by some of its adherents. There seems to be an understandable loss of nerve about explicitly explaining eternal conscious torment to prospective responders. Whether this is from a desire to emphasize the positive, or because the destiny of hell is dreadful to contemplate and difficult to explain, I do not know.

I was an example of this phenomenon and I have observed it many times among evangelicals. To those who know about hell, you can hear the oblique references to it in the preaching and evangelism of proponents as they speak of God's justice, or "death," or "separation from God." I have been collecting evangelistic presentations and tracts for years. They usually avoid any clear reference to the traditional position. The vague presentations speak of "death" and "judgment" without clarification. It would be an interesting research topic to find out what the hearers of such presentations actually thought was being said about the consequences of failing to turn to Christ.

It is also common for evangelical believers to offer their own explanations to fellow believers of what "hell" will involve as separation from God. I have noticed that few adopt a literal understanding of the passages. They have their own way of understanding "hell" that often seems to soften the picture, but they rarely make this clear to those who are most in danger of it. (One traditionalist told me that he thought God would keep the lost in a permanent state of suspended animation, a kind of frozen coma, while claiming he was holding to biblical teaching.) I can understand this reticence. The matter is indeed sobering and dreadful. If strongly emphasized, it may not open up responsiveness to God. I am sympathetic with this desire to focus on the positive and minimize the negative. When I became an ordained minister of the gospel, I felt the inhibition myself. I became increasingly uncomfortable about my own failure of nerve about hell.

Evangelical proponents of the traditional hell can become very vocal and clear, however, when this doctrine is challenged by fellow Christians. All their vagueness and reticence drops away in a strong push-back against a denial of the gospel. The resurgence of conditionalism has ignited a publishing push-back by traditionalists. Their theological justification for the traditional "hell" leads them to positions that are hard to find anchored in biblical texts, in speculative explanations such as the eternal impenitence of the wicked as compelling ongoing punishment, and the infinite punishment of finite humans justified by offence against an infinite God.[6] These explanations open up a number of objections, inviting people to challenge them on logical or scriptural grounds. They are rationalizations to explain how and why God keeps alive and in ongoing punishment those who reject him. I doubt that this underlying rationale of eternal conscious punishment is ever included in their gospel presentations.

Thus the traditionalist view of hell *can* lead to vagueness in the presentation of the gospel and so mislead hearers about the issue of salvation. If the gospel is an invitation to abundant life (John 10:10) and also a warning of the consequences of missing this salvation, then a failure to be clear about either will make the communication of the gospel message significantly foggy. To appreciate that the gift of God is eternal life in Christ Jesus our Lord, we must also understand the nature of this death that the wages of sin brings (Rom 6:23).

The other problem of the traditional view of hell is that it can so easily make the gospel sound like bad news. The logic of a God who will punish so severely, despite the claim that he is loving and gracious, usually escapes the unconvinced. This severe doctrine has often been felt to be an impediment to gracious evangelism. It can so easily turn the loving invitation of God into a fearful threat to comply.

---

6. For example, see Morgan, "Annihilationism," 210–12.

The conditionalist evangelist has no reason to deny God's justice or to avoid the issue of consequences for those who reject grace. God's final judgment can be communicated as part of the full and confident proclamation of the gospel, since the conditionalist is not burdened by notions of infinite penalties and eternal misery. We are able to make the straightforward and reasonable claim that eternal life is ultimately found only in relationship with the source and giver of life—the living God. When people reject the offer of eternal life, God sadly withdraws it. His gift of temporal life has been given with freedom, but ongoing and greater blessings require our faith union with the life-giver. God is entitled to withdraw the gift of life that he provided, when we do not agree to the only condition for continuance. As the Teacher in Ecclesiastes put it: "the dust returns to the earth as it was, and the breath returns to God who gave it" (Eccl 12:7).

The conditionalist approach to evangelism also meets a challenge from the opposite direction, against the false hopes of universalism.

2. Confronting False Hopes

Conditionalist evangelism removes the false hope of a Christ-less immortality or an easy dissolution after death and issues a strong challenge for decision.

One possible consequence of this reticence about the nature of "hell" is to leave open other future possibilities in the back of the minds of unbelievers, and some Christians. It is thought that eventually this separation from God, unpleasant for a while, will be overcome or forgiven. The "universal salvation" option comes into play when endless existence is presupposed. Hell, if it exists, is understood as reserved for the "Adolf Hitlers" of this world. Most people don't consider it likely or reasonable that God should send them to hell in this sense. In my country (Australia) there seems to be a kind of popular pagan hope of immortality, usually displayed at secular funerals. A vague hope of immortality, combined with no sense of divine judgment and no hearing about endless hell, all combine to dull the hearing of the good news of Christ.

The conditionalist evangelist takes the statement of St. Paul in its full import: "The wages of sin is death" (Rom 6:23). The end result of sin apart from the grace of God is the opposite of life, an utter end in the judgment and mercy of God. We recall that it was never God's purpose for people to continue to live forever outside his fellowship, as Genesis 3:22–23 indicates:

"He must not be allowed to reach out his hand and take also from the tree of life and eat, and live forever."

Unless we make clear to our hearers that the only hope for ongoing, eternal life after death is through the life-giving power of God received in union and fellowship with the Lord by faith, then we have not fully communicated the options before them. Conditionalist gospel presentations will remove this deluded hope of immortality apart from God and his Son in the understanding of the Christian way. This forces a choice between life with God forever, in submission and love to God through the grace of his Son, or a self-chosen end to one's existence.

At this point an objection arises to our minds, and in fact, it can occur in our evangelism. Is not this destiny of annihilation and an absolute end a weakening of God's judgment? Will it not lessen people's concern about repentance? Will not some people welcome this destiny as a kind of preferable euthanasia after a life lived apart from any concern with God?

Traditionalists have indeed lodged this objection to conditional immortalism. I think it is probably the first, instinctive reaction to the conditionalist view. It is charged that we are weakening the judgment of God, letting people off, and presenting a lenient view of God's final reckoning. Eternal conscious punishment is thus seen to be essential to the morality of divine justice. One writer says, "something would be profoundly wrong with a world where its Hitlers could, when the time of reckoning drew near, just step off into nescience."[7]

It is true that this conclusion is sometimes drawn. I have had this initial response from some people with whom I have been sharing the gospel. They seemed relieved and almost ready to welcome rejecting God now on these terms of eternal annihilation. However, the evangelist must convey two truths clearly in order to meet this response in an evangelistic way.

First, we must make clear that we are not talking about the avoidance of divine judgment. This is why I don't use the term "Annihilationism" to describe the view I hold. The conditionalist evangelist will not present the option of an easy, unaccounted-for end to a life of rebellion against God, as if it is a matter of "eat, drink, be merry, sin away now, and then it will be all over without accountability." The conditionalist will remind the hearers that there will be a final and awesome encounter with God, a judgment on how we have lived our lives. There will be no reason to think that this encounter with God by unrepentant rebels will be easy or pleasant.

Let us also recall that conditionalism does not lessen the seriousness of the penalty of rebellion, since the real loss or punishment that the

---

7. Talbot, "The Morality of Everlasting Punishment," 120.

unrepentant face is their clear awareness on that Day that have chosen the infinite loss of God and the blessedness that accompanies the Lord. As Stephen H. Travis explains, summing up the drift of New Testament depictions of the final judgment, "The experience of those who refuse to respond to this gospel is not so much an experience of retributive punishment as the negation of all that is offered in Christ."[8] The fact that people in the process of rejecting God lose the capacity to desire what God offers, does not lessen the reality of final judgment.

Conditionalists believe that suffering is not the essence or whole of punishment. There is a punishment in loss, as well as a punishment that entails suffering. Nigel Wright puts it well:

> Hell is ... an ultimate, final encounter with God. ... The torment of hell consists in beholding God at the last, looking upon his beauty, majesty, and infinite love and knowing that through one's own deliberate fault all of this has been made forfeit and lost. In short, hell is the *infinite loss of God*. ... Our loss is as great as is God himself, since his eternal purpose has been to be our God and to become all in all to us ... our theology is personally and relationally defined not as torment in some eternal concentration camp, but as a falling out of the hands of the one who loves us.[9]

The traditionalist magnifies the suffering of this loss to an eternal degree and feels that only by an eternal conscious punishment will the reality of divine justice be served. The conditionalist puts the focus on the loss of God, not on the ongoing punishment of those who have lost the highest end of their lives.

The gospel is thus presented as an offer of real life, an invitation to enter into a deeper and richer fulfillment, with God, and on God's terms. The gospel offers more than avoidance of some punishment or even the gift of a new status ("salvation"). The gift of salvation is God himself, who is "Life" with all its blessings. The real wages of sin is the loss of God and the death that comes with this fact. The consequences of missing this offer are the built-in results of allowing evil or disruption to continue. Sin or separation from God is the pathway to destruction, in partial ways now and in the end, complete and absolute. To lose God is an infinite loss: "What greater punishment can there be?"[10] The gospel offers life and to reject it is to choose death. "Evil culminates in the extinction of its victims," observed

---

8. Travis, *Christ and the Judgement of God*, 325.
9. Wright, "A Kinder, Gentler Damnation?" 232–33.
10. Marshall, "Divine and Human Punishment in the New Testament," 221.

Pétavel-Olliff.[11] "Wandering from the Source of life, the sinner takes his slow funereal way towards eternal death."[12]

The conditionalist gospel presentation will confront the unbeliever with a sobering challenge about life and ultimate destiny, but will not affront the human sense of justice in the way that traditional eternal punishing does. In the conditionalist presentation, God gives life on condition of living with him and for him, and when this is rejected, despite all efforts to rescue humans from perishing, the gift of life in relationship with God is withdrawn. Pétavel-Olliff again puts it well: "According to the Bible, life is a sacred trust, which God withdraws from those who abuse it. The Creator forces no one to remain seated at the banquet of life."[13]

The universalist evasion of human responsibility is ruled out by the conditionalist view of life, death, and eternity. If sin is ultimately self-destruction, then grace and salvation is about true life. The challenge for the conditionalist evangelist is to present the gospel as the word of life (1 John 1:1).

3. The Gift of Full and Eternal Life with God

Conditionalist evangelism frames the gospel as the offer of life—abundant life with God.

Much traditional evangelism has focused on the negative prospects for failing to turn to God. The traditionalist view of hell places the emphasis on punishment, and takes immortality as a given. The focus of judgment is on punishing. It is locked into a preoccupation with retribution and individual sins. Conditionalist evangelism focuses on sin (broken relationship with God) rather than sins (*expressions* of broken relationship). Sin brings the loss of life with God, and ultimately the loss of the gift of life itself—death in all its finality as an absolute end of existence.

The biblical message is that humans are made to live in relationship with God. We have physical life from God, but "Life" in biblical understanding is more than physical existence with its blessings and challenges; it is being alive in the blessing of God's presence, experiencing his love and friendship. We could put this into an equation: "Life = Physical existence from God + Knowing God and all the blessings that flow from God." As Jesus said, "I have come that they may have life, and have it to the full" (John 10:10).

---

11. Pétavel-Olliff, *The Struggle for Eternal Life*, 85.
12. Ibid., 13.
13. Ibid., 27.

The conditionalist evangelist is offering "life," abundant and eternal life. We remind people or inform them that it is in knowing God personally, in union with him through the life, death, and resurrection of his Son, Jesus Christ, that we receive a new, eternal life. The problem that Christ came to remove is the breach of relationship between humans and God, which has disrupted their connection to the source of their life. This rebellion or "sin" has brought death into our world in various forms. People can be physically alive, though afflicted with spiritual death. They are essentially "dead men walking," under sentence of ultimate death. The time will come when their enjoyment of physical existence will come to an absolute end. It is given conditionally to be used for God and in union with God. We may pursue many worthwhile activities and derive much satisfaction from life without God, but finally we will face the reality that there is no life forever without relationship with God, who is the life-giver and purpose of life. Separated from God we will finally encounter God and his justice, and face the inevitable consequences of our disconnection from the source of "life." Our existence will come to an end forever in what the Bible terms "eternal destruction" (2 Thess 1:9).

The conditionalist evangelist will frame the problem of sin primarily in relational and personal terms, as a rupture in union with God, the source of our lives. This differs from the moralistic, legal, and judicial framework on the sin issue held by many traditionalists. Sin will be seen as a self-destructive power, which will ultimately destroy us absolutely. Our contemporary Western world may not respond to an invitation to debate the ethical and moral scales of value as we talk of sins, but they may be on our wavelength when we draw attention to the widespread experiences of futility and self-destruction in human life. John Wenham found that approaching the issue of sin and judgment this way had power in evangelism: "In personal talks I often find myself explaining the self-destructive power of sin and of its ultimate power to destroy absolutely. I explain that that is how God has made the world. Judgment expresses his wrath and the abominable thing which he hates."[14]

The conditionalist evangelist has the challenge of explaining how Christ offers abundant life and what this life entails. This is the positive blessing of the gospel: to know God and enjoy him forever. How God in Christ rescues us from sin and death, and lifts us into the fellowship of life—this is the positive motivation. In this way of evangelism, the "hell" or judgment aspect is not a difficulty to the conscience of the unbeliever, who can understand that to reject God is to reject what God, and only God, can

---

14. Wenham, *Facing Hell,* 251.

offer—eternal life. The challenge to the evangelist is to present the nature of life with God now and forever in its fullness, and to show what Christ did to provide this hope.

How did God in Christ bring this abundant life and enable us to be delivered from death? How did Christ deal with the problem of sin? The Bible clearly uses the category of Christ as our substitute. Sin brings a penalty or consequence, estrangement from God and liability to judgment, and ultimately destruction. The good news is that God in Christ has acted dramatically and decisively to enable people to come back to relationship with God, to find forgiveness for sin. As the new Adam offering the covenant sacrifice that effects the new covenant, Christ does for us what we cannot do for ourselves. He is both substitute and representative.

Our view of "hell" and our understanding of Christ's atoning work can be closely connected. I believe that there is a strong connection between the way that evangelicals have applied the penal substitutionary theory of the atonement and the hold of the traditional view of hell on the minds of many in the evangelical wing of the church. For churches in the Western, Reformed, and evangelical tradition, penal substitution is usually dominant. An objection to conditionalism can arise from this view of the atonement. In this view, the main work of Christ was to bear for us the punishment of our sins.[15] If God's justice upon sinners was an infinite punishment for guilt, then it took the Son of God with his union of divine and human natures to suffer this penalty on the cross. This was the nature of his atoning suffering. Since Christ was not annihilated, however, the traditionalist may argue that conditionalism cannot be the correct view of the destiny of the lost. David Wells argues this way:

> To be commensurate with the offense, God's response must be correspondingly infinite. Annihilationism looks instead for a finished, finite, temporal response. An infinite response, however, is what we see occurring at the Cross. Christ stood in the place of those whom he represented, and bore their punishment. In so doing, was he annihilated? Of course not. What we see is Christ bearing their actual punishment, and he could exhaust it because he himself was the eternal and infinite God. He did not bear a punishment merely like that which sinners deserved, one that was merely analogous to theirs.[16]

---

15. See Stephen Travis's discussion in *Christ and the Judgement of God*, 181–82.
16. David Wells, "Everlasting Punishment," *Christianity Today* 31, March 20, 1987, 42, cited in Morgan, "Annihilationism," 212.

Let us notice what is happening here. The traditional understanding of infinite punishment in hell is being reinforced by appeal to the view that there was a strict equivalence in punishment between the penalty incurred by human sins and the infinitely powerful atoning suffering of the God-Man, Christ, on the cross. It is a neat and mathematical kind of theology, but it seems to go beyond the scriptural texts, building an equivalence of punishment upon them. At this point it is worth challenging the application of a strict, penal substitutionary atonement theory as the logical basis for final judgment.

The conditionalist sees the work of Christ as bearing the consequences of human sin as our representative substitutionary Savior, without necessarily applying a substitutionary mathematical equivalence of sins to be punished. Care needs to be taken in viewing the atonement in these terms. Evangelicals often push St. Paul further than he actually goes in this matter. Hastings Rashdall observed long ago that while "it is clearly St. Paul's conception that Christ has paid that penalty (sin in some way demands death) in order that man may not have to pay it ... he never uses the preposition *anti* (instead of) but always *huper* (on behalf of) in this connexion. Christ is always said to have suffered 'on behalf of' men, not 'instead of' them."[17] Stephen Travis offers a careful analysis of this topic, especially in regard to St. Paul, concluding:

> Rather than saying that in his death Christ experienced retributive punishment on behalf of humanity, Paul more often says that he entered into and bore on our behalf the destructive consequences of sin. Standing where we stand, he bore the consequences of our alienation from God. In so doing he absorbed and exhausted them so that they should not fall on us. It is both true and important to say that he "was judged in our place"— that he experienced divine judgment on sin in the sense that he endured the God-ordained consequences of human sinfulness. But this is not the same to say that he bore our punishment[;] ... judgment is not inflicted by God "from outside," but is the intrinsic outworking, under God's control, of the consequences of human choices and actions. ... Paul's primary category for understanding salvation and condemnation is that of relationship or non-relationship to God.[18]

The conditionalist evangelist will also see the atoning work of Christ our substitute as the key to new life, but without needing to have an

---

17. Rashdall, *The Idea of Atonement in Christian Theology*, 92–93.
18. Travis, *Christ and the Judgement of God*, 199.

equivalence of sins punished. The real problem of sin—the real consequence or "hell"—is the state of God-forsakenness or abandonment by God. The judgment on sin is the loss of God's presence and blessings; this is hell. In Christ, God bore our sin's consequences—God-forsakenness. As the one in whom all humanity is created and finds life, Christ the new human entered into the state of God-forsakenness for the sake of lost people. This involved his death as an experience of God-forsakenness. God "took his own judgment," observed P. T. Forsyth.[19]

The conditionalist evangelist holds that a God-forsaking life leads to a God-forsaken (God-less, life-less) death. But Christ dealt with this failure of humanity, so that we need not face it. The problem was death, the loss of God and the gifts of God in life. The salvation achieved by Christ is therefore the opposite state of life with God. The other part of Christ's renewing work, his resurrection, will now assume central importance in gospel presentations.

4. The Resurrection is Central to the Gospel

Conditionalist evangelism unites the life, death and resurrection of Christ in his saving work for us.

One result of a strong emphasis on the atoning death of Christ on the cross is that the resurrection of Jesus is somewhat eclipsed, and becomes a corollary and a vindication. Concentration on the cross as the key is a mark of much modern evangelicalism—it is a crucicentric movement.[20] A conditionalist view of the gospel can also help avoid one of the oft-noticed imbalances of a penal substitutionary understanding of the atonement, in which the cross is the place where the atonement was achieved and the resurrection of Christ is secondary.

The conditionalist evangelist will keep the death and resurrection together as two parts of the saving work of the Lord. "The work of salvation involves both cross and resurrection."[21] St. Paul brings the two parts together: "He was delivered over to death for our sins and was raised for our justification" (Rom 4:25). The goal of the work of Christ is to bring humanity back to life with God—life in union with God, reconciled and renewed.

The resurrection of Christ can be seen as part of the large New Testament theme of Christ as the new Adam, who recapitulates the plight of humanity and through his obedience, all the way to the cross, enables the reversal of the sin problem. This is how St. Paul unfolds the work of Christ

19. Forsyth, *The Cruciality of the Cross*, 206.
20. See Clifford and Johnson, *The Cross is Not Enough*, chapter 1.
21. Ibid., 245.

in Romans chapters 4, 5, and 6. Christ's resurrection is not a corollary of his saving work; it is central to it. When the glorious Christ of the Revelation announces himself to the seer in the book of Revelation chapter 1, it is his victory over death that is the key achievement (Rev 1:17–18). He has freed us from our sins by his blood and holds the keys of death and Hades in his risen power.

Jesus is not simply a separate divine person doing something wonderful for us on the cross, suffering in our place so that we don't have to suffer the same thing later on. We are participants by faith in the great work of renewal that Christ accomplishes as our Lord and Savior, our human representative in the new creation. We are united with him as he offers true obedience to God on our behalf and enters into the plight of sinners held captive by the problem of "death."

The resurrection of Christ brings the resurrection of human nature in himself, because he is the new Man, the source of life. As Thomas Torrance puts it, "The resurrection is the affirmation and restoration of humanity."[22] He is the new Adam who heads the race in the new creation opened up by his death and resurrection (1 Cor 15:45–49). We are united with him and rise with him in the new creation. He is not our substitute in the sense of replacing us but as representing us. We are bound up with his work and victory on our behalf. St. Paul carefully uses *"on behalf of,"* not *"instead of,"* to describe the work of Christ for us (1 Thess 5:10; Gal 1:4).

Christ's resurrection is a vital part of his victory over sin and death, in which we share. He is our representative and substitute. Constantine Campbell explains, "Dying and rising with Christ means that believers identify with his representative death and resurrection, and it facilitates a change of lordship as the believer dies to the dominion of sin and death and enters new life in the realm of Christ."[23] When Christ died, he was not an innocent third party substituting for mankind in the face of divine punishment. He was the Son of God and head of humanity dealing with sin and human failure as man and as God. Christ as Messiah is qualified to be the substitute because he is the representative human. Another apt way of putting it: "Christ actualized the full surrender to God that we could will but not actualize."[24]

In sharing the gospel message, the conditionalist will invite people to leave the realm of sin and death, and come under the Lordship of Christ, and through union with him, to share in his resurrection life. There will be

---

22. Torrance, *Atonement,* 238.
23. Campbell, *Paul and Union with Christ,* 352.
24. John. V. Dahms, quoted in ibid., 352.

no other way to enter the new age of God other than in union with the Lord Jesus Christ in his victory over the power of sin and death.

The good news of Christ offers the lifting of the penalty of death, the wages of sin. Central to our evangelism will be the proclamation of the resurrection of Christ, which portends and promises our own coming resurrection (1 Cor 15:20–28). In presenting the gospel message, the conditionalist will invite people to become part of God's renewal of creation. We will not offer people a spiritual escape from moral failure but an engagement in the real world, which God is going to renew.

5. The Renewal of Creation

Conditionalist evangelism fits well with a biblical theological gospel presentation that highlights the renewal of creation as the plan of God.

A conditionalist way of communicating the good news coheres with a narrative approach to evangelism, which essentially frames the message as "what God is doing to renew the world." The work of God in Christ is to renew the cosmos, as the source of life in the new creation (Eph 1:9–10). The individual's response to Christ is placed into the wider story of God's work to restore his world.

In much of the Western world, this entry point may be more fruitful than older methods of evangelism, which focused on personal guilt and assumed belief in God's reality and moral principles as the framework for discussion. Evangelism has often used the starting point of individual guilt or sins, and the need for a personal relationship with God. The work of Christ is set forth in relation to individual needs and decisions. Threats of hell and endless separation from God in a miserable existence may have had more impact in former ages, when shared beliefs about God and eternity could be assumed. The work of Christ on the cross is often presented as his own individual, personal substitution in punishment for the sinner's guilt, without explaining that all humanity and nature subsists in him as the eternal Word or Logos.[25] Evangelistic presentations can fail to explain how in Christ, the Creator is renewing humanity and the very creation ultimately.

An evangelistic framework that uses the large biblical-theological narrative of the Bible may have more traction these days. Tim Keller observes that we can offer the biblical good news of how an individual can get right

---

25. "Because he is the eternal Word of Logos in whom all humanity coheres, for him to take human nature upon himself means that all humanity is assumed by his incarnation; all humanity is bound up with him, he died for all humanity and all humanity died in him." (Torrance, *Atonement*, 182).

with God, and we can also explain the biblical good news of what God will fully accomplish in history through the salvation of Jesus: "This is to understand the question as 'What hope is there for the world?'"[26]

There is a great awareness today of ecological issues. Salvation, explained as renewal of the cosmos, including humanity in relationship with God the Creator working through and in the world in his divine Son, Jesus Christ, has a potential resonance as an entry point and framework for the gospel. A conditionalist evangelist may find that the explanation of sin as death-dealing alienation from God opens up a new discussion. It places the gospel as good news for a dying creation. Life in Christ is a world-renewing plan of God—will people accept God's powerful offer of new life in and through Christ in the new creation that is coming?

The consequences of staying in the old order of sin and death—cut off from God and passing away, under God's justice—are simple, straightforward, and fair. There is one way to the resurrection and eternal life can only be found in God's gracious gift through Christ. Why not join God's movement for the renewal of creation?

Another point of evangelistic contact is the problem of evil. The existence of evil, suffering, and death is often the main stated objection to Christianity. The conditionalist evangelist, however, can frame the good news as an answer to the problem of evil: the victory of Christ over sin, evil, and death—in fact, the ultimate victory of God in the renewal of creation. The "Christus Victor" model of salvation is clearly proclaimed in the conditionalist view of final judgment as the destruction of all evil from God's creation (1 Cor 15:28; Rev 21:4). The challenge to the unbeliever is to see his or her own place in the big problem of sin and death. Presenting the gospel as the removal of evil, sin and suffering from the world meets head-on the modern Western mind-set of justice and ecological focus.[27]

The conditionalist evangelistic presentation that uses the "renewal of life" framework also helps to keep the work of God in Christ closely related to the call to obedience and renewal by the Holy Spirit. The goal of God in salvation is not a clearing of our eternal "sin account" but the renewal of human lives, now and forever. The new life in Christ starts now; the powers of the age to come has begun to change us. Sanctification forms part of this story of renewal. The good news is not all about what happens when you die.

The Christian gospel is about experiencing fellowship with God now and becoming part of God's renewal process for the whole world. The power

---

26. Keller, *Center Church*, 32–37.

27. The Letter of Paul to the Romans, particularly in the summary of redemption in Romans 8, can be looked at from one aspect, as the way that God addresses the problem of sin, evil and death in his creation, bringing justice and renewal.

of new life, eternal life, is part of our message. In Christ we become a new creation. The conditionalist evangelist will also challenge and hopefully intrigue the lost by the invitation to experience now the fullness of the abundant life in Christ.

CONCLUSION

In this part of Christian history, the task of evangelism has been released from the heavy burden of the unsound doctrine of eternal conscious torment through the labors of Edward Fudge and others in the conditionalist movement. Our challenge now is to develop creative and compelling ways to offer life in Christ alone to our world.

Communicating the good news of Jesus Christ from a theology of conditional immortality can take different forms. Conditionalists will have a range of views about the atonement and different ways of presenting the multifaceted good news of salvation. Common to all conditionalist evangelism, however, will be a message of salvation in Christ that is unburdened and unhindered by the terrible doctrine of eternal conscious punishment of the impenitent lost. There will be a positive proclamation of the abundant life that is found in Christ now and for eternity. The work of God will be set in its cosmic context of renewal and justice. The issue of eternal life as found only in Christ will challenge hearers to see the choice before them. The victory of the Lord Jesus Christ, the new head of humanity, over sin, evil, and death in his death and resurrection, will be confidently communicated. The gracious gift of life from God can be emphasized, along with the inherently reasonable withdrawal of life by God when his offer of eternal life is declined. This wonderful gift of life with God now and forever will be at the center of conditionalist gospel explanations.

We will remind people of the God who is the giver of life, who calls us from self-destructive deathly ways, who has acted in Jesus Christ to renew his world and who now offers us life in all its abundance, from him and with him forever. The invitation is to choose well—to choose life in Christ.

20

How to Talk about the Afterlife (If You Must)

Ten Theses to Guide Debates among Traditionalists, Conditionalists, and Universalists

— DAVID C. CRAMER —

David C. Cramer is a PhD candidate in the Department of Religion at Baylor University with an emphasis on theology and ethics. He is co-editor of The Activist Impulse: Essays on the Intersection of Evangelicalism and Anabaptism *and has written numerous essays and reviews on topics ranging from systematic theology and religious pluralism to death and dying, gender, violence, and immigration. His work has been published in a number of academic and popular outlets, including* Christian Scholar's Review, The Mennonite Quarterly Review, Priscilla Papers, The Christian Century, *and* Sojourners. *David, his wife Andrea, and their two young children live in Waco, Texas, where they are members of Hope Fellowship Mennonite Church.*

David originally presented the following paper at the Rethinking Hell conference, 2014.

While describing the universalism of several church fathers in the 26th chapter of the third edition of his masterful work, *The Fire that Consumes*, Edward Fudge offers a most succinct and helpful summary of the issue of debate regarding personal eschatology. Fudge writes, "The three major views of final punishment can be identified and distinguished by the purpose that one ascribes to the fire of hell: whether the fire is *consuming* (conditionalist), *torturing* (traditionalist), or *purifying* (restorationist)."[1] It is as simple and straightforward as that. And yet, often when discussing this topic, the issues quickly become complex and the debates quickly heat up (apologies for the pun). Indeed, perhaps no one knows better than Fudge how talking about the afterlife can quickly get you into hot water. And perhaps no one has navigated such discussions with more grace, wisdom, and charity.

In honor of Fudge's seventieth birthday and in the spirit of Fudge's writing and speaking, this essay proposes and defends ten theses that should guide debates about the afterlife, especially debates among evangelical traditionalists, conditionalists, and universalists (or, in Fudge's terminology, restorationists). Instead of defending any one particular viewpoint, then, this essay offers a roadmap for debates on these issues among evangelicals. I argue that, if these theses were adhered to by proponents of the respective viewpoints on the afterlife, not only would debates be more fruitful and productive but evangelical Christian unity would be maintained in the midst of such debates. And though I imagine Fudge will not agree entirely with what follows (perhaps especially those places where I critique his work!), I hope that these theses will be offered and received in the same irenic spirit that so characterizes his work.[2]

THESIS 1: EVERY VIEW OF THE AFTERLIFE INVOLVES SOME AMOUNT OF SPECULATION.

In this debate as with so many others, there are always proponents of each position who insist that their position is simply the "biblical" one—as though everyone else is too dense or stubborn to recognize what Scripture clearly teaches. But while advocates of each position are encouraged to offer the biblical support for their view, I tend to agree with Reinhold Niebuhr who once wrote that "it is unwise for Christians to claim any knowledge of either the furniture of heaven or the temperature of hell; or to be too certain about any details of the Kingdom of God in which history is consummated."[3]

Fudge seems to at least partially concur with this sentiment when he writes concerning the level of certainty necessary to adopt a view,

> We do not live our lives waiting for theories or answers that resolve every potential problem. Most often, we operate on a

---

1. Fudge, *The Fire That Consumes* (2011), 274.

2. This essay develops two guest posts I made on Scot McKnight's blog, Jesus Creed. See Cramer, "How to Talk about the Afterlife," parts 1 and 2.

3. Niebuhr, *Nature and Destiny of Man*, 2:294.

> level that will make sense to anyone who ever has served on a civil jury: not proof *beyond a reasonable doubt* (the standard in a criminal trial . . .), but proof *by the greater weight and preponderance of the evidence*. This standard of judgment weighs the evidence to determine which alternative view, if either, is shown to be more likely.[4]

In other words, we can weigh the respective biblical evidence for various views and judge which view we believe best fits the evidence; but at the end of the day, we must recognize that the Bible may very well underdetermine an answer to a question it was not written to directly address.[5] As Fudge writes, "It cannot be said too strongly, clearly, and often: Jesus did not come to satisfy our curiosity or to make us as wise as God. He came to reveal God—and to call men and women to faith and obedience."[6]

Thus, if we are going to try to develop a theory, we are going to have to go beyond the words on the page and into the realm of theological speculation—albeit speculation that is faithful to the words on the page. Again, Fudge writes, "No human being on earth is perfectly objective. We all have blind spots, although in different areas. The most that any of us can do is pray for wisdom and guidance, commit ourselves to proper methods of interpretation, and do the best job that we can."[7] This leads me to my second thesis.

THESIS 2: THEOLOGICAL POSITIONS CANNOT BE REDUCED STRICTLY TO BIBLICAL EXEGESIS.

After following debates on the afterlife for a while, one can get the impression that if we could just dig in a little deeper into the meaning of the word *aiōnios* or *gehenna* we would finally have the answer to all of our questions. But, while understanding terms in their original language and context is important, it is not the magic key to unlocking the mysteries of the eschaton.

Although in the quotes above Fudge seems to acknowledge the limitations of exegesis, at times he appears to forget this point when assessing the work of others. So, for example, after discussing the views of N. T. Wright and Greg Boyd on the afterlife, Fudge concludes, "Both Wright and Boyd acknowledge that their proposals are based on speculation rather than

---

4. Fudge, *The Fire That Consumes* (2011), 375; emphasis in original.
5. For more on biblical underdetermination (though in the context of a different debate), see Cramer, "Creating a Culture of Equality."
6. Fudge, *The Fire That Consumes* (2011), 279.
7. Ibid., 32.

exegesis."[8] By stating it this way, he makes it seem as though one *either* deals with exegesis *or* falls into speculation. But I would suggest that, especially with evangelical scholars such as Wright and Boyd, exegesis and speculation are not mutually exclusive, but rather speculation picks up where exegesis leaves off.

This, I take it, is why after commending Fudge's work in his foreword to *The Fire That Consumes*, Richard Bauckham concludes, "In my view, we very much also need a fully theological study of the wider contexts and implications of this particular issue within biblical theology. Especially I find it impossible to ignore its relationship to the doctrine of God."[9] This statement from a leading New Testament scholar acknowledges the fact that theology and exegesis have always had a cyclical relationship: biblical exegesis gives rise to theological speculation while also providing a check on it, but theology also provides a test for proper exegesis.

Fudge repeatedly notes, for example, that Origen's views on the afterlife were based on speculation. He writes that, "In his writings, Origen speculates that the fire of hell is a purifying and refining fire";[10] that "Origen based his speculations on elements of human nature and the divine nature";[11] and that "Origen's defenders insist that he offered his ideas as mere speculations or possibilities, not as matters of settled doctrine."[12] All of these observations are correct as far as they go, but they seem to miss the cyclical way Origen relates exegesis and theology in his *Peri Archon* or *On First Principles*. While space prohibits an in-depth review of this massive tome, a brief explanation may be instructive.[13]

Origen begins his preface to *On First Principles* by proclaiming, "All who believe and are convinced that grace and truth came by Jesus Christ . . . and who know Christ to be the truth (in accordance with his own saying, 'I am the truth' . . .), derive the knowledge which calls men to lead a good and blessed life from no other source but the very words and teachings of Christ."[14] For Origen, Christ's teachings—by which he means not only the direct words of Jesus while on earth but also the teachings of Moses and the prophets inspired by the Logos—form the foundation for the Chris-

8. Ibid., 143.
9. Ibid., x.
10. Ibid., 273.
11. Ibid., 274.
12. Ibid., 275.
13. For more on Origen's approach, see de Lubac, *History and Spirit*, and Martens, *Origen and Scripture*.
14. Origen, *On First Principles*, I.Preface; 1.

tian faith. However, Origen notes that there is a great diversity of opinions on matters great and small regarding Christian doctrine. As such, his first matter of business is to "lay down a definite line and unmistakable rule" in regard to these matters in order to establish "that that only is to be believed as the truth which in no way conflicts with the tradition of the church and the apostles"—a rule he lays down in the remainder of the preface, following the "plain terms" of the apostles.

This rule of faith includes the affirmations that God is the creator, that Christ Jesus "was begotten of the Father," "that the Holy Spirit is united in honor and dignity with the Father and the Son"; that the soul "will be rewarded according to its deserts after its departure from this world"; that "there will be a time for the resurrection of the dead"; "that every rational soul is possessed of free will and choice"; that a "devil and his angels and the opposing spiritual powers" exist; that "this world was made and began to exist at a definite time and that by reason of its corruptible nature it must suffer dissolution"; "that the scriptures were composed through the Spirit of God"; that there are incorporeal objects; and that "there exist certain angels of God and good powers." Origen declares, "Everyone therefore who is desirous of constructing out of the foregoing a connected body of doctrine must use points like these as elementary and foundation principles."[15] Here, then, his theological speculation is clearly constructed on the foundation of the plain text of Scripture.

Thus, while affirming these plain teachings as his rule of faith, Origen's purpose in the rest of *On First Principles* is to investigate the "grounds" of these plain statements. He explains that the apostles themselves did not offer the grounds of their statements so that instead these grounds might "be investigated by such as should merit the higher gifts of the Spirit and in particular by such as should afterwards receive through the Holy Spirit himself the graces of language, wisdom and knowledge." With still other doctrines, the apostles offered the what, while "keeping silence as to the how or why." Again, Origen explains that "their intention undoubtedly [was] to supply the more diligent of those who came after them, such as should prove to be lovers of wisdom, with an exercise on which to display the fruit of their ability." These people he describes as "those who train themselves to become worthy and capable of receiving wisdom." In short, Origen is describing the task of the systematic or philosophical theologian: working within the parameters of Scripture and the orthodox Christian faith, the theologian is tasked with offering "clear and cogent arguments" in order to "discover the truth about each particular point and so [to] produce . . . a single body of

---

15. Ibid., I.Preface; 2–7.

doctrine, with the aid of such illustrations and declarations as he shall find in the holy scriptures and of such conclusions as he shall ascertain to follow logically from them when rightly understood."[16]

For Origen the goodness and justice of God is a foundational theological belief derived from a holistic reading of Scripture. He thus often rebuts the literal readings of heretics, but he does so not because they are literal *per se* but because they are used to defend a morally deficient view of God. In other words, Origen's theology derives from his scriptural interpretation, but once so derived his theology can also come back around to identify bad exegesis. And this leads me to my third thesis.

THESIS 3: CHRISTIAN PHILOSOPHERS AND THEOLOGIANS SHOULD BE GIVEN THE BENEFIT OF THE DOUBT WHEN REASONING ABOUT THE MEANING OF IMPORTANT CONCEPTS (LOVE, JUSTICE, ETC.).

When Paul decries the "philosopher of this age" in 1 Corinthians 1:20, he is clearly not talking about *Christian* philosophers; rather, he is talking about those pagan philosophers "who are perishing" (v. 18). Scripture has a high regard for Christian wisdom and clear thinking, guided by the Holy Spirit. It should not count against philosophers and theologians that they are trying to be logical or consistent in their views or trying to trace out the implications and entailments of various understandings of Scripture. Of course, even Christian philosophers and theologians can give in to the temptation to fall into the presuppositions of pagan or secular philosophy, but we should not assume they have from the outset. Note, however, that giving them the benefit of the doubt does not mean agreeing with their conclusions; it simply means not being suspicious of them strictly because they are using so-called "human wisdom."

Of course, rarely does one criticize the philosopher who advocates one's own position. Usually this criticism is saved for the philosopher defending an opposing position. So, for example, Fudge writes of early Christian apologists that they

> wanted to show their pagan neighbors the reasonableness of the biblical faith. . . . They wrapped their understanding of Scripture in the robes of philosophy, choosing from the vocabulary of worldly wisdom the words that sparkled and adorned it best.

---

16. Ibid., I.Preface; 7.

> Paul had often warned against contemporary philosophy... but these apologists, zealous for their new-found faith, set out to battle pagan thinkers on their own turf.[17]

However, when narrating the recovery of conditionalism, Fudge describes John Locke as an "influential philosopher and ardent advocate of unhampered thought" who "was an outspoken defender of the divine origin of Scripture."[18] But, while Locke rejected the Platonism of the early apologists, his project was largely consistent with how Fudge describes theirs: to show his pagan neighbors the reasonableness of the biblical faith, as suggested by the title of Locke's last work, *On the Reasonableness of Christianity*. Indeed, Locke's Socinian or Arian Christology suggests that he too wrapped his understanding of Scripture in the robes of philosophy—albeit Enlightenment rather than Platonic philosophy.

Rather than jumping to 1 Corinthians 1 when a Christian philosopher presents an argument, then, we should consider the merits of the argument itself. While Fudge is certainly correct that the story of the fall "teaches that our sense of moral rightness can be a deceitful guide, and that we must listen to God's voice instead,"[19] Christians also affirm that in Christ "there is a new creation" (2 Cor 5:17, NRSV) and that we have been transformed by the renewing of our minds so that we "may discern what is the will of God—what is good and acceptable and perfect" (Rom 12:2, NRSV). I personally want to listen to what the Christian philosopher or theologian discerns about "what is good and acceptable and perfect," then, because in so doing I just may hear the voice of the Holy Spirit.

THESIS 4: MINORITY READINGS OF SCRIPTURE SHOULD BE GIVEN SPECIAL ATTENTION.

As we are try to listen carefully to, and discern the voice of, the Spirit, I believe that we must pay particularly careful attention to scriptural readings that go against the grain of our tradition. If we do not listen to such readings, then we cannot truly claim to be "reformed and always reforming." This, of course, does not mean that minority readings are necessarily more likely to be true. At the same time, I have found that those with minority views often know their position and opposing positions better than those who hold majority views.

---

17. Fudge, *The Fire That Consumes* (2011), 20.
18. Ibid., 331.
19. Ibid., 368.

As a Christian pacifist, for example, I often encounter others who dismiss my views with quick references to the Old Testament wars of Yahweh, or Jesus clearing the temple with a whip, or John's instructions to the Roman soldiers, or Paul's teaching on the state in Romans 13, as though I had not ever considered those passages before as well as every other passage that might possibly pertain to the question of Christians and violence. But when the tables are turned and I offer biblical arguments for pacifism, often at least some of them are unfamiliar to my interlocutor. I imagine the situation is similar for conditionalists and universalists. Precisely because minority readings are less familiar, therefore, they should be given special consideration.

THESIS 5: THE POSITION ONE ACTUALLY HOLDS MUST BE DISTINGUISHED FROM WHAT WE BELIEVE TO BE THE "GOOD AND NECESSARY CONSEQUENCES" OF THAT POSITION.

Roger Olson once wrote in the context of debates between Calvinists and Arminians about the distinction between the views one actually holds and what we may believe to be the "good and necessary consequences" of that view. Olson explains, "So, for example, Reformed theologians have often argued that works righteousness . . . is a good and necessary consequence of Arminian belief in the necessity of free response to the gospel for salvation. While I disagree, I accept that as fair criticism *so long as* the critic clearly says (in some way) 'This is not what Arminians believe; it is what their belief logically entails.'"[20] In the same way, a conditionalist might believe that the "good and necessary consequence" of eternal conscious torment is a sadistic view of God or that the "good and necessary consequence" of universalism is an elimination of divine judgment and justice. These criticisms are fair so long as those making them are clear that, for example, the one holding to eternal conscious torment does not actually advocate divine child abuse, and the one holding to universalism does not actually advocate eliminating divine judgment and justice.

---

20. Olson, "Fair and Unfair Criticisms"; emphasis in original.

THESIS 6: THE PRACTICAL DIFFERENCES AMONG THESE VIEWS SHOULD NOT BE OVERESTIMATED.

Whether an unbeliever suffers forever, is completely destroyed, or suffers for a really long time, this is not a state of affairs that one would desire. So if our evangelism is going to be predicated on the fate of those who do not accept Christ (which I do not believe should be our *primary* motivation anyway), then there should not be a practical difference between the major evangelical views of the afterlife. Even if one believes that ultimately all will be saved, one would still want to save people from all the unnecessary suffering they would face in the penultimate afterlife. And as Christians, we would hopefully want all to experience the fullness of kingdom-living now, which should be motivation enough for evangelism regardless of our views of the afterlife.

To my mind, the argument that the eternal suffering of the lost is necessary to motivate evangelizing them is most revealing about the one making the argument.[21] Fudge tells the story of John Wenham, whose evangelical zeal was initially deflated after changing from a traditionalist to a conditionalist view. "But," writes Fudge, "as [Wenham] prayed about it, he 'realized that rescue from torment was not a primary motive for evangelism, rather one wished to see God glorified through the loving response of a sinner to the one who loved him.'"[22] If this is our primary motivation for evangelism (which I believe it should be), then it will not be affected by one's particular view of the afterlife.

This is not to say that there are not *any* practical ramifications of one's view of final punishment. Since Jesus instructs us to be perfect as our heavenly Father is perfect (Matt 5:48), I suspect that those who hold the traditional view are less likely to reject certain forms of torture (like waterboarding), while those who hold to conditionalism are probably less likely to reject capital punishment (although even here there are numerous other considerations that might mitigate such correlations). This leads me to my next, and in many ways corresponding, thesis.

---

21. There is especial irony when such an argument is made by an Edwardsian Calvinist; see McDermott, "Will All Be Saved?" 243.

22. Fudge, *The Fire That Consumes* (2011), 345.

THESIS 7: THE THEOLOGICAL DIFFERENCES AMONG THESE VIEWS SHOULD NOT BE UNDERESTIMATED.

Most of us believe that God loves everyone and that God is perfectly just. But clearly, what one who believes in eternal conscious torment, one who believes in final destruction, and one who believes in ultimate universal reconciliation mean by terms like "love" and "justice" are going to radically differ.

On the eternal conscious torment view, one has to reconcile one's definition of love and justice with the notion that God torments (or allows to be tormented) unbelievers eternally (that is, after all, the very definition of the term "eternal conscious torment"). Other views of God necessarily follow from eternal conscious torment, such as that God does not ultimately get everything he desires: minimally, that all should be saved (1 Tim 2:4; 2 Pet 3:9). Of course, one might say that God desires some things more than he desires all to be saved, but then that too is saying something about God and his character. Moreover, as Greg Boyd points out, this view ends with a "dualism . . . throughout eternity," which seems in tension with the biblical idea that God will be "all in all" (1 Cor 15:28).[23]

On the annihilationist view, one has to reconcile one's view of love and justice with the notion that God destroys (or allows to cease existing) unbelievers at the second death. One also has to deal with some of the same theological ramifications as the eternal conscious torment view just discussed (though not the eternal dualism issue).

On the universalist view, one has to reconcile one's definition of love and justice with the notion that God will give second (and possibly third, fourth, fifth . . .) chances to those who die in utter defiance toward God and utter hatred toward fellow human beings. Even if these postmortem chances include much suffering, as evangelical universalists argue, this view is clearly working with a different notion of love and justice than the other views.

The question then becomes: Which notion of love and justice is most consistent with the whole scope and tenor of Scripture (as well as those nitty-gritty details of Scripture that the exegetes deal with)?

Moreover, the third edition of *The Fire That Consumes* alerted me to another significant theological difference that I had not considered before.[24] In chapters 16 and 17 on "Golgotha," Fudge argues that "eschatology is an

---

23. Boyd, "The Case for Annihilationism."

24. For a development of this argument, see Bawulski, "The Annihilationist's Theological Problem."

aspect of Christology"[25] and, thus, that "the Passion of Jesus Christ uniquely revealed God's judgment against sin—the same judgment that those who knowingly and persistently reject Christ now will face at the end of the world."[26] However, practically, since Fudge has already concluded that the fate of the lost is complete annihilation, he is led to conclude that "Jesus' death involved total destruction."[27]

Fudge notes Robert Peterson's response that on Fudge's view Christ was destroyed "either in his wholeness (two natures) or ... in his human nature only," but, argues Peterson, the first option "would mean that the Trinity was reduced to a Binity for three days," while the second entails that Christ's "two natures be divided for three days, which the definition given at Chalcedon says cannot happen."[28] Instead of explaining how his view avoids this dilemma, Fudge resolutely responds, "While Christians may legitimately look to a variety of sources for assistance in understanding Scripture teaching and discerning its proper application, of which tradition is one, in the event of a clash, evangelicals should always receive Scripture as possessing greater authority than any other source of guidance."[29] But while this response is an evangelical truism, it does not get Fudge off the hook of the profound theological ramifications of his argument.

If the Trinity is reduced to a Binity at the destruction of one of its persons, then that will have profound implications for notions of divine immutability, which itself has strong support from Scripture. Minimally, it would entail that the resurrected Christ was recreated by God *ex nihilo* (after being totally destroyed), which would result in a novel version of Arianism.[30] Fudge concedes, "We ultimately recoil from such a thought, that the Son of God could truly have perished—even for a moment," but he continues, "Yet is this not the same difficulty we face in accepting Jesus' humiliation in becoming a *man*?"[31] Contra Fudge, I would argue that it is not the same. The incarnation teaches a self-chosen act of humility that is fully consistent with God's eternal nature, whereas the view of Christ's temporary annihilation teaches a profound disruption of God's otherwise eternal nature.

---

25. Fudge, *The Fire That Consumes* (2011), 171.
26. Ibid., 174.
27. Ibid., 181.
28. Ibid., 185.
29. Ibid.
30. Moreover, from a strictly biblical standpoint, it is surprising that Fudge does not discuss in this context (or anywhere in his book) Jesus' statement to the thief on the cross: "Truly I tell you, today you will be with me in Paradise" (Luke 23:43, NRSV).
31. Fudge, *The Fire That Consumes* (2011), 182–83; emphasis in original.

On the other hand, if Christ's natures were divided at death, then it is difficult to see how the Son's death and resurrection really are the pattern for humanity, since unlike humans who are utterly destroyed at death, Christ merely separated his divine nature from his human one before reuniting with it days later. I imagine there are other ways conditionalists might deal with this issue,[32] but from my standpoint, this is one of those cases where, while affirming the ultimate authority of Scripture, I would with Origen conclude that something has gone awry with my own exegesis if it leads me to such theological conclusions. After all, contrary to popular belief, the formulations of the Councils were not foreign Greek interpositions into biblical Christianity; rather, they were attempts by the church to work out the Christological entailments of the biblical witness.

THESIS 8: EACH OF THESE POSITIONS HAS BOTH SUBTLE, SCHOLARLY ARTICULATIONS AND SHALLOW, POPULAR DESCRIPTIONS; CARE SHOULD BE TAKEN TO DISTINGUISH THE TWO.

It is always best to take on the best form of an argument and try to refute it than to merely refute popular forms of an argument. However, since popular forms are so *popular*, it is sometimes necessary to discuss and refute those too; this is acceptable so long as one specifies that in so doing one is not taking on the best version of the argument. So, if popular formulations of eternal conscious torment suggest a sadistic view of God, it is acceptable to point out the flaws in that view. And if popular formulations of universalism suggest a lax view of God, it is acceptable to point out the flaws in that view too. But the most subtle forms of eternal conscious torment try to avoid divine sadism, and the most subtle forms of universalism try to avoid divine laxity; and in debating these issues eventually one will have to deal with these more sophisticated views head on.

32. During the question and answer period after his plenary talk at the 2014 Rethinking Hell conference in Houston, Texas, conditionalist Glenn Peoples offered a novel response to this objection based on the doctrine of divine timelessness. In short, Peoples argued that the eternal (timeless) *Logos* is distinct from the incarnate, temporal *Logos*, such that nothing that could happen to the incarnate *Logos*—including being "completely destroyed" or "metaphysically annihilated"—could possibly have any effect on the eternal *Logos*. It would take me beyond the purposes of this paper to evaluate the adequacy of this explanation other than simply to register my doubt that many conditionalists will adopt Peoples's line of reasoning, based as it is on classical theism, which many conditionalists reject in favor of a more personalistic, biblical theism (though, as I have suggested in this paper, these categories are not as distinct as such conditionalists might imagine).

Here Fudge's treatment of universalism offers a good example. Although he mentions what he calls the "liberal Protestant" universalism of previous centuries that "ignored sin, dismissed the atonement, overlooked judgment, and denied hell,"[33] he goes on to discuss individually a number of more careful articulations of evangelical universalism. One wishes that others from all sides would follow Fudge's lead here.

THESIS 9: WE ALL HAVE MOTIVATIONS FOR HOLDING THE VIEWS WE HOLD, BUT UNLESS SOMEONE EXPLICITLY STATES HIS OR HER MOTIVATION FOR HOLDING A VIEW, IT IS BEST TO LEAVE DISCUSSION OF MOTIVATIONS OUT OF IT.

Yes, some universalists and conditionalists probably grew up in oppressive fundamentalist churches from which they are trying desperately to break away. Yes, some who hold to eternal conscious torment cannot stand the idea of someday worshiping next to Hitler and bin Laden in heaven. But not everyone who holds to these views does so for the same reasons or with the same motivations. Speculating on one's motivations, then, is just another form of the old *ad hominem* fallacy, and fallacies are generally best to avoid.

Having just commended Fudge's treatment of universalists, I must also draw attention to his closing arguments in that chapter. Fudge notes that "every sensitive Christian probably wishes that universalism could be true,"[34] which, though not stated directly, implies that universalists might hold their view as a form of wish-fulfillment (an argument that, as I already suggested, could be turned on any of the views, depending on what one's wish is for one's enemies). But further, Fudge suggests that "the traditional theory of unending conscious torment continues as a major incentive driving believers to universalism and potential believers to unbelief."[35] While this statement may very well be true in many cases, it again implies a motivation for universalists besides their desire to seek the truth.

Indeed, Fudge uses this motivation argument as a kind of backdoor argument for conditionalism: "The only absolute answer to universalism is conditionalism, or some other variety of biblical annihilationism."[36] In other words, if you really want to guard against the idea of ultimate reconciliation,

---

33. Fudge, *The Fire That Consumes* (2011), 280.
34. Ibid., 284.
35. Ibid., 285.
36. Ibid., 286.

you should embrace conditionalism. Of course, since conditionalism holds that God resurrects persons who have previously been totally destroyed, Fudge overstates his argument: God could always decide to resurrect the damned after their second death to reconcile them to himself. But beyond that point, these kinds of pragmatic considerations are generally red herrings in these debates.

We should stick to the actual arguments made by respective adherents of the various views rather than speculating about the motivations one has for holding to her respective view. As Fudge reminds us, "we all are part of a great family of faith. . . . Because we are talking to family members, it is important for us to forbear making personal accusations or judging the motives of others in the conversation."[37] And this leads to my tenth and final thesis.

THESIS 10: NONE OF THESE POSITIONS IS CLEARLY UNORTHODOX OR UNEVANGELICAL.

By stating that none of these positions is clearly unorthodox or unevangelical, I am arguing for the principle of charity in these discussions. In other words, if someone claims to present their view as an orthodox or evangelical Christian, I am obliged to consider her such unless and until I discover compelling evidence to the contrary. Of course, this is not to deny that there has been a dominant view in the Christian tradition generally or the evangelical tradition more specifically. But it is also true that (perhaps because one view has been most often assumed) none of these views has been universally and univocally ruled out by these traditions. There have always coexisted minority views, and while some particular denominations or institutions have settled on one view or another, the major stream of Christianity has always allowed for some variance.[38] And even within evangelicalism, there has been a history of competing views, although today that story has largely been suppressed.

The fact is that universalist Gregory of Nyssa was one of the most important fathers of the church, being venerated as a saint in Catholicism, Eastern Orthodoxy, and pretty much every other Christian tradition that believes in venerating saints, including Protestant ones. In modern times, Robin Parry titled his book *The Evangelical Universalist*, which does not leave a lot of room for ambiguity about his commitment to evangelical

37. Ibid., 15.
38. This point is argued persuasively in von Balthasar, *Dare We Hope*.

Christianity.[39] On the conditionalist side, one would be hard pressed to find a more well-respected evangelical churchman than John Stott. And Fudge's own evangelical credentials are, of course, unassailable. It goes without saying that adherents to the traditionalist view are to be found throughout the tradition.

In short, personal eschatology just has not been the focus or core of Christian teaching and doctrine, and that's probably how it should be. This is why I included the parenthetical in this essay's title. I have seen how debates about this topic can become all-consuming (another bad pun), especially for those who hold minority positions. But as Fudge notes, "Upon consideration, fair-minded people will realize that the differences between evangelical traditionalists and conditionalists regarding hell are miniscule by comparison with the first-level truths they hold in common."[40] I am not sure whether he would include evangelical universalists in this statement as well, although I cannot see why he would not. As he states elsewhere, "The message of final punishment is not the gospel."[41] And so, since it cannot be said often enough, I conclude by once again quoting Fudge's important reminder:

> Only at the cross of Jesus can one truly read Scripture in the light of God's judgment—whether one seeks to know of divine mercy or divine wrath. Questions not answered there must remain unanswered in this life. It cannot be said too strongly, clearly, and often: Jesus did not come to satisfy our curiosity or to make us as wise as God. He came to reveal God—and to call men and women to faith and obedience.[42]

May we all seek to be faithful to that call, even as we continue to enjoy spirited debates together as sisters and brothers in Christ.

---

39. MacDonald, *The Evangelical Universalist*, 2nd. ed.
40. Fudge, *The Fire That Consumes* (2011), 376.
41. Ibid., 377.
42. Ibid., 279.

21

Taking Conditionalism to the People

— JIM WOOD —

Jim Wood is a graduate of Pacific Union College (Theology) and has been serving in media ministry since 1985. He has worked with Angwin, California-based LLT Productions since 1998. He is writer and associate producer of The Seventh Day: Revelations from the Lost Pages of History, *a five-part documentary series hosted by Hal Holbrook. He is co-producer of* Hell and Mr. Fudge *and is currently working on a documentary presentation of conditionalism.*

Jim originally presented the following paper at the Rethinking Hell conference, 2014.

For those of us who are actively engaged in the traditionalist-universalist-conditionalist conversation, the relevant issues loom large within our intellectual horizons. The truth is, however, that what seems so important to us has attracted minimal attention "on the street." Out there in the real world few people recognize that there is any serious debate about the ultimate fate of the lost.

Traditionalism maintains its popularity among conservative Christians, but its status as the default view transcends religious boundaries. According to a 2008 report by the Pew Research Center, a poll of 35,000

Americans showed that the majority (59 percent) assumes that this worst of all possible views of eternity is true.[1]

Universalism has gained ground within liberal and progressive religious groups. According to Richard Bauckham, "Among the less conservative, universal salvation, either as hope or as dogma, is now so widely accepted that many theologians assume it virtually without argument."[2] Theologians aside, universalism is a popular and easy assumption for the unaffiliated post-modern or post-Christian classes.

Conditionalism, on the other hand, remains very much a minority view at the lay level. In spite of its deep roots within historical Christianity, it is largely unknown, often misrepresented, and widely misunderstood. As a result, most people are left with a picture of (a) a sovereign God who is so offended by sinners that His unmitigated wrath far surpasses the demands of justice (traditionalism) or (b) a God whose love for sinners ultimately denies the validity of free will and negates the concept of divine justice (universalism).

Teaching conditionalism is authentic gospel ministry. It exposes the fallacies of the alternative views, and that certainly needs to be done. But above and beyond that, it exalts the character of God and the atoning ministry—the life, the death, and the resurrection—of Christ. John Stott had it right when he wrote, "Christian integrity consists partly in a resolve to unmask the caricatures, but mostly in personal loyalty to Jesus, in whose mind the saving cross was central."[3]

Taking conditionalism to a wider audience would be an important mission if only to correct false impressions of God or to bring spiritual topics into the arena of public dialogue. But there's more to it.

A truly biblical view of the nature of man, the wages of sin, the judgment, divine justice joined to mercy offers peace and assurance to believers who live in fear—for themselves or their loved ones—of eternal conscious torment in hell.

Many thoughtful and sincere individuals have admitted that the doctrine of eternal torment and its corollaries have been major factors in their rejection of Christianity. The conditionalist alternative can offer these people new reasons to reconsider their relationship to God and the claims of the gospel.

---

1. Pew Research Center, "U.S. Religious Landscape Survey."
2. Bauckham, "Universalism," 47.
3. Stott, *The Cross of Christ*, 43.

CHALLENGES

As conditionalists, we face an uphill battle in our "evangelistic" efforts. Going up against the *status quo* means first recognizing the challenges that must be faced.

Diverse Audiences

First of all, there is the diversity of the intended audience. It includes adherents of the full gamut of Christian faiths, Jews, Muslims, and confirmed secularists whether atheist/agnostic or postmodern/"spiritual." The diversity becomes even more complex when cultural and generational differences are factored in.

The default strategy might be to write off the non-Christian audience and target the Christian subgroups deemed most likely to be receptive. The genuine evangelical heart, however, cannot be satisfied with such a narrow focus. We cannot restrict the gospel—including the good news about God's plan for the eternal future—to a select class or territory.

Traditionalist Gatekeepers

Within the evangelical community, pastors and evangelists who adhere to traditionalism stand ready to protect their flocks from what they see as heresy. Like gatekeepers at the entrance to their fortress, they vigorously defend against alternative views like conditionalism and its alter ego, annhilationism. This is just as true on the institutional and denominational levels.

John Gerstner is surely an extreme example, but his work is at least suggestive of the Traditionalist tone. Gerstner devoted much of his academic life to the study of traditionalist icon Jonathan Edwards, so it's no surprise that he was an aggressive gatekeeper. His *Repent or Perish* is a fierce defense against conditionalism. Here are a few of his comments:

> If the evangelical will hold to God, he knows he must hold to hell. If he parts with hell, he know he parts with Jesus Christ, his God and Savior. If he loves God, he must love hell, too.[4]

> When a conservative believer attacks hell, he has ceased to be a conservative believer, if a believer at all.[5]

---

4. Gerstner, *Repent or Perish*, 31.
5. Ibid.

> This is the reason I wrote this book. Not because I love hell and hate its annihilation, but because I hate attempts to annihilate God and His Son, Jesus Christ. . . . Annhilationism attempts just that.[6]

Media Bias

Writers, producers, and publishers feed the public's infatuation with the occult and the supernatural. Intentional or not, this is a market-driven bias toward some of the foundational principles of traditionalism, favoring natural immortality and spiritualism. From comedies like *Ghostbusters* (1984) to romantic dramas like *The Ghost and Mrs. Muir* (1947) and *Ghost* (1990) to edgy thrillers like *The Sixth Sense* (1999), the big screen has served up a long menu of films that have set the tone for prime-time television fare. According to Ranker.com, "Currently, there are more genuinely creepy television shows airing than ever before."[7]

Immortal Soulism

Conditionalists are swimming against the strong current of immortal soulism. The popularity of this belief is barely short of universal. The idea that death is not death, that deceased loved ones are alive and well in heaven with Jesus, that dying is simply a transition to life in a new dimension—this has become a form of folk religion. It is deeply rooted in our cultural DNA.

A Culture of Vengeance

You don't have to look far to find examples of injustice. Crimes that go unsolved, convicted criminals who somehow get off easy, and penalties that seem not to fit the crime offend our human instinct for balance and fairness. Victims find themselves powerless against justice systems that go to great lengths to protect the rights of criminals.

On a larger scale we sympathize with multitudes of fellow human beings who are victimized by dictators, tyrants, and radical ideologies. There's little we can do to bring relief to the abused, widowed, and orphaned masses whose lives are a living hell.

---

6. Ibid., 185.
7. Ranker, "Creepiest Shows on TV Right Now."

Frustration over the injustices in the world around us feeds our desire to see things put right. Many people find solace in the hope that God, in His vengeance, will eventually reward the perpetrators of evil with unending conscious torment in the eternal flames.

The attitude of vengeance also crops up in the form of sectarian triumphalism as church members see themselves and their congregation or denomination as the exclusive repository of truth. They expect God's favor to the exclusion of other believers who may differ with them on points of church structure, doctrine, or standards of behavior. They expect victory over their rivals and write them off as bound for hell.

The desire for disproportionate punishment is fed by widespread traditional teachings about hell. It leads to a view of a God who is ultimately unfair and unjust—a made-up God designed for a culture of vengeance.

The King James Bible (KJV)

For some Christians the KJV is still the default choice among English-language Bibles. And for many who favor the modern translations the KJV is deeply embedded in their memories. Bible verses memorized in childhood still echo the seventeenth-century poetry and prose of the old standard. For many conservative Christians the KJV still rules.

The KJV poses a challenge to a correct understanding of concepts vital to a conditionalist outlook. This is because of the archaic use of important key words. One representative example is "soul." For many people this word is identified with dualistic notions of man's nature.

By modern standards, "soul(s)" is overused in the KJV. As the English translation of the Hebrew *nephesh* and the Greek *psuché*, it occurs 626 times. The translators of *The New International Version* (NIV) have a much more scientific, sophisticated, and nuanced understanding of the original. They use "soul(s)" only ninety-seven times. For example, the KJV translates Genesis 2:7 as "man became a living soul," whereas the NIV renders it "man became a living being." Likewise, while in the KJV Genesis 35:18 reads, "her soul was in departing," in the NIV it reads, "she breathed her last."

The Popularity of Universalism

Traditionalism drives people to universalism. Compared with a picture of an angry and vengeful God and the prospect of eternal conscious torment, the prospect of universal salvation is very appealing. This alternative understanding of how God will ultimately deal with the lost dates back at least to

Origen (c.185–c.254). While there are several versions of universalism, in its best-known forms it allows for judgment and a finite period of punishment. The punishment may be purgative, or it may be a type of moral restitution, but when it's over, it's over. There's a happy ending for everybody—even the evil angels.

Universalism distorts one's view of the nature of sin, the plan of salvation, the character of God, and the principle of free will. It spiritualizes or otherwise reinterprets key Bible passages. But on the surface, at least, it's an attractive option to traditionalism—especially to people who know nothing about conditionalism.

Unfamiliarity with Conditionalism

Although conditionalism's roots go back to the first Christian centuries, it has not been the dominant view since at least the time of Augustine. Its holistic view of man, its denial of natural immortality, and its rejection of the doctrine of eternal torment make it inimical to what the Roman Catholic Church has traditionally taught. And, despite some conditionalist rumblings, the Protestant churches born in the Reformation have retained a modified, but easily recognizable form of the traditional doctrine.

Beginning in the mid-nineteenth century the Seventh-day Adventists and a handful of other groups (notably the Advent Christians) have taught the conditionalist view. But Clark Pinnock has suggested that conditionalism's identification with Adventists may be a black mark against it. "It seems that a new criterion of truth has been discovered which says that if Adventists . . . hold any view, that view must be wrong."[8]

Traditionalist scholars are aware that conditionalism exists and are sure that they disagree with it—but they seem not to understand it well. J. I. Packer observed that for conditionalists "the question of salvation is less agonizing than we thought because after judgment day the unsaved will not exist."[9] What's more, opponents of conditionalism misrepresent its tenets because, supposedly, "the great majority of those who hold to conditional immortality of the wicked do not subscribe to the doctrine of biblical inerrancy."[10]

In spite of misunderstanding and misrepresentation, recent decades have seen a burgeoning interest in conditionalism. But that seems to have

---

8. Pinnock, "The Conditional View," 161.
9. Packer, "Evangelicals and the Way of Salvation," 123–24.
10. Walvoord, "Response to Clark H. Pinnock," 167–68.

been most apparent among theologians; within the general population conditionalism is still largely unknown.

Biblical Illiteracy

In the Spring 2014 issue of *Biola Magazine* author Kenneth Berding elaborates on what he calls "a famine of Bible knowledge."[11] His article stands with several others in decrying the decline of biblical literacy.[12] The American Bible Society's *State of the Bible: 2014* poll, conducted by the Barna Group, documents the negative trends not just in Bible reading but in attitudes toward—and belief in—the Bible.[13]

Given the direction of current literature and data, it may seem counterintuitive to suggest that the Bible is widely perceived as the source of traditional doctrines like hell and eternal torment. Nevertheless, this seems to be the case. People assume that the Bible teaches these doctrines—an assumption that may find its roots in nothing more than a passing comment by a friend, a line in a movie, or a common expletive like "go to hell." Without the corrective effects of careful study of God's Word, the assumptions about what the Bible teaches are perpetuated from generation to generation.

METHODS

Communicating the conditionalist message in the face of these challenges is an uphill battle. While there are a few signs of progress here and there, there have been no breakthroughs big enough to capture the attention of the masses. So far no individual, group, or alliance of groups has put together a well-coordinated, multi-pronged effort. What would such an effort look like? Perhaps something like this:

The Press

The issues that fire the enthusiasm of conditionalist apologists have yet to become front-page news in the secular press. But there are opportunities to get conditionalist principles into print. Thought-leaders out there in the

---

11. Berding, "The Crisis of Biblical Literacy," 18.
12. See, for example, Watson, "High Rate of Biblical Illiteracy 'No Surprise'"; Mohler, "The Scandal of Biblical Illiteracy."
13. Barna Group, "The State of the Bible: 2014."

real world read beyond the front-page headlines of newspapers and the lead articles in news magazines.

Local newspapers exist in cities large and small, and they are often published in print and online editions. These all have readers—and content is still king. Editors still look for quality material.

The content of opinion pages and guest columns runs the gamut from silly to serious, from cosmic to microcosmic, from practical to whimsical. Thoughtful essays and letters to the editor touching on ultimate issues can find an audience of sober-minded readers. But communicating through the secular press should not stop with articles and essays.

Edward Fudge's *The Fire That Consumes* has become the standard apologetic work on conditionalism. He wrote his recent *Hell: A Final Word* for a general audience. Fudge has led the way, setting standards for reaching both academic and popular audiences. Has the last book on conditionalism now been written—for either scholars or laymen?

Public Events

Seminars and debates in public venues can reach a niche audience—attracting the people who are most interested in the very issues that lie at the heart of conditionalism. Streaming over the Internet—either live or on demand—can extend the reach of these events.

Broadcast

Radio and television spots, while expensive, are where big-time advertisers commit the lion's share of their budgets. They learn where their target audience is, and they go there. Which stations or channels. Which time slots. Which locations. A serious strategy for sharing the conditionalist message will take all this into account.

There are other opportunities in broadcast media, including talk shows and news features. Effective publicity strategies will include specific efforts to book interviews for conditionalist authors and other spokespersons.

The Internet

Online potential for conditionalists ranges from full-blown websites to personal blogs; content-specific forums; social media and video-sharing sites.

The web is hungry for rich content, and offers great opportunities for repurposing content originally prepared for other forms and formats.

Theatrical

Hell and Mr. Fudge (LLT Productions) is a dramatic film based on the life of Edward Fudge and has a clear conditionalist message. A platinum award-winner at the Houston International Film Festival in 2012, the film played theaters and other public venues during 2013. The DVD is widely available in Christian bookstores as well as in department store chains and online outlets.

Hellbound? from director Kevin Miller is a documentary approach to the eternal fate of the lost. Although Edward Fudge was interviewed during production, he and his conditionalist viewpoint did not make it through to the final cut. *Hellbound?* turned out to be an unabashed promotion of universalism. Like *Hell and Mr. Fudge*, it enjoyed a limited public release before going to DVD distribution.

These are diverse examples of theatrical productions dealing with hell and the hereafter. Films like these can reach an audience that may never be reached through more conventional methods.

Integrated Publicity

Promoting a single, memorable message via multiple channels is standard practice for both aspiring and incumbent politicians. Campaigners pump out their slogans from the street level to the national level. From bumper stickers to billboards, from print ads to radio and television spots, from "snail mail" to email and internet ads—they try to saturate their target audience with their message. Does it work? Sure. "I like Ike" still echoes in the memories of 1950s-era voters.

Well-planned and well-executed advertising campaigns may have some benefit as stand-alone efforts. But the real potential can be achieved when multiple promotional channels are coordinated with other methods of communication.

MESSAGE

Stake Out a Clear Biblical Position

In order for conditionalism to be understood and appreciated, we must present it as distinct from the alternative views. With the vengeance of a sovereign God at one extreme, and the divine love that overpowers both justice and human free will at the other, there is plenty of territory in the center.

No one has done more to stake out that territory for conditionalists than Edward Fudge. There he has set the standard of truth, insisting that our understanding of eternal realities be based on the Bible. This is fundamental. The single most distinguishing characteristic of conditionalism must not be the qualifications or abilities of its apologists but its firm foundation on the words of sacred Scripture.

Common Ground

While emphasizing the uniqueness of conditionalism we must not fail to adequately represent the things we have in common with those who hold other views of the eternal future. The radical, counter-intuitive demands of the gospel are central in the thinking of most serious Christians. The Bible's revelation of God's love and mercy unite us with all believers.

We need to keep things in perspective. What we believe and teach is important, but there is no salvation in "isms." A system of doctrines—such as conditionalism—can bring us an appreciation of God's character, assurance of His perfect justice, and confidence in His plan of salvation. But belief in this doctrinal system cannot save us or anyone else. It cannot take the place of our personal, voluntary acceptance of Jesus Christ as our only hope, our only Savior.

History of Conditionalism

We cannot appeal to church tradition in support of conditionalism, but we can show that conditionalism is not a newcomer to the theological stage. Talking about its rich history from the time of the church fathers onward will help to validate conditionalism in the minds of people for whom it is a completely new set of ideas about God, judgment, and eternity.

Intersecting Issues

A key element in defending and promoting conditionalism is to show how well it fits into the big picture. This is a great advantage. Consider the logical tension created by traditionalist teachings that have the souls of the dead in heaven or hell prior to the judgment. Catholicism solves this problem with the particular judgment and purgatory. Conditionalism avoids the problem by leaving death, judgment, and reward/punishment in logical sequence, merging them perfectly into the larger eschatological scenario of the parousia, the resurrection, etc.

Traditionalism, with its disembodied souls surviving the death of the body, leaves the door wide open for spiritualism. The possibility of communication with the dead is appealing to those who mourn the loss of loved one, and it suggests to inquiring minds that spirits from "the other side" can offer authoritative revelations. We should teach conditionalism's holistic view of the nature of man as a protective against spiritualism.

It's also valuable to point out how conditionalism moderates one's understanding of the Atonement, the sovereignty of God, and man's free will.

The Fate of the Lost

We need to picture, in achingly vivid terms, the terrible cost of being lost. We don't need lurid images of sinners in flames, writhing in agony. We need visions of the redeemed reveling for all eternity in the presence of the triune God and the angels, united forever with loved ones and the saints of all ages. We don't need an endless cacophony of screams from lost souls in torment. We need to help sinners imagine the bitter, unassuageable loss that will be experienced by all who reject their only hope for eternal life.

And we need to crown our efforts to portray the fate of the lost by describing, as well as humanly possible, the immeasurable eternal loss to the Creator, Father, and Redeemer—whose limitless power, boundless love, and infinite sacrifice were not enough to win the hearts of those He ultimately had to let go into oblivion.

22

Articulating and Promoting Conditionalism in the Twenty-First Century

— Christopher M. Date —

Christopher M. Date lives in the Pacific Northwest with his wife, Starr, and their four sons. Although a software engineer by trade, he is a passionate student of Scripture and theology, and hopes one day to teach as part of Christian academia. To that end he is presently pursuing a BS in Religion from Liberty University, after which he intends to move on to graduate and postgraduate studies. He is the co-editor of Rethinking Hell: Readings in Evangelical Conditionalism *and is the principal blogger and podcaster of the Rethinking Hell project. Having MC'd the inaugural Rethinking Hell conference celebrating the life and work of Edward Fudge, he delivered the opening plenary speech at the second Rethinking Hell conference in June of 2015.*

INTRODUCTION

In November of 2013, I was asked to speak to a small group of a dozen or so friends and fellow conditionalists who gathered at a Baptist church in southern California for what we were calling the first-ever Rethinking Hell symposium. We were acutely aware of the state of affairs described by Jim Wood in his contribution to this volume: Lay evangelicals are largely unaware of conditionalism, and of the vigorous debate between its scholarly Christian advocates and those of a more traditional understanding of hell. Meanwhile—and largely to blame—influential traditionalist pastors, evangelists, and academics serve as gatekeepers treating conditionalists like liberals at best, and as heretics at worst, limiting their participation in the marketplace of ideas and not permitting them to teach at—and at times even attend—conservative churches and seminaries.

So we met that fateful November weekend to discuss strategies for how to overcome the various obstacles preventing conditionalism from being taken seriously by the evangelical community at large. We authored a "Statement on Evangelical Conditionalism" to clarify what it is we as the conditionalist community actually believe, in contrast to what it is we're often mistakenly thought to believe, "in order to foster greater clarity as we engage in dialogue with fellow evangelicals."[1] We began earnestly planning our inaugural conference at which, the following year in Houston, we would go on to engage in that dialog while celebrating the life and ministry of Edward Fudge, to whom we are all so indebted. We discussed our publication and media plans which included what would become our first book, *Rethinking Hell: Readings in Evangelical Conditionalism*, as well as this, our second book, and additional books, videos, and more.

In my presentation I did not focus on what we as Rethinking Hell can do, nor necessarily what we as the larger conditionalist community can do. Instead, I aimed to equip my fellow conditionalists *as individuals*, as members of their own, more closely-knit faith communities, with what I hope will feature as elements of their own personal strategies for advocating and promoting our shared belief that eternal life is found only in Christ. My firm conviction was that if one embraces and applies these principles, one will be a more winsome and persuasive agent of change—and a healthier follower of Christ overall. With that conviction as strong now as it was then, I commend these principles to you, the reader.

THE REAL CHALLENGE

It's important that conditionalists first understand the challenge that truly lies before us. Until shortly before that 2013 symposium, I had been thinking primarily in terms of how we can change evangelical minds in the present, but a friend and fellow contributor to this volume, Ronnie Demler, awoke me to the reality that that's not really the challenge before us. He said, "As far as I can tell, conditionalism was even more popular and just as well defended in the mid-nineteenth century. It's worth asking why the movement dwindled in influence and what (if anything) can be done to prevent

---

1. Rethinking Hell, "Statement on Evangelical Conditionalism," 1.

it from happening again." I realized immediately that Ronnie was right. The challenge before us is not changing evangelical minds today; rather, the challenge before us is securing a significant place for conditionalism within the evangelical world of tomorrow.

Consider the words of Jacob Blain, a Baptist minister in Buffalo, New York, who published a book promoting conditionalism as early as 1853 entitled, *Death not Life: or the Destruction of the Wicked*. In his introduction he writes at length about several mainstream, conditionalist leaders in America and England, their published works, and the many who followed them and embraced our view. Then he says this:

> In brief, the number who now hold the view is so large, and so decided in spreading light, that all efforts to stop its progress must be vain, and a general investigation must soon take place: at least in the United States and Canada. When that comes, the doctrine of endless woe must soon fall, for it can no more stand before the light of God's word, than Dagon before the ark of God. It shows great weakness or ignorance of the theological book-world, to say this doctrine has been investigated. Had it been in the field of controversy as Universalism has, it would have triumphed long since.[2]

One can easily picture a conditionalist in our day saying the very same kinds of things; many evangelicals as of late have argued cogently for conditionalism. I have often felt the same way Blain did, as if we were witnessing an irreversible change of tide. The words of fellow contributor Glenn Peoples, in his open letter to traditionalists, ring true: "if this theological disagreement were a war, you [traditionalists] would be losing. Christians are turning away from your point of view. . . . In particular, the doctrine of annihilationism now has more evangelical adherents than it has, I believe, ever had before."[3] I think Glenn's probably right.

However, Blain probably thought *he* was right, and yet, alas, efforts to stop the progress of conditionalism were *not* in vain, and the movement *did* dwindle. As Max Sotak noted in his 2013 book, more than a century and a half after Blain,

> Most traditionalists have never read or heard a serious biblical defense of conditional immortality by an evangelical who believes it. Instead, the arguments of conditionalists are presented by traditionalists in a popular and abbreviated form so they can be disposed of without much difficulty. Most evangelicals are

2. Blain, *Death not Life*, vi.
3. Peoples, "An Open Letter to My Traditionalist Friends."

exposed to conditional immortality by reading books about cults.[4]

The great evangelical investigation Blain expected to soon take place in the U.S. and Canada hasn't happened; the doctrine of endless woe hasn't fallen; conditionalism has not triumphed.

So, although I feel much like Blain did, and although I suspect what Peoples said in his open letter is correct, nevertheless the past century and a half of conditionalist history gives me pause. Demler is right: we must ask ourselves why conditionalism dwindled and fell again into disrepute. We must then try to figure out what, if anything, we can do to ensure that it doesn't happen again, how it is that we can help make Blain's eager expectation a reality in the decades to come.

CONDITIONALISM IN NINETEENTH-CENTURY AMERICA

In early nineteenth-century America, the Second Great Awakening was in full swing and many Christians had a renewed passion for reexamining traditional beliefs as had been done three centuries earlier during the Protestant Reformation. Perhaps the earliest noteworthy American conditionalist from this century was Henry Grew. He pastored a Baptist church for four years until 1811 when he resigned or was fired because he insisted that only faithful members of the congregation should be allowed to lead it in praise and worship.[5]

A quarter of a century later in 1837, Methodist George Storrs—the first man mentioned by Jacob Blain leading up to the excerpt above—happened upon a pamphlet advocating conditionalism which, he discovered later, was written by Grew.[6] For the next three years Storrs continued in the Methodist Church, but by 1840 he had become convinced of conditionalism and so resigned.[7] Not long thereafter, Storrs published the first edition of his *Six Sermons* advocating conditionalism, which was popular and prolific.[8]

---

4. Sotak, *Damning Assumptions*, 7.
5. Grew was fired according to Watchtower, "Working in the 'Field'—Before the Harvest"; he resigned according to the editor of *The Telescope* 2:41 (March 11, 1826), and Benedict, *A General History of the Baptist Denomination in America, and Other Parts of the World*, 530.
6. Watchtower, "Working in the 'Field'—Before the Harvest."
7. Zackrison, *In the Loins of Adam*, 132–33.
8. Penton, *Apocalypse Delayed*, 16.

The Millerite movement was at this time becoming a national phenomenon, coming to be known as Adventism in 1845. Grew and Storrs became major players, which at least in part explains why Adventists embrace conditionalism today.[9] Adventist George Stetson was associated with Storrs early in his ministry, and later with Adventist Jonas Wendell, one of whose presentations in 1869 was attended by none other than the infamous Charles Taze Russell, who credited Wendell's presentation as having restored his faith in the Bible.[10]

It was Russell who would go on to start the Bible Student movement, which later came to be known as Jehovah's Witnesses, and whose formative influences included Grew, Storrs, Stetson, and Wendell.[11] Since then, conditionalism has often been associated with the Jehovah's Witnesses who reject the doctrine of the Trinity as Grew did, and with the Seventh-day Adventists who have doctrines that tend to encourage isolation from evangelicals in general. Both groups are branches of this nineteenth-century Millerite movement, which garners criticism for additional reasons beyond conditionalism and the peculiarities of these two of its branches.

Conditionalism's association with the Jehovah's Witnesses, the Adventists, and the Millerite movement more broadly probably contributed to its decline in America. It couldn't have helped that in the sixteenth century John Calvin had swayed public opinion against mortalism by associating it with the Anabaptists.[12] It couldn't have helped that in the seventeenth century conditionalism became associated with the Socinians.[13] It couldn't have helped that, as Edward Fudge notes, in the eighteenth century "popular attacks on the traditional doctrine of hell sprang from its seeming incompatibility with human hope rather than from concern for actual Bible teaching," and it couldn't have helped that it came to be associated with Arianism, liberalism and modernism.[14]

So although—and thankfully—the traditional hell was being questioned in the nineteenth and twentieth centuries in England where these associations were not as damning to the conditionalist cause, conditionalism was increasingly dismissed in America. Edward Fudge explains,

> for most of the twentieth century, American evangelicals in general avoided questions regarding final punishment, neither

---

9. Zackrison, *In the Loins of Adam*, 132; Penton, *Apocalypse Delayed*, 16–17.
10. Penton, *Apocalypse Delayed*, 15–16.
11. Ibid., 5–6.
12. Fudge, *The Fire That Consumes* (2011), 312.
13. Ibid., 332.
14. Ibid., 333, 337, 340–41.

entering the study themselves nor allowing others to enter.... British evangelicals in general experienced neither the American fear of the modernist disease that threatened orthodox belief, nor the reactionary fundamentalism that many Americans considered its only cure. As a result, British evangelicals both within and without the state church have been more willing to consider the biblical evidence for the final extinction of the wicked.[15]

One additional conditionalist from nineteenth-century America deserves attention. In 1879, the fifth volume of *Dickinson's Theological Quarterly* contained an article addressing the doctrine of conditional immortality. It began by implicitly criticizing conditionalists for preferring alternatives to the label "annihilationism," and for saying the traditional view of hell violates principles of God's justice and mercy. But the author goes on to speak fairly highly of a conditionalist named William Huntington. The author writes,

> The Rev. William R. Huntington, D.D., whose book we have chosen for notice, is in good standing doubtless, as a presbyter of the Protestant Episcopal Church ... thought not possessing great force, [he] is clear as crystal, a remark that applies both to the statement of his propositions and to his reasonings.... The marvellous thing about this book is the *spirit of candour* that prevails in it. His bearing is, for the most part, that of a Christian gentleman. He makes but few flings, and seldom applies opprobrious epithets to those whose views he opposes, and is ready to give them the credit of an honest love of the truth. Persons who are at all familiar with the literature upon this subject will understand us when we draw the contrast between the spirit of this book and the vituperative bitterness and unfairness manifested by very many of those who have undertaken the work of writing down the commonly accepted views of future retribution. This characteristic makes it exceedingly difficult for anyone who is not a sympathising partisan to read their productions. A person who is listening to the argument of another finds it hard to possess himself in perfect patience, if his opponent every now and then shakes his fist in his face, or flings at him some reproachful charge or insinuation.[16]

On the other hand, the author criticizes Huntington for not speaking firmly of his convictions:

15. Ibid., 342–43.
16. Paterson, *Dickinson's Theological Quarterly*, 347; emphasis in original.

> The force of Dr. Huntington's reasoning, as it strikes us, is very greatly weakened by the *air of uncertainty* which he throws over his conclusions . . . a mind disquieted with doubts on the subject discussed can hardly draw comfort from his hesitating words. All he proposes to do, and all he professes to have done is to weigh "*the comparative probability*" of the truth of the three doctrines of endless punishment, of restoration, and of extinction. And the result reached is, that the first is pronounced to be "the least likely," the second "the less likely," and the last, "the likeliest" of the three.[17]

The article goes on to offer a number of responses to Huntington's arguments for conditionalism, but it is the above statements about him personally to which I want to call our attention. They, as well as the legacy of Grew, Storrs, Stetson, and Wendell, can teach us something as conditionalists in the twenty-first century who wish to avoid whatever mistakes may have been made by conditionalists in the nineteenth. It's important that we take to heart the words George Santayana penned in 1905, and which have become so famous (if misquoted) since: "Those who cannot remember the past are condemned to repeat it."[18] So I will return to these historical details shortly, and explain the lessons we have to learn as I see them, as I now move on to share with you some of the principles I think we need to embrace in articulating and promoting conditionalism today.

PART OF THE EVANGELICAL FAMILY

First we must be—and behave like—part of the evangelical family. It may seem as though we have already been doing this as a movement. After all, most of us would self-identify as evangelicals, and would heartily affirm the earliest Christian creeds and those doctrines recognized by most as being essential to evangelical Christianity. This is certainly important; our critics need to see that we are not Arians or Socinians, or Jehovah's Witnesses like Charles Taze Russell and his successors. They need to see that we are not a liberal or emergent movement, questioning the authority of Scripture or trying to change its message to suit our surrounding culture. They need to see that while some of us are Adventists or members of other communities whose history can be traced back to the nineteenth-century Millerites, we come from many other denominations and faith communities whose status as evangelical can hardly be questioned. We are Presbyterians, Baptists,

---

17. Ibid., 348; emphasis in original.
18. Santayana, *The Life of Reason*, 284.

Pentecostals, Anglicans, Episcopalians, non-denominational, members of the Churches of Christ, and everything else in between.

"In Non-Essentials, Liberty"

There is more, however, to being part of the evangelical family than simply believing and affirming the essentials of evangelical Christianity. For one thing, we need to treat the topic of hell as a secondary issue, one which ought not to be cause for division or for otherwise leaving our churches and denominations for others in which conditionalism is more readily embraced. I know this may be a tough pill to swallow; for some of you, the traditional doctrine of hell is an offense to the character of a just and loving God, a blight on the church that prompts revulsion and ridicule as often as it does repentance. For in it, God renders the risen lost immortal for apparently no other purpose than to undergo everlasting physical, emotional, and spiritual torment the likes of which, we're told, is worse than we can possibly imagine. I understand why it might be difficult to remain in churches and denominations in which this is the official teaching, or at least the dominant one.

What would happen, however, were we to abandon our faith communities in favor of those who already think like us? The history of conditionalism in the nineteenth century furnishes us with a partial answer to that question. Had Henry Grew not left his Baptist church, perhaps his peers would have brought him back into Trinitarian orthodoxy, and perhaps he would have eventually gotten them to rethink hell. Had George Storrs not left his Methodist church and joined the Millerite movement which later spawned the Jehovah's Witnesses, perhaps he would have been an agent for change within the more mainstream church. Instead, these and other conditionalists left their churches, and conditionalism went on to become associated with Adventism and the Jehovah's Witnesses in the minds of twentieth- and twenty-first-century evangelicals.[19]

History aside, if we don't remain in our present communities insofar as we're permitted to, who will change their minds? I am aware of only one other convinced conditionalist in my church and I've never heard him speak out about it. If I were to leave for some other church in which conditionalism is more commonly embraced, who would remain to change the minds of those I'd be leaving behind? And what if there were others who shared my

---

19. Of course, it is conceivable that Grew and Storrs may not have been allowed to remain in good standing with their former churches, so I'm admittedly speculating.

view and who left with me? What if all of us left our churches to congregate with one another? What would that communicate?

My passion in speaking and writing about this topic, the thing that drives me to spend a seemingly inordinate amount of time articulating, promoting, and defending conditionalism, is unity in the body of Christ. Leaving our faith communities and joining others in which our view is more widely accepted will have the opposite effect. If we want to be seen as the faithful members of our evangelical family that we truly are, we should not abandon our various communities to fellowship exclusively or primarily with likeminded conditionalists. If we do, we'll be seen as divisive and as fostering disunity.

"In Essentials, Unity"

Embracing this principle of behaving like part of the evangelical family demands additionally that, in treating this issue as secondary, we speak and write on the essentials and not only on the topic of hell. This is something Glenn Peoples pointed out in the first anniversary episode of the Rethinking Hell podcast—and it is something which, I must confess, I need to more fully embrace.[20] It will matter little if we refuse to divide over hell if that's all we ever talk about. What's more, we must visibly stand side-by-side with our fellow evangelicals in defense of the essentials, showing ourselves to be every bit as much the stalwart defenders of evangelical Christianity as our traditionalist peers. I suspect that this is a major reason why John Stott, John Wenham, and other noteworthy conditionalists including Edward Fudge have been so successful in persuading their audiences to start rethinking hell.

While we are calling for the widening of the evangelical tent to include conditionalism, we're not asking that it be widened to include a liberal doctrine of Scripture, or Unitarianism, or denials of other essentials of the faith. Nor as a movement are we calling evangelicals to distort the teaching of Scripture into something more readily embraced in our postmodern culture. It needs to be clear, both from our words and from our deeds, that in the war of worldviews we are fellow soldiers fighting shoulder to shoulder with traditionalists for the Christian faith once and for all delivered to the saints. If that isn't apparent, it will fuel the fear and the circle-the-wagons mentality of traditionalists who are understandably wearied by the constant attacks on the faith and authority of Scripture.

---

20. Date, "Episode 32."

"In All Things, Charity"

Finally, we need to be charitable and respectful in how we articulate our view. This isn't always easy. Again, some of you have understandably very strong feelings about the traditional view of hell, the picture you think it paints of God, and what you think is its destructive impact on both our efforts to evangelize the lost as well as on the faith of many who are troubled by it. As a result, many of us will describe the traditional view using language that may accurately capture it, language which even traditionalists themselves have historically used, such as that God will torture the lost for eternity. And our emotional reactions to those who advocate such a view, and to their attacks upon our character and exegesis, sometimes drive us to speak uncharitably to and about those who promote and defend it.

Recall, however, that 1879 article and its author's warm opinion of the conditionalist he was critiquing. "The marvellous thing about [Dr. Huntington's] book," the author writes, "is the spirit of candour that prevails in it. His bearing is, for the most part, that of a Christian gentleman. He . . . is ready to give them the credit of an honest love of the truth." Dr. Huntington may not have changed the mind of the article's author, but consider how much more unlikely we are to change minds if we aren't equally charitable and irenic. As the author astutely observes, "A person who is listening to the argument of another finds it hard to possess himself in perfect patience, if his opponent every now and then shakes his fist in his face, or flings at him some reproachful charge or insinuation."

It won't matter how accurate we are in articulating our view and that of our critics, nor will it matter how justified is our emotional response to the traditional hell, if people can't hear what we're saying because their emotions are clouded by their reaction to our behavior. One may never change a traditionalist's mind no matter how respectful one is, but one can be sure to change fewer minds than otherwise possible if one comes across as rude, obnoxious, and uncharitable.

If we want to change minds of today and of tomorrow, then we may need to strategically avoid referring to and describing their view using terminology to which they object, such as the word "torture." We may need to avoid saying their view makes God out to be "monstrous" or "vindictive." You may feel that those characterizations are accurate, but so what? Isn't it more important that we have a positive, lasting impact? Besides, if we're truly part of the evangelical family, we ought to treat traditionalists *as* family, and not as opponents.

So let us not merely affirm the essentials of the Christian faith, and merely claim that hell is a secondary, non-essential issue unworthy of division. Let us demonstrate that we are genuine members of the evangelical family by remaining in our existing faith communities as much as possible, and by lovingly, charitably, and patiently articulating and promoting conditionalism when possible, while remaining united with our traditionalist brothers and sisters in fellowship, and in defense of the faith.

A BIBLICAL CONVICTION

After first embracing the principle of behaving like part of the evangelical family to which we belong, we must secondly articulate conditionalism on biblical grounds, using biblical precision, leaving no room for misunderstanding or mischaracterization. Putting the first principle into practice will put us in a much better position to have fruitful opportunities to articulate and promote conditionalism. Such opportunities, however, will be less fruitful, and may even backfire, if it isn't readily apparent that Scripture authoritatively dictates our convictions, if we don't articulate them with biblical precision, and if we give our critics the opportunity to misunderstand or mischaracterize our position.

The Primacy of Scripture

The traditional view of hell may produce legitimate concerns about justice and the character of God, and those concerns may have been what first spurred many conditionalists to wonder if the understanding of hell we received from tradition might not be found in the pages of the Bible.[21] Our commitment to the authority of Scripture, however, and its witness to the final destruction of the lost, is what forced us to reject the traditional contention that they will instead live forever in hell. Our words must demonstrate that reality.

Arguments from justice and God's character can be legitimate ones, and I don't think we should feel pressured to exclude them altogether from the reasons we offer in commending our view. However, they ought to be treated as secondary to the explicit biblical testimony concerning man's mortality and the nature of final punishment. Just think of how many times conditionalists have been accused of sentimentality and emotionalism. Traditionalists will, consciously or not, latch on to any reason to reject our view,

---

21. This was not the case with me. I did not question the justice of the traditional view when I began seriously considering conditionalism, nor did I see it as inconsistent with the character of God. Indeed, to this day I remain convinced that at least certain formulations of the traditional view would be just. I just don't see it in Scripture.

no matter how cogent our thinking, no matter how solid our exegesis. It's human nature. No doubt we're guilty of it at times, too, when it comes to other issues. We must avoid this pitfall; we must not repeat what I think has been this mistake made by some conditionalists in the past.

Now, what I'm about to say may be a bit controversial, and not every reader will agree, but I remain convinced of its wisdom: If a conditionalist is asked what she believes about hell and why, and if she can't explain it and appeal first to biblical texts concerning the destiny of the lost before appealing to justice, the character of God, and other related reasons, then I would prefer that she simply explain what she believes the Bible teaches without offering a defense at all, other than to say that she's convinced that it's the consistent testimony of Scripture. Perhaps she can ask for a rain check and a future opportunity to provide the biblical basis for conditionalism; or perhaps she could recommend some good books and resources that promote and defend our view. Articulating a concise and compelling biblical case for the final destruction of the unsaved, however, isn't all that hard to do, and every conditionalist should endeavor to learn how to do it, and to present that case first before appealing to any other reasons for rethinking hell.

The Importance of Biblical Language

Next, we ought to articulate what we believe clearly and with biblical precision. This may be challenging for us because we aren't monolithic in the way we interpret certain texts or envision the punishment of hell. Nevertheless, I think there are some mistakes that have been made in the past, and from which we need to learn.

First, I think we ought to refer to the punishment awaiting the lost as death, rather than as cessation of existence. This is important for a few reasons, not the least of which is that the Bible speaks primarily in terms of death, rather than cessation of being. Beyond that, critics often object to our view on the grounds that Jesus Christ didn't cease to exist when he died, and since he suffered what we deserve in our place, the punishment of hell cannot be "cessation of being." Additionally, I think it's difficult to make a case that words like "death" and "destruction" in Scripture necessarily carry the meaning of ceasing to be, but it's very easy to demonstrate that they carry the meaning of ceasing to live.

Second, while the merciful nature of God may furnish one with a reason for questioning the traditional view, we need to emphasize that the second death will not be inflicted by God primarily as an expression of his mercy. Whether God will actively execute the lost, or whether he will allow them to die by unplugging them from the source of life, or however else one views this fate, the final destruction of the impenitent is not an act of mercy or a form of "divine euthanasia" that rescues the lost from ongoing torment. Rather, the terrible "cosmic death penalty" of the unsaved in hell is an expression of God's holy wrath, like the destruction of Sodom and Gomorrah.[22]

Third—and here I might ruffle some feathers—I think we need to emphasize that our view is not that the risen lost will be punished *and then die*, but rather that their death *will be* their ultimate punishment. I understand the feeling many of us have that at least some unsaved people (Adolf Hitler, for example) ought to suffer in hell. I understand the desire to make room for the belief that some will suffer more than others in order to account for so-called "degrees of punishment." The solution, however, is to see pain as being part of the process by which the lost will be punished with death, rather than as the punishment itself which will then be followed by death. Just as a death row criminal will suffer psychological torment while being strapped into the electric chair, and unimaginable physical pain when the switch is flipped, so, too, might the risen lost suffer emotional, spiritual, and physiological agony in hell as part of their execution. In either case the punishment is ultimately death.

If we do not carefully formulate what we believe about this issue and carefully articulate it, we will create two or three weaknesses in our position, opportunities which have been and will continue to be seized by our critics. If some duration of pain will exhaust the penalty due sinners in hell, then after suffering for their sins, why will they go on to die? If pain is what will primarily constitute final punishment, why does Scripture so consistently and repeatedly emphasize death? And if the punishment for sin will be torment, and not the death in which it will terminate, how can "eternal punishment" consist in anything other than an eternity of torment? On the other hand, if we speak biblically about final punishment, articulating our view as one in which the unsaved will suffer as part of the process by which they are punished by being deprived of life forever, then we can answer each of those questions easily.

Our challenge is to secure a lasting place for conditionalism in the evangelical community. Therefore, having established ourselves as genuine members of the evangelical family by our words and deeds, let us build our case on a clear and precise exposition of the central biblical texts, while

---

22. Rethinking Hell, "Statement on Evangelical Conditionalism."

avoiding the mistakes that have given our critics an opening to misrepresent our viewpoint.

PERSUASIVE CONVICTION

Having embraced the first and second principles of being active members of the evangelical family and articulating conditionalism on biblical grounds and with precision, we thirdly need to promote and defend conditionalism persuasively, and with conviction. This principle entails that we present the most persuasive arguments possible for our position, and that we present our position, not merely as one legitimate interpretation of the biblical data, not even as the likeliest, but as the clearly intended meaning of its authors.

Remember what the author of that 1879 *Dickinson's* article said about Huntington's presentation: "The force of Dr. Huntington's reasoning, as it strikes us, is very greatly weakened by the air of uncertainty which he throws over his conclusions . . . a mind disquieted with doubts on the subject discussed can hardly draw comfort from his hesitating words." I understand that there may be some who sincerely are not completely convinced, but many of them seem content to remain unconvinced instead of going on to study the issue further, and there are many others who simply feign uncertainty. Perhaps this is in order to avoid losing one's job or causing division. Whatever the reason for one's uncertainty, and however genuine it is, if one thinks conditionalism is a plausible or likely interpretation of the biblical data, one should endeavor to seriously study the issue until one can confidently land on a position, and then argue for it with conviction. Otherwise one's audience is likely to fall back on tradition as a reason for accepting what they're told is merely a less likely interpretation of the biblical material.

One's Own Petard

Once able to articulate conditionalism with conviction, we can do several things to make our case more persuasive. First, we can hoist our traditionalist critics by their own petards, incorporating their own proof-texts and objections into the case we present for our position. Conditionalists often present a case such as that offered by Glenn Peoples in *Rethinking Hell: Readings in Evangelical Conditionalism*: the Bible teaches that immortality is a gift God will give only to the saved, that eternity will be free of sin and of sinners, that Christ died as a substitute in the place of sinners, and that those who reject him will be destroyed.[23] Such a case is compelling, to be sure, but we must remember that traditionalists think there are texts which so clearly teach eternal torment that our case must be rejected, no matter how otherwise powerful.

Robert Peterson, for example, rejects the argument for conditionalism from the biblical teaching about immortality on the grounds that some texts appear to him to require belief in universal immortality:

> I do not accept traditionalism because I believe in the immortality of the soul. Rather, I believe in the immortality of human beings (united in body and soul after the resurrection of the dead) because the Bible teaches that there will be "eternal punishment" for the lost and "eternal life" for the saved (Mt 25:46).[24]

Similarly, Christopher Morgan admits that the biblical vision of eternity is a persuasive argument for conditionalism, but says, "a better approach is to ask: What do the Scriptures teach about the final victory of God? The Bible seems to teach that God's ultimate victory is compatible with the endless punishment of the wicked. The final chapters of Revelation contrast the final state of the redeemed with that of the wicked."[25]

Proof-texts like Matthew 25, Revelation 20, Mark 9:48, and others will linger in the minds of many traditionalists, preventing them from being moved by our case, and so I think we need to include several of these texts in that case, demonstrating conclusively that they are better support for our view. That's why in my first two debates my opening statements focused primarily on them. It was actually texts like these which, despite being so frequently cited as support for the traditional view, most contributed to my "conversion" to conditionalism, even before I came to appreciate the case typically offered for it. Too often conditionalists are put on the defensive by these texts, told our case fails because of them. We need to turn the tables on traditionalists by including these texts in *our* case. Let us put *them* on the defensive, and from the outset prevent them from rejecting our case based on these texts.

What's more, it's not only traditionalist arguments from Scripture that we can anticipate and proactively leverage as our own. How often have we been told that conditionalism doesn't allow for degrees of punishment, as readers were told in that 1879 *Dickinson's* article? Let us consider incorporating that into our positive case by pointing out how insignificant

---

23. Peoples, "Introduction to Evangelical Conditionalism," 11–23.
24. Fudge and Peterson, *Two Views of Hell*, 88–89.
25. Morgan, "Annihilationism," 217.

differences in degree of punishment become when stretched out over eternity, and how the very idea of degrees militates against the notion that every sin against an infinitely holy God deserves an infinite punishment. Or take the oft-repeated refrain that Jesus didn't cease to exist on the cross. We can turn that against our critics by pointing out that the Bible emphasizes Jesus' death, the very thing traditionalists deny awaits the risen lost.

These and other exegetical, theological, and philosophical arguments offered by traditionalists can and should be used to argue positively for our view. Our critics will be left with little justification for rejecting the rest of our persuasive case for conditionalism. Of course, they might still reject it based on the traditional view's dominance in the Christian tradition, which brings me to my next point.

Early Church Fathers

There are some areas in which I think we as a community have work to do, so that we can leverage its fruits as we articulate and promote conditionalism today and in the future. We need an up-to-date, in-depth, scholarly analysis of the early church writings on the topic of immortality and final punishment, one that doesn't seek for and produce mere sound-bite quotes from church fathers that sound like they favor conditionalism. What Edward Fudge includes in his *The Fire That Consumes* is good, as was Froom's *The Conditionalist Faith of our Fathers*. The early church was cited by nineteenth-century conditionalists as well, and yet the myth persists that the earliest Christians universally taught the eternal conscious torment of the lost in hell.

The conditionalist community today must decisively demolish this myth. We must produce the modern-day version of Froom's work, one which thoroughly examines the Fathers' writings, demonstrating how clearly they teach the final destruction of the impenitent, tackling head on those things they said which traditionalists point to as evidence that they taught otherwise. The fruit of our labor will be definitive proof that conditionalism was taught earliest and most consistently, and persisted for a while even as its alternatives—universalism and traditionalism—arose in the development of Christian thought.

Supplementary Arguments

Other work remains to be done as well. I said earlier that I think we need to demonstrate that conditionalism has as its foundation Scripture, first and foremost. Challenges to the traditional view on the basis of proportional justice and the character of God, I said, need to be presented as secondary to the biblical data concerning final punishment. However, I don't think this means that we should avoid those issues altogether. I think they can and should be used to supplement the biblical case for conditionalism, but we should carefully craft the best arguments possible as a community.

The simplistic argument that an infinite punishment is disproportionate to a finite lifetime of sinning just won't do, since annihilation is an infinite punishment insofar as the punishment of death will last forever. We need to be more careful than that, in this case perhaps distinguishing between the sense in which annihilation is infinite in seriousness and deprivation, and the sense in which it is finite in experience and therefore more just. It is no secret that I don't know what a carefully crafted, persuasive case for conditionalism from justice and the character of God looks like; I can at this point only encourage us as a community to work on one together. Once we have a good grasp of it, we can deploy it as a secondary argument buttressing the foundation of our case, which is Scripture.

We must also incorporate conditionalism into a wider, more systematic theology and philosophy, and leverage the fruit of our labor in making our case. This is important for at least two reasons. First, theologians want to see how an alternative view impacts and fits within its larger theological context. John Stackhouse makes this point in his contribution to this volume; focusing exclusively on exegesis makes for a powerful biblical case that ought to be convincing but too often fails to persuade the theologically minded.

Second, it is not only traditionalists with whom we have to contend, but universalists as well. Robin Parry's *The Evangelical Universalist* has received praise for the philosophical, theological, *and* biblical case it makes for universalism. Our position is exegetically far superior to its alternatives, and for some of us like myself that's all that's required. Unfortunately that won't be enough to persuade others. To overcome what is perceived by universalists to be the philosophical and theological superiority of their view on the one hand, and to overcome the strong pull of tradition and peer pressure toward traditionalism on the other hand, we must focus on incorporating conditionalism, with its overwhelmingly strong exegetical support, into an overarching and compelling theological and philosophical worldview.

Embracing Diversity

More precisely, what is called for is a variety of such worldviews featuring conditionalism. After all, our community is as diverse as any group of evangelicals who share a particular view. Conditionalism will feature differently in a Reformed conditionalist's systematic theology than in an Arminian's, and differently in a futurist's eschatology than in a preterist's. As we do the hard work on the one hand of demonstrating to our critics how conditionalism fits into a bigger theological picture, we must on the other hand embrace our diversity in advancing the conditionalist cause, not making our view of final punishment so dependent upon any other doctrine that those who reject it must likewise reject this one.

One author ties conditionalism so intimately to premillennialism, for example, that postmillennialist and amillennialist traditionalists are likely to reject our view of final punishment simply because they are not premillennialists.[26] Not to be outdone, I probably make the mistake of giving nearly the opposite impression that only preterists and amillennialists can be conditionalists. Some argue so passionately for mortalism or "soul sleep" that dualist traditionalists often reject conditionalism thinking the two positions must necessarily go together.

I understand the passion with which we hold our various convictions. I feel very strongly that preterism and either amillennialism or postmillennialism most accurately captures the meaning of the biblical data, and I will zealously argue with futurists and premillennialists when it comes to the timing of future events. However, in articulating and promoting conditionalism, I make an effort to put those areas aside, recognizing that they aren't ultimately germane to the debate over final punishment.

The fact is that embracing conditionalism does not require changing one's understanding of the millennium, or the constitution of human nature, or of the intermediate state, or of a host of other issues. We are as theologically diverse as evangelical traditionalists, with representatives of every side of every in-house debate over the non-essentials. We are Calvinists, Arminians and other non-Calvinists, and Open Theists. We are premillennialists, postmillennialists, and amillennialists. We are futurists, preterists, and idealists. We are dispensationalists and covenantalists. We are cessationists and continuationists. We are credobaptists and paedobaptists. We are complementarians and egalitarians. We are young-earth creationists, old-earth creationists, progressive creationists, and theistic evolutionists. We are dualists and we are and physicalists. There are those among us who

---

26. Mealy, *The End of the Unrepentant*.

think the devil and his angels will be tormented forever, and those of us who think they will be destroyed with the rest of impenitent mankind.

These and other areas of intramural disagreement are worth debating, even passionately. But we need to celebrate the diversity among us, and avoid as much as possible arguing for our particular stance on any of these issues when we articulate, promote, and defend conditionalism. If we do not, we risk giving our critics the impression that one must change any number of one's views in order to embrace it, and that will make it all the more challenging for them to change their minds.

Best Foot Forward

Finally, we must avoid really bad arguments, and where there are multiple competing explanations of certain texts, we should offer first those that are least likely to be met with incredulity.

I've seen conditionalists offer a number of what I think are bad arguments for our shared view, but two in particular come to mind. Ezekiel 18:4 says "the soul who sins shall die," and some conditionalists have said, "See? The soul is mortal and can die, too." In its context, however, this text says nothing of the sort. God is instead saying that any individual Israelite would be punished with death for his own sins, and not for this sins of his father.

When challenged with Matthew 25:46, some conditionalists have said that it's the outcome or consequences of the punishment that are eternal, but traditionalists have—legitimately I think—seized the opportunity to point out that Jesus says it is the punishment itself which is eternal, not the result of the punishment. We must be more careful, and affirm that the punishment itself is, indeed, eternal, but that the noun "punishment" refers to the outcome of the verb "punish," in the way "translation" may refer to the product of the verb "translate." Remember: It is human nature to latch on to the weakest link in an argument presented to us, and we need to identify and avoid bad arguments so as to avoid giving our critics any foothold from which to reject the case for conditionalism.

As for offering first those explanations of texts least likely to be seen with incredulity where multiple competing explanations exist, I'm going to ruffle some feathers again but I think a really good example of this is Matthew 25:46 and its "eternal punishment." I know some conditionalists are convinced that the word translated "eternal" really means something like "age-lasting" or "characteristic of the age to come," and I'm not saying they shouldn't offer these as plausible interpretations of the text. However, traditionalists will find these interpretations to be unlikely and ad hoc, and it will prove far more persuasive to explain first that if the more common understanding of "eternal" is the correct one, annihilation is an eternal punishment since the punishment of death lasts forever. Only then should the other, seemingly less credible explanations be offered. Similarly, we shouldn't argue that in Revelation the phrase "forever and ever" just means a very long time, and we should instead point out that this is symbolic imagery, highlighting the OT imagery promising destruction upon which Revelation draws. As a community we should identify other such texts where competing conditionalist explanations exist, endeavoring individually to offer as first the ones least likely to be cause for scoffing on the part of our traditionalist peers.

We want to have a lasting impact by building a momentum that won't wane as it did in the late nineteenth century. So having first demonstrated that we are genuine members of the evangelical family, and having gone on to articulate our position primarily from its biblical foundation and with the precision afforded by it, let us promote and defend conditionalism persuasively, and with conviction.

CONCLUSION

Remember the very similar sentiments expressed by two conditionalists separated by a century and a half: Blain who said in 1853, "the number who now hold the view is so large, and so decided in spreading light, that all efforts to stop its progress must be vain," and Peoples who said just a few short years ago, "if this theological disagreement were a war, you [traditionalists] would be losing ... the doctrine of annihilationism now has more evangelical adherents than it has, I believe, ever had before." Then reflect upon the widespread disdain for conditionalism that characterized the intervening years.

If we hope to have a lasting impact, and not merely enjoy a brief resurgence of conditionalism only to watch it fade once again into obscurity, we may need to do some things differently. Yes, we have some things going for us that nineteenth-century conditionalists did not; the internet, blogs, and podcasts can be leveraged to ensure that Christians whose exposure to conditionalism would have been limited in the past have access today to lucid thinking and persuasive argumentation. But these and other modern innovations won't get us far if we don't take to heart the three principles I've laid out in this chapter.

We need to remain an active part of the evangelical family. We need to articulate conditionalism on biblical grounds, using biblical precision, leaving no room for misunderstanding or mischaracterization. And we need to promote and defend conditionalism persuasively, and with conviction.

Bibliography

Ackroyd, Peter R. *Exile and Restoration: A Study of Hebrew Thought of the Sixth Century B.C.* Louisville, KY: Westminster John Knox, 1968.
Alcorn, Randy. *If God Is Good: Faith in the Midst of Suffering and Evil.* Colorado Springs, CO: Multnomah, 2009.
Allen, Jimmy. *What Is Hell Like? And Other Sermons.* Dallas: Christian Publishing, 1965.
Allen, Leslie C. *Jeremiah.* The Old Testament Library. Louisville, KY: Westminster John Knox, 2008.
Ankerberg, John, with John Weldon. "Response to James I. Packer." In *Evangelical Affirmations*, edited by Kenneth S. Kantzer and Carl F. H. Henry, 137–48. Grand Rapids: Zondervan, 1990.
Anselm. "Fifth Meditation." In *Saint Anselm's Book of Meditations and Prayers*, 62–68. London: Burns and Oates, 1872.
Appelman, Hyman. "Hell—What Is It?" In *Great Preaching on Hell*, edited by Curtis Hutson, 135–50. Murfreesboro, TN: Sword of the Lord, 1989.
Aquinas, Thomas. *Summa Theologica*, vol. 27. Translated by T. C. O'Brien. Cambridge: Cambridge University Press, 2006.
Atkinson, Basil F. C. *Life and Immortality: An Examination of the Nature and Meaning of Life and Death as They Are Revealed in the Scriptures.* Taunton, UK: Phoenix, n.d.
Augustine of Hippo. "The City of God." In *A Select Library of the Nicene and Post-Nicene Fathers of the Christian Church*, edited by Philip Schaff, ix–511. Vol. 2. Buffalo, NY: The Christian Literature Company, 1887.
Bacchiocchi, Samuele. *Immortality or Resurrection? A Biblical Study on Human Nature and Destiny.* Berrien Springs, MI: Biblical Perspectives, 1997.
Baird, Joseph Arthur. *The Justice of God in the Teaching of Jesus.* New Testament Library. London: SCM, 1963.
Barker, William S. William S. Barker to Edward Fudge, August 23, 1983, Correspondence, Edward Fudge Papers. Center for Restoration Studies MS #76. Milliken Special Collections, Brown Library. Abilene Christian University, Abilene, TX.
Barna Group. "The State of the Bible: 2014." *American Bible Society.* 9 April 2014. Online: http://www.americanbible.org/uploads/content/state-of-the-bible-data-analysis-american-bible-society-2014.pdf.
Barnes, Albert. *Isaiah II.* Notes on the Old Testament. Grand Rapids: Baker, 1968.
Barrett, C. K. *Essays on John.* Louisville, KY: Westminster John Knox, 1982.

Bassler, Jouette M. *Navigating Paul: An Introduction to Key Theological Concepts.* Louisville, KY: Westminster John Knox, 2007.

Bauckham, Richard. "Early Jewish Visions of Hell." *JTS* 41.2 (1990) 355–85.

———. "Emerging Issues in Eschatology in the Twenty-First Century." In *The Oxford Handbook of Eschatology,* edited by Jerry L. Walls, 671–90. Oxford: Oxford University Press, 2008.

———. "Foreword to Third Edition." In *The Fire that Consumes: A Biblical and Historical Study of the Doctrine of Final Punishment,* by Edward Fudge. 3rd ed. Eugene, OR: Cascade, 2011.

———. *Theology of the Book of Revelation.* New Testament Theology. Cambridge: Cambridge University Press, 1993.

———. "Universalism: A Historical Survey." *Themelios* 4.2 (1978) 47–54.

Bauer, Walter. *A Greek-English Lexicon of the New Testament and Other Early Christian Literature.* Revised and edited by Frederick W. Danker. 3rd ed. Chicago: University of Chicago Press, 2000.

Bawulski, Shawn. "Annihilationism, Traditionalism, and the Problem of Hell." *Philosophia Christi* 12.1 (2010) 61–79.

———. "The Annihilationist's Theological Problem." Paper presented at the Rethinking Hell Conference, 12 July 2014, Lanier Theological Library, Houston, TX.

Baxter, Richard. *The Saints' Everlasting Rest.* 6th ed. Glasgow: Collins, 1831.

Benedict, David. *A General History of the Baptist Denomination in America, and Other Parts of the World.* Vol. 1. Boston: Lincoln & Edmands, 1813.

Berding, Kenneth. "The Crisis of Biblical Literacy & What We Can Do About It." *Biola Magazine,* Spring 2014, 16–22.

Berkhof, Louis. *Systematic Theology.* New combined ed. Grand Rapids: Eerdmans, 1996.

Blackwell, Ben C. *Christosis: Pauline Soteriology in Light of Deification in Irenaeus and Cyril of Alexandria.* Wissenschaftliche Untersuchungen zum Neuen Testament 2.314. Tübingen: Morh Sieback, 2011.

———. "Immortal Glory and the Problem of Death in Romans 3:23." *JSNT* 32.3 (2010) 285–308.

Blackwell, Ben C., and Kris A. Miller. "Theosis and Theological Anthropology." In *The Ashgate Research Companion to Theological Anthropology,* edited by Joshua Farris and Charles Taliaferro, 303–18. Burlington, VT: Ashgate, 2014.

Blain, Jacob. *Death not Life: Or the Destruction of the Wicked.* 7th ed. Buffalo, NY: Jacob Blain, 1857.

Blanchard, John. John Blanchard to Edward Fudge, May 24, 1993, Correspondence, Edward Fudge Papers. Center for Restoration Studies MS #76. Milliken Special Collections, Brown Library. Abilene Christian University, Abilene, TX.

Blocher, Henri. "Everlasting Punishment and the Problem of Evil." In *Universalism and the Doctrine of Hell,* edited by Nigel M. de S. Cameron. Grand Rapids: Baker, 1992.

Boa, Kenneth D., and Robert M. Bowman Jr. *Sense & Nonsense about Heaven & Hell.* Grand Rapids: Zondervan, 2007.

Boettner, Loraine. *The Reformed Doctrine of Predestination.* Philadelphia: Presbyterian and Reformed, 1973.

Bonar, Andrew A. *Memoir and Remains of the Rev. Robert Murray M'Cheyne.* 2nd ed. Dundee, UK: Middleton, 1845.

Borchert, G. L. "Wrath, Destruction." In *The Dictionary of Paul and His Letters*, edited by Gerald Hawthorne and Ralph Martin, 991–93. Downers Grove, IL: IVP Academic, 1993.
Bowles, Ralph G. "Does Revelation 14:11 Teach Eternal Torment?" In *Rethinking Hell: Readings in Evangelical Conditionalism*, edited by Christopher M. Date, Gregory G. Stump, and Joshua W. Anderson, 138–54. Eugene, OR: Cascade, 2014.
Boyd, Gregory A. "The Case for Annihilationism." *ReKnew* blog. 19 January 2008. Online: http://www.reknew.org/2008/01/the-case-for-annihilationism/.
———. *Satan and the Problem of Evil: Constructing a Trinitarian Warfare Theodicy*. Downers Grove, IL: IVP, 2001.
Boys, John. *An Exposition of the Several Offices*. New York: Stanford and Swords, 1851.
Brady, Ignatius C., et al. "Immortality." In *New Catholic Encyclopedia*. Vol. 7, edited by Thomas Carson and Joann Cerrito, 347–54. New York: Gale, 2003.
Bremmer, Jan N. "Orphic, Roman, Jewish and Christian Tours of Hell: Observations on the Apocalypse of Peter." In *Other Worlds and Their Relation to This World: Early Jewish and Ancient Christian Traditions*, edited by Tobias Nicklas et al., 305–21. Leiden; Boston: Brill, 2010.
Brenneman, Todd. *Homespun Gospel: The Triumph of Sentimentality in Contemporary American Evangelicalism*. New York and Oxford: Oxford University Press, 2013.
Bright, John. *A History of Israel*. 4th ed. Louisville, KY: Westminster John Knox, 2000.
Brown, Colin. Colin Brown to Edward Fudge, May 4, 1988, Correspondence, Edward Fudge Papers. Center for Restoration Studies MS #76. Milliken Special Collections, Brown Library. Abilene Christian University, Abilene, TX.
Brown, Warren S., Nancey Murphy, and H. Newton Malony, eds. *Whatever Happened to the Soul? Scientific and Theological Portraits of Human Nature*. Theology and the Sciences. Minneapolis, MN: Augsburg/Fortress, 1998.
Bruce, F. F. F. F. Bruce to Edward Fudge, November 20, 1972, Correspondence, Edward Fudge Papers. Center for Restoration Studies MS #76. Milliken Special Collections, Brown Library. Abilene Christian University, Abilene, TX.
———. F. F. Bruce to Edward Fudge, January 18, 1975, Correspondence, Edward Fudge Papers. Center for Restoration Studies MS #76. Milliken Special Collections, Brown Library. Abilene Christian University, Abilene, TX.
———. F. F. Bruce to Edward Fudge, July 31, 1975, Correspondence, Edward Fudge Papers. Center for Restoration Studies MS #76. Milliken Special Collections, Brown Library. Abilene Christian University, Abilene, TX.
———. F. F. Bruce to Edward Fudge, September 9, 1987, Correspondence, Edward Fudge Papers. Center for Restoration Studies MS #76. Milliken Special Collections, Brown Library. Abilene Christian University, Abilene, TX.
———. *The Gospel of John*. Grand Rapids: Eerdmans, 1983.
———. *Paul, Apostle of the Heart Set Free*. Grand Rapids: Eerdmans, 1977.
———. "Paul on Immortality." *Scottish Journal of Theology* 24 (1971) 457–72.
Bruner, Frederick Dale. *The Gospel of John: A Commentary*. Grand Rapids: Eerdmans, 2012.
Buis, Harry. *The Doctrine of Eternal Punishment*. Philadelphia: Presbyterian & Reformed, 1957.
Calvary Chapel Deer Park. "What We Believe." Online: http://www.calvarychapeldeerpark.org/what-we-believe.

Calvin, John. *Commentaries on the Epistle of Paul the Apostle to the Hebrews*. Translated by John Owen. Edinburgh: Calvin Translation Society, 1853.

———. *The First Epistle of Paul the Apostle to the Corinthians*. Translated by John W. Fraser. Grand Rapids: Eerdmans, 1960.

———. *Institutes of the Christian Religion, Volumes 1 & 2*, edited by John T. McNeill, translated by Ford Lewis Battles. Lousiville, KY: Westminster John Knox, 2011.

———. "Psychopannychia." In *Selected Works of John Calvin: Tracts and Letters*, edited and translated by Henry Beveridge. Vol. 3. Grand Rapids: Baker Book House, 1983.

———. *Tracts Relating to the Reformation*. Translated by Henry Beveridge. Vol. 3. Edinburgh: Calvin Translation Society, 1851.

———. *Treatises Against the Anabaptists and Against the Libertines*, trans. Benjamin W. Farley. Grand Rapids: Baker Book House, 1982.

Campbell, Constantine R. *Paul and Union with Christ: An Exegetical and Theological Study*. Grand Rapids: Zondervan, 2012.

Carson, D. A. *The Gagging of God: Christianity Confronts Pluralism*. Grand Rapids: Zondervan, 1996.

———. *The Gospel according to John*. Grand Rapids: Eerdmans, 1991.

Charles, R. H. *The Book of Enoch*. London: SPCK, 1966.

———. *The Old Testament Apocrypha and Pseudepigrapha*. 2 vols. Oxford: Oxford University Press, 1991.

Charlesworth, James H., ed. *The Old Testament Pseudepigrapha*. 2 vols. New Haven: Yale University Press, 1983, 1985.

Clifford, Ross, and Phillip Johnson. *The Cross Is Not Enough: Living as Witnesses to the Resurrection*. Grand Rapids: Baker, 2012.

Code, Lorraine. *Ecological Thinking: The Politics of Epistemic Location*. Oxford: Oxford University Press, 2006.

Constable, Henry. *The Duration and Nature of Final Punishment*. Reprint of London edition. Boston: Advent Christian Publication Society, n.d. circa 1883.

Craig, William Lane, and James Porter Moreland. *Philosophical Foundations for a Christian Worldview*. Downers Grove, IL: IVP, 2003.

Cramer, David C. "Creating a Culture of Equality as Witness to the Truth: A Philosophical Response to Gender Difference." *Priscilla Papers* 24.3 (2010) 18–22.

———. "How to Talk about the Afterlife (If You Must), Part 1." *Jesus Creed* blog. 12 July 2011. Online: http://www.patheos.com/blogs/jesuscreed/2011/07/12/how-to-talk-about-the-afterlife-if-you-must-1/.

———. "How to Talk about the Afterlife (If You Must), Part 2." *Jesus Creed* blog. 14 July 2011. Online: http://www.patheos.com/blogs/jesuscreed/2011/07/14/how-to-talk-about-the-afterlife-if-you-must-2/.

Crockett, William, and Stanley N. Gundry, eds. *Four Views on Hell*. Grand Rapids: Zondervan, 1996.

Crofford, J. Gregory. *The Dark Side of Destiny: Hell Re-Examined*. Eugene, OR: Wipf & Stock, 2013.

Cryderman, Lyn. Lyn Cryderman to Edward Fudge, November 5, 1990, Correspondence, Edward Fudge Papers. Center for Restoration Studies MS #76. Milliken Special Collections, Brown Library. Abilene Christian University, Abilene, TX.

Cullmann, Oscar. *Immortality of the Soul or Resurrection of the Dead? The Witness of the New Testament*. London: Epworth, 1958.

Cyril of Jerusalem. "The Catechetical Lectures of S. Cyril, Archbishop of Jerusalem." In *A Select Library of the Nicene and Post-Nicene Fathers*, edited by Philip Schaff and Henry Wace, lix–143. Vol. 7. New York: The Christian Literature Co., 1894.

Danby, Herbert. *Tractate Sanhedrin: Mishnah and Tosefta: The Judicial Procedure of the Jews as Codified Towards the End of the Second Century A.D.* London: SPCK, 1919.

Date, Christopher M. "Cross Purposes: Atonement, Death and the Fate of the Wicked." *Rethinking Hell* blog. August 12, 2012. Online: http://www.rethinkinghell.com/2012/08/cross-purposes-atonement-death-and-the-fate-of-the-wicked.

———. "Episode 32: A Year of Rethinking Hell." *Rethinking Hell* podcast. 29 July 2013. Online: http://www.rethinkinghell.com/2013/07/episode-32-a-year-of-rethinking-hell.

———. "Episode 65: Immortal." *Theopologetics* podcast. 27 October 2011. Online: http://www.theopologetics.com/2011/10/27/episode-65-immortal/.

———. "Obfuscating Traditionalism: No Eternal Life in Hell?" *Rethinking Hell* blog. October 12, 2013. Online: http://www.rethinkinghell.com/2013/10/obfuscating-traditionalism-no-eternal-life-in-hell.

Date, Christopher M., Gregory G. Stump, and Joshua W. Anderson. *Rethinking Hell: Readings in Evangelical Conditionalism*. Eugene, OR: Cascade, 2014.

Dayton, Donald W., and Robert K. Johnston. *Varieties of American Evangelicalism*. Knoxville, TN: University of Tennessee Press, 1991.

De Lubac, Henri. *History and Spirit: The Understanding of Scripture according to Origen*. Translated by Anne Englund Nash. San Francisco: Ignatius, 2007.

Driscoll, Mark. "Heaven and Hell." Sermon. Delivered on February 27, 2011. *YouTube*. Online: https://www.youtube.com/watch?v=RPOQoyA87hE.

Dryden, J. de Waal. "Immortality in Romans 2:6–11." *JTI* 7.2 (2013) 295–310.

Duncan, Ligon. "Speaking Seriously and Sensitively about Hell to the Sons of this Age and the Next." *Reformation 21*. Online: http://www.reformation21.org/blog/2011/03/speaking-seriously-and-sensiti.php.

Dyrness, William A., and Veli-Matti Kärkkäinen. *Global Dictionary of Theology: A Resource for the Worldwide Church*. Downers Grove, IL: IVP, 2008.

Edwards, David L., and John R. W. Stott. *Evangelical Essentials: A Liberal Evangelical Dialogue*. London: Hodder & Stoughton, 1988.

Edwards, Jonathan. "The Eternity of Hell Torments." In *The Works of President Edwards*, Vol. 4, 266–79. New York: Leavitt, Trow & Co., 1844.

———. "A History of the Work of Redemption." In *The Works of President Edwards*, Vol. 1, 293–516. New York: Leavitt, Trow & Co., 1844.

———. "The Justice of God in the Damnation of Sinners." In *The Works of Jonathan Edwards, Volume 19: Sermons and Discourses, 1734–1738*, edited by M. X. Lesser, 339–76. New Haven, CT: Yale University Press, 2001.

———. "The Salvation of All Men Strictly Examined." In *The Works of Jonathan Edwards*, Vol. 1, 1–294. Boston: Jewett, 1854.

———. *The Wrath of Almighty God: Jonathan Edwards on God's Judgment against Sinners*. Edited by Don Kistler. Morgan, PA: Soli Deo Gloria, 1996.

Elliott, Mark W. *Isaiah 40–66*. Old Testament XI. Ancient Christian Commentary on Scripture. Downers Grove, IL: IVP, 2007.

Ellis, Aaron. *Bible vs. Tradition: In Which the True Teaching of the Bible is Manifested, the Corruptions of Theologians Detected, and the Traditions of Men Exposed*. 2nd ed. New York: Bible Examiner, 1853.

Ellis, E. Earle. *Christ and the Future in New Testament History*. Leiden: Brill, 2000.
Erickson, Millard J. *Christian Theology*. 2nd ed. Grand Rapids: Baker Academic, 1998.
———. *The Word Became Flesh: A Contemporary Incarnational Christology*. Grand Rapids: Baker, 1991.
Eskridge, Larry. *God's Forever Family: The Jesus People Movement in America*. Oxford: Oxford University Press, 2013.
Evans, C. Stephen, ed. *Exploring Kenotic Christianity: The Self-Emptying of God*. New York: Oxford University Press, 2006.
Faber, Frederick W. *Notes on Doctrinal and Spiritual Subjects*. Vol. 2. London: Richardson and Son, 1866.
Fairbairn, Donald. *Life in the Trinity: An Introduction to Theology with the Help of the Church Fathers*. Downers Grove, IL: IVP, 2009.
Fee, Gordon D. *The First Epistle to the Corinthians*. Grand Rapids: Eerdmans, 1987.
Ford, Desmond. Desmond Ford to Edward Fudge, October 5, 1983, Correspondence, Edward Fudge Papers. Center for Restoration Studies MS #76. Milliken Special Collections, Brown Library. Abilene Christian University, Abilene, TX.
Forsyth, Peter Taylor. *The Work of Christ*. London: Hodder & Stoughton, 1910.
———. *The Cruciality of the Cross*. New Creation: Australia, 1994.
Fretheim, Terence. *Exodus, Interpretation: A Bible Commentary for Teaching and Preaching*. Louisville: John Knox, 1991.
Froom, LeRoy Edwin. *The Conditionalist Faith of Our Fathers*. 2 vols. Washington, DC: Review & Herald, 1965.
Fudge, Edward W. "Bible Scholars and Church Leaders Endorse [*Hebrews: Ancient Encouragement for Believers Today*]." *Edward Fudge Ministries*. Online: http://edwardfudge.com/written-ministry/books/hebrews-ancient-encouragement-for-believers-today/bible-scholars-and-church-leaders-endorse/.
———. "Divine Rescue: Endorsements." *Edward Fudge Ministries*. Online: http://edwardfudge.com/written-ministry/books/the-divine-rescue/divine-rescue-endorsements/.
———. "The Final End of the Wicked." In *Rethinking Hell: Readings in Evangelical Conditionalism*, edited by Christopher M. Date, Gregory G. Stump, and Joshua W. Anderson, 29–43. Eugene, OR: Cascade, 2014.
———. *The Fire that Consumes: A Biblical and Historical Study of the Doctrine of Final Punishment*. 1st ed. Fallbrook, CA: Verdict, 1982.
———. *The Fire that Consumes: A Biblical and Historical Study of the Doctrine of Final Punishment*. 3rd ed. Eugene, OR: Cascade, 2011.
———. *Hell: A Final Word; The Surprising Truths I Found in the Bible*. Abilene, TX: Leafwood, 2012.
———. "Putting Hell in Its Place." *Christianity Today* 20.22, August 6, 1976, 14–17.
Fudge, Edward, and Robert Peterson. *Two Views of Hell: A Biblical & Theologiacl Dialogue*. Downers Grove, IL: IVP, 2000.
Gaffin, Richard. *The Centrality of the Resurrection: A Study in Paul's Soteriology*. Grand Rapids: Baker, 1978.
Galli, Mark. "Heaven, Hell, and Rob Bell: Putting the Pastor in Context." *Christianity Today*, 2 March 2011. Online: http://www.ctlibrary.com/ct/2011/marchweb-only/rob-bell-universalism.html.
Gatch, Milton M. *Death: Meaning and Mortality in Christian Thought and Contemporary Culture*. New York: Seabury, 1969.

Geisler, Norman L. *If God, Why Evil? A New Way to Think about the Question.* Bloomington, MN: Bethany House, 2011.

Geisler, Norman L., and Frank Turek. *I Don't Have Enough Faith to Be an Atheist.* Wheaton, IL: Crossway, 2004.

Gerhard, Johann. "The Eternity of Future Punishment." In *Gerhard's Sacred Meditations*, translated by C. W. Heisler, 291–96. Philadelphia, PA: Lutheran Publication Society, 1896.

Gerstner, John. John Gerstner to Edward Fudge, July 11, 1990, Correspondence, Edward Fudge Papers. Center for Restoration Studies MS #76. Milliken Special Collections, Brown Library. Abilene Christian University, Abilene, TX.

———. *Repent or Perish.* Ligonier, PA: Soli Deo Gloria, 1990.

Getz, Gene. Gene Getz to Edward Fudge, June 11, 1982, Correspondence, Edward Fudge Papers. Center for Restoration Studies MS #76. Milliken Special Collections, Brown Library. Abilene Christian University, Abilene, TX.

Gill, John. "Mark 9." In *The New John Gill Exposition of the Entire Bible.* Reproduced at Studylight.org Commentaries, http://www.studylight.org/com/geb/view.cgi?bk=40&ch=9.

Goldingay, John. *Old Testament Theology.* Vol. 1. Downers Grove, IL: IVP Academic, 2003.

———. *Theological Diversity and the Authority of the Old Testament.* Grand Rapids: Eerdmans, 1987.

Gombis, Timothy G. "A Radically New Humanity: The Function of the *Haustafel* in Ephesians." *JETS* 48.2 (2005) 317–30.

Goppelt, Leonhard. *Theology of the New Testament Volume 1: The Ministry of Jesus in Its Theological Significance.* Translated by John Alsup. Grand Rapids: Eerdmans, 1981.

Gorman, Michael J. *Apostle of the Crucified Lord: A Theological Introduction to Paul and His Letters.* Grand Rapids: Eerdmans, 2004.

———. *Cruciformity: Paul's Narrative Spirituality of the Cross.* Grand Rapids: Eerdmans, 2001.

———. *Inhabiting the Cruciform God: Kenosis, Justification, and Theosis in Paul's Narrative Soteriology.* Grand Rapids: Eerdmans, 2009.

———. *Reading Paul.* Eugene, OR: Cascade, 2008.

Gorra, Joe. "Honoring Alvin Plantinga." *Evangelical Philosophical Society* blog. 23 May 2010. Online: http://blog.epsociety.org/2010/05/honoring-alvin-plantinga.html.

Goss, Leonard George. Leonard George Goss to Edward Fudge, November 10, 1982, Correspondence, Edward Fudge Papers. Center for Restoration Studies MS #76. Milliken Special Collections, Brown Library. Abilene Christian University, Abilene, TX.

Graham, Billy. *The Heaven Answer Book.* Nashville, TN: Thomas Nelson, 2012.

Green, Joel B. *Body, Soul, and Human Life: The Nature of Humanity in the Bible.* Studies in Theological Interpretation. Grand Rapids: Baker Academic, 2008.

Gundry-Volf, Judith. "Universalism." In *The Dictionary of Paul and His Letters*, edited by Gerald Hawthorne and Ralph Martin, 956–61. Downers Grove, IL: IVP Academic, 1993.

Guthrie, Donald. "Transformation and the Parousia." *Vox Evangelica* 14 (1984) 39–51.

Hagenbach, Karl. Rudolf. *A Text-Book of the History of Doctrines.* Translated by C. W. Buch. Vol. 1. New York: Sheldon & Co., 1861.

Hamilton, Victor P. "peger." In *Theological Wordbook of the Old Testament*, edited by R. Laird Harris, Gleason L. Archer Jr., and Bruce K. Waltke. 2 vols. Chicago: Moody, 1980.

Hannah, Vern A. "Death, Immortality and Resurrection: A Response to John Yates, 'The Origin of the Soul.'" *EQ* 62.3 (1990) 241–51.

Hanson, Paul D. *The People Called: The Growth of Community in the Bible*. San Francisco: Harper and Row, 1986.

Haraburda, Scott S. *Christian Controversies: Seeking the Truth*. Spencer, IN: Meaningful, 2013.

Harmon, Kendall. Kendall Harmon to Edward Fudge, August 17, 1991, Correspondence, Edward Fudge Papers. Center for Restoration Studies MS #76. Milliken Special Collections, Brown Library. Abilene Christian University, Abilene, TX.

Hasel, Gerhard F. *Old Testament Theology: Basic Issues in the Current Debate*. Rev. ed. Grand Rapids: Eerdmans, 1972.

Heath, Chip, and Dan Heath. *Made to Stick: Why Some Ideas Survive and Others Die*. New York: Random House, 2007.

Hodge, Charles. *Systematic Theology*. Vol. 3. New York: Scribner's Sons, 1898.

Hopkins, Gerard Manley. *The Sermons and Devotional Writings of Gerard Manley Hopkins*. 2nd ed. New York: Oxford University Press, 1967.

Hudson, C. F. *Debt and Grace, as Related to the Doctrine of a Future Life*. New York: Cowles and Company, 1857.

Hughes, Philip E. *The True Image: The Origin and Destiny of Man in Christ*. Grand Rapids: Eerdmans, 1989.

Hui-Neng. *The Sutra of Hui-Neng, Grand Master of Zen*. Translated by Thomas Cleary. Boston: Shambhala, 1998.

Hunter, James Davison. *Evangelicalism: The Coming Generation*. Chicago: University of Chicago Press, 1987.

Irenaeus. *The Demonstration of the Apostolic Teaching*. Translated by J. Armitage Robinson. London: SPCK, 1920.

Jacob, Edmond. *Theology of the Old Testament*. New York: Harper & Row, 1958.

Jacoby, Douglas A. "Heaven and Hell: Terminal Punishment." *International Teaching Ministry of Douglas Jacoby*. Online: http://www.douglasjacoby.com/wp-content/uploads/Hell-Jacoby.pdf.

———. *What Happens After We Die? The Long-Neglected Biblical Teaching on What Happens After Death*. Spring, TX: Illumination, 2012.

———. *What's the Truth About Heaven and Hell? Sorting Out the Confusion about the Afterlife*. Eugene, OR: Harvest House, 2013.

Jensen, Robert. *Systematic Theology Volume 2: The Works of God*. Oxford: Oxford University Press, 1999.

Johnson, Alan F. *1 Corinthians*. Downers Groves, IL: IVP Academic, 2004.

Joyce, Gilbert C. "Annihilation." In *Encyclopedia of Religion and Ethics*, vol. 1, edited by James Hastings, 544–49. Edinburgh: T. & T. Clark, 1908.

Justin Martyr. "Dialogue of Justin with Trypho, a Jew." In *The Ante-Nicene Fathers*, Vol. 1, edited by Alexander Roberts and James Donaldson, 194–270. Buffalo: The Christian Literature Co., 1885.

Juza, Ryan P. "Echoes of Sodom and Gomorrah on the Day of the Lord: Intertextuality and Tradition in 2 Peter 3:7–13." *BBR* 24.2 (2014) 227–45.

Kant, Immanuel. *Lectures on Ethics*. Translated by Louis Infield. Indianapolis: Hackett, 1963.
Kantzer, Kenneth S. and Carl F. Henry, editors. *Evangelical Affirmations*. Grand Rapids: Zondervan, 1990.
Keller, Timothy. *Center Church: Doing Balanced, Gospel-Centered Ministry in Your City*. Grand Rapids: Zondervan, 2012.
Kessler, John. "The Shaking of the Nations: An Eschatological View." *JETS* 30 (1987) 159–66.
Kinnaman, David, and Gabe Lyons. *unChristian: What a New Generation Really Thinks about Christianity . . . and Why It Matters*. Grand Rapids: Baker, 2007.
Kline, Meredith G. "Creation in the Image of the Glory-Spirit." *WTJ* 39.2 (1977) 250–72.
Koukl, Greg. "Hell, Yes!: The Terrifying Truth." *Stand to Reason* (Audio CD).
Kreitzer, Larry J. "Resurrection." In *The Dictionary of Paul and His Letters*, edited by Gerald Hawthorne and Ralph Martin, 805–12. Downers Grove, IL: IVP Academic, 1993.
Kuhn, Thomas S. *The Structure of Scientific Revolutions*. 2nd ed. Chicago: University of Chicago Press, 1970.
Lactantius. "The Divine Institutes." In *The Ante-Nicene Fathers*, Vol. 7, edited by Alexander Roberts and James Donaldson, 9–223. Buffalo: The Christian Literature Co., 1886.
Ladd, George Eldon. *The New Testament Pattern of Truth*. Grand Rapids: Eerdmans, 1968.
———. *A Theology of the New Testament*. Grand Rapids: Eerdmans, 1974.
Lamont, Michèle. *How Professors Think: Inside the Curious World of Academic Judgment*. Cambridge: Harvard University Press, 2009.
Latham, John W. "The Use of the Old Testament in 1 Corinthians 15:44–49." *The American Journal of Biblical Theology* 14.10. Online: http://www.biblicaltheology.com/Research/LathamJW01.pdf.
Lewis, C. S. *Mere Christianity*. New York: Harper-Collins, 1972.
———. *The Problem of Pain*. London: Macmillan, 1973.
———. "The Weight of Glory." In *The Weight of Glory and Other Addresses*, 25–46. New York: HarperOne, 2001.
Liddell, Henry George, et al. *A Greek-English Lexicon*. Oxford: Clarendon, 1996.
Liebreich, Leon J. "The Compilation of the Book of Isaiah." *JQR* 46 (1956) 259–77.
Lightfoot, J. L. *The Sibylline Oracles: With Introduction, Translation, and Commentary on the First and Second Books*. Oxford: Oxford University Press, 2007.
Longman, Tremper III, and Daniel G. Reid. *God Is a Warrior*. Studies in Old Testament Biblical Theology. Grand Rapids: Zondervan, 1995.
Luther, Martin. "Assertio Omnium Articulorum M. Lutheri per Bullam Leonis X. Novissimam Damnatorum" (Assertion of all the articles of M. Luther condemned by the latest Bull of Leo X). *D. Martin Luther's Werke*, Vol. 7:131–32. Weimar: Böhlaus, 1897.
Lutzer, Erwin W. *One Minute After You Die*. Chicago: Moody, 1997.
MacArthur, John. "Bell's Inferno." *Grace to You* blog. Online: https://www.gty.org/Resources/Print/Blog/B110421.
———. "The Furnace of Fire." Sermon. *Grace to You*. Online: https://www.gty.org/resources/print/sermons/2304.

———. "The Resurrection of Jesus Christ: The Main Event in Redemptive History." Sermon. Delivered on April 12, 2009. *Grace to You*. Online: http://www.gty.org/resources/sermons/90-374/the-resurrection-of-jesus-christ-the-main-event-in-redemptive-history.

———. "The Truth About Hell." *Grace to You*. Online: http://www.gty.org/resources/sermons/80-376/the-truth-about-hell.

MacDonald, Gregory. *The Evangelical Universalist*. Eugene, OR: Cascade, 2006.

MacDuff, John. *The Footsteps of Jesus: Or, Things to be Sought and Things to be Shunned*. London: Griffith, Farran, Okeden & Welsh, 1885.

Magen, Yitzhak. *The Stone Vessel Industry in the Second Temple Period: Excavations at Hizma and the Jerusalem Temple Mount*. Jerusalem: Israel Exploration Society, 2002.

Marcus, Joel. *Mark 8–16*. The Anchor Yale Bible. New Haven, CT: Yale University Press, 2009.

Marsden, George M. *Fundamentalism and American Culture: The Shaping of Twentieth-Century Evangelicalism 1870–1925*. Oxford: Oxford University Press, 1980.

Marshall, Christopher D. "Divine and Human Punishment in the New Testament." In *Rethinking Hell: Readings in Evangelical Conditionalism*, edited by Christopher M. Date, Gregory G. Stump, and Joshua W. Anderson, 207–27. Eugene, OR: Cascade, 2014.

Marshall, I. Howard. "The New Testament Does Not Teach Universal Salvation." In *Universal Salvation? The Current Debate*, edited by Robin A. Parry and Christopher H. Partridge, 55–76. Grand Rapids: Eerdmans, 2004.

Martens, Peter W. *Origen and Scripture: The Contours of the Exegetical Life*. New York: Oxford University Press, 2012.

Martin von Cochem. *The Four Last Things: Death, Judgment, Hell, Heaven*. Reprint. London: Forgotten, 2013.

Maynard, Arthur H. "ΤΙ ΕΜΟΙ ΚΑΙ ΣΟΙ." *NTS* 31.4 (1985) 582–86.

McDannell, Colleen, and Bernhard Lang. *Heaven: A History*. 2nd ed. New Haven, CT: Yale University Press, 1988.

McDermott, Gerald R. "Will All Be Saved?" *Themelios* 38.2 (2013) 232–43.

McGee, J. Vernon. "Hell—Fact or Fiction?" Online: http://www.oneplace.com/ministries/thru-the-bible-sunday-sermon/listen/hellfact-or-fiction-159826.html.

Mealy, J. Webb. *The End of the Unrepentant: A Study of the Biblical Themes of Fire and Being Consumed*. Eugene, OR: Wipf and Stock, 2013.

Middleton, J. Richard. *A New Heaven and a New Earth: Reclaiming Biblical Eschatology*. Grand Rapids: Baker Academic, 2014.

———. "The Role of Human Beings in the Cosmic Temple: The Intersection of Worldviews in Psalms 8 and 104." *CTR* 2.1 (2013) 44–58.

Mikolaski, S., ed. *The Creative Theology of P. T. Forsyth*. Grand Rapids: Eerdmans, 1969.

Mohler, Albert. "Is Hell for Real?" In *Is Hell for Real or Does Everyone Go to Heaven?* edited by Christopher W. Morgan and Robert A. Peterson, 11–22. Grand Rapids: Zondervan, 2011.

———. "Modern Theology: The Disappearance of Hell." In *Hell under Fire: Modern Scholarship Reinvents Eternal Punishment*, edited by Christopher W. Morgan and Robert A. Peterson, 15–41. Grand Rapids: Zondervan, 2004.

———. "The Scandal of Biblical Illiteracy: It's Our Problem." *AlbertMohler.com*. 29 June 2004. Online: http://www.albertmohler.com/2004/06/29/the-scandal-of-biblical-illiteracy-its-our-problem-2/.

Moltmann, Jürgen. *The Coming of God: Christian Eschatology*. London: SCM, 1996.

———. *The Crucified God: The Cross of Christ as the Foundation and Criticism of Christian Theology*. Minneapolis, MN: Fortress, 1974.

———. *God in Creation*. Minneapolis, MN: Fortress, 1993.

Moloney, Francis J. *the Gospel of John*. Sacra Pagina. Edited by Daniel J. Harrington. Collegeville, MN: Liturgical, 2005.

Moo, Douglas J. "Paul on Hell." In *Hell under Fire: Modern Scholarship Reinvents Eternal Punishment*, edited by Christopher W. Morgan, & Robert A. Peterson, 91–109. Grand Rapids: Zondervan, 2004.

Moody, Raymond A. Jr. *The Light Beyond*. New York: Bantam, 1988.

Moore, Clifford H. *Ancient Beliefs in the Immortality of the Soul: Our Debt to Greece and Rome*. New York: Cooper Square, 1963.

Moreland, J. P. *The God Question: An Invitation to a Life of Meaning*. Eugene, OR: Harvest House, 2009.

Morey, Robert A. *Death and the Afterlife*. Minneapolis, MN: Bethany House, 1984.

Morgan, Christopher W. "Annihilationism: Will the Unsaved Be Punished Forever?" In *Hell Under Fire: Modern Scholarship Reinvents Eternal Punishment*, edited by Christopher W. Morgan and Robert A. Peterson, 195–218. Grand Rapids: Zondervan, 2004.

Morgan, Christopher W., and Robert A. Peterson, eds. *Hell under Fire: Modern Scholarship Reinvents Eternal Punishment*. Grand Rapids: Zondervan, 2004.

Murphy, Nancey C. *Bodies and Souls, or Spirited Bodies?* Cambridge: Cambridge University Press, 2006.

———. *Reasoning and Rhetoric in Religion*. Valley Forge, PA: Trinity, 1994.

Murphy-O'Connor, Jerome. *Paul: A Critical Life*. Oxford: Clarendon, 1996.

Murray, Michael J. "Heaven and Hell." In *Reason for the Hope Within*, 287–317. Grand Rapids: Eerdmans, 1999.

Neusner, Jacob, trans. *The Babylonian Talmud: A Translation and Commentary*. Vol. 1. Peabody, MA: Hendrickson, 2011.

———. *The Mishnah: A New Translation*. New Haven; London: Yale University Press, 1988.

———. *The Tosefta*. 6 vols. New York: Ktav, 1981.

Newman, John H. *Newman on the Bible: Commentaries on Scripture*. Edited by William Park. New York: Scepter, 2006.

Nickelsburg, George W. E. *Resurrection, Immortality, and Eternal Life in Intertestamental Judaism and Early Christianity*. Cambridge: Harvard University Press, 2007.

Niebuhr, Reinhold. *The Nature and Destiny of Man*. Vol. 2: Human Destiny. New York: Scribner's, 1964.

Noll, Mark A. *The Scandal of the Evangelical Mind*. Grand Rapids: Eerdmans, 1994.

Nysse, Richard. "Yahweh Is a Warrior." *WW* 7 (1987) 192–201.

Olbricht, Thomas H. *He Loves Forever: The Enduring Message of God from the Old Testament*. Joplin, MO: College, 2000.

Olley, John W. "'No Peace' in a Book of Consolation. A Framework for the Book of Isaiah?" *VT* 49 (1999) 351–70.

Olson, Roger E. *Against Calvinism*. Grand Rapids: Zondervan, 2011.

———. "Fair and Unfair Criticisms of Calvinism and Arminianism." *Patheos* blog. 20 June 2011. Online: http://www.patheos.com/blogs/rogerolson/2011/06/fair-and-unfair-criticisms-of-calvinism-and-arminianism/.

Origen. *On First Principles*. Translated by G. W. Butterworth. Notre Dame, IN: Ave Maria, 2013.

Ortlund, Dane. "Inaugurated Glorification: Revisiting Romans 8:30." *JETS* 57.1 (2014) 111–33.

Ortlund, Gavin. "Image of Adam, Son of God: Genesis 5:3 and Luke 3:38 in Intercanonical Dialogue." *JETS* 57.4 (2014) 673–88.

Osborne, Grant R. *Romans*. Downers Grove, IL: IVP Academic, 2003.

Pace, William. William Pace to Edward Fudge, July 28, 1983, Correspondence, Edward Fudge Papers. Center for Restoration Studies MS #76. Milliken Special Collections, Brown Library. Abilene Christian University, Abilene, TX.

Packer, James I. "Does Everyone Go to Heaven?" In *Is Hell for Real or Does Everyone Go to Heaven?* edited by Christopher W. Morgan and Robert A. Peterson, 58–72. Grand Rapids: Zondervan, 2011.

———. "Evangelicals and the Way of Salvation: New Challenges to the Gospel: Universalism, and Justification by Faith." In *Evangelical Affirmations*, edited by Kenneth S. Kantzer and Carl F. H. Henry, 107–31, 133–36. Grand Rapids: Zondervan, 1990.

Padgett, Alan G. "The Body in Resurrection: Science and Scripture on the 'Spiritual Body' (1 Cor 15:35–58)." *WW* 22.2 (2002) 155–63.

Papaioannou, Kim. *The Geography of Hell in the Teaching of Jesus: Gehenna, Hades, the Abyss, the Outer Darkness Where There is Weeping and Gnashing of Teeth*. Eugene, OR: Pickwick, 2013.

Paterson, H. Sinclair, ed. *Dickinson's Theological Quarterly*. Vol. 5. London: Dickinson, 1879.

Payson, Edward. *Sermons*. London: Holdsworth and Ball, 1831.

Payton, Donald. *Getting the Reformation Wrong: Correcting Some Misunderstandings*. Downers Grove, IL: IVP Academic, 2010.

Penton, M. James. *Apocalypse Delayed: The Story of Jehovah's Witnesses*. 3rd ed. Toronto: University of Toronto Press, 2015.

Peoples, Glenn A. "An Open Letter to My Traditionalist Friends." *Right Reason* blog. 19 June 2011. Online: http://www.rightreason.org/2011/an-open-letter-to-my-traditionalist-friends/.

———. "Introduction to Evangelical Conditionalism." In *Rethinking Hell: Readings in Evangelical Conditionalism*, edited by Christopher M. Date, Gregory G. Stump, and Joshua W. Anderson, 10–24. Eugene, OR: Cascade, 2014.

———. "The Mortal God: Materialism and Christology." In *The Ashgate Research Companion to Theological Anthropology*, edited by Joshua R. Farris and Charles Taliaferro, 331–45. Farnham, UK: Ashgate, 2015.

Pétavel-Olliff, Emmanuel. *The Struggle for Eternal Life: or The Immortality of the Just, and the Gradual Extinction of the Wicked*. London: Kellaway, 1876.

Peterson, Robert. "Does the Bible Teach Annihilationism?" *Bibliotheca Sacra* 156 (1999) 13–27.

———. "A Traditionalist Response to John Stott's Arguments for Annihilationism." *JETS* 37.4 (1994) 553–68.

Pettingell, John H. Τὰ Μέλλοντα: *Views and Reviews in Eschatology; A Collection of Letters, Essays, and Other Papers Concerning the Life and Death to Come.* Yarmouth, ME: Scriptural Publication Society, 1887.
Pew Research Center. "U.S. Religious Landscape Survey: Religious Beliefs and Practices." *Pew Research Center Religion & Public Life.* 1 June 2008. Online: http://www.pewforum.org/2008/06/01/u-s-religious-landscape-survey-religious-beliefs-and-practices/.
Phelps, Elizabeth Stuart. *The Gates Ajar.* Boston: Fields, Osgood, & Co., 1869.
———. *Beyond the Gates.* Boston: Houghton, Mifflin, & Co., 1883.
Pink, A. W. *The Sovereignty of God.* Grand Rapids: Baker, 2002.
Pinnock, Clark H. Clark Pinnock to Edward Fudge, December 19, 1989, Correspondence, Edward Fudge Papers. Center for Restoration Studies MS #76. Milliken Special Collections, Brown Library. Abilene Christian University, Abilene, TX.
———. "The Conditional View." In *Four Views on Hell*, edited by William Crockett and Stanley N. Gundry, 135–178. Grand Rapids: Zondervan, 1996.
———. "The Destruction of the Finally Impenitent." In *Rethinking Hell: Readings in Evangelical Conditionalism*, edited by Christopher M. Date, Gregory G. Stump, and Joshua W. Anderson, 56–73. Eugene, OR: Cascade, 2014.
Pinnock, Clark H., and Robert Brow. *Unbounded Love: A Good News Theology for the 21st Century.* Downers Grove, IL: IVP, 1994.
Piper, John. *A Godward Life: Savoring the Supremacy of God in All of Life.* Sisters, OR: Multnomah, 1997.
———. "Hijacking Back Your Brain from Porn." *Desiring God.* Online: http://www.desiringgod.org/articles/hijacking-back-your-brain-from-porn.
Polanyi, Michael. *Personal Knowledge: Towards a Post-Critical Philosophy.* Chicago: University of Chicago Press, 1958.
Preuss, Dietrich Horst. *Old Testament Theology.* Vol. 1. Edingurgh: T. & T. Clark, 1995.
Pyne, Robert A. Robert A. Pyne to Edward Fudge, January 16, 1991, Correspondence, Edward Fudge Papers. Center for Restoration Studies MS #76. Milliken Special Collections, Brown Library. Abilene Christian University, Abilene, TX.
Quient, Nicholas R. "Paul and the Particularity of Resurrection: A Theological Exegesis of Limited Resurrection in Pauline Theology." Manuscript. 2015.
Ranker. "The Creepiest Shows on TV Right Now." Online: http://www.ranker.com/list/creepiest-shows-on-tv-right-now/ranker-tv. Accessed September 25, 2014.
Rashdall, Hastings. *The Idea of Atonement in Christian Theology.* London: Macmillan, 1919.
Rethinking Hell. "Chris Date and Phil Fernandes Debate Hell (HD)." *YouTube.* Online: https://www.youtube.com/watch?v=PaPz33dVPvc.
———. "Endorsements." Online: http://www.rethinkinghell.com/about/endorsements.
———. "Statement on Evangelical Conditionalism." Online: http://www.rethinkinghell.com/Rethinking-Hell_Statement-on-Evangelical-Conditionalism.pdf.
Rice, John R. "Hell—What the Bible Says about It." In *Great Preaching on Hell*, edited by Curtis Hutson, 11–48. Murfreesboro, TN: Sword of the Lord, 1989.
Ritchie, George. *Return from Tomorrow.* Eastbourne, UK: Kingsway, 1978.
Roetzel, Calvin J. *The Letters of Paul: Conversations in Context.* 5th ed. Louisville, KY: Westminster John Knox, 2009.
Roller, John H. *The Doctrine of Immortality in the Early Church.* Charlotte, NC: n.p., 1999.

Russell, David M. *The "New Heavens and New Earth": Hope for the Creation in Jewish Apocalyptic and the New Testament*. Studies in Biblical Apocalyptic Literature 1. Philadelphia: Visionary, 1996.

Russell, David S. *The Method and Message of Jewish Apocalyptic*. Philadelphia: Westminster, 1964.

Santayana, George. *The Life of Reason: Or, the Phases of Human Progress*. New York: Scribner's Sons, 1905.

Saville, Andy. "Arguing with Annihilationism: An Assessment of the Doctrinal Arguments for Annihilationism." *Scottish Bulletin of Evangelical Theology* 24.1 (2006) 65–90.

Schaff, Philip. *The Creeds of Christendom: With a History and Critical Notes*. Vol. 3. New York: Harper & Brothers, 1882.

Schnelle, Udo. *The Human Condition: Anthropology in the Teachings of Jesus, Paul, and John*. Minneapolis, MN: Fortress, 1996.

———. *Theology of the New Testament*. Translated by M. Eugene Boring. Grand Rapids: Baker, 2009.

Schwarz, Hans. *Eschatology*. Grand Rapids: Eerdmans, 2000.

Scott, J. J. Jr. "Immortality." In *The Dictionary of Paul and His Letters*, edited by Gerald Hawthorne and Ralph Martin, 431–33. Downers Grove, IL: IVP Academic, 1993.

Seitz, Christopher R. "Isaiah 40–66." *New Interpreter's Bible*. Vol. 6. Nashville, TN: Abingdon, 2001.

Seymour, Charles. "Hell, Justice, and Freedom." *International Journal for Philosophy of Religion* 43.2 (1998) 69–86.

Shedd, William G. T. *Dogmatic Theology*, vol. 1. New York: Scribner's Sons, 1888.

Simons, Menno. *The Complete Works of Menno Simons*. Elkhart, IN: Funk and Brother, 1871.

Smart, James D. "A New Interpretation of Isaiah lxvi. 1–6." *ExpTim* 46 (1935) 420–24.

Sotak, Max H. *Damning Assumptions: What Advocates of Endless Torment Take for Granted*. n.d.: Sotakoff, 2013.

Sproul, R. C. *The Character of God: Discovering the God Who Is*. Ann Arbor, MI: Vine, 1995.

———. *Chosen by God*. Wheaton, IL: Tyndale House, 1986.

———. *Truths We Confess: A Layman's Guide to the Westminster Confession of Faith*, vol. 1. Phillipsburg: Presbyterian and Reformed, 2006.

Spurgeon, Charles H. *The New Park Street Pulpit Sermons*. Vol. 4. London: Alabaster and Passmore, 1858.

———. *Sermons of the Rev. C. H. Spurgeon*. 2nd series. New York: Sheldon, Blakeman & Co., 1857.

———. *Sermons of the Rev. C. H. Spurgeon*. 4th series. New York: Sheldon, Blakeman & Co., 1858.

Stackhouse, John G. Jr. John Stackhouse to Edward Fudge, January 18, 1993, Correspondence, Edward Fudge Papers. Center for Restoration Studies MS #76. Milliken Special Collections, Brown Library. Abilene Christian University, Abilene, TX.

———. *Need to Know: Vocation as the Heart of Christian Epistemology*. Oxford: Oxford University Press, 2014.

Stockman, Edward A. *Our Hope, or Why Are We Adventists*. Boston: Advent Christian Publication Society, 1899.

Storm, Howard. *My Descent into Death: And the Message of Love Which Brought Me Back.* Forest Row, UK: Clairview, 2000.

Stott, John R. W. *The Cross of Christ.* Downers Grove, IL: IVP, 1986.

———. "Judgment and Hell." In *Rethinking Hell: Readings in Evangelical Conditionalism*, edited by Christopher M. Date, Gregory G. Stump, and Joshua W. Anderson, 48–55. Eugene, OR: Cascade, 2014.

Strack, H. L., and Günter Stemberger. *Introduction to the Talmud and Midrash*, translated and edited by Markus Bockmuehl. 2nd Fortress Press ed. Minneapolis, MN: Augsburg Fortress, 1996.

Stephens, Mark B. *Annihilation or Renewal? The Meaning and Function of New Creation in the Book of Revelation.* Wissenschaftliche Untersuchungen zum Neuen Testament 2.307. Tübingen: Morh Sieback, 2011.

Swindoll, Charles R. *Growing Deep in the Christian Life: Essential Truths for Becoming Strong in the Faith.* Grand Rapids: Zondervan, 1995.

Talbot, Mark R. "The Morality of Everlasting Punishment." *Reformation & Revival* 5.4 (1996) 117–34.

Taylor, Jeremy. "Contemplations of the State of Man, in This Life and in That Which Is to Come." In *The Whole Works of the Right Rev. Jeremy Taylor*, Vol. 1, 350–98. London: Bohn, 1851.

Terry, Milton S., trans. *Sibylline Oracles.* New York: Eaton & Mains, 1899.

Thielicke, Helmut. *A Little Exercise for Young Theologians*, translated by Charles L. Taylor. Grand Rapids: Eerdmans, 1962.

Thiselton, Anthony C. *1 Corinthians: A Shorter Exegetical & Pastoral Commentary.* Grand Rapids: Eerdmans, 2006.

———. "Claims about 'Hell' and Wrath." In *Rethinking Hell: Readings in Evangelical Conditionalism*, edited by Christopher M. Date, Gregory G. Stump, and Joshua W. Anderson, 174–77. Eugene, OR: Cascade, 2014.

———. *The Living Paul: An Introduction to the Apostle's Life and Thought.* Downers Grove, IL: IVP Academic, 2009.

Thomas, Robert L. "Jesus' View of Eternal Punishment." *The Master's Seminary Journal* 9.2 (1998) 147–67.

Tomasino, Anthony J. "Isaiah 1.1—2.4 and 63–66, and the Composition of the Isaianic Corpus." *JSOT* 57 (1993) 81–98.

Torrance, Thomas F. *Atonement: The Person and Work of Christ.* Milton Keynes, UK: Paternoster, 2009.

Tozer, A. W. *The Knowledge of the Holy: The Attributes of God: Their Meaning in the Christian Life.* New York: Harper and Row, 1971.

Travis, Stephen H. *Christ and the Judgment of God: The Limits of Divine Retribution in New Testament Thought.* 2nd ed. Milton Keynes, UK: Paternoster, 2008.

Vines, Jerry. "Sermon on John 3:16." In *Whosoever Will: A Biblical-Theological Critique of Five-Point Calvinism*, edited by David L. Allen and Steve W. Lemke, 13–28. Nashville, TN: B&H, 2010.

Von Balthasar, Hans Urs. *Dare We Hope "That All Men Be Saved"? With a Short Discourse on Hell.* Translated by David Kipp and Lothar Krauth. San Francisco: Ignatius, 1988.

Wallace, J. Warner. "Is There an Eternal Conscious Hell?" *Please Convince Me.* Online: http://pleaseconvinceme.com/2012/is-there-an-eternal-conscious-hell/.

Walls, Jerry L. *Purgatory: The Logic of Total Transformation*. New York: Oxford University Press, 2012.
Walvoord, John F. "The Literal View." In *Four Views on Hell*, edited by William Crockett and Stanley N. Gundry, 11–28. Grand Rapids: Zondervan, 1996.
———. *Major Bible Prophecies: 37 Crucial Prophecies That Affect You Today*. Grand Rapids: Zondervan, 1991.
———. "Response to Clark H. Pinnock." In *Four Views on Hell*, edited by William Crockett and Stanley N. Gundry, 167–70. Grand Rapids: Zondervan, 1996.
Watchtower Bible and Tract Society. "Working in the 'Field'—Before the Harvest." *Watchtower*, October 15, 2000, 25–30.
Watson, Navar. "High Rate of Biblical Illiteracy 'No Surprise.'" *National Catholic Reporter*, March 28, 2014.
Watts, John D. W. *Isaiah 1–33*. Word Biblical Commentary, vol. 24. Waco, TX: Word, 1985.
Wengst, Klaus. *Das Johannesevangelium: 2. Teilband: Kapitel 11–21*. Stuttgart: Kohlhammer, 2007.
Wenham, John. "The Case for Conditional Immortality." In *Universalism and the Doctrine of Hell*, edited by Nigel M. de S. Cameron, 161–91. Grand Rapids: Baker, 1992.
———. *Facing Hell: The Story of a Nobody; An Autobiography, 1913–1996*. Carlisle, UK: Paternoster, 1998.
———. *The Goodness of God*. Downers Grove, IL: IVP, 1974.
Wenkel, David H. "Wild Beasts in the Prophecy of Isaiah: The Loss of Dominion and Its Renewal through Isaiah as the New Humanity." *JTI* 5.2 (2011) 251–64.
Werblowsky, R. J. Zwi and Geoffrey Wigoder. "Geihinnom." In *The Oxford Dictionary of the Jewish Religion*, edited by Adele Berlin, 285. 2nd ed. New York: Oxford University Press, 2011.
Wesley, John. *Explanatory Notes upon the New Testament*. 4th American ed. New York: Soule and Mason, 1818.
Westermann, Claus. *Isaiah 40–66*. Philadelphia: Westminster, 1969.
———. *What Does the Old Testament Say about God?* Atlanta, GA: John Knox, 1979.
White, James. *The Sovereign Grace of God: A Biblical Study of the Doctrines of Calvinism*. Lindenhurst: Reformation, 2003.
Whitefield, George. *The Christian's Companion: Or, Sermons on Several Subjects*. London: n.p., 1739.
Williamson, G. I. *The Westminster Confession of Faith for Study Classes*. Philadelphia: Presbyterian and Reformed, 1964.
Willison, John. *The Whole Works of the Reverend and Learned Mr. John Willison*. Vol. 1. Edinburgh: Moir, 1798.
Wise, Michael O., Martin G. Abegg Jr., and Edward M. Cook, eds. *The Dead Sea Scrolls: A New Translation*. New York: HarperOne, 2005.
Witherington III, Ben. *Conflict and Community in Corinth: A Socio-rhetorical Commentary on 1 and 2 Corinthians*. Grand Rapids: Eerdmans, 1995.
Witherington III, Ben, and Darlene Hyatt. *Paul's Letter to the Romans: A Socio-Rhetorical Commentary*. Grand Rapids: Eerdmans, 2004.
Worthen, Molly. *Apostles of Reason: The Crisis of Authority in American Evangelicalism*. New York: Oxford University Press, 2013.

Wright, Guy. "Billy Graham Talks about Eternal Life." *The Pittsburgh Press*, September 27, 1952, 2.

Wright, N. T. *Evil and the Justice of God*. Downer's Grove, IL: IVP, 2006.

———. *How God Became King: The Forgotten Story of the Gospels*. New York: HarperOne, 2012.

———. *New Heavens, New Earth: The Biblical Picture of Christian Hope*. Grove Biblical Series. Cambridge: Grove Books, 1999.

———. *The Resurrection of the Son of God*. Christian Origins and the Question of God. Vol. 3. Minneapolis, MN: Fortress, 2003.

———. *Surprsed by Hope: Rethinking Heaven, the Resurrection, and the Mission of the Church*. London: SPCK, 2007.

Wright, Nigel G. "A Kinder, Gentler Damnation?" In *Rethinking Hell: Readings in Evangelical Conditionalism*, edited by Christopher M. Date, Gregory G. Stump, and Joshua W. Anderson, 228–33. Eugene, OR: Cascade, 2014.

Yarbrough, Robert. "Jesus on Hell." In *Hell under Fire: Modern Scholarship Reinvents Eternal Punishment*, edited by Christopher W. Morgan, & Robert A. Peterson, 67–90. Grand Rapids: Zondervan, 2004.

Zackrison, Edwin. *In the Loins of Adam: A Historical Study of Original Sin in Adventist Theology*. Lincoln, NE: iUniverse, 2004.

Zens, Adam. "Closing Statement on Hell and Annihilation Debate." *YouTube*. Online: https://www.youtube.com/watch?v=LoY77z6WiSc.

Zens, Jon. "Do the Flames Ever Stop in Hell?" *Free Grace Broadcaster* 64, March/April 1978, 1–8.

———. *Christ Minimized? A Response to Rob Bell's Love Wins*. Omaha, NE:, 2012.

Zuck, Roy B. *A Biblical Theology of the Old Testament*. Chicago, IL: Moody, 1991.

Zuckermandel, M., and S. Liebermann. *Tosephta: Based on the Erfurt and Vienna Codices*. Jerusalem: Bamberger & Wahrmann, 1937.

Scripture and Ancient Works Index

OLD TESTAMENT

Genesis

1.	78, 123
1–2	93n11, 105
1:20–31	121–22
1:26	117
1:26–27	109
1:26–28	131, 140
1:27–28	127
1:28	117, 123
2.	97, 100, 122
2:7	91, 98, 118, 119, 127, 343
2:17	28, 99n44
3:3	110
3:7	122n19
3:14–19	122n19, 124
3:17	99n44
3:19	91, 99n44
3:22–23	312
3:24	299
4.	91
5:1–3	127
5:3	127
6:3	91
6:4	215
6–9	91
7.	97
15:11	167
15:16	147
19	101
19:24	126
21	91
30:30–43	118
31:1	118
31:8–12	118
35:16–21	91
35:18	343
45:5	144n8
45:8	118
45:13	118
50:20	144n8, 146

Exodus

3:2–6	126
4:21	144n8
15:18	188n31
16:10	125
19:6	130
19:16–19	124
21:15	92n5
21:16	92n5
21:17	92n5
21:22–25	45
22:19	92n5
23:3	300
24:16	125
24:17	125
24:18	125
28:3	218n12
34	44
34:6	44n20, 230, 232, 233

Exodus (continued)

34:6–7	43

Leviticus

10:1–2	126
13	108n94
18:21	168n25
19:15	300
20:2–5	168n25
21:9	92n5
24:17–21	45
24:19–22	300
26:12	133

Numbers

14:14–18	43
16:19	126
16:35	126
22:28	144n10
35:18–21	92n5

Deuteronomy

1:16–17	300
4:34	125
12:31	168n25
18:10	168n25
19:16–21	45
25:1–3	45
26:1–11	105n73
26:8–9	42n16
28:1–6	147
28:15–19	147
29:23	91n3
30	72
30:15–30	51
30:18	72
32:32	91n3

Joshua

6:17	98
7:12	98, 98n38

Judges

1:17	98, 98n37
4.	37
5:4–5	124
12:6	306
14:1–4	144n8

1 Samuel

	46
1:19	111
2:6	230, 232, 232n24, 233
16:14–16	144n9

2 Samuel

	46
14:14	279
22:5	92
24:1	144n9

1 Kings

	46
2:10	175
8:13	228
11:43	175
17:4	144n10
18:38	126
19:11–12	125
22:19–23	144n9

2 Kings

	46
1:10	126
6:5–19	69
19:35	167
23:10	138, 169

1 Chronicles

	46
21:1	144n9
21:2	144n9
21:26	126
29:11	143

2 Chronicles

	46
7:1–3	126
20:6	143
28:3	138

Scripture and Ancient Works Index   391

33:6	138
35:21	76

Ezra

	46

Nehemiah

	46
9:17	43

Esther

	46

Job

1:16	126
3:13	175
14:1	94n12
14:10–14	92
14:11	92
26:2	97
29:20	120
34:21	92
37:9	125
37:13	125
40:6–14	125
42:2	143

Psalms

	46
1	72
6:5	92
7:12–16	203n13
8:3	121
8:3–8	121
8:4	121
8:4–8	131
8:5–6	122
8:5–8	140
8:6	105n78, 113, 117, 121
9:11a	92
9:13–14	92
9:15–16	203n13
9:17	226
16	197
18:6	125
18:7–15	124, 125
19	93n9
19:1	119
21:4–5	119
21:8	119
22:28	143, 144
29:9	144n10
30:9	92
33:12–22	93n9
37:10	147
44:25	96, 108n94
49:14	92, 227, 228
49:20	92n6
58:7–11	138
76:10	144n8
86:15	43
88:10–11	92
89:15	120
89:17	120
89:27	120
89:29	120
89:36–37	120
89:39	120, 127
89:44	120
103:8	43
103:14–17	119
103:15	92
103:15–16	147
103:19	146, 188n31
103:20–21	144n9
104	122
104:4	144n9
104:29	122
104:35	123
108	122
110	121, 150
110:1–2	121
110:2	106
110:5	121
110:5–6	106, 106n82
115:3	143
115:17	92
116	233, 235
116:1	230, 232, 233
116:3	235
116:6	226
116:8	235
116:8–9	235
136	44n22

Psalms (continued)

139	208
139:16	144
145:8	43

Proverbs

1:4	218
1:7	51, 218, 218n12
2:21–22	147
10:25	147
12:7	147
12:28	92
16:4	144n8
16:33	144n6
21:1	144n8
24:15–20	147

Ecclesiastes

3:11	300
3:19	93
8:17c	300
9:5	93
9:5–6	175
12:7	312

Isaiah

1.	161, 162, 165
1:2	161, 162
1:20	161
1:24	164
1:28	161, 165
1:31	162
1–39	160
2.	139n55
2:10	139n55
2:19	139n55
2:21	139n55
3:10–11	46
6:3	119, 140
9–10	91n3
11:9	140
13:19	91n3
20:2–4	97
20:5	97
24:6	136, 138
29:5–6	124
30:27	100–101
30:27–33	138
30:30	125
33:1	46
33:1–13	136
33:14	135, 171
33:16–24	136
34:3	167
34:10	31
35:18	92
36–37	31, 166
37:26	31
40:5	119
40:8	119
40–66	160
44:28	144n8
45:1–4	144n5
45:7	146
46:8	165
46:9–10	143, 144
47:3	97n28
48:8	165
52:11	133
53:5	103n62
56–66	160
59:18	164
60:1–3	137
60:11	137
60:19	126, 137
63:1–6	137
65	74
65:17	137
65:17–18	74
65:21	74
66	160, 161, 162, 163, 165
66:1	126
66:1–2	121, 138
66:1–5	136
66:1–6	162
66:2	163
66:3	163, 165
66:4	163, 165
66:5	163
66:6	164
66:14	108n94, 136, 138, 163, 164
66:15	138
66:15–16	101, 165
66:16	165, 169

66:17	163	18:23	93
66:18	126	18:32	93
66:18–19	138	20:47–48	30
66:18–23	164	23:26	97n28
66:22–24	137, 219	23:29	97n28
66:23	167	32:4	144n10
66:23–24	225	33:11	93
66:24	xxii, 31, 46, 135–36n52, 136, 138, 159–71, 214n1, 227–28, 229, 301	37	127
		37:26–27	133
		47:1–12	132–33

Jeremiah

Daniel

2:11	128	2:31–45	121
2:13	133	2:37	121
3.	47	2:38	121
5:19	46	2:44	121
7:30–34	138	3:25	126
7:31	168	4:23	226
7:31–33	169	6:22	144n10
7:32	169	7.	121
7:32–33	168	7:13	202n10
7:37–39	133	7:14	121
8:7	144n10	7:18	121
18:10–13	46	7:26–27	121
19:1–13	168	12:1–3	93n10
19:2–6	138	12:2	26, 102, 113, 116n10, 139, 230, 231, 233, 234
19:6–7	169		
25:27–33	138	12:3	139
25:31	164	12:12	114
30:16	46		
31:40	169		

Hosea

49:18	91n3	1–3	47n28
50:29	46	1:9	46
50:40	91n3	2:3	97
		2:4	46
		4:7	114

Lamentations

	47
3:37	144

Joel

2:13	43

Ezekiel

Amos

1:4–28	124	2:6	47
16:46–49	91n3	4:6–12	47–48n29
16:49	47	4:11	91n3
16:50	91n3	4:14–15	47–48n29
16:53	91n3	5:5–6	30
16:56	91n3		
18:4	99n44, 368		

Scripture and Ancient Works Index

Amos *(continued)*

14418	14418

Jonah

4:2	43

Nahum

1:37	147

Habakkuk

2:14	140
2:16	114
3:3–15	124
3:4	125

Zephaniah

2:9	91n3

Haggai

2.	137
2:6	137n53
2:13	108n94

Zechariah

13:9	230, 231, 232
14:8	133

Malachi

4:1	226
4:1–3	75, 136
4:1–6	30

NEW TESTAMENT

Matthew

2:29ff	76n14
3:7	186
3:8	186
3:10	172, 186
3:10–12	29, 240n31
3:12	30, 186, 263, 264
5:22	172, 214n3, 240n31, 240n32
5:29	172, 214n3
5:29–30	240n32, 241
5:30	172, 214n3
5:48	332
6:10	70
7:11	240n31
7:13	262
7:13, 14	29, 72
7:16	239
7:19	29, 186
7:24–27	239
8:11–12	195
10:15	91n3
10:28	18, 28, 46, 72, 116, 135–36n52, 139, 148, 169, 172, 196, 214n3, 214n5, 240–41n32, 262
11:20–23	241
11:23	193, 240–41n32
11:23–24	91n3
12:28	188n31
13	76
13:3–9	239
13:24–30	239
13:30	29
13:37–43	139
13:37–44	77
13:40–42	29
13:42	240n31
13:47–50	239
13:49, 50	29
13:49–50	139
13:50	240n31
16:18	193
16:21	103n63
18:8	30, 99n41, 240n31
18:9	214n3, 241
18:34, 35	29
21:23	188n31
21:33	239
22:1–10	239
22:2–15	236
22:11–14	239
22:13	237, 240
22:32	108n94
22:37–40	306
23:15	214n3, 240–41n32, 241
23:23	306
23:33	214n3
24:36	236

24:42–51	239	14:62	202n10
24:43	236		
25	364	## Luke	
25:1–13	236, 239		
25:10–12	237	1:37	144
25:12	237	2:9	118n16
25:13	236	3:9	186
25:14–30	239	3:9–17	240n31
25:30	214n2	3:17	263
25:31–46	33, 139, 172, 239	3:38	127
25:33	240–41n32	4:33–34	76n14
25:41	30, 99n41, 214n2	6:43–49	239
25:41–46	240, 240n31	6:47–49	239
25:46	30, 214n4, 242, 303, 364, 368–69	8:5–8	239
		8:52	116n10
26:2–3	239	9:22	103n63
27:52	175	9:26	114
27:53	176	9:54	126
28:12–14	239	10:12	91n3
		10:15	193, 240–41n32
## Mark		12:4–5	172
		12:5	214n3, 240–41n32
1.	77	12:10	208
1:15	188n31	12:13–34	119
1:21–28	75	12:32–48	239
1:34	75	12:36	236
3:29	30	12:39	236
4:3–9	239	12:46	236
4:26	188n31	12:54–56	239
5:7ff	76n14	13:3	214n5
8:11–13	239	13:6–9	239
8:31	103n63	13:7	186
9:43	214n3, 240n31, 263	13:22–30	239
9:43–45	240n32, 241	13:25–28	236
9:43–48	29, 172	13:27	237
9:44	170	13:27–28	237, 240
9:44–48	31	13:28	195
9:45	214n3	14:15–24	236
9:46	170	14:16–24	236, 239
9:47	214n3	14:17	236
9:47–48	46, 135–36n52	15:4–7	239
9:48	170, 170–71, 186n27, 214n1, 364	15:8–10	239
		15:11–32	239
12:1–9	239	16	194–95
12:19	214n5	16:1–18	301
12:27	108n94	16:19–31	172, 239
13:26–27	202n10	16:23	240–41n32, 241, 300
13:33–37	239	16:23–26	194
14:58	132	17:29	91n3

Luke (continued)

17:29–30	137
17:32–33	137
18:2–5	241
19:12–27	239
20:9–16	239
20:34–36	139
20:38	108n94
23:43	334n30
23:46	70n9

John

	xxii, 172–73
1:4	116
1:29	203n15
2:14–22	132
3:3	188, 188n31
3:5	182, 188, 188n31
3:13	33, 299, 303
3:16	28, 44, 178, 183, 185, 188, 214n5, 255, 261, 266, 299
3:36	179
4:7–24	132–33
4:15	186n28
4:49	176
5:21	177
5:21–29	140
5:24	173n2, 179, 181
5:25	176, 299
5:26	116, 252
5:28–29	113, 175, 176, 180, 266
5:29	178
5:29b	113
6.	281
6:12	177
6:15	186
6:26	186
6:27	177, 181n16, 185, 186
6:39	184
6:39–40	185
6:40	176
6:48	181
6:49	176
6:49–51	181
6:50	139, 181, 256
6:53	116
6:53–54	181
6:58	139
6:63	182
7:16–17	303
8:24	72, 184
8:30–31	105n75
8:51	173n2, 182
9:22	302
10:8	184n23
10:10	177, 184, 184n23, 185, 311, 315
10:11	175, 184
10:12	184
10:28	184
11:4	173n2
11:11	175
11:13	173n2
11:14	176
11:16	174
11:21	174
11:24	174
11:25	174–75, 179, 182
11:25–26	256, 273
11:26	139, 174–75, 182
11:31	174
11:32	174
11:33	174
11:50	177
12:1	177
12:17	176, 177
12:25	178, 184
12:34–36	135
12:42–43	302
14:6	72
14:19	180
14:22	178
15:1–8	185–86
15:16	144n7
17	37
17:2	183
17:5	140
17:12	184
21:14	177

Acts

1:6	133
1:7c	133
1:11	202n10
2.	197

Scripture and Ancient Works Index 397

2:22–23	144n8
2:29–31	197
2:34	33, 299, 303
3:20	139n55
3:21	66
4:27–28	144n8
7:24	130
7:25	130
7:59	70n9
7:60	175
10:34	300
10:43	105n75
13:36	116n10, 175
13:46	95
13:49	95
17:22–34	128
17:28	94
20:27	5
23:8	234
24:15	113
24–29	119

Romans

1–8	68
1:17	129
1:18–25	128
1:21	120
1:22–25	120
1:23	94, 128, 130
1:32	99n41
2:6–7	259
2:6–10	131
2:7	94, 95, 101, 107n90, 113, 114, 128, 129, 140
2:11	300
2:12	100n45
3:22	105n75
3:23	128
3:24	129
3:31	105n79
3:38	208
4–6	320
4:17	98, 105n75
4:25	319
5.	102
5:12–21	95n20, 101, 129
5:21	95
6:2	135
6:5	139
6:9	135, 139
6:21f	99n41
6:22	95
6:23	28, 72, 95, 129, 148, 189, 256, 299, 311, 312
7:5	99n41
8:6	99n41
8:9–11	140
8:10–11	129
8:11	120, 182
8:13	256
8:15	131
8:17–30	120, 129
8:18–23	124
8:18–28	68
8:18–30	140
8:19–22	117
8:21	67
8:23	96, 131
8:26	69
8:28	145
8:29	133
8:29–30	134
8:30	133
9:22	106n84
9:29	91n3
11:16	105
12:2	330
12:19	151
13.3	331
14:15	100n45
16:25–26	30

1 Corinthians

1.	330
1:18	100n45, 329
1:20	329
1:21	105n75
1:28	105n79
2:6	105n79
3:16	133
5:1–5	95
6:1–11	95
6:13	105n79
6:19	133
7:3–4	95
7:39	175

1 Corinthians (continued)

8:11	100n45
10:9	101n54
11:2–16	96
11:7	133
11:7–34	96
11:30	175
13	37
13:6	302
13:8	105n79
13:10	105n79
13:11	105n79
14:22	105n75
15	90, 97n29, 98, 102, 107, 112–15, 120
15:1–11	103–4
15:11	105n75
15:11–34	103
15:12–34	104–7
15:12–53	299
15:18	100n45, 116n10
15:20–28	321
15:21–23	127
15:21f	99n41
15:24	105n79, 121
15:24–28	118, 140, 150
15:26	105n79, 116, 201n8
15:28	27, 299, 322, 333
15:35–49	118
15:35–55	118n15
15:35–57	103, 107–11
15:35–58	107n92
15:40–49	133
15:42–50	127
15:42–55	140
15:44–49	128
15:45	127
15:45–49	320
15:45b	127
15:47–49	127
15:49	126
15:50	67
15:50–57	116
15:52–53	260
15:53–54	299
15:54–55	96
18:20	116n10

2 Corinthians

2:15	100n45
2:15–17	101
2:16	99n41
3:7–18	120
3:18	120, 133, 140
4:3	100n45
4:4–6	128
4:9	100n45
4:16	96
4:17	120
4:17–18	114
5:1–4	136
5:1–10	96, 97
5:5–6	96
5:17	131, 330
6:16–18	133
7:10	99n41

Galatians

1:4	135, 320
1:8	98n35
1:8–9	98
2:6	300
3.	37
4:5	131
5:19–21	183
6:7–8	98, 105n73
6:8	73, 95, 99, 99n39

Ephesians

1:5	131, 134
1:7	134
1:9–10	321
1:10	134
1:11	145
1:20–23	132
2:1	134
2:1–10	44
2:2–3	134
2:5	134
2:5–7	132
2:10	131, 144n7
2:11	131
2:15	132
2:15–17	105n79
2:16	131

2:19	131, 135
2:20	135
2:20–22	132
2:21	131
2:22	131
4:3–6	304
4:8–9	208
4:18	116, 134
4:24	132
5:5–6	102
5:22—6:9	132
5:27	133
6:9	300
6:12	135

Philippians

1:9	218
1:23	96n26
1:28	100n45, 102, 106n84
2:5–10	140
2:5–11	95n20, 106
2:6–11	121
2:8	102
2:9–11	27
2:12–13	144n7
3:10	139
3:10–11	135
3:11	139
3:19	100n45, 102, 106n84, 114
3:20–21	133
3:21	133

Colossians

1:12–13	134
1:13	135
1:14	134
1:15	127
1:15b	120
1:20	27, 134
1:27	134
2:13	134, 135
2:15	140
2:20	135
3:3	135
3:3–4	116
3:4	134
3:10	128, 131

| 3:25 | 300 |

1 Thessalonians

1:9–10	99
2:16	147
4:13–17	175
4:13–18	107
4:17	178
5:3	99, 106n84
5:10	320

2 Thessalonians

1–2	139
1:5–10	139
1:7	139
1:9	30, 99, 99n43, 106n84, 139n55, 262, 316
1:10	118n16, 139
2:1–4	139
2:3	106n84
2:3–4	100
2:5–11	100
2:8	100, 139
2:10	100n45
2:13–14	139

1 Timothy

1:10	107n90
1:11	114
1:16	95
1:17	94
2:4	333
4:7	131
4:8	131
4:9	131
4:10	131
6:9	100n45, 106n84
6:11–19	119
6:12	95
6:16	78, 94, 107n90, 299
6:17–19	131

2 Timothy

1:10	94, 113, 140, 259
2:13	147
3:16	191n2

Titus

1:2	95
2:13	118n16
3:7	95

Hebrews

1:3	118n16
1:3a	121
1:14	203n16
2:4	121
2:5–10	140
2:6	121
2:6–9	131
2:7–9	122
2:9	105n78, 121
2:9–11	114
2:10	131
2:14	140
2:14–15	135
3:1–6	130
3:3–6	130–31n40
5:9	30
6:2	30, 306
9:8–26	136
9:11a	136
9:12	30
9–12	136
9:24	136
9:27	199
10:1	136
10:2	266
10:12	136
10:13	136
10:26–27	264–65
10:27	136, 274
10:31	77
11:10	136
11:34a	126
11:35	139
12:18–29	136
12:22	136–37
12:25–29	136
12:26	137n53
12:28	136–37
12:29	266

James

1:9–12	119
1:15	28, 99n41
1:18	28
2:1	300
2:9	300
5:20	99n41

1 Peter

1:7c	119
1:22–25	119
2:5	133
2:9	130
3:10	67, 75
3:15–16	304
4:6	208
5:12–21	133–34

2 Peter

1:3–4	116
1:4	130
1:16–17	118n16
2:1—3:3	137
2–3	137
2:5	137
2:6	30, 31, 91n3, 136, 137
2:12	92n6, 99n39, 262
3:5–7	48
3:6	137
3:7	137, 138
3:7–13	137
3:9	101n54, 105n76, 133, 137, 333
3:12	137
3:13	137

1 John

	xxii, 172–73
1:1	315
2:17	258
3:2	118n16, 133
3:8	76
3:14	179, 181
3:15	182
4:7–16	44
4:18	51

5:12	183	20:11–15	200–201
5:16	99n41	20:13–15	266
5:16–17	183	20:14	174
		20:14–15	26

2 John

	xxii, 172–73
1:8	178

20–22	202
21	137
21:3	140
21:4	322
21:5	79, 133
21:8	73, 99n41, 139, 174, 201n9
21:9	133
21:22	133
21:22–27	140
21:27	201n9
22:3	79
22:5	126, 202n12
22:15	201n9

3 John

	xxii, 172–73

Jude

3.	113, 245
4–18	137
7.	30, 91n3, 99n41, 137
24	133

Revelation

	xxii, 31, 79, 117, 173–74, 369
1:12–16	137
1:17–18	320
1:18	191, 192–93, 196, 199
2.	73
2:11	99n41, 174
4:1	70
5:6	203n14
6:7–8	200
6:10	27
6:15–16	139n55
11:8	91n3
14	99n41
14:6	113
14:9–11	201–4, 210
14:10–11	29
14:11	28, 31, 147
14:14	201
14:14–20	137–38
19:11–16	137, 147
19:13–16	149
19:17–21	138
19:20	299
20	364
20:6	26, 99n41, 251
20:9	126
20:10	29, 299

SEPTUAGINT

Numbers

21:3	98

Joshua

6:17	98
7:12	98

Judges

1:17	98

Psalms

8:5–6	122
8:6	105n78
110:1	105n78

Isaiah

22:13	107n89

Daniel

4:30b	97n28

Galatians

1:8–9	98

Hebrews

2:7–9	122
2:9	105n78

APOCRYPHA / DEUTEROCANONICAL TEXTS

1 Esdras

1:24 [22]	218
3:10–26	102
7:117–119	102

2 Esdra

2:8	91n3

3 Maccabees

2:5	91n3

Judith

16:17	7, 170, 218, 224, 242

Letter of Jeremiah

1:41	218n12

Sirach

7:17	170
17	93n11
17:27–28	93
17:30	93
22:12	93

Testament of Reuben

6:3	99

Wisdom of Solomon

1:15	108n93
7:1–6	93–94

PSEUDOEPIGRAPHA

1 Enoch

	219
10:13	215, 216
10:13–15	215, 224n19
10:13–16	216
21:3	215
21:6	216
21:7	215
21:10	216
22:2	215
22:11	216
27	168
27:1	216
38:5–6	216
46:4–6	216
54:1	215
54:1–5	216
69:27	76n16
91:1	224n19
91:9	215, 216
103:7	215
103:10	216
108:4–5	215
108:5	216

4 Ezra

7:75–101	217

Jubilees

7.28	218
7.29	218
22.22–23	218
36:10	224n19
36.10	218

DEAD SEA SCROLLS

1CD (Damascus Document)

	220
2:6	220
2.5	220
2.6	224n19

Scripture and Ancient Works Index 403

1QHa (Thanksgiving Hymn)

	220
4:19	220
4:25	220
14:21–22	220
14.21	224n19

1QM (War Rule)

	220
14:17–18	220
14:18	239

1QS (Community Rule)

	220
1:10	220
2:7	220
2:7–15	220–21
2:8	220
2:12–17	221
2:15	220, 238
2.15	224n19
4:12	220, 238
4:12–14	238
4:13–17	220
4:14	220, 221, 238
4.14	224n19
5:13	238
5.13	224n19

4Q174

fl_3ii:1	220, 224n19

4Q223–224

f2ii:52-iii:1	218n11

4Q257

5:12–13	238

4Q286

f7ii:7	238
f7ii:10	221, 224n19, 238

4Q287

f6:4	220
f6:9	221

4Q418

f69ii:4–8	238
f69ii:6	224n19
f69ii:7	220
f69ii:8	224n19

4Q491

f1_3:4	220
fl_3:4	224n19, 238

4Q496

f3:5	220, 224n19, 238

Hodayot

	220

Pesherim

	220

PHILO OF ALEXANDRIA

On the Creation

XLVI, 135	94n15

JOSEPHUS

Jewish Antiquities

18.12–17	234

Jewish War

2:163–66	234

MISHNAH

Eduyyoth

2.10	225

Parah

1.1	222

Scripture and Ancient Works Index

Sanhedrin

10.1	225
10.3	232n24

Shabbat

1.4	234

Yadayim

4.6	235n28

TOSEPHTA

Sanhedrin

13.1	226, 228, 229
13.1–5	225
13.2	226, 228, 229
13.3	226, 229, 230, 232n24, 234
13.4	227, 228, 229
13.5	227, 228, 229

BABYLONIAN TALMUD

Baba Batra

115b-116a	235n28

Berakhot

4:2	223
28b	237
I.2	223

Menahoth

65ab	235n28

Rosh Hashana

17a	228, 235

Shabbat

153a	236

Sibylline Oracles

1.101	217
1.103	217
2.292	217
2.303	217
2.303–12	217
2.305	217
2.312	217
2.332	217
2.344	217
4.186	217
4.43	217
94–106	217n10

Yohana ben Zakkai

ARNb.31

b.31	235n28

b.RH 16b-17a

	224n18

Sanhedrin

1.19b-d	235n28
1.2–4	235n28

CLASSICAL AUTHORS

Plato

Phaedo	248, 249

GREEK AND LATIN TEXTS

Ambrose

Of the Holy Spirit

3.44	100n47

Anselm

"Fifth Meditation"

66	256

Anti-Nicene Fathers

1411	135

Apostles' Creed

	143, 143n2

Athenagoras of Alexandria

Apology

    248

Treatise on the Resurrection

    248

Augustine

The City of God

21.3	270–71
21.4	266
21.9.2	266
Book XXI	249

The City of God

20.19.2	100n45

Catechetical Lectures

15:9	100n45

Chrysostom

Homilies on 2 Thessalonians 3

    100n45

Cyril of Alexandria

    166

Cyril of Jersalem

Catechetical Lectures

15.9	100n45

"The Catechetical Lecutres"

NPNF 7:139	265

Irenaeus

The Demostration of the Apostlic Preaching

72. 133	119n18

Against Heresies

2.34.2	119n17
2.34.3	135

Jerome

Isaiah 40–66

291	166

Lactantius

"The Divine Institutions"

217	263

Nicene Creed

    143

Origen of Alexandria

On First Principles

2.3.2	110n104
preface	327–28

A Select Library of the Nicene and Post-Nicene Fathers of the Christian Church

2:453	270–71
2:454	266
2:461	266

Tertullian

The Prescription aganist Heretics

7.	248n27

Thomas Aquinas

The Catecheical Instructions of St. Thomas Aquinas

Article 11	265

Summa Contra Gentiles

    250

Summa Theologica

82

Thomas More

Utopia

251

Westminster Confession of Faith

2.2 144

PROTESTANT AUTHORS

Athanasian Creed

143

Calvin, John

Commentaries on the Epistle of Paul the Apostle to the Hebrews

123n21

Institutes of the Christian Religion

193 252n54

Psychopannychia

251
454–455 115n5

Tracts Relating to the Reformation

414	251n45*46, 251n49
415	251n47
416	251n48
436	252n51
439	252n52
443–44	252n56
446	251n50

Treatises Against the Anabaptists

33	253n57
33–34	253n58
34	253n59
119	251n44

127 252n53

Edwards, Jonathan

"A History of the Work of Redemption"

265

"The Justice of God in the Damnation of Sinners"

82–83

"The Salvation of All Men Strictly Examined"

230 260

The Wrath of the Almighty

356 149n17

Locke, John

On the Reasonableness of Christianity

330

Luther, Martin

"Assertio Omnium Articulorum M. Lutheri per Bullam Leonis X, Novissi Damnitorum

article 27, 131–132 115n5

Simons, Menno

The Complete Works of Menno Simmons

273 258

Spurgeon, Charles

The New Park Street Pulpit Sermons

22 258

Sermons of the Rev. C. H. Spurgeon, 2nd series
275   265

Sermons of the Rev. C. H. Spurgeon, 4th series
217   258

Wesley, John

Explanatory Notes upon the New Testament
758   257

Whitefield, George

The Christian's Companion
170–71   258

Subject Index

A

Abihu, 126
Abraham, 41–42
Adam
    as living being, 108–9, 127
    loss of glory of God, 128–29
    original sin, 102, 105
    as representative of fallen man, 127–34
Advent Christians, 344
Adventism, 253, 354
advertising campaigns, 347
afterlife
    biblical exegesis on, 326–29
    minority readings of scripture on, 330–31
    speculation in forming views, 325–27
    theses guiding debates among traditionalists, conditionalists, and universalists, 325–38.
    See also annihilation; eternal torment; Hades; hell; immortality; judgment
aggadah (Jewish discussions), 221, 222
ahab (love), 44n19
aiōnios (eternal), 30, 33, 73, 99n41
a'isqhsei (*understanding*), 218, 242
aiwuios (eternal). *See aiōnios* (eternal)
Akiba, 224
Alcorn, Randy, 264
Allen, Jimmy, 49
ambivalent passages, 301

American evangelism, 9, 11
Anabaptists, 251, 252, 253, 354
anakainos (continuous renewal), 131
Anastasis fresco, Chora, Istanbul, 208
anathema (cursed), 98
Anderson, Joshua W., 14
anistēmi/ anastasis (resurrection), 176
Ankerberg, John, 22, 256
annihilation
    acceptance of, 352
    Akiba's belief concerning, 224
    biblical framework for, 112–16
    biblical texts supporting, 266
    concepts of in Greek, 99n42–43, 100
    conditionalists' view of, 257–59
    of death, 103, 107–11
    distinction between conditional immortality and, 58n17
    evangelical adherents, 21–25
    evangelical message and, 313
    evangelical opposition to, 21–22, 24
    as expression of God's wrath, 361–62
    Fudge's view of, xxi, 20
    implication concerning character of God, 333
    as infinite punishment, 84, 366
    Pauline evidence for, 99–102
    philosophical advantages of, 84–85
    references in Apocalyptic Judaism, 216
    references in Qumran Judaic texts, 220–21, 238

410   Subject Index

annihilation *(continued)*
  references to in Rabbinic literature, 229
  as shameful disinheritance, 135–40
  Stott's defense of, 58
  Tiessen's journey to, 19–31
  traditional gatekeepers against, 341–42
  traditional view of, 18–21, 262–64
  use of the term, 14, 18–19, 66.
  See also conditional immortality
    terminal punishment
Anselm, Saint, 81, 86, 256, 300
Ante-Nicene fathers, 248
anthrōpoktonos (murder), 182
anthropologic monism, 95–98
aparche (first fruits), 105
Apocalyptic Judaism, 215–19, 229, 230
apocalyptic literature, 301
Apocrypha, 93–94, 99
Apollinarianism, 290
apollumi (to kill, destroy)/ *apōleia* (loss, destruction), 100n48, 106n84, 177, 178, 180, 183–85, 187, 214
apothnēskō (to die), 174, 180, 181, 182, 183
Appleman, Hyman, 257
appolumenois (destroy, kill), 101n54
Arianism, 354
Aristotelianism, 250
Arnobius, 244
Athanasius (bishop of Alexandria), 248
Athenagoras of Alexandria, 248
Atkinson, Basil, 12, 22
Augustine, Saint, 5, 7, 85–86, 249, 267, 270

B

Bacchiocchi, Samuele, 92, 95, 97n26
Baird, Joseph Arthur, 285
baptism for the dead, 106, 114
Barker, William, 56
Barth, Karl, 4n2, 8
basanismos/brasanos (torment), 202
Bassler, Jouette M., 103n60, 106n85

Bauckham, Richard, xxi, 12, 14, 116–17, 327, 340
Bauer, Walter, 100, 105n79
Bawulski, Shawn, 85, 291
Baxter, Richard, 260, 265
Belgic Confession, Article 37, 260
believers. *See* righteous souls
Bell, Rob, 35, 266, 292
Bell, W. F., 35
Berding, Kenneth, 345
Beyond the Gates (Phelps), 9n7
Bible Student movement, 354
biblical cosmology. *See* Hebraic cosmology
biblical language, 361–63
biblical literacy, 345
biblical obstacles to acceptance, 300–301
biblical theology
  chesed of God and, 43–45
  core of, 41–43
  definition of, 39–40
  method of, 190–92
  story of God, 40–41
Biola Magazine, 345
Blackwell, Ben C., 128, 129n35, 130
Blain, Jacob, 352, 353, 369
Blanchard, John, 59
Blocher, Henri, 60, 271
Bloesch, Donald, 207
blogs, 346
Boa, Kenneth, 270
body
  Greek view of, 70
  redemption of, 96–97
  of resurrected beings, 107–11, 133, 260, 263, 265, 266
  soul's connection to, 95. *See also* death
Bowles, Ralph, xxiiii, 28, 202, 307–23
Bowman, Robert, 270
Boyd, Gregory, xxi, 326–27, 333
Boys, John, 272
Brandyberry, James, xxii–xxiii, 243–54
Brenneman, Todd, 9
Bride of Christ, 96
broadcast media, 346

Brow, Robert, 8n4
Brown, Colin, 58
Bruce, F. F.
  on eternal life, 181n16–17
  forward to Fudge's books, 54, 55, 58
  on John 6, 39, 185n25
  on kingdom of God, 188n31
  letters to Fudge, xxi, 54
  on mortal man, 95
  on resurrection, 107, 110n105
  students of, 57, 58
  view of conditionalism, 285
Buckareff, Andrei A., 207

C

Caiaphas, 177
Cain, 91
callousness, 88–89
Calvary Chapel Deer Park statement of faith, 261
Calvin, John
  on basis of Christian arguments, 5
  critique of, 245
  discussion of baptism, 8
  Fudge's refutation of, 7
  on immortal soul and hell, 70n9, 115, 250–53, 354
  on theatre of divine glory, 122
  training as lawyer, 12
Campbell, Constantine, 320
Canaanite genocide, 48
capital punishment, 295–96
Carson, D. A., 87, 184, 188n32
"Case against Conditionalism, The" (Harmon), 59–60
Centrality of the Resurrection, The (Griffin), 34
chesed (lovingkindness) of God, 43–45, 51–52
Christadelphians, 302
Christian apologists, 329–30
Christianity Today
  advertisement for *The Fire That Consumes*, 56–57
  articles by Fudge in, xx
  hearing for conditionalism, 243
  as means of promotion of conditionalism, 13
  as mirror of evangelicalism, 20
  review of *The Fire That Consumes*, xxi
  Zens article refuting Fudge, 33
Christian philosophers, 329–30
Christians. *See* righteous souls
Christ Minimized? (Zens), 35
Christology, 290–91
christosis (life in Christ), 116
Churches of Christ (COC), 296
COC. *See* Churches of Christ (COC)
Code, Lorraine, 4, 11
conditional evangelism
  attitude necessary for, 359–60
  biblical conviction as basis of, 360–63
  consistent and confident gospel of, 311–12
  false hopes of universalism vs., 312–15
  focus on essentials, 357–58
  focus on renewal of creation, 321–23
  framing of the gospel, 315–19
  implications of, 366
  need for re-examination of early church fathers, 365
  as part of the evangelical family, 356–60
  resurrection as central to gospel, 319–21
  statement of, 351
  supplementary arguments for, 365–66
  use of biblical language, 361–63
  use of persuasive conviction, 363–69. *See also* conditional immortality/conditionalism
conditional immortality/conditionalism
  acceptance of, 243–44, 285–88
  advice for future path of, 282–93, 305–6
  articulation and promotion of, 350–370
  association with Jehovah's Witnesses and Adventism, 7, 19, 254, 264, 302, 344, 354, 357

conditional immortality/conditionalism *(continued)*
  bad arguments for, 368–69
  biblical obstacles to acceptance, 295, 300–301
  challenges to teaching of, 341–45, 351–53
  concerns about present followers, 280–82
  contemporary reactions to, 244–46, 294–95
  as controversial doctrine, 115–16
  definition of, xxi, 309–10
  description of traditionalist view of hell, 48–49, 50
  distinguishing between annihilation and, 58n17
  distinguishing between scholarly and popular descriptions, 335
  doctrinal obstacles to acceptance, 295, 299–300
  ecumenical creeds on, 6
  evangelical opposition to, 21
  evangelism and, 310–323
  Fudge's contribution to, xxi, xxiiii, 348
  general knowledge of, xxiii, 3–4, 344–45, 350–53
  history of, 348
  Hughes argument for, 24
  implications of, 26–28, 69–70, 129–30, 142, 150–51, 289–92, 340, 366
  Jacoby's journey to acceptance of, 297–98
  message of, 348–49
  method for teaching, 345–48
  as minority view, 340
  motivation for belief in, 336–37
  need for philosophical contributions, 80–82
  in nineteenth century evangelism, 10, 353–56
  as orthodox and evangelical view, 337–38
  philosophical problems with traditionalism, 82–89
  psychological obstacles to acceptance, 295, 301–2
  reestablishment of in Reformation, 250
  reevaluation of related doctrines, 289–92
  rejection of, 9–12
  revival of, 254
  root of opposition to, 246–54
  scriptural foundation of, 28–29, 46
  strategy for affecting acceptance of, 12–15, 302–5, 350–370
  support of, 8–9, 11–12, 58
  theocentricity of, 94
  Tiessen's journey to, 19–31
  traditionalists' response to, 244, 268, 311, 313, 341–42
  two kinds of resurrection, 129
  use of the term, 14–15, 18, 66
  view of death of Jesus, 290–91
  view of hell, 324
  view of soul and death, 116, 207. *See also* annihilation; conditionalist evangelism; terminal punishment
Conditionalist Faith of Our Fathers, The (Froom), 244, 365
conferred immortality, 66
Constable, Henry, 67, 285
Constantine, 248
consuming fire, 220–21
contemporary reactions, 244–46
content-specific forums, 346
Continuing Sin Thesis (CST), 86–89
corporal punishment, 295–96
corruption, 124, 128–29. *See also* death; sin
cosmic disinheritance, 135–40
cosmic temple, 121–24
cosmology. *See* Hebraic cosmology
cosmos. *See* creation
Craig, William Lane, 269–700
Cramer, David, xxiiii, 324–38
creation
  continuity and discontinuity in concept of, 116–17
  as God's temple, 130
  praise of God, 122

Subject Index   413

redemption of, 120, 140
renewal of, 66–79, 116–18, 120,
    140, 321–23
Crisp, Tom, 288
Criswell Theological Review, 24, 58
Crofford, Gregory, 194, 206, 208, 210
Crouch, Andy, 13
crown of life, 119
cruelty, 88–89
Cryderman, Lyn, 56
Cullmann, Oscar, 33
cultural mandate, 122–23
culture, 287
culture of vengeance, 342–43
Curtis, O. A., 207
Cyril of Jerusalem, 265

D

damned. *See* unbelievers
    wicked
Daniel, 102n58
Dante Alighieri, 300
darkness, kingdom of, 134–35
Dark Side of Destiny, The (Crofford),
    210
Date, Christopher M., xix–xxiiii, 14,
    25, 269, 274, 350–70
David (king of Israel), 43, 230, 233
Davis, Stephen T., 207
Dawkins, Richard, 282
the dead
    baptism for, 106, 114
    location of before resurrection,
        201–4, 207, 210, 297, 299
    status of before resurrection,
        115–16, 295, 299. *See also* annihilation; glorification; judgment;
        resurrection; death
    as absence of life, 33–34, 188
    annihilation of, 94, 105–7, 110–11,
        113, 120, 259
    in Apocrypha, 93–94
    contrasted with eternal life, 180–83
    doctrine of as final chance, 204–5
    as end of sin, 154, 315–16
    as end of the sinner, 72–75, 91–92,
        99, 100

entrance into the world, 91, 102,
    105, 127, 316
as eternal punishment, 368–69
as expression of God's wrath,
    361–62
Greek view of, 69, 94n15, 116
intermediate state, 115–16, 295,
    299. *See also* Hades; Sheol
interplay between temporal and
    eschatological death, 174–76,
    188–89
of Jesus Christ, 44, 113, 134–35,
    136, 174, 290–91, 317–19,
    334–35, 361, 363, 365
Jesus' triumph over, 140
John's depiction of, 173–78
judgment of, 200–201
in Old Testament, 92–93
Paul's view of, 69, 98–102
Philo on, 94n15
as punishment for sin, 362
relationship to worship, 92–94
as result of sin, 72–73, 74–75, 91,
    98–102, 135–40, 146–48, 189,
    256, 312, 314
resurrection preceded by, 107–8
as separation, 116, 315–16
sowing of the body, 114
traditional definition of, 116
universality of, 91–98, 105, 111. *See
    also* Hades
"Death and Resurrection in Scripture"
    (W. F. Bell), 35
Death and the Afterlife (Morey),
    244–45
*Death not Life
    or the Destruction of the Wicked*
    (Blain), 352
Demler, Ronnie, xxiiii, 255–76,
    351–52, 353
demons, 75–76
destroy, 46
destruction, 98–102
"Destruction of the Finally Impenitent, The" (Pinnock), 58
Deutero-Isaiah, 160
Dickinson's Theological Quarterly,
    355–56, 363, 364

disobedience. *See* sin
diversity of audience, 341, 367–68
Divine Comedy, The (Dante), 300
divine nature, 129–30
divine punishment, 45–48, 146–48.
　See also annihilation; eternal torment; hell; terminal punishment
Divine Rescue, The (Fudge), xx
divine sovereignty
　biblical witness to, 143–45
　evil and, 145–46
　punishment for sin and, 146–53
　restoration of all things and, 153–55
doctrinal obstacles to acceptance, 299–300
dogmatics, 40n6
"Do the Flames Ever Stop in Hell" (Zens), 33
doxa (glory), 118–24, 128–29. *See also* glory
Driscoll, Mark, 259
Dryden, J. de Waal, 131–32
dualism
　of eternal kingdoms, 333. *See also* traditionalism
　Paul's refutation of, 95–98
　Philo's belief in, 94n15
　view of body and soul, 18, 70–71, 78, 95, 116, 117, 175–76, 246–47, 249, 299, 343

E

early church fathers, 365. *See also* Scripture Index
ecumenical creeds
　affirmation of, 356
　Anabaptists' stand on, 251
　consideration of alternative views and, 304
　doctrinal confusion established by, 300
　lack of position on fate of unbelievers, 28
　Plato's influence on, 248
　as source for arguments, 6
　on sovereignty of God, 143
Edwards, David L., 11, 22, 27, 58

Edwards, Jonathan
　on death and hell, 50, 51, 82–83, 260, 265, 270
　evidence in arguments of, 8
　Infinite Seriousness Thesis, 86
　influence of, 51, 291, 341
egeirō/egersis (resurrection), 176
Eichrodt, Walther, 41
Eliezer ben Hyrcanus, 226, 232n24
Elisha, 69–70
Ellis, E. Earle, 98, 106n84
enemies of God. *See* unbelievers wicked
Erickson, Millard, 290
eschatology
　renewal of creation, 66–79, 116–18, 321–23
　salvation linked to, 95, 128, 129
　theophanies, 124–26, 136
　works-oriented realization of, 132. *See also* annihilation; conditional immortality; hell; holistic eschatology; judgment; New Heavens, New Earth; *parousia*; resurrection; Second Coming
Eskridge, Larry, 9
eternal glory, 114, 118–19
eternal life. *See* immortality
eternal torment
　background to Jesus' teaching, 213–15
　believers and unbelievers' view of, 36–37, 51
　change in thinking concerning, 279–80
　character of God vs., 43–48, 88–89, 204–5
　conditionalists' view of, 30–31, 257–58
　elements that don't fit, 71–74
　as factor in acceptance of universalism, 343
　as factor in rejection of Christianity, 340
　Gospels on, 239–41, 242
　Greek influence on concept of, 29, 33, 38

implication concerning character of God, 333
incorporation of concept into Christianity, 246–53
infinite evil problem, 85–87
infinite punishment problem, 83–85
influencing thinking about, 302–5
lack of Scriptural evidence for, 6, 191
problematic status principle, 82–83, 85, 86, 300
problem of cruelty, malice, and callousness, 88–89
problem of injustice, 87–88
proportionality of punishment vs., 205–6
Qumran Judaism on, 238–39
Rabbinic theology concerning, 230–34
references in Apocalyptic Judaism, 216–19
Scriptural proof text, 201
traditional evangelical teaching on, 308, 310–12
traditionalists' understanding of, 18–21, 255–57, 258–66
traditional understanding of, 256–76, 309, 310, 315
Yohanan ben Zakkai's view of, 223–24. *See also* hell; second death
eternity, 363
Eternity magazine, 243
evangelical affirmations conference, 20–23
Evangelical Book Club, xxi, 57, 58, 244
Evangelical Essentials (Stott), 58, 244
evangelicalism
annihilation doctrine and, 20–21
competing views within, 337
conditional immortality teaching in, 310–323
conditionalists' identification with, 356–60
core biblical truths, 309
crucicentric movement, 319

definition of, 309
diversity of audience, 341
factors preventing reconsideration of doctrine of hell, 9
focus and motivation of, 332
in nineteenth century evangelism, 10, 353–56
Reformed tradition as basis of, 8
teaching on hell, 307–9
view of conditionalism, 20–21, 285–86
view of universalism, 23. *See also* conditional evangelism
Evangelicalism (Hunter), 10n8
"Evangelicals and the Way of Salvation" (Packer), 21
Evangelical Theological Society, 13
Evangelical Theology Group of AAR, 13
Evangelical Universalist, The (Parry), 337, 366
evil
extinction of, 66–79, 133, 299
God's sovereignty and, 145–46
exile of Jews, 43, 45–47
exodus, 42–43, 181
experience, 209–10

F

Faber, Frederick, 260
Fackre, Gabriel, 207
Fairbairn, Donald, 130
faithful followers. *See* righteous souls
fall of man, 91, 102, 105, 122, 127, 316
Fee, Gordon D., 103n64, 106
Fernandes, Phil, 269
Fire That Consumes, The (Fudge)
criticism of, 59–60
on eschatology as aspect of Christology, 333–34
forward to, 55, 58, 327
hermeneutical principles in, 5–7
influence of, xxi, 3–4, 7–12, 20–21, 24, 32, 35, 308
larger context of, 9–12
promotion of, 12–15
quotes from church fathers, 365
Rabbinic sources, 221

Fire That Consumes, The (Fudge) (continued)
- reevaluation of doctrine of hell, 141–42
- as standard apologetic work on conditionalism, 346
- style of, 4–5, 38
- success of, 56–58, 60–61, 244, 244n2
- summary of issues of debate on personal eschatology, 324
- third edition of, 53
- weakness of, 7–9

First Enoch, 215–16. *See also* Scripture Index
First Isaiah, 160
Flechtner, J., 99n40
flood, 41n13, 48, 91, 137
Flowers, David D., 35
Ford, Demond, 56–57
forgiveness of sins, 134–35, 317–19
Forsyth, P. T., 207, 319
Free Grace Broadcaster, 33
Froom, LeRoy Edwin, 12, 244–45, 254, 365
Fudge, Edward William
- advice to Tiessen, 26
- on Anabaptists, 251
- on attacks on conditionalism, 354
- on biblical interpretation, 326–27
- on Calvin, 253
- on Christian apologists, 329–30
- commendation of post-mortem salvation, 210
- contribution to discussion of hell, xxiii, 17, 38–39, 280, 283, 285, 348
- credentials of, 12
- criticism of, 49
- equating hell and Gehenna, 195
- on eschatology as aspect of Christology, 333–34
- as evangelical, 338
- on evangelicals avoidance of final punishment, 354–55
- on grace of God, xix
- Hell
  - A Final Word, 191, 364
- influence of, xix, xxiii, 20–21, 24, 30–31, 32, 35, 38, 297, 308, 323
- on intermediate state, 115
- jigsaw metaphor, 191
- legacy of, 15–16
- letters to, 54–61
- on level of certainty for adoption of views, 325–26
- on motivation for evangelism, 332
- on parable of Lazarus, 47
- personality of, xix–xx, 54, 65
- promotion of theology of, 12–15
- quotes from church fathers, 365
- recognition of his contributions, xxi–xxii, xxiii, 53–54, 254, 351
- reevaluation of doctrine of hell, 141, 205
- reference to Isaiah 66 24, 159
- on status of doctrine of hell, 338
- style of writing, 4–7
- summary of issue of debate on personal eschatology, 324
- treatment of universalism, 336–37
- view of Christ's death, 334–35
- view of hell, xxi, 78
- works of, xx, xxi. *See also Fire That Consumes, The* (Fudge); *Hell and Mr. Fudge* (film)

Fulbert, Saint, 209
fundamentalist-modernist controversy, 10

G

Gaffin, Richard, 34
Galli, Mark, 13
Gamaliel, 226
Gates Ajar, The (Phelps), 9n7
Gehenna
- compared to winepress, 138
- Hades distinct from, 195–96, 204
- Jesus' description of, 34–35, 46
- judgment of wicked at, 168–69
- as lake of fire, 200
- length of punishment in, 224–25, 227–28, 229, 240
- as place of the dead, 219

references to in Rabbinic literature, 222, 227, 228, 229, 241
translation of, 18
use of term in Sibylline Oracles, 217
Geisler, Norman, 263, 266
Gentiles, 225, 226–28, 229
Gerhard, Johann, 272
Gerstner, John, 59, 60, 245–46, 341–42
Getz, Gene, 55–56
Gill, John, 256, 265
Global Dictionary of Theology, 24
glorification, 34, 133–34, 138–40
glory
  of God, 120, 128–29
  of Jesus Christ, 119–20, 131, 140
  judgment theophanies, 124–26
  life and image associated with, 120, 133
  link to immortality, 114, 118–19
  man's glorification, 138–40
  man's loss and regaining of, 122, 128–29
  man's worship and, 122
  spectrum of expression of, 118–19, 120
  temple associated with, 118–24
God
  adoption of believers, 131
  believers' participation in life of, 116
  biblical description of, 40–41
  character of vs. eternal torment, 204–5
  Christians' relationship with, 315–21
  desire for all to repent, 206–7
  establishment of kingdom of, 121
  glory of, 120, 128–29
  holiness of, 44
  immortality of, 94
  judgment of wicked, 164–67, 171. *See also* hell; judgment
  justice of and divine punishment, 44, 45–48
  love of, 43–45, 51
  patience of, 287
  plan of, 120, 140, 321–23
  promise of restoration, 153–55
  relationship to creation, 108n93
  rule of, 70
  self-revelation of, 39, 41–43
  as source of life, 91, 119
  sovereignty of, 143–55
  theophanies of, 124–26, 136, 138–40, 165
  triumph of, 299, 364
  view of death, 93
  wrath of, 47n29, 361–62
God Delusion, The (Dawkins), 283
God's Forever Family (Eskridge), 9
Goldingay, John, 91–92
Gombis, Timothy G., 132
good and necessary consequences of beliefs, 331
Goodness of God, The (Wenham), 8, 55, 291
good works, 131–32
Gorman, Michael, 96, 97, 104, 130
gospel, 113, 114
Gospel Coalition, 13
Gospels, 18, 239–41. *See also* Scripture Index
Goss, Leonard George, 57
Graham, Billy, 55, 57, 259, 261
Great Divorce, The (Lewis), 207
Greek philosophy
  belief in immortal soul, 29, 33, 94n15, 246–49, 299
  dualism of, 70–71, 78, 116, 117, 175–76, 246, 249
  influence on concept of hell, 29, 38
  influence on doctrine of Trinity, 33
  view of redemption, 69
Green, Joel, 91, 108, 109n99
Green, Michael, 11, 285
Gregory of Nyssa, 337
Grew, Henry, 353–54, 356, 357
Grice, Peter, xxii, 112–40
"Guide Me O Thou Great Redeemer" (Williams), 209
Guthrie, Donald, 133

H

Hades

Hades *(continued)*
    emptying of at last judgment, 200–201
    Gehenna distinct from, 195–96, 204
    as hell, 241
    Jesus' possession of keys to, 198–200
    Jesus' references to, 193–94
    judgment of, 200–201
    in Luke 16, 194–95
    proportionality of punishment in, 206
    as realm of the dead, 200, 201–4, 207, 210, 297, 299
    in Revelation 1
    18, 192–93, 196, 199
    as Sheol, 197
    translation of, 300
Hagar, 91
Hagenbach, K. R., 33
halakhah (rulings on obedience), 221–22
Hamilton, Victor P., 167
Hannah, 230, 232, 233
Hanson, Paul D., 162
happōsh'im (ones who rebelled), 165–67
Harmon, Kendall, 59–60
Harper, Roger, xxii, 190–210
Harrowing of Hell, The (MacCulloch), 207
Hasel, Gerhard F., 40, 41
heaven, 69–70, 71, 122, 126
"Heaven to Earth
    The Believer's Hope in the Resurrection" (Flowers), 35
Hebraic cosmology, 118–24
hell
    Apocalyptic Judaism's terminology, 215–19
    change in thinking concerning, 279–80
    church members search for understanding of, 50–51
    conditionalist view of, 319, 324
    description in Isaiah 66
    24, 159–71
    as divine punishment, 146–53
    elements that don't fit, 71–74
    as essential topic for evangelism, 307–9
    as expression of God's wrath, 361–62
    extinction of evil, 66–79
    as factor in rejection of Christianity, 340
    Fudge's view of, xxi, 20
    Gehenna as, 200–201
    Greek influence on concept of, 38
    infinite evil problem, 85–87
    new Rabbinic theology concerning a third group, 230–34
    place of, 168–69
    popular problem with, 36–38
    problematic status principle, 82–83
    problem of cruelty, malice, and callousness, 88–89
    problem of injustice, 87–88
    problem of language about, 48–51
    problem of restoration in traditionalist view, 153–55
    problems of divine sovereignty in traditionalist view, 146–53
    Qumran Judaism's view of, 220–21
    Rabbinic sources concerning, 221–37
    as secondary issue for evangelism, 357
    Tertullian's view of, 248
    traditional evangelical teaching on, 308, 310–12
    traditional understanding of, xx–xxi, 18–21, 25–26, 48–50, 66–67, 71, 109n103, 141, 147–48, 255–68, 309, 310, 315, 324
    universalist view of, 324–25
    use of the term, 17–18
    Yohanan ben Zakkai's view of, 235–37. *See also* annihilation; conditional immortality/conditionalism; eternal torment; terminal punishment
*Hell
    A Final Word* (Fudge), 191, 346

Subject Index   419

Hell and Mr. Fudge (film), xx, 38, 53, 192, 205, 347
Hellbound? (film), 347
Hell Under Fire (Zondervan), xxi, 37
Henry, Carl, 20, 21
Highfield, Ron, xix
Hillelites, 230–37
historical theology, method of, 191
Hitchens, Christopher, 282
Hodge, Charles, 273
Hoekema, Anthony, 252
holistic eschatology, 116–18
holy angels, 202, 203, 204
Holy Spirit
　changing views of hell and, 50–51
　as giver of life, 97, 99, 182
　intercession of, 69
　as living water building the temple, 133
　role in creation, 78–79
　role in redemption, 69
Homer, 246
Homespun Gospel (Brenneman), 9
honor
　of Jesus Christ, 131
　link between immortality and, 114
　mans fall from, 122
Hopkins, Gerard, 266
hormah (destruction), 98n37
Horton, Michael, 13
hoton, 105n77
Howson, Peter, 208
Hughes, Philip Edgecumbe
　belief in dualism, 115
　as conditionalist, 21, 22, 244
　on doctrine of man, 115n7, 128
　response to criticism of annihilationism, 245
　support of conditionalism, 11
　view of hell, 23–24
humans. *See* man
Hunter, James Davidson, 10n8
Huntington, William, 355–56, 363
Hyatt, Darlene, 101n56

I

ICOC. *See* International Churches of Christ (ICOC)

idolatry, 120
image
　glory associated with, 120, 133
　of God in man, 121–23, 122n19, 127–28, 133–34
　Jesus as image of God, 127–28
imago Dei, 121–23, 122n19, 127–28
immortality
　as attribute of God, 78, 94, 119
　biblical framing of, 116
　contrasted with *apollumi*, 183–85
　contrasted with eschatological death, 180–83
　creation of at resurrection, 177
　definition of, 101
　as gift from God to believers, 18, 28, 33, 72–74, 78, 94, 95, 97, 119, 140, 257–58, 259–61, 288, 289, 299, 308, 309–10, 312, 313, 315–19, 351, 363
　glory associated with, 120
　Greek view of, 94n15
　human anthropology and, 107n90, 109
　John's concept of, 178–80
　justification associated with, 101
　link to resurrection, 109, 114, 178
　present and future, 178–80, 188
　reward of the spiritual, 99
　of the soul, 94n15, 299
　traditionalists' understanding of, 257–69, 259–61, 262–68, 274–75, 315
　use of term in New Testament, 33. *See also aiōnios*; immortal soul
immortal soul
　annihilation implying, 14
　biblical view of, 74, 78
　Calvin's view of, 250–53, 354
　as change to nature of final judgment and work of Christ, 71–72
　conflict with Scripture, 74
　controversy over concept of, 115–16
　Greek philosophy, 18, 29, 33, 69, 70–71, 78, 94n15, 246–49, 252, 299

420 Subject Index

immortal soul *(continued)*
  incorporation of concept into Christianity, 246–53, 342
  Philo on, 94n15
impenitent. *See* unbelievers wicked
imperishability, 120
indoctrination, 299–300
infinite evil problem, 85–87
infinite punishment problem, 83–85
Infinite Seriousness Thesis (IST), 86, 88, 89
infinite sin, 82–85, 300
iniquity. *See* sin
injustice problem, 87–88
innatism, 244n3, 246–53
Institutes of the Christian Religion (Calvin), 252
Instone-Brewer, David, xxii, 213–42
integrated publicity, 347
intermediate state
  controversy concerning, 115–16
  place of the dead, 295, 299. *See also* Hades; Rich Man and Lazarus parable; Sheol
International Churches of Christ (ICOC), 296, 298, 304–5
Internet, 346–47
Isaac, Gordon L., xxii, 65–79
Isaiah (Book of)
  66
  24 in Mark 9
  48, 170–71
  author of, 160
  historical background of Isaiah 66, 162–67
  structure of, 160–62. *See also* Scripture Index
Ishamel, 91
Israel, 42–43, 123–24
IST (Infinite Seriousness Thesis), 86, 88, 89
"Is the eternal punishment of the lost literally unending?" (Fudge), 54

J

Jacob, 118
Jacob, Edmond, 40, 46

Jacoby, Douglas, xxiiii, 15n17, 66, 294–306
Jehoshaphat, 143
Jehovah's Witnesses
  conditionalism associated with, 7, 19, 254, 264, 302, 354
  establishment of, 354, 357
Jeremiah, 163, 168–69
Jerome, 166
Jesus Christ
  annihilation of Satan at His coming, 100–101
  approaches to the call to followers, 281
  comparison of physical and spiritual food, 186–87
  death and resurrection of, 44
  death of, 113, 134–35, 136, 174, 290–91, 317–19, 334–35, 361, 363, 365
  description of Gehenna, 34–35, 46
  description of judgment, 34–35
  dominion over all things, 121
  exaltation of, 119, 121
  as faithful son, 140
  on fate of fruitless, 186
  feeding of 5000, 177
  glory of, 119–20, 130–31, 140
  glory of angel at birth of, 118
  healing of man with unclean spirit, 75–76
  on hell, 214
  as image of God, 127–28
  on life and death, 181, 182
  as life-giving spirit, 108–9
  ministry of, 76–78
  mission of, 326
  Nicodemus and, 188
  parable of the sower, 76
  parables on judgment, 239–41
  possession of keys of death and Hades, 193–200, 203, 204, 208, 320
  presence in Hades, 202, 203
  reaping of Earth, 201–2
  reconciliation through, 102, 293, 317–21

restoration of image of God in man, 127–34
as resurrection and life, 174, 182–83, 184
resurrection of, 42–43, 97, 103–4, 111, 113, 119, 132, 176, 177, 192–93, 199, 319–21, 334
Rich Man and Lazarus parable, 5, 47, 172, 193–94, 197, 198–99
role in redemption, 72–73
Second Coming, 68, 77, 100–101, 118, 133, 138–39, 177, 201–2
Sermon on the Mount, 45
as source of eternal life, 72–74, 78, 94, 95, 97, 119, 140, 257–58, 259–61, 288, 289, 299, 308, 309–10, 312, 313, 315–19, 351
subjection to God the Father, 106
transfiguration of, 118, 130
use of words of Isaiah, 170
victory over all enemies, 105–7, 140, 320
vine metaphor, 185–86
as warring judge, 137–38, 148, 149, 150
words of as cornerstone of faith, 192–93
Jews, 222–29, 240–41, 242
Job, 143
Joel, 43
John Paul II (pope), 258
Johnson, Alan F., 103n61, 105–6, 107n89
John the Baptist, 186
John the Beloved, 51, 173–78, 178–80, 192
John XXII (pope), 252
"Joint Statement of the World Evangelical Alliance and the Seventh-day Adventist Church," 19m3
Jonah, 43
Jonathan, Stephen, 207
Jonathan, Targum, 135–36n52
Joseph (son of Jacob), 118, 146
Joshua ben Hananiah, 222, 225, 226, 227–28
Josiah, 169

Journal of Evangelical Theology Society, 20
Jubilees, 218–19
Judaism, 95, 220–21, 229, 230, 237–39
judgment
according to works, 96, 200
of Assyria, 100–101, 171
as cleansing of creation, 71, 75–78, 79, 186
conditionalist view of, 312, 313–15, 316–19
extinction of evil, 66–79
final judgment as exclusion, 187–88
Gospels and Qumran view of, 238–41
John's depiction of, 180–88
justice of, 27, 146
length of punishment, 224–25, 227–28, 229
limitations of, 43–44
Messianic vision in First Enoch, 76n16
nature of, 26–28, 98–102, 106, 137–40
Paul's imagery of, 100
place of, 168–69
of Sodom and Gomorrah, 91
studies of, 173
theophanies bringing, 124–26
of unbelievers, 164–67, 168–69, 171, 179–80
Yohanan ben Zakkai's view of, 235–37. *See also* annihilation; eternal torment; hell; immortality; justice
of God, 146
in Old Testament, 45–48
terminal punishment as, 154–55
of traditional view of hell, 82
justification, 101, 129
Justin Martyr, 115

K

kainos anthropos (man as a new creation), 131
Kaiser, Walther C., Jr., 41
Kant, Immanuel, 88
Kantzer, Kenneth, 21

katargeo (destroyed, annihilated), 105–6
katargesei (annihilation), 100
Keeble, Marshall, 49
Keller, Tim, 13
kenotic Christology, 10
kingdom of God, 121, 188
King James Bible, 343
Kinkade, Thomas, 9
koimaomai (to sleep), 175, 177
Koukl, Greg, 262
Kreitzer, Larry J., 95n22
Kuhn, Thomas, 4, 9, 12

L

Lactantius of Nicomedia, 248, 263
Ladd, George Eldon, 40n7, 70
Lamont, Michèle, 4, 11
Lang, Bernhard, 9–10n7
Last Day. *See* judgment
Last Judgment parable, 172
Last Things, The (Bloesch), 207
Latham, John W., 127
Lawless One. *See* Satan
Lazarus, raising of, 174
Leaven, xx
Lewis, C. S., 86, 207, 258
lex talionis, 45–46, 82
liberalism, 354
Lichfield Mysteries, 209
Liebreich, Leon J., 161, 167
Lie of Hell, The (Harper), 210
life, 91, 97–98, 119. *See also* eternal life
Life in Christ (White), 207
light, kingdom of, 134–35
Lindbeck, George, 207
literal interpretations, 5
Lloyd-Jones, Martyn, 244
Locke, John, 330
the lost. *See* unbelievers wicked
love, 43–45, 51
Love Wins (R. Bell), 35
Lucado, Max, xx
Luther, Martin, 7, 115, 250, 253, 287
Lutzer, Erwin, 263

M

MacArthur, John, 191, 259, 265–66
MacCulloch, J. A., 207
MacDonald, Gregory, 105n79
MacDuff, John, 257
malice, 88–89
man
  death as universal for, 91–98, 105, 111
  dominion over all things, 121–23
  fall from grace, 91, 102, 105, 122, 127, 316
  fate of, 126–34
  glorification of, 34, 133–34, 138–40
  Greek dualistic view of, 18, 70–71, 78, 95, 115–16, 117, 175–76, 246–47, 249, 299, 343
  as image of God, 121–23, 122n19, 127–28, 133–34
  Jewish concept of, 95, 97
  as new creation and temple of God, 123–24, 131–34
  Paul's teaching on, 95–98
  renewal of image of God in, 128–29
  Scriptural understanding of, 69, 70–71
  stewardship and exaltation of, 121–23. *See also* righteous souls; unbelievers; wicked
Marcus, Joel, 170
Marcus Aurelius, 248
Mariottini, Claude, xxii, 159–71
Marsden, George, 11
Marshall, I. Howard, 12, 106, 107n90
Martha, 174, 182
Martin of Cochem, 271
Mary (mother of Jesus), 144
Mary (sister of Martha), 174
McDannell, Colleen, 9–10n7
McGee, Vernon, 264
McGrath, Alister, 14
M'Cheyne, Robert Murray, 256
McKnight, Scot, 14
McRay, Rob, xxii, 36–52
media bias, 342
Micah, 207
Middleton, J. Richard, 117, 122, 125, 135

Midrashim, 222
Miller, Kevin, 347
Miller, Kris A., 130
Millerite movement, 354, 357
minority readings of Scripture, 330–31
Mishnah, 222. *See also* Scripture Index
mistranslation, 300–301
modernism, 354–55
Mohler, Albert, 37, 49–50, 264
Molinists, 146n13
Moloney, Francis J., 184n23–24, 185
Moltmann, Jürgen, 97, 110, 116, 117
Moo, Doug, 274
Moreland, J. P., 262–63
Morey, Robert, 244–45, 275n81
Morgan, Christopher, 264, 364
"Mortal God, The" (Peoples), 290
mortalism, 354. *See also* conditional immortality; conditional immortality/conditionalism
mortality, 91–92, 95–98, 128–29. *See also* death
Moses, 43, 51, 69, 124, 125, 130
motivations, 336–37
Murphy, Nancey, 4n2
Murray, Michael, 86
Murrell, Adam, xxii, 141–55

N

Nadab, 126
National Association of Evangelical Essentials, 20–23
near-death experiences, 210
Nebuchadnezzar, 121, 168
Nehemiah, 43
neos anthropos (new man), 131
nephesh (soul), 95, 343
Nestorianism, 290
new Adam, 109n100, 317, 319–20
new creation
believers as, 123–24, 131–34
Christ as head of, 320
continuity and discontinuity in, 116–17
New Heaven and a New Earth, A (Middleton), 117

New Heavens, New Earth
biblical foundations of, 68–71
establishment of, 137
as recreation of perfect habitation of God, 78–79
requirements for, 68
traditional elements that don't fit, 71–74
as world without evil, 74–79
Newman, Cardinal, 271
New Testament
background for interpretation of, 5–6
core teaching of, 41, 42n15
references to hell, 18. *See also* Gospels; Scripture Index
New Wineskins, xx
Nickelsburg, George W. E., 102n58
Niebuhr, Reinhold, 325
No Other Name (Sanders), 207

O

Olbricht, Thomas H., 44, 47n29
Old Testament
core teaching of, 41–43, 44
as governing background for New Testament interpretation, 5–6
theme of justice and divine punishment, 45–48. *See also* Scripture Index
olethros (destruction, ruin, death), 99, 99n41, 100, 106n84
Olley, John W., 165–66
Olson, Roger, 331
oluthrios (annihilation), 99n42–43, 100
omnipotence. *See* divine sovereignty
On First Principles (Origen), 327–29
onto-ethical immortality, 132–34
Open Theists, 146n13
optimal grace, 205
orgē (destruction), 99n40
Origen of Alexandria, 110n104, 327–29, 344
Ortlund, Gavin, 127, 133
Osborne, Grant, 101
Our Man in Heaven (Fudge), 54

P

Pace, William, 56
Packer, J. I., 21–22, 48, 264, 344
Padgett, Alan, 107, 109
Papaioannou, Kim, xxii, 172–89, 194
parousia, 100–101, 118, 133, 138–39, 177, 201–2
Parry, Robin, 337, 366
Paul
   on annihilation of death, 94–111
   on death, sin, and destruction, 34, 98–102
   on death and resurrection of Jesus, 113
   on glory, 118, 120
   on immortality of God, 94
   on immortality of soul, 259–60
   on mortal man, 95–98
   relationship with Christ, 97n26
   on resurrection, 102–11, 246
   on subjection of all thing to God, 150–51
   view of death, 69
   view of redemption, 68–69
   on work of salvation, 319–20
Payson, Edward, 260
peger (corpse), 167
penal substitutionary atonement, 317–19
Peoples, Glenn, xxiiii, 279–93, 335n32, 352–53, 358, 363, 369
Petavel, E., 309
Pétavel-Olliff, Emmanuel, 314–15
Peterson, Robert, 259, 262, 266, 284, 291, 334, 364
Pharisees, 234n25
Phelps, Elizabeth Stuart, 9n7
philosophical contribution, 81–89
philosophy. *See* Greek philosophy
phthora (corruption), 99
Pinnock, Clark
   on acceptance of Adventism, 344
   belief in post-mortem salvation, 207
   as conditionalist, 22
   letter to Fudge, 58
   Mohler on, 50
   support of conditionalism, 8n4, 12
   use of "conditional immortality," 18
   view of hell, 24
Piper, John, 258
Plantinga, Alvin, 288
Plato, 18, 246–48, 252
Plotinus, 249
Plug, Allen, 207
Polanyi, Michael, 4, 11
post-mortem salvation
   Gospels and Qumran's view of, 238–42
   Harper's view of, 199, 205, 207, 208–10
   implication concerning character of God, 333
   Rabbinic theology concerning, 230–37, 241–42
praise, 92–94, 122
Presbyterion journal, 244
press, 345–46
Problem of Hell, The (Buckareff, Plug, Davis), 207
Prodigal Son parable, 195
proof-texting, 5
psuché/psyche (soul, mind), 95, 108n97, 175, 343
psychological obstacles to acceptance, 301–2
public events, 346
punishment
   according to works, 259, 364–65
   conditionalist view of, 314–15
   death as, 362
   length of, 219, 224–25, 227–28, 229, 240
   proportionality of, 45, 82, 205–6, 217
   for sins against infinite being, 86, 300. *See also* annihilation; eternal torment; Hades; hell; terminal punishment
purgatory, 205, 206, 249–50
Purgatory (Walls), 207
purity, 95–96
"Putting Hell in Its Place" (Fudge), 33
Pyne, Robert, 59

Q

Quient, Nicholas Rudolph, xxii,
  90–111
Quistorp, Heinrich, 253
Qumran Judaism, 220–21, 229, 230,
  237–39

R

Rabbinic sources, 221–37, 237–41. *See also* Scripture Index
Rachel, 91
radio, 346
Rahner, Karl, 207
Ranker.com, 342
Rashdall, Hastings, 318
reconciliation
  extent of, 66
  process of, 75–78
  through Jesus Christ, 102, 131, 293
  traditionalist view of hell and, 153–55
  uniting of all things in Christ, 134–35
reconciliationism, 27
redemption
  of the body, 96, 120
  of creation, 120, 140
  extent of, 68–71, 117–18
  process of, 75–78
  qualifications for, 134–35
  reconstitution of image of God in man, 128
Reformed tradition, 8
Relevant magazine, 13
repentance, 241, 242
Repent or Perish (Gerstner), 59, 245–46, 341–42
restorationists. *See* universalism
Restoration Movement (RM), 296
restoration of all things, 66, 153–55
resurrection
  of believers, 96–98, 104–7, 111, 113–15, 118, 127, 133–34, 139–40
  centrality to gospel, 319–21
  of the dead, 33–34, 260
  as future event, 105n77, 174
  giving of eternal life in, 178–80, 188
  glory associated with, 120, 129, 133–34
  of Jesus Christ, 44, 103–4, 111, 113, 119, 132, 176, 177, 192–93, 199, 319–21, 334
  John's depiction of, 175–78
  link between immortality and, 109, 114
  nature of, 97–98, 178
  nature of the body, 107–11, 133, 260, 263, 265, 266
  Paul's teaching on, 96, 102–11, 113–16
  renewal of image of God in man, 129–30
  Sadducees' rejection of, 234
  statement in Old Testament, 93n10
  timing of, 33–34
  types of, 129, 176, 179–80, 185
  of unbelievers, 118, 265
  of the unjust, 113
  as work of God, 97
Rethinking Hell (Date, Stump, Anderson), 14, 28, 351, 363
Rethinking Hell Conference, xxi–xxii, 53–54, 80, 115, 298, 350
"Rethinking Hell" website, 24–25
Revelation, 173, 301
Reymond, Robert L., 244
Rice, John, 258
Rich Man and Lazarus parable, 5, 47, 172, 193–94, 197, 198–99
Ridderbos, Herman, 252
righteous souls
  adoption by God, 131, 134–35
  animosity of wicked toward, 163, 164
  at Christ's return in glory, 118
  definition of in Isaiah 66, 163
  glorification of, 34, 133–34, 138–40
  image of God within, 127–28
  immortality as gift from God, 18, 28, 33, 72–74, 78, 94, 95, 97, 108n93, 119, 140, 257–58, 259–61, 288, 289, 299, 308, 309–10, 312, 313, 315–19, 351, 363

righteous souls *(continued)*
  as new creation and temple of God, 123–24, 131–34
  partakers of divine nature, 129–30
  path of, 72–73
  place of after death, 197
  protection of, 126, 137
  resurrection of. *See* resurrection
  reward for, 71–72, 101, 146–47, 201
  transformation of, 134–35
  view of eternal punishment, 36–37, 50–51
Ritchie, George, 210
RM. *See* Restoration Movement (RM)
Robertson, Pat, 57
Roetzel, Calvin, 102–3
Russell, Charles Taze, 354, 356
Russell, David S., 168

S

Sadducees, 234
salvation
  Greek vs. Pauline view of, 69
  Judeo-Christian concept of, 70–71
  link to eschatology, 95, 128, 129
  as matter of destination in traditional view, 71–72, 78
  as paramount to Paul, 113–14
  Scriptural description of, 72
  as work of Christ, 317–21. *See also* soteriology
sanctification, 322
Sanders, John, 207
Santayana, George, 356
Satan, 100, 135, 299
Saville, Andy, 84–85
Schaff, Phillip, 244
Schnelle, Udo, 108
School Disputes, 230–34
Scripture
  Anabaptists' stand on, 251
  decline in biblical literacy, 345
  Fudge's reliance on, 5–6
  interpretation of, 5–6
  post-mortem salvation consistent with, 208
  primacy of, 348–49, 360–61
  as source of Fudge's arguments, 5, 15–16. *See also* Scripture Index
Searching Together journal, 35
Second Coming, 68, 77, 100–101, 118, 133, 138–39, 177, 201–2
second death
  lake of fire, 73, 200
  parallel to temporal death, 180–83, 188–89
  resurrection and, 175. *See also* annihilation; eternal torment; hell; terminal punishment
Second Great Awakening, 353
Seitz, Christopher R., 166
sentimentality, 9, 11
Sermon on the Mount, 45
Seth, 127
Seventh-day Adventists
  conditionalism associated with, 7, 19, 344, 354, 357
  view of hell, 264, 302
Seymour, Charles, 86
Shammaites, 230–34, 237
Shedd, William G. T., 143n3
Sheol, 197, 218, 297, 300. *See also* Hades
Shrewd Manager parable, 301
Sibylline Oracles, 217, 219, 222
Simons, Menno, 258
sin
  affect on community, 96
  conditionalist vs. traditionalist view of, 315–16
  deserving of hell, 241
  elimination of, 124
  entrance into the world, 91, 102, 105, 124
  forgiveness for, 134–35
  infinite sin, 82–85, 300
  mortality associated with, 128–29
  punishment for, 362
  of Satan, 100
  wages of, 72–73, 74–75, 91, 98–102, 135–40, 146–48, 189, 256, 312, 314
sinners. *See* unbelievers wicked
Six Sermons (Storrs), 353

sleep, 97n26, 104, 116, 175
Smart, James D., 162
social media, 346
Socinians, 253, 264, 354
Sodom and Gomorrah, 47, 91, 101, 126, 137, 203, 362
soma pneumatikon (spiritual body), 108–9
Sons of Korah, 126
Sotak, Max, 352
soteriology, 95, 113–14, 128, 129. *See also* salvation
soul
   biblical view of, 74
   Greek belief in immortal of, 29, 33, 94n15, 117, 246–49, 299, 343
   Jewish concept of, 95, 97
   Paul's view of, 95–98
   as psychosomatic unity, 69, 70–71
soul sleep, 197
Sound of His Voice, The (Fudge), xx
sower, parable of, 76
Spiegel, James S., xxii, 80–89
spiritualism, 342, 349
Sproul, R. C., 256
Spurgeon, Charles, 7, 50, 258, 265
Stackhouse, John G., Jr., xxii, 3–16, 60–61, 66
"Statement of Evangelical Conditionalism," 351
State of the Bible 2014 (American Bible Society poll), 345
status principle, 82–83, 85, 86, 300
Stemberger, Günter, 222n16
Stephens, Mark B., 117
Stetson, George, 354, 356
Stockman, Edward A., 79n19
Storm, Howard, 210
Storrs, George, 353–54, 356, 357
Stott, John
   belief in dualism, 115
   on Christian integrity, 340
   as conditionalist, 21, 22, 244
   as evangelical, 338
   letter to Fudge, 58
   revelation of his conditionalist views, 22–23, 26, 27, 285

support of conditionalism, 11
Structure of Scientific Revolutions, The (Kuhn), 9
Stump, Gregory G., xxii, 14, 53–61
Swinburne, Richard, 12
Swindoll, Chuck, 261
systematic theology, 39–40, 191

T

tabernacle, 123–24
Table Talk magazine, 256
Talmuds, 222
Targums, 222
Tartarus, 217, 219, 241, 300
Taylor, Jeremy, 272
television, 346
telos (end), 105–11
tempest theophanies, 124–26
temple
   believers as, 131–34
   glory associated with, 118–24
   of God, 119
   man's access to, 136
terminal punishment
   acceptance of, 295
   biblical portrayal of, 72–73
   definition of, 295–96
   extinction of evil, 66–79
   Jacoby's journey to acceptance of, 297–98
   as requirement for New Heavens, New Earth, 68
   sovereignty of God and, 154–55
   use of the term, 15, 66. *See also* annihilation; conditional immortality/conditionalism; second death
"Terminal Punishment" (Jacoby), 298
Tertullian of Carthage, 67, 248
thanatos (death), 18, 173–74, 177, 178, 180, 181, 182, 183
theatrical productions, 347
theologians, 329–30
theological paradigm shifts, 9–12
theological tradition, 6
theophanies, 124–26, 136–40, 165–66. *See also* Second Coming
theosis (life in God), 116, 130

Thielicke, Helmut, 306
Thiselton, Anthony
  on 1 Corinthians 15 12–34, 104
  on annihilation of death, 110
  on contrast between perishable and imperishable, 110
  on death, 106
  on life, 107n89
  on old and new humanity, 109n100
  on Paul's references to death and destruction, 18, 100
  support of conditionalism, 12
  translation of *katargeo*, 105n79
  translation of *katargesei*, 106
Thomas, 174
Thomas, Robert, 263
Thomas Aquinas
  on basis of Christian arguments, 5
  on fate of the lost, 249–50, 265
  Infinite Seriousness Thesis, 86, 300
  view of eternal punishment, 82
Thomas More, 251
Threshold (seminary newsletter), 56
Tiessen, Terrance L., xxii, 17–31
time, 54–55, 97n26, 104
Topheth, 138, 168–69
Torrance, Thomas F., 130, 320, 321n25
Tosephta, 222. See also Scripture Index
Tozer, A. W., 143n3
tradition, 208–9
traditionalism
  attempt to resolve the issues of eternal torment in hell, 268–76
  culture of vengeance, 342–43
  difficulty in accepting new ideas, 287
  distinguishing between scholarly and popular descriptions, 335
  dualism of, 70–71, 78, 116, 117
  elements of judgment that don't fit, 71–74
  evangelical confirmation of, 302
  evangelistic message of, 308, 310–12
  gatekeepers of, 341–42, 351
  Greek influence on, 29. See also Greek philosophy
  impact of language of hell, 50–51
  infinite evil problem, 85–87
  infinite punishment problem, 83–85
  interpretation of Scripture, 6–7
  as orthodox and evangelical view, 337–38
  popularity of, 336–40
  popular problem with hell, 36–38
  problematic status principle, 82–83, 85, 86, 300
  problem of cruelty, malice, and callousness, 88–89
  problem of God's sovereignty, 146–53
  problem of infinite evil, 83–85
  problem of injustice, 87–88
  problem of language about hell, 48–50
  problem of restoration, 153–55
  problems of divine sovereignty, 146–53
  response to conditionalists, 244, 268, 311, 313, 344, 368–69
  spiritualism and, 349
  theses guiding debates among conditionalists, universalists, and, 325–38
  Tiessen's use of the term, 18–19
  view of death, 295–96
  view of hell and divine punishment, xx–xxi, 18–21, 25–26, 29, 48–50, 66–67, 109n103, 141, 147–48, 255–68, 309, 310, 315, 324, 340. See also eternal torment
  view of immortality, 14, 18, 29, 71, 342
transformation, 134–35
Travis, Stephen H., 314, 318
Trinity Evangelical Divinity School, 20–23
Trito-Isaiah, 160, 162–67, 170
True Image, The (Hughes), 23–24, 244
Turek, Frank, 263
Tyndale, William, 253

U

ultimate reconciliation, 248
unbelievers
    animosity toward faithful, 163, 164
    definition of in Isaiah 66, 163–64
    destruction of, 262–66
    fate of, 18, 27–28, 99, 106, 113, 114, 123, 131, 135–40, 181–83, 185–86, 188, 195–96, 199, 201, 256, 309
    judgment of, 164–67
    punishment of, 71–72, 146–53, 159–71, 224–25, 227–28, 229, 240, 262–68. *See also* wicked
Unbounded Love
    A Good News Theology for the 21st Century (Pinnock and Brow), 8n4
universalism
    belief in immortal soul, 14
    biblical support of, 47, 95n20
    conditionalism associated with, 7
    conditionalism's argument against, 312–15, 366–67
    difficulty for, 105n75
    distinguishing between scholarly and popular descriptions, 335
    evangelical opposition to, 23
    followers of, 292
    Fudge on, 336–37
    implication concerning character of God, 333
    lack of Scriptural evidence for, 6, 46, 101n55
    motivation for belief in, 336–37
    as orthodox and evangelical view, 337–38
    popularity of, 340, 343–44
    post-mortem salvation and, 208
    problems of, 109n103
    sovereignty argument, 154n22
    theses guiding debates among traditionalists, conditionalists, and, 325–38
    view of judgment and hell, 324–25, 344
unquenchable fire, 168–69, 186
unrepentant. *See* unbelievers
wicked
unrighteous. *See* unbelievers
    wicked
unrighteousness. *See* sin
Utopia (More), 251

V

Valley of Hinnom, 168–69, 219, 241. *See also* Gehenna
video-sharing sites, 346
vine metaphor, 185–86
Vines, Jerry, 257
Von Rad, Gerhard, 41

W

Wallace, J. Warner, 262
Walls, Jerry, 205, 207
Walvoord, John, 262, 275n81
Watts, Isaac, 7
website, 12–13, 24–25, 346
Wells, David, 317
Wendell, Jonas, 354, 356
Wengst, Klaus, 174
Wenham, John W.
    approach to evangelism, 316
    as conditionalist, 22
    correspondence with Bruce, 58
    correspondence with Fudge, 55, 61
    criticism of, 49
    defense of conditional immortality, 8
    evangelical opposition to, 23
    forward for Fudge's books, 55
    The Goodness of God, 291
    on Harmon's paper, 60
    on motivation for evangelism, 332
    on Stott's discussion of conditionalism, 58n17
    on Stott's distinction between annihilationism and conditional immortality, 58n17
    support of conditionalism, 11
    view of hell, 264
Wesley, Charles, 209
Wesley, John, 5, 257
Westermann, Claus, 40–41, 42n15

Whatever Happened to Hell?
(Blanchard), 59
What's the Truth About Heaven and Hell (Jacoby), 298
White, Edward, 207, 285
White, Ellen, 19
Whitefield, George, 258
wicked
animosity toward faithful, 163, 164
definition of in Isaiah 66, 163
destruction of, 262–66
fate of, 27–28, 99, 106, 113, 114, 123, 131, 135–40, 181–83, 185–86, 188, 195–96, 199, 201, 215, 256, 309
path of, 72–73
punishment of, 71–75, 146–53, 159–71, 210, 224–25, 227–28, 229, 240, 262–68
Wideness in God's Mercy, A (Pinnock), 207
Williams, W., 209
Willimon, W., 207
Willison, John, 257
Wise and Foolish Virgins parable, 194–95

Witherington III, Ben, 101n56, 106n88, 108n97
Wolters, Albert, 117
Wood, Jim, xxiiii, 339–49, 350
World Evangelical Alliance, 28
worship. *See* praise
Wright, Christopher, 13–14
Wright, Nigel, 314
Wright, N. T., 6, 13, 68, 69, 117, 326–27

Y

Yahweh. *See* God
Yancey, Philip, 13
Yarbrough, Robert, 37, 49
Yohanan ben Zakkai, 222–24, 226, 235–37, 240

Z

Zens, Adam, 261
Zens, Jon, xxii, 32–35
zēsete (future of live), 180
zōē (life)/ *zaō* (to live), 178, 180
zōopoiō/ zoopoieo (to create life), 177, 182
Zuck, Roy, 39

www.ingramcontent.com/pod-product-compliance
Lightning Source LLC
Chambersburg PA
CBHW052049290426
44111CB00011B/1670